Beginning Latin for College Students

Charles Chamberlain

University of California, San Diego

cognella®

SAN DIEGO

Bassim Hamadeh, CEO and Publisher
Seidy Cruz, Senior Field Acquisitions Editor
Anne Jones, Project Editor
Alia Bales, Production Editor
Jess Estrella, Senior Graphic Designer
Trey Soto, Licensing Coordinator
Ursina Kilburn, Interior Designer
Natalie Piccotti, Director of Marketing
Kassie Graves, Senior Vice President of Editorial
Jamie Giganti, Director of Academic Publishing

cognella® | ACADEMIC PUBLISHING
3970 Sorrento Valley Blvd., Ste. 500, San Diego, CA 92121

Contents

AVISO TO TEACHERS

The following remarks are intended for teachers; students will probably find them too technical to be useful.

In ordering the material, I begin with basics and gradually move to higher-level grammar. Each chapter usually covers one topic. Note that some chapters are heavier and some lighter than others. The heavier ones are chapters 23, 25, 28, 41, and 56; lighter are chapters 11, 16, 26, 33, 39, 44, 48, and 66. You may need more time for some, less for others.

I often present topics without going into all the details. For example, verbs are always presented in vocabulary lists with all their principal parts even before these can all be used. However, principal parts not yet usable are printed in non-bold type. Note that not until chapter 47 does the full story for so-called **ūnus nauta** adjectives appear, although many of the words themselves have been used before. Similarly, the concept of semi-deponent is not explained until chapter 56 even though the semi-deponents **audeō** and **gaudeō** are used earlier.

Macrons appear throughout the book, but not over so-called hidden quantities as in **cōgnōscō**.

Once a word has been introduced in a vocabulary, it will be considered as required vocabulary and will appear thereafter in bold type. Glossed sentences contain words not presented in vocabulary lists; such words are therefore printed in non-bold type. I have sometimes used non-required vocabulary when giving illustrative examples in the body of chapters. They are printed in bold type and always have a translation. Vocabulary specific to the chapter topic is found at the beginning of vocabulary lists.

The titles of the passages found at the end of some chapters are my own invention, an attempt to indicate context.

I have combed more than 150 works of thirty-eight Latin authors to find sentences and passages suitable for this book. My goal was to include only verbatim bits. However, I have taken the occasional license of omitting the subordinator of an originally subordinate clause or of omitting a parenthetical expression.

INTRODUCTION

Latin was the language spoken by the ancient Romans from roughly 400 BC until about 500 AD. During this long period, the language underwent many changes. This book is based on Latin as it was spoken and written from about 200 BC to 100 AD. We are fortunate to have many writings from this three hundred–year period, a time many call the high point of Latin literature. These are the writings I used to construct this book.

We Latin teachers hear many strange things from well-meaning parents and interested bystanders, one of which is that "all languages come from Latin." This is incorrect as a moment's thought will reveal. Chinese and Hindi did not descend from Latin. However, a group of languages called the Romance languages did come from Latin: Spanish, Italian, French, Romanian, Portuguese, and some lesser known ones. Notice that English is not on that list. English did not descend from Latin but from Anglo-Saxon. However, English did absorb thousands of Latin or Latin-based words over the course of its development; hence, you will often be able to guess the meaning of a Latin word from its English derivative—and vice versa. One of the joys of learning Latin.

Another bit of folk wisdom often heard is that Latin is good preparation for law school or medical school or seminary. There is some truth to this one. The law still has Latin terms and phrases, often mispronounced, but still valid. As for medicine, much of the early scientific vocabulary was taken from Latin or Greek, so knowing Latin can help with medical and scientific terminology, at least of the older type. (Quark is not Latin.) For the Catholic priesthood, Latin is still the official language of the church and is still spoken as a kind of universal language among the higher ranks of the clergy. (However, the Bible was not written in Latin, another common misconception.) But the bottom line is that as a preparation for these vocations, Latin has a less direct influence than it once did. Its contribution is more subtle. I tell people Latin is a good preparation for life.

PRONUNCIATION

Although we don't know exactly how Latin was pronounced, we have a general idea. As you can imagine, there are no audio recordings from ancient Rome. As a result, the guide to pronunciation that follows will be approximate. Imagine trying to learn a modern language without ever hearing it spoken. You might learn a lot of vocabulary and grammar, but your pronunciation would often be faulty, perhaps even unintelligible to a native speaker. This is our situation with regard to Latin. We know a lot about the vocabulary and grammar, but if we could time travel back to ancient Rome and try to converse, we would have to ask the natives to pardon our Latin.

In general, the individual Latin vowels, -**a**-, -**e**-, -**i**-, -**o**- and -**u**-, sounded much as they do in Spanish or Italian. (Notice I do not include French.)

a	=	as in "mama"
e	=	as in "melee"
i	=	as in "machine"
o	=	as in "go"
u	=	as in "pooh"

Several common vowel pairs (called diphthongs) require special notice:

ae	=	as in "eye"
au	=	as in "ow"
ei	=	as in "eh"
oe	=	as in "oi"
ui	=	as in "whee"

Many of the consonants are also similar to modern Spanish or Italian (and sometimes even English). However, there are differences, so do not be surprised if familiar Latin words or names sound strange in their original pronunciation.

The consonants -**c**- and -**g**- in Latin are both "hard"; that is, the -**c**- is pronounced as in "cat" and the -**g**- as in "go." Those of you who know Spanish or French will need to reboot the common combination of -**qu**- to sound like "quack," not like "queso" or "quelle." The -**r**- was probably trilled as in Spanish, not gargled as in French. Finally, there is the consonant -**v**-. The evidence is conclusive that in our period of Latin this letter was pronounced like an English -**w**-, thus producing what sounds like a recurring case of lisping in Caesar's famous remark **veni vidi vici**. (Don't forget to make the -**c**- in **vici** hard!)

When you utter Latin, do not obssess over your accent. Make the adjustments I just laid out and you will be fine. In spite of all our research, any of us, even professors, would no doubt be laughed at by an ancient Roman hearing us speak. (For those of you who were exposed to Latin in the Catholic church, be advised that the pronunciation of so-called "church Latin" is heavily influenced by the pronunciation of Italian.)

Each of the vowels, -**a**-, -**e**-, -**i**-, -**o**- and -**u**-, had both a long and a short pronunciation. Contrary to what you might think, these terms mean simply that the long version took longer to pronounce than the short version. This is a distinction beginners can ignore, although the Romans were sensitive to it. (In fact, if we could travel to ancient Rome, we would have to be careful not to mix the two up; but we are not time travelers.) Sometimes the length of a vowel is all that differentiates two words with identical spelling. Consider the word **anus**: With a short -**a**- it means "old woman," with a long -**a**- something else.

STRESS/ACCENT

However, there is one place where an awareness of vowel length will be important: when it dictates where to place the stress on a Latin word. Every Latin word has a stress (or accent) on one of its syllables. Words of two syllables are stressed on the first syllable:

égo   níhil   ámo   víta

Words of three or more syllables are stressed either on the second or third syllable from the end according to the following rule:

(a) If the second syllable from the end contains a long vowel, it gets the stress;

(b) if that vowel is short, stress the third syllable from the end.

Examples will clarify (a long vowel has a dash above it):

(a)	**amīcus**	**fortūna**	**natūra**	**aliēnus**	**accūso**
(b)	**ánimus**	**cógito**	**dóminus**	**óculus**	**vídeo**

Throughout the book, a long vowel will be marked with a dash (called a macron) above it; if there is no macron, the vowel is short. (Notice that your instincts, based on English, will lead you to stress most of these Latin words properly.)

There is one more factor to consider:

(c) A short vowel followed by two consonants counts as long and will thus receive stress.

Examples are as follows:

(c)	**exspécto**	**senténtia**	**argéntum**	**aetérnus**	**puélla**

Once again, your instincts probably guided you to the proper pronunciation.

THE STRUCTURE OF LATIN

Every language, including Latin, requires that you learn its grammar, vocabulary, and idioms. In addition to these tasks, Latin presents English speakers with an entirely different grammatical structure, one that will take getting used to. Even if you have studied other languages, such as French or Spanish, the structure of Latin will be new. Briefly, it can be described as follows:

▼ **In English, the order of the words determines the meaning;
in Latin, the ending of words—not their order—determines the meaning.**

To see this in action, consider the following three-word sentences about a man, a dog, and a bite:

1. Man bites dog.
2. Dog bites man.
3. Man dog bites.
4. Dog man bites.
5. Bites man dog.
6. Bites dog man.

I have written every possible permutation of a three-word sentence to illustrate how dependent we are in English on word order. Sentences 1 and 2 make sense; the others do not. Sentences 1 and 2 make sense because English grammar requires the subject to come before the verb. Note that when "man" precedes "bites," we understand it to be the subject; when "dog" precedes "bites," it must be the subject. However, when two possible subjects precede a verb, as in sentences 3 and 4, confusion results. If one is the subject, what is the grammatical function of the other? In the last two, the verb comes before both nouns, so the reader is forced to guess at a subject, and the result is chaos.

Unlike English, Latin does not rely on word order to convey meaning but on information contained in the endings of words—especially nouns, adjectives, and verbs. Thus, Latin words will appear in various formations, called inflections, but not necessarily in any fixed order. (As a general rule, Latin verbs come at the end of a sentence, but they are not required to.) Here are the Latin versions of sentences 1 and 2:

1. **vir mordet canem.**
2. **canis mordet virum.**

All three Latin words have English derivatives. From the word for "man" (**vir**), we get "virile," from "dog" (**canis**) we get "canine," and from "bite" (**mordet**) we get "mordant," which means "biting." Note how the endings on the words for "man" and "dog" change depending on their grammatical function. In sentence 1, **vir** is the subject and **canem** is the direct object, while in 2, **canis** is the subject and **virum** is the object.

I have deliberately used English word order for ease of understanding, but be aware: A Latin author could put those words in any order without changing the basic meaning. Thus, sentence 1 could be expressed in six different arrangements:

(a) **vir mordet canem.**
(b) **canem mordet vir.**
(c) **mordet vir canem.**
(d) **mordet canem vir.**
(e) **vir canem mordet.**
(f) **canem vir mordet.**

All six arrangements mean basically the same thing—a man bites a dog—although each has a slightly different emphasis. The same would be true for **canis mordet virum** (Dog bites man), but I leave that to your imagination.

Long experience has shown me that this basic fact of the Latin language will underlie many of the translation difficulties you encounter in the first year. Therefore your first year and beyond will be spent training yourself to adapt to a new way of reading and thinking, one that relies on the endings of words, not their order.

For the sake of simplicity, I used sentences of only three words. However, a well-written passage of English usually contains longer sentences. Just for fun, I have chosen, almost at random, a normal-length English sentence from a recent novel and scrambled the words as follows:

> and had blue since the clothes afternoon changed
> now dress was she handsome a wearing.

The lines have a haunting beauty, but any attempt to reconstruct the original sentence is probably doomed. You might eventually arrive at a sensible meaning, but how could you say whether it is the only possible one? Now I will add a brief grammatical description to each word. It contains the kind of information that a Latin-inflected ending will convey. If you have some basic knowledge of grammar, you should be able to make sense of the scramble. This process will give you some idea of what "solving" a Latin sentence is like. (If you are unfamiliar with the terminology, don't worry; by the end of this year it will be an old friend.)

and	joins compound predicate
had	part of predicate
blue	modifies "dress"
since	preposition governing "afternoon"
the	modifies "afternoon"
clothes	direct object of "changed"
afternoon	object of preposition "since"
changed	part of predicate
now	modifies second part of compound predicate
dress	direct object of "wearing"
was	part of predicate
she	subject of sentence
handsome	modifies "dress"
a	modifies "dress"
wearing	part of predicate

The answer follows chapter 66.

Here is another one:

> when she then she room the night the heard next woke
> in coughing someone in.

when	subordinates second clause to first
she	subject of main clause
then	modifies "woke"
she	subject of subordinate clause
room	object of preposition "in"
the	modifies "night"
night	object of preposition "in"
the	modifies "room"
heard	predicate of subordinate clause
next	modifies "room"
woke	predicate of main clause
in	preposition
coughing	modifies "someone"
someone	direct object of "heard"
in	preposition

The answer follows chapter 66.

Verbs of the Second Conjugation/Present Tense/Principal Parts

Latin verbs belong to four families called "conjugations." When I say "called," I do not mean that the ancient Romans used these names. Most Romans were as unaware of the grammatical principles of their language as we are of ours. The names used in this book were developed during late antiquity by teachers and scholars as a shorthand way of referring to grammatical categories.

The subject of a Latin verb is indicated by a variable ending. By learning the pattern of endings of each conjugation, you acquire mastery over the hundreds of verbs belonging to that conjugation. Here is the pattern for the second conjugation:

Second Conjugation

hab-e-ō	I have
hab-ē-s	you have
hab-e-t	he/she/it has
hab-ē-mus	we have
hab-ē-tis	you have
hab-e-nt	they have

I have broken up the words with dashes to emphasize a common pattern. A Latin verb often consists of (1) a root, (2) a connecting vowel, and (3) an ending. In general, the root remains unchanged while the other two elements can vary. Note the unchanging element of this pattern: **hab**-; it carries the basic meaning "have." Then comes the connecting vowel -**e**-, which appears in every form. Finally come various endings that indicate the subject. Notice that, unlike English, where the subject comes before the verb, ("we have"), in Latin the subject is indicated at the end of the verb. In effect you must learn to mentally scan inflected words backward.

As you will see in later verb patterns, the endings -ō, -s, -t, -mus, -tis, -nt are used repeatedly. Practice saying and writing this verb until you don't need to look. Then substitute another second conjugation verb and practice. All you need to establish the pattern in your mind is one verb. All others will fit that model.

Latin has no equivalent to our so-called "progressive" and "emphatic" forms. Thus, **habeo** can also be translated "I am having" or "I do have" depending on the context. Here is a table:

Second Conjugation

hab-e-ō	I am having, I do have
hab-ē-s	you are having, you do have
hab-e-t	he/she/it is having, does have
hab-ē-mus	we are having, we do have
hab-ē-tis	you are having, you do have
hab-e-nt	they are having, they do have

In addition to these six forms, Latin verbs also have two command forms (imperatives) and one infinitive form, to be translated with "to."

Singular		Plural	
hab-ē	have!	**hab-ē-te**	have!
	hab-ē-re	to have	

Unlike English, Latin distinguishes between an imperative addressed to one person and that addressed to several. This will require you to step back mentally and decide how many people you are addressing when you give a command. By the same logic, if you are asked to translate the command "have!" into Latin, you may use either **habē** or **habēte** since the English word could imply either one.

PRINCIPAL PARTS OF VERBS

In order to fully manage a Latin verb, you must also understand the concept of principal parts, even though you will only be using two of them for a while. A fully conjugated Latin verb is built on four different bases, called principal parts. Here are the first two:

(1) the first person present form, such as **habeō** or **videō**
(2) the present infinitive form, such as **habēre** or **vidēre**

The first principal part tells you what the root of the verb is, in this case **hab-** or **vid-**. The second principal part tells you what conjugation the verb belongs to, in this case the second conjugation. For completeness, I have included in the vocabulary all the principal parts of a verb; however, until chapter 23 only the first two principal parts will concern us, and they will be printed in bold type.

CHAPTER 1: VOCABULARY

habeō, habēre, habuī, habitus	*have, hold*
maneō, manēre, mansī, mansūrus	*(a)wait, remain*
taceō, tacēre, tacuī, —	*be quiet*
timeō, timēre, timuī, —	*fear*
valeō, valēre, valuī, valitūrus	*be well, be strong*
videō, vidēre, vīdī, vīsus	*see*
ego	*I*
est	*he/she/it is*
mē	*me*
nihil / nil	*nothing*
nōn	*not*
quid	*what*
tē	*you (object)*
valē /valēte	*goodbye*

CHAPTER 1: LATIN TO ENGLISH SENTENCES

1. **nihil habēs.**   PLAUT ASIN 189
2. **manē.**   PLAUT AMPH 931
3. **quid timēmus?**   CIC PHIL 12.16
4. **valē, valē.**   PLAUT ASIN 592
5. A. **vidēs?**   B. **videō.**   PLAUT MOST 1105
6. A. **manē.**   B. **nōn maneō.**   PLAUT BACC 572-3
7. A. **tacē.**   B. **nōn taceō.**   PLAUT CAS 826
8. **nihil timent.**   CIC PRO FLACC 44
9. **videō ego tē.**   PLAUT PERS 284
10. A. **quid ego videō?**   B. **quid vidēs?**   PLAUT MEN 1062
11. **nōn vidēs?**   AUCHER 4.68

CHAPTER 1: GLOSSED LATIN TO ENGLISH SENTENCES

1. nunc **nihil habet.**   nunc: now   PLAUT TRUC 217
2. sī **valēs,** bene **est; ego valeō.**   sī: if   CIC FAM 14.8

                              bene: well

CHAPTER 1: ENGLISH TO LATIN SENTENCES

1. We do not have you.   CIC ATT 3.7.1
2. A. Wait.   B. What is it?   PLAUT CAS 733
3. I do not fear.   SENR C 1.8.1
4. You (plural) fear nothing.   CATULLUS 23.8
5. I see nothing.   TER ADEL 266
6. He does not see me.   PLAUT AMPH 331
7. A. Do you see me?   B. I see you.   PLAUT MG 376
8. We see nothing.   SEN E 110.7
9. What do you see?   PLAUT RUD 162
10. They are not quiet.   CIC CAEC DIV 21

2 Verbs of the First Conjugation/Present Tense

The -a- conjugation has traditionally been called the first conjugation merely because it was usually presented first. I am introducing it second because it is not quite as regular as the second conjugation. Once again there will be a root, a connecting vowel, and an ending. However, the very first form has a slight glitch—no connecting vowel.

First Conjugation

am-ō	I love	
am-ā-s	you love	
am-a-t	he/she/it loves	
am-ā-mus	we love	
am-ā-tis	you love	
am-a-nt	they love	

am-ā	love!	**am-ā-te**	love!

am-ā-re	to love

Notice that the same batch of endings is used to indicate the subject of the verb. As you proceed through this book, you will find that many Latin endings are repeated in similar contexts, thus reinforcing their meaning in your mind. You should be warned that the vowels that link endings to roots also carry crucial information; this will become more of a factor later.

CHAPTER 2: VOCABULARY

amō, amāre, amāvī, amātus	*love, be in love*
cōgitō, cōgitāre, cōgitāvī, cōgitātus	*think*
exspectō, exspectāre, exspectāvī, exspectātus	*await, wait for*
laudō, laudāre, laudāvī, laudātus	*praise*
negō, negāre, negāvī, negātus	*deny, say no, refuse*
properō, properāre, properāvī, properātus	*hurry*
putō, putāre, putāvī, putātus	*think*
rogō, rogāre, rogāvī, rogātus	*ask (for), beg (for)*

nunc	*now*
quis	*who*
sed	*but*
sī	*if*
tū	*you (subject)*

CHAPTER 2: LATIN TO ENGLISH SENTENCES

1. **tē amō.** PLAUT MOST 303
2. **quid cōgitās?** PETR 72.5
3. **tē exspectō.** TER ADEL 322
4. **nunc ego tē laudō.** PLAUT EPID 150
5. **sed nunc properō.** CIC ATT 5.17.2
6. **quid nunc putās?** CIC FAM 11.24.1
7. **tē rogō.** PLAUT PSEUD 971
8. **nōn amās mē?** PLAUT CAS 978
9. **cōgitāte nunc.** CIC VER 2.185
10. **quis negat?** CIC PRO PLANC 63
11. **quid rogās?** PLAUT MERC 214
12. **tū mē amās, ego tē amō.** PLAUT MOST 305
13. **quid exspectātis?** CIC VER 2.191

CHAPTER 2: ENGLISH TO LATIN SENTENCES

1. You love nothing.   PLAUT MG 625
2. We are waiting for you.   CIC ATT 4.2.7
3. What are you waiting for?   SEN E 76.6
4. If you deny, I deny.   PLAUT AUL 137
5. Hurry (plural)!   PLAUT CAS 766
6. What are you asking me?   PLAUT BACC 801
7. He denies nothing.   [QUINT] DECL 19.5

3 Nouns of the First Declension/Cases/Prepositions

Like verbs, Latin nouns have different endings, called inflectional endings, which indicate their grammatical function. By grammatical function, I mean whether the word is used as the subject of a sentence (near its beginning, as in "Life can be harsh"), the object of a verb (near its end, as in "I admire her life"), or the object of a preposition (as in "In my life, I love you more"). Your job will be to memorize the endings that go with each noun. All Latin nouns fall into one of five families, traditionally called declensions. Here is a common representative noun of the first declension. By learning this pattern, you achieve power over hundreds of other first declension nouns:

Singular		Plural	
vīt-a	life	**vīt-ae**	lives
vīt-ae	of life	**vīt-ārum**	of lives
vīt-ae	to/for life	**vīt-īs**	to/for lives
vīt-am	life	**vīt-ās**	lives
vīt-ā	by/with/from life	**vīt-īs**	by/with/from lives
vīt-a	life	**vīt-ae**	lives

Once again, I have broken up the words with dashes to bring out the endings more clearly. As with verbs, there is an unchanging element, the root. By itself, it signals "life" but no more. The various endings signal the word's grammatical function.

The first form is called the **nominative case** and tells you that the word is the subject of a verb. The next form, the **genitive case**, generally indicates possession; it can usually be translated with "of." The **dative case** is used for the indirect object of a verb, the **accusative case** for the direct object, and the **ablative case** functions in general as a prepositional case. The final case is the **vocative**, when you use the noun in direct address. The next table shows what I mean:

Case	Singular		Plural	
nominative	**vīt-a**	life	**vīt-ae**	lives
genitive	**vīt-ae**	of life	**vīt-ārum**	of lives
dative	**vīt-ae**	to/for life	**vīt-īs**	to/for lives
accusative	**vīt-am**	life	**vīt-ās**	lives
ablative	**vīt-ā**	by/with/from life	**vīt-īs**	by/with/from lives
vocative	**vīt-a**	life	**vīt-ae**	lives

You have probably noticed that some of these endings are repeated: The -**ae** appears four times and the -**īs** twice. This ambiguity will be a constant feature of Latin endings. You might suppose that, if one has chosen to have a language with inflectional endings, these endings ought to be clear and unambiguous so that there would be no confusion between a word used as subject and one used as an indirect object. I cannot argue with your logic. However, Latin was not created by a group of linguistic experts but grew up over centuries in the minds and mouths of millions of speakers. As a result, the various families of nouns and verbs traded around with each other over time and thus display some ambiguities and irregularities. For now, we will concentrate on the regularities, leaving the ambiguities for later. In general, when a word has several possibilities, like **vītae**, the surrounding sentence will provide enough grammatical clues to determine whether it means "of life," "to/for life," or "lives." Be advised, however, that you need to keep all the possibilities present in your mind as you read a sentence. And, when asked what possibilities an ambiguous form has, you should be able to say what they are.

In addition to case, Latin nouns also have number—singular and plural—and gender—feminine, masculine, or neuter. Most first declension nouns (**but not all!**) are feminine and will be signaled in the vocabulary by the abbreviation "f." after the word. If you do not know the gender of a noun, you cannot fully understand its use in Latin sentences.

One type of Latin word that does not decline is the preposition. Rather than attempt to define a preposition, I will simply give some examples in English: "toward," "in," "on," "through," and many others. In English, a preposition governs a noun, which is then called the "object of the preposition." Latin prepositions also have nouns as objects, but the noun will appear in either the accusative or ablative case. There is no way to predict which case a particular preposition requires; it must simply be memorized.

NOTE ON PROPER NOUNS

Just as nouns have different inflections, so too do proper nouns, that is, names. It may strike you as odd that one's own name can be subject to various spellings, but it is perfectly in keeping with the logic of inflected languages. So if your name is **Livia**, you may find your-self referred to as **Liviam** (accusative) or **Liviae** (genitive or dative). In fact, several women named **Livia** would be referred to with plural endings: **Liviās video** "I see the Livias." Though a name may have a variety of forms when written in Latin, your translation of it should always restore it to its nominative form.

For convenience, all proper nouns in this book will begin with a capital letter, although this is a modern convention that has no relation to ancient Latin. The Romans used only capitals; lowercase letters were not invented until much later. (Also, they did not leave spaces between words, and punctuation was optional or lacking!)

▎ CHAPTER 3: VOCABULARY

fortūna, ae, f.	fortune, Fortune
lacrima, ae, f.	tear
litterae, ārum, f. pl.	a letter (epistle), letters
patria, ae, f.	homeland
puella, ae, f.	girl
sententia, ae, f.	(settled) opinion
via, ae, f.	road, way
vīta, ae, f.	life
mūtō, mūtāre, mūtāvī, mūtātus	change
spectō, spectāre, spectāvī, spectātus	watch, look at, view
vocō, vocāre, vocāvī, vocātus	call; invite
ad	to, toward (prep. + acc.)
in	in (prep. + abl.)
itaque	and so
longa	long
per	through (prep. + acc.)
quō	(to) where, whither
tua	your

CHAPTER 3: LATIN TO ENGLISH SENTENCES

1. **quō properās, Aurōra? manē.**   OV A 1.13.3
2. **itaque tuās litterās exspectō.**   CIC ATT 11.16.3
3. **valē, puella.**   CATULLUS 8.12
4. **longa via est; properā!**   OV TRIST 1.1.127
5. **vītam rogat.**   SENR C 7.3.3
6. **per lacrimās spectō.**   OV HER 6.71
7. **sed quō vocat mē patria?**   SEN OED 296
8. **nunc, nunc properāte, puellae!**   OV F 2.745
9. **manēte in sententiā.**   CIC PHIL 14.3
10. **mē ad vītam vocās.**   CIC ATT 3.7.2
11. **mūtat via longa puellās.**   PROP 1.12.11

CHAPTER 3: GLOSSED LATIN TO ENGLISH SENTENCES

1. **sed mē patria** sollicitat.   sollicitō: worry   CIC FAM 10.1.1
2. **mē ad** cēnam **vocā.**   cēna, ae, f.: dinner   TER PHOR 1053
3. **ad** dominam **properō.**   domina, ae, f.: mistress   OV A 3.6.2
4. **vīta** vigilia **est.**   vigilia, ae, f.: being awake at night   PLINY NH PR 18
5. **nōn est** mea, **sed tua** culpa **est.**   mea: my   MART 11.79.3
                                         culpa, ae, f.: fault
6. **ad** mētam **properāte** simul.   mēta, ae, f.: finish-line   OV AA 2.727
                                         simul: at the same time

CHAPTER 3: ENGLISH TO LATIN SENTENCES

1. I love Casina.   PLAUT CAS 225
2. I praise your fortunes.   PLAUT RUD 523
3. I remain in (my) opinion.   CIC ATT 9.10.8
4. I do not change (my) opinion.   SEN E 10.1
5. He remains in (his) homeland.   CIC ATT 10.10.2
6. Terentia invites Pomponia.   CIC ATT 2.3.4

Nouns of the Second Declension: Masculine

The second family of Latin nouns shows more variation than the first. For one thing, it contains both masculine and neuter nouns. As a general rule, the masculine nouns end in -**us** and the neuter nouns end in -**um**, but this rule will eventually be amended. Unfortunately, there is no sure way to predict the gender of a Latin noun, so it must simply be noted and memorized. Here is a representative masculine noun of the second declension:

Case	Singular		Plural	
nominative	**anim-us**	mind	**anim-ī**	minds
genitive	**anim-ī**	of mind	**anim-ōrum**	of minds
dative	**anim-ō**	to/for mind	**anim-īs**	to/for minds
accusative	**anim-um**	mind	**anim-ōs**	minds
ablative	**anim-ō**	by/with/from mind	**anim-īs**	by/with/from minds
vocative	**anim-e**	mind	**anim-ī**	minds

As with the first declension, certain endings appear more than once: the -**ī**, the -**ō**, and the -**īs**. However, a well-written Latin sentence will be structured so that there is no ambiguity, as you will see. Note that if you are asked to translate the word "**animī**" with no other information given, the correct answers will be "of mind" (genitive singular) or "minds" (nominative plural) or "minds" (vocative plural). It is important to keep the various possibilities in your mind, even though in a real sentence only one of them can be correct.

Many masculine nouns of the second declension end not just in -**us**, but in -**ius**. These nouns contain a slight exception to the previous table. Their vocative singular ends not with the expected -**e**, but, anomalously, with an -**ī**. Here is a table with the unexpected form underlined:

Case	Singular		Plural	
nominative	**fīli-us**	son	**fīli-ī**	sons
genitive	**fīli-ī**	of son	**fīli-ōrum**	of sons
dative	**fīli-ō**	to/for son	**fīli-īs**	to/for sons
accusative	**fīli-um**	son	**fīli-ōs**	sons
ablative	**fīli-ō**	by/with/from son	**fīli-īs**	by/with/from sons
vocative	<u>**fīl-ī**</u>	son	**fīli-ī**	sons

Although the only difference is the vocative singular, it is a very common phenomenon since this family includes many Roman men's names like **Gāius**, **Lūcius**, **Iūlius**, and hundreds more.

CHAPTER 4: VOCABULARY

amīcus, ī, m.	*friend*
animus, ī, m.	*mind, heart*
deus, deī, m.	*god*
fīlius, fīliī, m.	*son*
inimīcus, ī, m.	*enemy (personal)*
mundus, ī, m.	*universe*
errō, errāre, errāvī, errātus	*wander; be wrong*
narrō, narrāre, narrāvī, narrātus	*tell, relate*
grātiam habeō	*be grateful*
igitur	*therefore*
Ītalia, ae, f.	*Italy*
mihi	*to/for me*
nātūra, ae, f.	*nature*
-ne	*(indicates a question)*
nec/neque ... nec/neque	*neither ... nor*
salvē/salvēte	*hello*
sine	*without (prep. + abl.)*

VOCABULARY NOTE   The word **deus** has several common alternate forms, underlined in the table that follows. Oddly, in classical Latin, there is no vocative singular!

Case	Singular	Plural
nominative	**de-us**	**de-ī / diī / dī**
genitive	**de-ī**	**de-ōrum**
dative	**de-ō**	**de-īs / diīs / dīs**
accusative	**de-um**	**de-ōs**
ablative	**de-ō**	**de-īs / diīs / dīs**
vocative	**—**	**de-ī / diī / dī**

CHAPTER 4: LATIN TO ENGLISH SENTENCES

1. **habēsne tū amīcum?**   PLAUT TRIN 89
2. **sed narrā mihi, Gāī, rogō.**   PETR 67.1
3. **errās, Lūcīlī.**   SEN E 21.2
4. **nec amīcum habeō nec inimīcum?**   SUET N 47.3
5. **habeō gratiam dīs.**   TER HEC 653
6. **nec nātūra sine deō est nec deus sine nātūrā.**   SEN BEN 4.8.2
7. **Fortūnae fīlius!**   HOR S 2.6.49
8. **nōn est igitur mundus deus.**   CIC ND 3.23

CHAPTER 4: GLOSSED LATIN TO ENGLISH SENTENCES

1. **sed properā, per deōs!**
2. occaecat **animōs Fortūna.**
3. **in** oculīs **animus** habitat.

4. superat **sententia** Sabīnī.

5. **amīcōrum litterae mē ad** triumphum **vocant.**

per: (prep. + acc.) by
occaecō (1): blind
oculus, ī, m.: eye
habitō (1): live, dwell

superō (1): prevail
Sabīnus, ī, m.

triumphus, ī, m.: victory parade

CIC AD BRUT 1.15.12

LIVY 5.37.1

PLINY NH 11.145

CAES BG 5.31.3

CIC ATT 6.6.4

CHAPTER 4: ENGLISH TO LATIN SENTENCES

1. Hello, friend.
2. I see your mind.
3. You are wrong, Clodius.
4. (Your) son is well.
5. I have a son.
6. Pompeius remains in Italy.
7. I am waiting for Servius.

TER EUN 560

SENR C 2.PR.3

CIC ATT 1.16.9

CIC AD BRUT 1.4A.4

QUINT DECL 335

CIC ATT 9.10.5

CIC ATT 10.10.4

Nouns of the Second Declension: Neuter

The second declension also contains neuter nouns. Neuter nouns have many of the same endings as masculine nouns, but with a few differences. Here is a typical neuter noun of the second declension:

Case	Singular		Plural	
nominative	**fāt-um**	fate	**fāt-a**	fates
genitive	**fāt-ī**	of fate	**fāt-ōrum**	of fates
dative	**fāt-ō**	to/for fate	**fāt-īs**	to/for fates
accusative	**fāt-um**	fate	**fāt-a**	fates
ablative	**fāt-ō**	by/with/from fate	**fāt-īs**	by/with/from fates
vocative	**fāt-um**	fate	**fāt-a**	fates

With neuters there are more ambiguous endings: the -**um**, the -**o**, the -**a**, and the -**īs**. In addition, the following rule applies to all neuter nouns in the language:

▼ **The nominative, accusative, and vocative of all neuter nouns are identical.**

The introduction of neuter nouns will complicate your reading of Latin. Previously, a noun ending in -**a** was pretty likely to be the nominative (like **amīca**), and a noun ending in -**um** was pretty likely to be the accusative (like **animum**). Now, however, the -**a** ending could signal nominative plural, accusative plural, or even vocative plural—if the noun is neuter. The only defense is to memorize the gender of all nouns. That way you will not get **vitia** ("faults") mixed up with **vīta** ("life").

CHAPTER 5: VOCABULARY

argentum, ī, n.	*silver, money*
aurum, ī, n.	*gold*
beneficium, iī, n.	*kindness, favor*
consilium, iī, n.	*advice, counsel, plan*
fātum, ī, n.	*fate*
officium, iī, n.	*duty, service*
verbum, ī, n.	*word*
vitium, iī, n.	*fault (of character)*
dō, dare, dedī, dātus	*give*
pugnō, pugnāre, pugnāvī, pugnātus	*fight*
teneō, tenēre, tenuī, tentus	*hold*
at	*but*
cum	*with (prep. + abl.)*
dīvitiae, ārum, f. pl.	*riches*
dominus, ī, m.	*owner, master*
et	*and*
meum	*my*
servus, ī, m.	*slave*

CHAPTER 5: LATIN TO ENGLISH SENTENCES

1.	**datisne argentum?**	PLAUT ASIN 712
2.	**aurum habet.**	PLAUT POEN 660
3.	**habētis consilium meum.**	SENR S 2.9
4.	**at vocat officium.**	PERS 6.27
5.	**verbīs laudō.**	CIC ATT 6.1.16
6.	**dīvitiās putās aurum et argentum?**	SENR C 2.1.1
7.	**ego argentum habeō.**	PLAUT CURC 530
8.	**nōn cum fātō pugnant.**	SEN QN 2.38.3
9.	**nōn dat beneficium servus dominō.**	SEN BEN 3.18.3

CHAPTER 5: GLOSSED LATIN TO ENGLISH SENTENCES

1. **vīta** vīnum **est.**

   vīnum, ī, n.: wine — PETR 34.7

2. **dat** signa **deus.**

   signum, ī, n.: sign — TIB 1.5.57

3. **in** forō operam **amīcīs dā.**

   opera, ae, f.: support — PLAUT TRIN 651

   forum, ī, n.: forum

4. **mē** quoque **fāta vocant?**

   quoque: (adverb) also, too — OV HER 6.28

5. **fāta sī vītam negant, habēs** sepulcrum.

   sepulcrum, ī, n.: tomb — SEN TROAD 511–2

6. **animum** dēbēs **mūtāre, nōn** caelum.

   dēbeo (2): ought — SEN E 28.1

   caelum, ī, n.: sky

CHAPTER 5: ENGLISH TO LATIN SENTENCES

1. Do you hold the money? — PLAUT PERS 413

2. Give the money to me. — PLAUT PERS 422

3. Do you (plural) have the gold? — PLAUT BACC 269

4. You give advice to me. — PLAUT MG 1114

5. It is a fault of the mind. — SEN CLEM 2.4.4

6 Adjectives of the First and Second Declensions

An adjective is a word that describes a noun. Like nouns and verbs, Latin adjectives also have various endings—and you have already learned them! That is, there is a large family of adjectives that have the same endings as nouns of the first and second declensions. The basic rule for using adjectives in Latin is as follows:

▼ **An adjective must agree with the noun it modifies in case, number, and gender.**

Notice that, although the adjective has to have the same case, number, and gender as the noun it modifies, it does not have to be right next to that noun. Also, adjectives can assume more endings than nouns, as the following table for **bonus** "good" will show:

Case	Singular			Plural		
	masc	*fem*	*neut*	*masc*	*fem*	*neut*
nominative	**bon-us**	**bon-a**	**bon-um**	**bon-ī**	**bon-ae**	**bon-a**
genitive	**bon-ī**	**bon-ae**	**bon-ī**	**bon-ōrum**	**bon-ārum**	**bon-ōrum**
dative	**bon-ō**	**bon-ae**	**bon-ō**	**bon-īs**	**bon-īs**	**bon-īs**
accusative	**bon-um**	**bon-am**	**bon-um**	**bon-ōs**	**bon-ās**	**bon-a**
ablative	**bon-ō**	**bon-ā**	**bon-ō**	**bon-īs**	**bon-īs**	**bon-īs**
vocative	**bon-e**	**bon-a**	**bon-um**	**bon-ī**	**bon-ae**	**bon-a**

You may be thinking that adjectives will always have the same endings as the nouns they modify. Unfortunately, it is not that simple. The table applies to the hundreds of adjectives of the first and second declensions, which are the only two declensions you know so far. Later, however, there will be adjectives of the third declension, to be introduced after you have learned nouns of the third declension. Their endings will not be the same as those of nouns in the first two declensions.

CHAPTER 6: VOCABULARY

aliēnus, a, um	*belonging to another, somebody else's*
bonus, a, um	*good*
longus, a, um	*long*
magnus, a, um	*big, great*
meus, a, um	*my, mine*
multus, a, um	*much; (plural) many*
nullus, a, um	*no, none*
plēnus, a, um	*full*
salvus, a, um	*unharmed*
tuus, a, um	*your(s)*
vērus, a, um	*true*
cūrō, cūrāre, cūrāvī, cūrātus	*care about, take care of*
gaudium, iī, n.	*joy*
glōria, ae, f.	*glory*
negōtium, iī, n.	*business, affair*
oculus, ī, m.	*eye*
quidem	*at any rate (emphasizes previous word)*
Rōma, ae, f.	*Rome*
satis / sat	*enough*
somnus, ī, m.	*sleep*
tibi	*to/for you*

CHAPTER 6: PRACTICE SENTENCES (ANSWERS FOLLOW CHAPTER 66)

1. **tuum consilium vērum est.**   CIC ATT 10.10.2
2. I praise your plan.   PLAUT PERS 548
3. I have no master.   SEN E 47.12

CHAPTER 6: LATIN TO ENGLISH SENTENCES

1. **aliēna negōtia cūrō.**   HOR S 2.3.19
2. **bone serve, salvē!**   PLAUT BACC 775
3. **longa est vīta sī plēna est.**   SEN E 93.2
4. **ego quidem meōs oculōs habeō.**   PLAUT MG 347
5. **multōs inimīcōs habēs.**   PLAUT AUL 580
6. **salva Roma, salva patria, salvus est Germānicus.**   SUET CAL 6.1
7. **aliēna vitia in oculīs habēmus.**   SEN IRA 2.28.8
8. **nullane habēs vitia?**   HOR S 1.3.20
9. **habeō, Neptūne, gratiam magnam tibi.**   PLAUT MOST 431
10. **glōria magna tua est.**   PROP 2.12.22
11. **sed nōn longa satis gaudia somnus habet.**   OV HER 15.126

CHAPTER 6: GLOSSED LATIN TO ENGLISH SENTENCES

1. **nunc** aurea **Rōma est.**	aureus, a, um: golden	OV AA 3.113
2. lenta īra **deōrum est.**	lentus, a, um: slow	JUV 13.100
	īra, ae, f.: anger	
3. per **magnōs, Brūte, deōs tē** ōrō.	per: (prep. + acc.) by	HOR S 1.7.33-34
	ōrō (1): beg	
4. **dī** pia facta **vident.**	pius, a, um: dutiful	OV F 2.117
	factum, ī, n.: deed	
5. **magnam fortūnam magnus animus** decet.	deceō (2): befit, suit	SEN CLEM 1.5.5
6. **sī** ita **putās,** tōtam ignōrās **viam glōriae.**	ita: thus	CIC PHIL 1.33
	tōtus, a, um: whole	
	ignōrō (1): be ignorant of	

CHAPTER 6: ENGLISH TO LATIN SENTENCES

1. He has a great mind.   SEN E 87.18
2. Your glory is true.   OV HER 17.243
3. I have no slave.   CIC ROSCAM 145
4. He is in great joy.   SEN E 23.4

7

Present Tense of **sum** and **possum**/Complementary Infinitive

In many languages, the verb "to be" is irregular, and Latin is no exception. The irregularity generally takes the form of a root that changes unexpectedly within a tense or from tense to tense. Since "to be" is a very common verb, perhaps the most frequently used verb in Latin, it must be thoroughly learned. Here is the present tense:

Present

su–m	I am	**su–mus**	we are
e–s	you are	**es–tis**	you are
es–t	he/she/it is	**su–nt**	they are

At least the endings are familiar, with the stipulation that the first person form can end in **-m**. There are also two imperatives and an infinitive:

es	be!	**este**	be!

esse	to be

The verb "to be" has certain peculiarities in its grammatical use, some of them quite different from modern American usage. In grammatical terms, the verb "to be" does not take a direct object (an accusative in Latin). In other words, the verb "to be" functions as a kind of grammatical equals sign so that whatever case appears on one side must appear on the other. Consider the following sentences:

amīcus sum.	I am a friend.	PLAUT PERS 293
tuus est servus.	He is your slave.	PLAUT AMPH 610
salvae sumus.	We (feminine) are safe.	TER EUN 834
ego bonus fīlius sum.	I am a good son.	[QUINT] DECL 4.18
dī sumus.	We are gods.	OV M 8.689

Note that, in certain circumstances, the forms **est** and **sunt** can be translated "there is" and "there are." Only the context can suggest when to use this construction. (In Latin, there is no "there" there.) Here are some examples:

nunc, nunc perīculum est.	Now, now there is danger.	PLAUT RUD 169
sunt enim multa vitia.	For there are many faults.	QUINT 11.3.31

Almost as common as **sum** is the word **possum**, which means "I am able" or "I can." In origin, **possum** was formed by combining the verb **sum** with the element **pot-**, meaning "able." It was once spelled **potsum**, but over the centuries the combination of **t** and **s** became **ss**. However, when the element **pot-** came before a vowel, the **t** remained. A table makes this all clearer:

Present

pos-sum	I am able	**pos-sumus**	we are able
pot-es	you are able	**pot-estis**	you are able
pot-est	he/she/it is able	**pos-sunt**	they are able

Beware: Although **possum** can be translated "I can," it is best to avoid that translation for the time being. If you stick with "I am able" you will be reminded that the infinitive form must follow. The infinitive generated by **possum** is called "complementary" because it completes the meaning of **possum**. In later chapters you will learn other verbs that can take a complementary infinitive.

CHAPTER 7: VOCABULARY

sum, esse, fuī, futūrus	*to be*
possum, posse, potuī, —	*to be able*
accūsō, accūsāre, accūsāvī, accūsātus	*blame; accuse*
aut	*or*
avāritia, ae, f.	*greed*
caecus, a, um	*blind*
certē	*certainly*

enim	*for (conjunction)*
ibi	*there (adverb)*
malus, a, um	*bad; evil*
perīculum, i, n.	*danger*
philosophia, ae, f.	*philosophy*
quam	*how*
ubi	*where*

CHAPTER 7: PRACTICE SENTENCES (ANSWERS FOLLOW CHAPTER 66)

1. **satis tibi est?** TER PHOR 1047
2. **nunc enim tū mea es.** PLAUT EPID 648
3. **tū pugnāre potes.** OV M 13.364
4. Where are you, slaves? PLAUT CIST 649
5. A. Are you bad? B. I am bad. PLAUT POEN 866
6. I cannot praise. CIC PRO MIL 33

CHAPTER 7: LATIN TO ENGLISH SENTENCES

1. **Fortūna caeca est.** CIC DE AMIC 54
2. **ubi sum, ibi nōn sum; ubi nōn sum, ibi est animus.** PLAUT CIST 211-2
3. **negōtiī nunc sum plēnus.** PLAUT PSEUD 380
4. **tē quidem satis laudāre nōn possum.** CIC PRO MIL 99
5. **nunc enim amās mē; amīcus nōn es.** SEN E 35.1
6. **ego tū sum, tū es ego.** PLAUT STICH 731
7. **quid enim sumus aut quid esse possumus?** CIC ATT 13.10.1
8. **accūsāre fāta possumus; mutāre nōn possumus.** SEN AD POLY 4.1
9. **at quam caeca avāritia est!** CIC PHIL 2.97
10. **exspectāre glōriam certē nullam potestis.** CIC REPUB 6.20
11. **dominīs servī beneficia possunt dare.** SEN BEN 3.18.4
12. **philosophia bonum consilium est.** SEN E 38.1
13. **nullum est enim perīculum.** CIC DE ORAT 1.209

CHAPTER 7: GLOSSED LATIN TO ENGLISH SENTENCES

1. **nōn sum, Classice,** tam **malus** poēta.

2. **nōn longa est** fābula.

3. **vērae** amīcitiae sempiternae **sunt.**

4. quantum **potes properā.**

5. **at** obscūrum **deō nihil potest esse.**

6. A. **nōn sum** īrāta. B. **nōn es?**
    A. **nōn sum.**

tam: so	
poēta, ae, m.: poet	MART 2.86.6
fābula, ae, f.: story	HOR S 1.1.95
amīcitia, ae, f.: friendship	CIC DE AMIC 32
sempiternus, a, um: eternal	
quantum: as much as	SEN E 4.1
obscūrus, a, um: dark	CIC ND 3.38
īrātus, a, um: angry	PLAUT POEN 404

CHAPTER 7: ENGLISH TO LATIN SENTENCES

1. I am your slave. — PLAUT CAS 738

2. Now where are you? — PLAUT BACC 149

3. You are full of advice. — PLAUT EPID 152

4. Certainly she is mine. — TER AND 933

5. For who can deny (it)? — MART 1.64.2

6. I am not able to hold (my) tears. — QUINT DECL 260

7. You (plural) are not able to give life. — PLINY E 2.20.8

8. For there are no bad gods. — AUG CD 8.13

8 Substantives

The short explanation of a substantive is that it is an adjective used as a noun. We do the same thing in English when we talk of "the good," "the bad," and "the ugly" or refer to the United States as the land of "the free" and the home of "the brave." As you can see, the way to create a substantive in English is to use the definite article with an adjective. But Latin has no definite article; therefore, the way to spot a substantive is to observe an adjective that is not modifying a noun.

For example, the adjective **malus, -a, -um** "bad" is often used alone as a substantive. Thus, **malus** by itself is "a bad man" and **malum** is "a bad thing," and **mala** are "bad things." (Depending on the context **mala** could also be "a bad woman.") Another very common Latin substantive is **vērum** meaning literally "a true thing," but more often "the truth." Another common substantive is the adjective **meus, -a, -um** used in the masculine plural **meī** (or **meōrum** or **meīs** or **meōs**) to mean "my dear ones" or "my close friends."

The possibility that an adjective is functioning as a substantive means you must proceed with more caution when dealing with an adjective. Do not assume that it is modifying a noun—it may be standing alone. Here are some examples of substantives; note that they all involve an adjective standing alone. The substantive may be singular or plural, masculine, feminine or neuter, and appear in any case:

1.	**magnum narrās.**	You relate a great thing.	HOR S 1.9.52
2.	**magna rogās.**	You ask for great things.	MART 11.58.2
3.	**stultī timent Fortūnam.**	Foolish people fear Fortune.	PUBLSYR S6
4.	**tacē, stulta.**	Be silent, foolish (woman).	PLAUT PERS 385

In sentence 1, **magnum** is accusative singular neuter; because it is neuter and singular, you can translate it with "thing." In sentence 2, **magna** is accusative plural neuter; because it is neuter and plural, you can supply the word "things." In sentence 3, **stultī** is nominative plural masculine; because it is masculine and plural, you can translate it with "foolish people" (or "fools"). In sentence 4, **stulta** is vocative singular feminine; because it is feminine and singular, you can translate it with "woman."

CHAPTER 8: VOCABULARY

beātus, a, um	*supremely happy*
cēterī, ae, a	*the rest*
stultus, a, um	*stupid, foolish*
summus, a, um	*highest*
gaudeō, gaudēre, gāvīsus sum	*rejoice*
iubeō, iubēre, iussī, iussus	*bid, order*
moveō, movēre, mōvī, mōtus	*move, rouse*
atque/ac	*and also*
bellum, ī, n.	*war*
causa, ae, f.	*cause; case*
dē	*about; from (prep. + abl.)*
ingenium, iī, n.	*mental character; talent*
locus, ī, m.	*place*
nisi	*unless, if not; except*
saepe	*often*
vērum, ī, n.	*truth*

CHAPTER 8: PRACTICE SENTENCES (ANSWERS FOLLOW CHAPTER 66)

1. **aliēna laudat.**   SEN HERC 341
2. **multa dare potes.**   SEN BEN 5.4.1
3. **cētera negāre nōn potes.**   CIC VER 3.132
4. Ask for great things.   MART 11.68.2
5. Greed is a bad thing.   CIC INVENT 1.95
6. If you (plural) can, praise the good.   SEN VIT BEAT 27.1

CHAPTER 8: LATIN TO ENGLISH SENTENCES

1. **nōn est sententia – vērum est.**   JUV 8.125
2. **multa mē movent.**   CIC HAR RESP 31
3. **vidēs enim cētera.**   CIC ATT 2.3.2
4. **nisi beātus est, in summō bonō nōn est.**   SEN E 71.18
5. **vīta nec bonum nec malum est; bonī ac malī locus est.** SEN E 99.12
6. **magna dī cūrant.**   CIC ND 2.167
7. **nōn est enim bonum nisi vērum est.**   SEN E 118.8
8. **stultī ac malī nōn gaudent?**   SEN E 59.17
9. **ingenium mala saepe movent.**   OV AA 2.43
10. **iubēs mē bona cōgitāre.**   CIC TD 3.35

CHAPTER 8: GLOSSED LATIN TO ENGLISH SENTENCES

1. **deī** hūmāna **nōn cūrant.**   hūmānus, a, um: human   CIC ND 1.123
2. **multa mē** sollicitant.   sollicitō (1): worry   CIC ATT 2.19.1
3. **tibi meōs** commendō.   commendō (1): entrust   CIC ATT 3.6
4. **multī** amīcās **habent.**   amīca, ae, f.: girlfriend   SEN E 122.14
5. **parvum parva** decent.   deceō (2): befit, suit   HOR E 1.7.44
6. **tē tua, mē** dēlectant **mea.**   dēlectō (1): delight   CIC TD 5.63
7. exiguum **nātūra** dēsīderat.   exiguus, a, um: tiny   SEN E 16.8
                                          dēsīderō (1): need
8. **bonī** improbīs, improbī **bonīs   improbus, a, um: base   CIC DE AMIC 74
   amīcī esse nōn possunt.**

CHAPTER 8: ENGLISH TO LATIN SENTENCES

1. Riches are not a good thing.   SEN PROV 5.2
2. Look toward the true good.   SEN E 23.6
3. Many praise you.   SEN E 7.12
4. War is the cause of bad things.   QUINT 5.10.73
5. I love the truth.   PLAUT MOST 181
6. I am silent about the rest.   CIC LEG AGR 2.24

Second Declension Nouns and Adjectives in **-er**

In addition to second declension nouns in -**us**, there is an important group whose nominatives end in -**er**. These -**er** nouns fall into two families, which can be conveniently represented by the nouns **puer** "boy" and **ager** "field":

Case	Singular	Plural	Singular	Plural
	puer		ager	
nominative	puer	puer-ī	ager	agr-ī
genitive	puer-ī	puer-ōrum	agr-ī	agr-ōrum
dative	puer-ō	puer-īs	agr-ō	agr-īs
accusative	puer-um	puer-ōs	agr-um	agr-ōs
ablative	puer-ō	puer-īs	arg-ō	agr-īs
vocative	puer	puer-ī	ager	agr-ī

Notice that **puer** retains the -**e**- in its root while **ager** loses its -**e**-. There is no way to predict whether such a noun will keep or drop the -**e**-. Only careful attention to the genitive form—which always reveals the root—will make it clear.

In addition, there is also a small but important group of adjectives that act like **puer** and **ager**. That is, the nominative masculine singular shows -**er**, with the feminine having either -**era** or -**ra**. Two tables will illustrate both patterns; notice that **līber** "free" keeps the -**e**- while **noster** "our" drops it:

Case	Singular			Plural		
	masc	*fem*	*neut*	*masc*	*fem*	*neut*
nominative	līber	līber-a	līber-um	līber-ī	līber-ae	līber-a
genitive	līber-ī	līber-ae	līber-ī	līber-ōrum	līber-ārum	līber-ōrum
dative	līber-ō	līber-ae	līber-ō	līber-īs	līber-īs	līber-īs
accusative	līber-um	līber-am	līber-um	līber-ōs	līber-ās	līber-a
ablative	līber-ō	līber-ā	līber-ō	līber-īs	līber-īs	līber-īs
vocative	līber	līber-a	līber-um	līber-ī	līber-ae	līber-a

Case	Singular			Plural		
	masc	*fem*	*neut*	*masc*	*fem*	*neut*
nominative	noster	nostr-a	nostr-um	nostr-ī	nostr-ae	nostr-a
genitive	nostr-ī	nostr-ae	nostr-ī	nostr-ōrum	nostr-ārum	nostr-ōrum
dative	nostr-ō	nostr-ae	nostr-ō	nostr-īs	nostr-īs	nostr-īs
accusative	nostr-um	nostr-am	nostr-um	nostr-ōs	nostr-ās	nostr-a
ablative	nostr-ō	nostr-ā	nostr-ō	nostr-īs	nostr-īs	nostr-īs
vocative	noster	nostr-a	nostr-um	nostr-ī	nostr-ae	nostr-a

CHAPTER 9: VOCABULARY

vir, virī, m.	*man; husband*
līberī, ōrum, m. pl.	*children*
aeger, gra, grum	*sick*
līber, era, erum	*free*
miser, era, erum	*wretched*
noster, tra, trum	*our(s)*
vester, tra, trum	*your(s)*

adiuvō, adiuvāre, adiūvī, adiūtus	*aid, help*
inquam, inquis, inquit	*I say, you say, he/she says*
aeternus, a, um	*eternal*
iam	*(by) now; soon; already*
in	*into (prep. + acc.)*
ita	*so, thus*
ō	*oh!*
semper	*always (adverb)*
valdē	*really, definitely (adverb)*

VOCABULARY NOTE   The verb **inquam** is a so-called "defective" verb because it does not have the full range of forms. These three are the major ones.

CHAPTER 9: PRACTICE SENTENCES (ANSWERS FOLLOW CHAPTER 66)

1. **spectāte, miserī!**   SEN AGAM 758
2. **habēs nostra consilia.**   CIC ATT 5.21.10
3. **vestrum cūrāte officium.**   PLAUT BACC 760
4. **nostrum, nōn nātūrae vitium est.**   SEN E 22.15
5. I (masculine) am wretched.   PLAUT PSEUD 80
6. Balbus is sick.   CIC ATT 13.47A.1
7. The mind is free.   QUINT DECL 282
8. I await your (plural) letters.   CIC FAM 14.16

CHAPTER 9: LATIN TO ENGLISH SENTENCES

1. **lībera es iam.**   PLAUT MOST 209
2. **ita nec beātus est vester deus nec aeternus.**   CIC ND 1.114
3. **multa miser timeō.**   OV A 1.4.45
4. **sī enim sunt virī bonī, mē adiuvant.**   CIC PRO CAEC 3
5. **salvī sunt, inquam, līberī tuī.**   SENR C 9.3.7
6. **valdē enim amō nostra atque nostrōs.**   CIC ACADPOS 18

7. **vidēre nostra mala nōn possumus.** PHAEDR 4.10.4
8. **lacrimae nōnne tē nostrae movent?** SEN PHAED 880
9. **ō vīta miserō longa!** PUBLSYR
10. **vitiīs enim nostrīs in animum per oculōs via est.** [QUINT] DECL 1.6
11. **animus aeger semper errat.** CIC TD 3.5

CHAPTER 9: GLOSSED LATIN TO ENGLISH SENTENCES

1. **servusne es** an **līber?** an: or PLAUT PSEUD 610
2. **tū** fortūnātus **es, ego miser.** fortūnātus, a, um: fortunate PLAUT MOST 48
3. apud **tē est animus noster.** apud: (prep. + acc) with PLAUT BACC 713
4. apud **bonum virum bonam causam habeō.** apud: (prep. + acc) with SEN BEN 4.40.3
5. inter **bonōs virōs ac deōs** amīcitia **est.** inter: (prep. + acc) between   amīcitia, ae, f.: friendship SEN PROV 1.5
6. **pugnant** vōta **nostra cum** vōtīs, **consilia cum consiliīs.** vōtum, i, n.: vow SEN E 45.6

CHAPTER 9: ENGLISH TO LATIN SENTENCES

1. I have your (plural) opinions. QUINT DECL 369
2. Am I not free? PLAUT CAS 736
3. Marcus Crassus is wretched. CIC TD 1.13
4. You have our opinions, my Livia. SUET CLAU 4.3
5. Hello, good man. PLAUT CAS 724
6. You are a great man. SEN PROV 4.2

CHAPTER 9: PASSAGES

DESCRIPTION OF A FRIEND

siccus, sobrius **est Aper** — quid ad mē?
    servum sīc **ego laudō, nōn amīcum.**

MART 12.30

---

siccus, a, um: dry
sobrius, a, um: sober
quid ad mē?: what's it to me?
sīc: thus

DINNER FOR ONE

nōn cēnat **sine** aprō **noster, Tite, Caeciliānus.**
    bellum convīvam **Caeciliānus habet.**

MART 7.59

---

cēnō, cēnāre: dine, feast
aper, aprī, m.: boar
bellus, a, um: fine
convīva, ae, m.: dinner guest

EPITAPH FOR A FAITHFUL WIFE

virum exspectō meum.

CIL 12.5193, 3

Nouns of the Third Declension: Masculine and Feminine

The third declension in Latin has the most variations of all the five declensions and contains nouns of all genders. We will start with the regular ones and gradually learn the more deviant ones. Following are some common nouns of the third declension:

Case	Singular			Plural	
nominative	**lex**	law		**lēg-ēs**	laws
genitive	**lēg-is**	of law		**lēg-um**	of laws
dative	**lēg-ī**	to/for law		**lēg-ibus**	to/for laws
accusative	**lēg-em**	law		**lēg-ēs**	laws
ablative	**lēg-e**	by/with/from law		**lēg-ibus**	by/with/from laws
vocative	**lex**	law		**lēg-ēs**	laws

Case	Singular		Plural	
nominative	**mīles**	soldier	**mīlit-ēs**	soldiers
genitive	**mīlit-is**	of soldier	**mīlit-um**	of soldiers
dative	**mīlit-ī**	to/for soldier	**mīlit-ibus**	to/for soldiers
accusative	**mīlit-em**	soldier	**mīlit-ēs**	soldiers
ablative	**mīlit-e**	by/with/from soldier	**mīlit-ibus**	by/with/from soldiers
vocative	**mīles**	soldier	**mīlit-ēs**	soldiers

Unlike the first and second declensions, which had several points of resemblance, the third declension endings seem to be a realm unto themselves. Note the repeated endings -ēs and -ibus. In fact, the genitive form **legum** looks as if it might be an accusative from the second declension. Note also that there is no fixed ending for the nominative singular in this declension.

The only way to avoid the potential ambiguities introduced by the third declension is to memorize (1) the nominative, (2) the genitive, and (3) the gender of every noun you encounter from now on. This was less crucial in the first and second declensions since their forms were so regular and predictable. Now, however, if you think that **legum** is the accusative singular of "law," not only will you miss its true grammatical function, but you may be led to misconstrue other words in the sentence. (I call this the "snowball of disaster" effect.)

The third declension also brings another difficulty, this time concerning adjectives. In chapter 6 you were told that an adjective must agree with its noun in case, number, and gender. This rule still holds, but look what happens when an adjective from the first and second declensions modifies a third declension noun. Each word must stay in its own declension; as a result, the endings no longer match. Consider the phrase "true love"—**amor vērus**:

Case	Singular		Plural	
nominative	**amor**	**vēr-us**	**amōr-ēs**	**vēr-ī**
genitive	**amōr-is**	**vēr-ī**	**amōr-um**	**vēr-ōrum**
dative	**amōr-ī**	**vēr-ō**	**amōr-ibus**	**vēr-īs**
accusative	**amōr-em**	**vēr-um**	**amōr-ēs**	**vēr-ōs**
ablative	**amōr-e**	**vēr-ō**	**amōr-ibus**	**vēr-īs**
vocative	**amor**	**vēr-e**	**amōr-ēs**	**vēr-ī**

The endings never match! And yet the adjective always agrees with the noun. Each word is stuck in its own declension and cannot leave it. Because **amor** is a third declension noun, it must keep third declension endings. Because **vērus** is an adjective of the first and second declensions, it too must keep to its declension. Now you can see why I have urged you to memorize endings and genders so carefully. Here is "true virtue"—**virtūs vēra**:

Case	Singular		Plural	
nominative	**virtūs**	**vēr-a**	**virtūt-ēs**	**vēr-ae**
genitive	**virtūt-is**	**vēr-ae**	**virtūt-um**	**vēr-ārum**
dative	**virtūt-ī**	**vēr-ae**	**virtūt-ibus**	**vēr-īs**
accusative	**virtūt-em**	**vēr-am**	**virtūt-ēs**	**vēr-ās**
ablative	**virtūt-e**	**vēr-ā**	**virtūt-ibus**	**vēr-īs**
vocative	**virtūs**	**vēr-a**	**virtūt-ēs**	**vēr-ae**

Once again the endings never match, yet each pair is identical in case, number, and gender. By now you are probably getting the message: the endings of adjectives do not at all necessarily match the nouns they modify. This feature of Latin will only multiply when you encounter fourth and fifth declension nouns. To be safe, you should memorize the nominative, genitive, and gender of all nouns.

CHAPTER 10: VOCABULARY

amor, amōris, m.	*love*
cōgitātio, cōgitātiōnis, f.	*thought*
dolor, dolōris, m.	*pain*
homō, hominis, m.	*human being, person, fellow*
lex, lēgis, f.	*law*
mōrēs, mōrum m. pl.	*moral character*
nēmō, nēminis, m.	*no one*
potestās, potestātis, f.	*power*
ratiō, ratiōnis, f.	*reason*
virtūs, virtūtis, f.	*virtue, excellence*
probō, probāre, probāvī, probātus	*approve (of); prove*
alius, a, ud	*(an)other, else*
ex / ē	*according to (prep. + abl.)*
populus, ī, m.	*people*
quam	*than*
rectus, a, um	*right*
sapientia, ae, f.	*wisdom*
studium, iī, n.	*zeal; study*
umbra, ae, f.	*shadow, shade*

CHAPTER 10: PRACTICE SENTENCES (ANSWERS FOLLOW CHAPTER 66)

1. **nēmō sine vitiō est.**   SENR C 2.4.4

2. **amāre nēminem potest.**   [QUINT] DECL 14.10

3. **nēmō igitur esse beātus potest.**   CIC DE FIN 2.87

4. **philosophia nōn vītae lex est?** SEN E 94.39
5. **nōn tū nunc hominum mōrēs vidēs?** PLAUT PERS 385
6. Thus is the life of human beings. TER ADEL 739
7. You are a wretched fellow. CIC DE FIN 2.24
8. Law is the highest reason. CIC DE LEG 1.18
9. We give laws to free peoples. CIC DE LEG 3.4

CHAPTER 10: LATIN TO ENGLISH SENTENCES

1. **philosophia studium virtūtis est.** SEN E 89.8
2. **amor timēre nēminem vērus potest.** SEN MED 416
3. **in potestāte itaque sunt servī dominōrum.** GAIUS 1.52
4. **bonum sine ratiōne nullum est.** SEN E 66.39
5. **tuō ex ingeniō mōrēs aliēnōs probās.** PLAUT PERS 212
6. **habēs ratiōnem meārum sententiārum.** CIC AD BRUT 1.15.11
7. **ibi potest valēre populus, ubi lēgēs valent.** PUBLSYR
8. **philosophia sapientiae amor est.** SEN E 89.4
9. **nōn est igitur summum malum dolor.** CIC DE FIN 2.104
10. **nec philosophia sine virtūte est nec sine philosophiā virtūs.** SEN E 89.8
11. **nihil enim aliud est virtūs quam recta ratiō.** SEN E 66.32
12. **līberae sunt enim nostrae cōgitātiōnēs.** CIC PRO MIL 79

CHAPTER 10: GLOSSED LATIN TO ENGLISH SENTENCES

1. **tot sine amōre virī,** tot **sunt sine amōre puellae.** tot: so many OV A 2.9.15
2. **deōs nēmō** sānus **timet.** sānus: sane SEN BEN 4.19.1
3. **quid enim manet** ex antīquīs **mōribus?** antīquus: ancient
ex: (prep. + abl) out of, from CIC REPUB 5.2
4. **in** Graeciā **multōs habent** ex **hominibus deōs.** Graecia, ae, f.: Greece
ex: (prep. + abl) out of, from CIC ND 3.39
5. **oculī sunt in amōre** ducēs. dux, ducis, m.: leader PROP 2.15.12
6. **laudās fortūnam et mōrēs** antīquae plēbis. antīquus: ancient
plebs, plēbis, f.: common people HOR S 2.7.22-3

CHAPTER 10: ENGLISH TO LATIN SENTENCES

1. We are humans, not gods.   PETR 75.1
2. No one is able to give a kindness to a bad man.   SEN BEN 5.12.4
3. The pain of my mind is great.   CIC FAM 13.77.3
4. Glory is the shadow of virtue.   SEN E 79.13
5. Our children are in our power.   GAIUS 1.55

CHAPTER 10: PASSAGES

CHATTIN' HER UP: ROMAN STYLE

mea voluptās, **mea** dēlicia, **mea vīta, mea** amoenitas,
meus ocellus, **meum** labellum, **mea** salūs, **meum** sāvium,
meum mel, **meum** cor, **mea** colustra, **meus** molliculus cāseus ...

PLAUT POEN 365-7

---

voluptās, tātis, f.: pleasure
dēlicia, ae, f.: sweetheart
amoenitas, tātis, f.: delight
ocellus, ī, m.: eye
labellum, ī, n.: lip
salūs, salūtis, f.: salvation
sāvium, iī, n.: kiss
mel, mellis, n.: honey
cor, cordis, n.: heart
colustra, ae, f.: first mother's milk
molliculus, a, um: soft little
cāseus, eī, m.: cheese

11

Nouns of the Third Declension: Neuter

The third declension also contains neuter nouns. Their endings are much like those of masculine and feminine nouns, with the characteristic neuter property: The nominative, accusative, and vocative are identical. Consider the word for "wound"—**vulnus**:

Case	Singular		Plural	
nominative	**vulnus**	wound	**vulner-a**	wounds
genitive	**vulner-is**	of wound	**vulner-um**	of wounds
dative	**vulner-ī**	to/for wound	**vulner-ibus**	to/for wounds
accusative	**vulnus**	wound	**vulner-a**	wounds
ablative	**vulner-e**	by/with/from wound	**vulner-ibus**	by/with/from wounds
vocative	**vulnus**	wound	**vulner-a**	wounds

Notice that the nominative form **vulnus** is rather different than the genitive form **vulneris**. The actual root of the word is **vulner-**, a fact that emerges clearly when you memorize the genitive and the nominative and the gender, as with the third declension masculine and feminine nouns. In fact, now you can see why it is a good idea to memorize the nominative, genitive, and gender of <u>all</u> Latin nouns. It's safer that way.

The same problem arises when a third declension neuter noun is modified by an adjective of the first and second declensions. However, the situation is somewhat better since the endings are occasionally identical. See the table for "great wound"—**vulnus magnum**:

Case	Singular		Plural	
nominative	vulnus	magn-um	vulner-a	magn-a
genitive	vulner-is	magn-ī	vulner-um	magn-ōrum
dative	vulner-ī	magn-ō	vulner-ibus	magn-īs
accusative	vulnus	magn-um	vulner-a	magn-a
ablative	vulner-e	magn-ō	vulner-ibus	magn-īs
vocative	vulnus	magn-um	vulner-a	magn-a

CHAPTER 11: VOCABULARY

corpus, corporis, n.	*body*
iter, itineris, n.	*journey*
pectus, pectoris, n.	*chest; heart*
scelus, sceleris, n.	*crime*
vulnus, vulneris, n.	*wound*
careō, carēre, caruī, caritūrus	*lack (+abl.)*
et … et	*both … and*
tūtus, a, um	*safe*

CHAPTER 11: LATIN TO ENGLISH SENTENCES

1. **dolōre corpus caret.** — SEN E 66.45
2. **et longum est iter et nōn tūtum.** — CIC FAM 14.12
3. **nullum scelus est in pectore nostrō.** — OV TRIST 3.6.25
4. **habet sine vulnere corpus.** — OV M 13.267
5. **per scelera semper sceleribus tūtum est iter.** — SEN AGAM 115

CHAPTER 11: GLOSSED LATIN TO ENGLISH SENTENCES

1. membra **sumus corporis magnī.**   membrum, ī, n.: limb   SEN E 95.52
2. **sceleris in scelere** supplicium **est.**   supplicium, iī, n.: punishment   SEN E 97.14
3. **rectum iter aliīs** monstrō.   monstro (1): show   SEN E 8.3
4. **sumus igitur hominēs; ex animō** constāmus **et corpore.**   CIC DE FIN 4.25

     consto (1): consist

CHAPTER 11: ENGLISH TO LATIN SENTENCES

1. Our mind is not a body.   AUG CD 8.5
2. There is a god in our heart.   OV PONT 3.4.93

CHAPTER 11: PASSAGES

KEEP YOUR SONS SAFE

fīlius autem
corporis egregiī **miserōs** trepidōsque parentēs
semper habet.

JUV 10.295-7

---

autem: you see
egregius, a, um: outstanding
-que: and
trepidus, a, um: trembling
parens, parentis, m. or f.: parent

12

Nouns of the Third Declension: I-Stems

There is a large group of third declension nouns called "i-stem" nouns because they contain an unexpected -i-. Such nouns can be masculine, feminine, or neuter. Although there are certain rules for predicting what third declension nouns will be i-stem, they are not worth learning yet. Instead, in your vocabulary, i-stem nouns will be marked with an asterisk (*).

The following tables contain the feminine i-stem **nox** "night" and the masculine i-stem **cīvis** "citizen." The form with the unexpected -i- is underlined:

Case	Singular		Plural	
nominative	**nox**	night	**noct-ēs**	nights
genitive	**noct-is**	of night	**noct-ium**	of nights
dative	**noct-ī**	to/for night	**noct-ibus**	to/for nights
accusative	**noct-em**	night	**noct-ēs**	nights
ablative	**noct-e**	by/with/from night	**noct-ibus**	by/with/from nights
vocative	**nox**	night	**noct-ēs**	nights

Case	Singular		Plural	
nominative	**cīvis**	citizen	**cīv-ēs**	citizens
genitive	**cīv-is**	of citizen	**cīv-ium**	of citizens
dative	**cīv-ī**	to/for citizen	**cīv-ibus**	to/for citizens
accusative	**cīv-em**	citizen	**cīv-ēs**	citizens
ablative	**cīv-e**	by/with/from citizen	**cīv-ibus**	by/with/from citizens
vocative	**cīvis**	citizen	**cīv-ēs**	citizens

As you can see, the letter -i- intrudes into only one form: the genitive plural.

The situation is more complicated in the case of neuter i-stem nouns, as the following tables show; the forms with the unexpected **-i-** are underlined:

Case	Singular		Plural	
nominative	**mare**	sea	<u>**mar-ia**</u>	seas
genitive	**mar-is**	of sea	<u>**mar-ium**</u>	of seas
dative	**mar-ī**	to/for sea	**mar-ibus**	to/for seas
accusative	**mar-e**	sea	<u>**mar-ia**</u>	seas
ablative	<u>**mar-ī**</u>	by/with/from sea	**mar-ibus**	by/with/from seas
vocative	**mare**	sea	<u>**mar-ia**</u>	seas

Case	Singular		Plural	
nominative	**animal**	animal	<u>**animāl-ia**</u>	animals
genitive	**animāl-is**	of animal	<u>**animāl-ium**</u>	of animals
dative	**animāl-ī**	to/for animal	**animāl-ibus**	to/for animals
accusative	**animal**	animal	<u>**animāl-ia**</u>	animals
ablative	<u>**animāl-ī**</u>	b/w/f animal	**animāl-ibus**	b/w/f animals
vocative	**animal**	animal	<u>**animāl-ia**</u>	animals

Here, the letter -i- appears in five forms. The word **mare** is especially tricky since the -**e** appears in the nominative and accusative but not in the ablative. (In this book, you will see only two neuter i-stem nouns: **mare** and **animal**.)

CHAPTER 12: VOCABULARY

*cīvis, cīvis, m. or f.	*citizen*
*fīnis, fīnis, m.	*end*
*mens, mentis, f.	*mind*
*mors, mortis, f.	*death*
*nox, noctis, f.	*night*
*vīs, –, f.	*force*

*vīrēs, vīrium, f. pl.	*strength*
doleō, dolēre, doluī, dolitūrus	*hurt; be pained*
aut … aut	*either … or*
carmen, carminis, n.	*poem*
dignus, a, um	*worthy, worthy of (+ abl.)*
medius, a, um	*middle (of)*
parvus, a, um	*small, little*
Rōmānus, a, um	*Roman*
sānus, a, um	*healthy; sane*
tōtus, a, um	*whole*

CHAPTER 12: PRACTICE SENTENCES (ANSWERS FOLLOW CHAPTER 66)

1. **nullum videō fīnem malī.**   CIC ATT 9.18.2
2. **corpus magnās habet vīrēs.**   SEN E 15.1
3. **in perīculō mortis est.**   CELS 2.8.P.50.12
4. **mors nec bonum nec malum est.**   SEN AD MARC 19.5
5. You love a good mind.   PETR 3.1
6. We do not think about death.   SEN AD MARC 9.2
7. The power of the people is great.   [SEN] OCT 185

CHAPTER 12: LATIN TO ENGLISH SENTENCES

1. **cīvis Rōmānus sum.**   CIC VER 5.162
2. **fīne carent lacrimae.**   OV PONT 1.2.27
3. **nulla sine deō mens bona est.**   SEN E 73.16
4. **carmina morte carent.**   OV A 1.15.32
5. **aut aegrum corpus est aut dolet aut caret vīribus.**   CIC DE FIN 5.47
6. **vīs magna est in hominum ingeniīs.**   CIC DE ORAT 2.38
7. **tōtum negōtium nōn est dignum vīribus nostrīs.**   CIC FAM 2.11.1
8. **nōn parvās animō dat glōria vīrēs.**   OV TRIST 5.12.37
9. **mens sāna in corpore sānō.**   JUV 10.356
10. **tōta vīta nihil aliud quam ad mortem iter est.**   SEN AD POLY 11.2

11. **nōn mortem timēmus sed cōgitātiōnem mortis.** SEN E 30.17
12. **puellam ad mediam noctem exspectō.** HOR S 1.5.82-3

CHAPTER 12: GLOSSED LATIN TO ENGLISH SENTENCES

1. Gallia **est plēna cīvium Romānōrum.** Gallia, ae, f.: Gaul CIC PRO FONT 11

2. **nōn est beneficium** iniūriae **fīnis.** iniūria, ae, f.: injury SEN BEN 6.26.1

3. ōtium **sine** litterīs **mors est.** ōtium, iī, n.: leisure SEN E 82.3
litterae, ārum, f. pl.: literature

4. **nōn sunt in** senectūte **vīrēs.** senectus, senectūtis, f.: old age CIC DE SENEC 34

5. **sapientia** perfectum **bonum est** perfectus, a, um: perfect SEN E 89.4
mentis hūmānae. hūmānus, a, um: human

CHAPTER 12: ENGLISH TO LATIN SENTENCES

1. You are both a good citizen and a good friend. CIC FAM 2.15.3
2. But there is no end of glory. SENR S 2.2
3. Death is a law of nature. SEN QN 6.32.12
4. There is great force in the virtues. CIC TD 3.36

13

First and Second Conjugations: Imperfect and Future Tenses

The imperfect tense is the most regular and predictable of the six Latin tenses. No matter what conjugation a verb belongs to, the endings of the imperfect remain the same for all. The name "imperfect" is chosen because the action of the verb is viewed as ongoing in the past, not completed. (Completed past time is expressed by the perfect tense, to be learned later.) Thus, one common translation for the imperfect is with "was/were … -ing" as in "I was having" or "They were loving." Unfortunately, the situation is more complicated, and you will find that many imperfect verbs can better be translated by a simple past in English, like "I had" or "They loved." The choice depends on the context of the sentence. When there is no context, either way is possible.

The following table gives both possible translations:

Imperfect

hab-ē-ba-m	I was having	I had
hab-ē-bā-s	you were having	you had
hab-ē-ba-t	he/she/it was having	he/she/it had
hab-ē-bā-mus	we were having	we had
hab-ē-bā-tis	you were having	you had
hab-ē-ba-nt	they were having	they had

Each form has been broken up with dashes to show how Latin builds verbs. First comes the root, indicating the root for the word "have," then the linking vowel -ē- characteristic of the -ē- conjugation, then a tense marker "**ba-**" for the imperfect, and finally the familiar endings (with the newcomer -**m** for the first-person singular).

More good news: There are no imperatives or infinitives! And you will find the same tense marker and endings for every other Latin verb, no matter which of the four conjugations it belongs to.

Imperfect

am-ā-ba-m	I was loving	I loved
am-ā-bā-s	you were loving	you loved
am-ā-ba-t	he/she/it was loving	he/she/it loved
am-ā-bā-mus	we were loving	we loved
am-ā-bā-tis	you were loving	you loved
am-ā-ba-nt	they were loving	they loved

So far, you have learned the present and imperfect tenses of the first and second conjugations. Now it is time to learn the future tense of these two. Once again, the endings to be learned are the same for both. As with the imperfect tense, there will be a root, a connecting vowel, a tense marker, and the endings you learned for the present tense: **-ō**, **-s**, **-t**, **-mus**, **-tis**, **-nt**.

Future

hab-ē-b-ō	I will have
hab-ē-bi-s	you will have
hab-ē-bi-t	he/she/it will have
hab-ē-bi-mus	we will have
hab-ē-bi-tis	you will have
hab-ē-bu-nt	they will have

There is a slight glitch here in that the tense marker changes slightly from **-b-** to **-bi-** to **-bu-**. However, as with the imperfect, there is no imperative or infinitive.

Future

am-ǎ-b-ō	I will love
am-ǎ-bi-s	you will love
am-ǎ-bi-t	he/she/it will love
am-ǎ-bi-mus	we will love
am-ǎ-bi-tis	you will love
am-ǎ-bu-nt	they will love

Another problem to look out for is how to remember that -**bō**, -**bis**, -**bit**, etc. indicate future, while **bam**, -**bās**, -**bat**, etc. indicate imperfect. A student once told me she remembered that the -**i**- was like "will" and the -**a**- was like "was." Maybe that will help you.

A good way to practice your verb endings is to jump from one tense to the next. Try muttering **amō**, **amābam**, **amābō**; **amās**, **amābās**, **amābis**; etc. Then **habeō**, **habēbam**, **habēbō**; etc.

CHAPTER 13: VOCABULARY

dēsīderō, dēsīderāre, dēsīderāvi, dēsīderātus	*need, require, miss*
excitō, excitāre, excitāvī, excitātus	*(a)rouse*
respondeō, respondēre, respondī, responsus	*answer, respond*
arma, ōrum, n. pl.	*arms*
autem	*you see; however*
dictum, ī, n.	*word*
ex / ē	*out of, from (prep. + abl.)*
factum, ī, n.	*deed*
iūdicium, iī, n.	*trial; judgment*
pax, pācis, f.	*peace*
-que	*and (attached to second item)*

CHAPTER 13: PRACTICE SENTENCES (ANSWERS FOLLOW CHAPTER 66)

1. **bellum habēbimus?**   SENR S 5.5
2. **nullum beneficium dabō.**   SEN BEN 2.15.2
3. **parvum habēbat fīlium.**   PHAEDR APP 3.3
4. **dī tē amābunt.**   PLAUT MEN 278
5. **pācis amor deus est.**   PROP 3.5.1
6. We will give advice to you.   CIC ATT 9.7A.1
7. Our son was fighting.   QUINT DECL 278
8. It remains and will always remain.   CIC DE LEG 1.1

CHAPTER 13: LATIN TO ENGLISH SENTENCES

1. **"in umbrā igitur," inquit, "pugnābimus."**   CIC TD 1.101
2. **vītam meam mōrēsque probābās.**   OV TRIST 2.89
3. **valēbunt autem semper arma.**   CIC FAM 9.17.1
4. **semper mortem exspectābam miser.**   TER HEC 422
5. **quid respondēbō līberīs meīs?**   CIC PRO MIL 102
6. **amīcum enim nostrum in iūdicium vocābās.**   CIC VER 4.25
7. **pācem cum hominibus habēbis, bellum cum vitiīs.**   PUBLSYR
8. **nullum neque officium neque studium meum dēsīderābis.**   CIC FAM 10.2.2
9. **tē ex somnō saepe excitābunt.**   CIC PRO SULLA 24
10. **mihi tua et facta et dicta laudābat.**   CIC FAM 13.24.2

CHAPTER 13: GLOSSED LATIN TO ENGLISH SENTENCES

1. **cīvēs cum cīvibus dē virtūte** certābant.   certō (1): compete   SALL C 9.2
2. **dī** fortūnābunt **vestra consilia.**   fortūnō (1): make prosperous   PLAUT TRIN 576
3. **in** balneō **carmen** recitābat.   balneum, ī, n.: bath house   PETR 91.3

     recitō (1): recite

4. **servīs** regna **dabunt,** captīvīs   regnum, ī, n.: kingship   JUV 7.201
   fāta triumphum.   captīvus, ī, m.: prisoner of war

     triumphus, ī, m.: victory parade

CHAPTER 13: ENGLISH TO LATIN SENTENCES

1. A good man will give a kindness.   SEN BEN 4.26.3

2. I will change my opinion.   CIC LEG AGR 2.16

3. Therefore I will await your letter.   CIC ATT 13.45.3

4. The mind was giving strength.   OV HER 10.27

5. I will not help crime.   SEN BEN 2.14.4

14

sum and possum: Imperfect and Future Tenses

As with the present tense, the imperfect and future of the verb "to be" are irregular, at least as compared with the other conjugations. However, there is a pattern to each of them as the following table shows:

Imperfect

eram	I was	erāmus	we were
erās	you were	erātis	you were
erat	he/she/it was	erant	they were

Future

erō	I will be	erimus	we will be
eris	you will be	eritis	you will be
erit	he/she/it will be	erunt	they will be

At least the endings are familiar, with the stipulation that the first-person form can be either -ō or -m. As always with **sum**, there is no direct object. Whatever case appears on one side of the **sum** equation appears on the other.

Moving to **possum**, we find that its imperfect and future are formed from those of **sum**:

Imperfect

pot-eram	I was able	**pot-erāmus**	we were able
pot-erās	you were able	**pot-erātis**	you were able
pot-erat	he/she/it was able	**pot-erant**	they were able

Future

pot-erō	I will be able	**pot-erimus**	we will be able
pot-eris	you will be able	**pot-eritis**	you will be able
pot-erit	he/she/it will be able	**pot-erunt**	they will be able

CHAPTER 14: VOCABULARY

ante	*(prep. + acc.) before*
***ars, artis, f.**	*art*
auctōritās, auctōritātis, f.	*authority*
contrā	*(prep. + acc.) against*
crīmen, crīminis, n.	*charge, crime*
Graecus, a, um	*Greek*
īra, ae, f.	*anger*
Iuppiter, Iovis, m.	*Jupiter*
pater, patris, m.	*father*
timor, timōris, m.	*fear*
tum	*(adverb) then*

CHAPTER 14: PRACTICE SENTENCES (ANSWERS FOLLOW CHAPTER 66)

1. **mea semper eris.** OV A 3.11B.17
2. **nullus līber erit.** PROP 2.23.24
3. **et iam plēna nox erat.** PETR 92.1

4. Nothing was safe. SENR C 2.5.2

5. He was not able to refuse. [QUINT] DECL 17.19

CHAPTER 14: LATIN TO ENGLISH SENTENCES

1. **potes, pater, et poteris et ego poterō.** PLAUT CAPT 933–4
2. **erās enim in animīs, in iūdiciīs nostrīs.** PLINY PANEG 21.3
3. **aut iam nihil est aut iam nihil erit.** PLAUT CAPT 921
4. **verbīs locus nōn erat.** SEN E 54.6
5. **in meō nullum carmine crīmen erit.** OV AA 1.34
6. **erat Ītalia tum plēna Graecārum artium.** CIC PRO ARCH 5
7. **īra Iovis magnī causa timōris erat.** OV F 5.248
8. **saepe tuā poterās, Leandre, carēre puellā.** OV AA 2.249
9. **nōn tū corpus erās sine pectore.** HOR E 1.4.6
10. **contrā hominum auctōritātem pugnāre nōn poterō.** CIC VER 3.209

CHAPTER 14: GLOSSED LATIN TO ENGLISH SENTENCES

1. **mors** sollicitī **fīnis amōris erit.** — sollicitus, a, um: worried OV HER 18.196
2. fortasse **erit,** fortasse **nōn erit;** interim **nōn est.** — fortasse: perhaps / interim: meanwhile SEN E 13.11

CHAPTER 14: ENGLISH TO LATIN SENTENCES

1. Death was before (my) eyes. OV HER 11.55
2. Certainly I will be unharmed. OV HER 20.178
3. Was I not able to prove the case? CIC DOMO SUA 57
4. He will not be able to be supremely happy. CIC TD 5.40
5. They will not be in our power. SEN E 85.11
6. Certainly our friend was a good man. SEN IRA 3.8.5

CHAPTER 14: PASSAGES

HOW TO SUCCEED IN ROMAN POLITICS

Gāius Laelius homō novus **erat,** ingeniōsus **erat,** doctus **erat,**
bonīs virīs et studiīs amīcus erat; ergō **in** cīvitāte prīmus **erat.**

AUCHER 4.19

---

novus, a, um: new
ingeniōsus, a, um: talented
doctus, a, um: learned
ergō: therefore
cīvitās, cīvitātis, f.: state
prīmus, a, um: first

15

Verbs of the Third Conjugation: Present System

We must now deal with the most irregular of the four Latin conjugations, the one traditionally called third conjugation. I do not designate it with a letter, because wherever you expect to see that letter, namely as a connecting vowel, it may appear as an -**e**, as an -**i**, or as a -**u**. Therefore, you should just observe the variations of this conjugation and try to memorize them as best you can. At least the endings are old friends.

Present

	vīv-ō	I live
	vīv-i-s	you live
	vīv-i-t	he/she/it lives
	vīv-i-mus	we live
	vīv-i-tis	you live
	vīv-u-nt	they live
vīv-e live!	**vīv-i-te**	live!
	vīv-e-re	to live

Note that the connecting vowel is sometimes an -**i**, sometimes a -**u**, and sometimes not there at all. However, as with all Latin verbs, the imperfect is quite regular:

Imperfect

vīv-ē-ba-m	I was living	I lived
vīv-ē-bā-s	you were living	you lived
vīv-ē-ba-t	he/she/it was living	he/she/it lived
vīv-ē-bā-mus	we were living	we lived
vīv-ē-bā-tis	you were living	you lived
vīv-ē-ba-nt	they were living	they lived

The future tense of the third conjugation is not formed like that of the first and second conjugations. Instead it has the following:

Future

vīv-a-m	I will live
vīv-ē-s	you will live
vīv-e-t	he/she/it will live
vīv-ē-mus	we will live
vīv-ē-tis	you will live
vīv-e-nt	they will live

Beware of these future forms! They will present difficulties when they appear in Latin sentences. If you forget that **vīvo** is a third conjugation verb, you may think **vīvet** is like **movet**, the present tense of a second conjugation verb. (You may also be led to the opposite error.) Consider the following sentence:

vīvit enim vīvetque semper.   For he lives and will live always.   PLINY E 2.1.11

Now that the third conjugation has entered the scene, it is vital to know what conjugation a verb belongs to.

CHAPTER 15: VOCABULARY

agō, agere, ēgī, actus — *drive; do; spend (of time)*

dēfendō, dēfendere, dēfendī, dēfensus — *defend*

dīcō, dīcere, dixī, dictus — *say; speak*

dīligō, dīligere, dīlexī, dīlectus — *esteem*

discō, discere, didicī, — — *learn*

neglegō, neglegere, neglexī, neglectus — *ignore, neglect*

quaerō, quaerere, quaesīvī, quaesītus — *seek, inquire*

regō, regere, rexī, rectus — *rule, control*

relinquō, relinquere, relīquī, relictus — *leave (behind)*

vīvō, vīvere, vixī, victus — *live*

doceō, docēre, docuī, doctus — *teach*

acerbus, a, um — *bitter*

bene — *well*

contentus, a, um — *content, content with (+ abl.)*

dum — *while*

ne ... quidem — *not even*

nec/neque — *and ... not*

parens, parentis, m. or f. — *parent*

prīmus, a, um — *first*

pulcher, chra, chrum — *beautiful, handsome*

quia — *because*

Venus, Veneris, f. — *Venus*

voluptās, voluptātis, f. — *pleasure*

VOCABULARY NOTE   The imperative singular of the verb **dico** is not **dīce** but **dīc**. See these examples:

dic, Marce Tulli.	Speak, Marcus Tullius.	CIC ATT 9.5.2
dic mihi.	Tell (to) me.	TER AND 763
dic — vivisne?	Say, are you alive?	PLAUT RUD 243

CHAPTER 15: PRACTICE SENTENCES (ANSWERS FOLLOW CHAPTER 66)

1. **timeō tibi dīcere vērum.**   OV HER 20.107
2. **quid nunc agētis?**   PLAUT PSEUD 504
3. **quaere meum patrem.**   PLAUT MEN 736
4. **quaerit enim ratiōnem animus.**   LUCR 2.1044
5. Control the mind.   HOR E 1.2.62
6. Leave wars to men.   OV M 12.476
7. I will say my opinion.   PLAUT CURC 702
8. I am able to defend cases.   HOR S 2.5.34
9. Greed was seeking money.   PLINY NH 33.4

CHAPTER 15: LATIN TO ENGLISH SENTENCES

1. **acerba fāta Rōmānos agunt.**   HOR EPO 7.17
2. **hominēs, dum docent, discunt.**   SEN E 7.8
3. **vitia nostra quia amāmus defendimus.**   SEN E 116.8
4. **vītam regit Fortūna, nōn sapientia.**   CIC TD 5.25
5. **magna dī cūrant, parva neglegunt.**   CIC ND 2.167
6. **dīligere parentēs prīma lex nātūrae est.** VALMAX 5.4.7
7. **nōn est bonum vīvere, sed bene vīvere.**   SEN BEN 3.31.4
8. **vērum ne dīs quidem dīcimus.**   SEN E 95.2
9. **pulcher es neque tē Venus neglegit.**   CATULLUS 61.191-2
10. **disce parvō esse contentus.**   SEN E 110.18
11. **relinque corporis atque animī voluptātēs.** SEN E 84.11

CHAPTER 15: GLOSSED LATIN TO ENGLISH SENTENCES

1. **nōn vītae sed** scholae **discimus.**   schola, ae, f.: school   SEN E 106.12
2. **virtūtēs discere vitia dēdiscere est.** dēdiscō (3): unlearn   SEN E 50.7
3. **sēro in perīculis est consilium quaerere.** sēro: too late   PUBLSYR

4. **pulchramque** petunt **per vulnera mortem.**

petō (3): seek

VERG G 4.218

5. **populī Rōmānī** nōmen salūtem**que dēfendite.**

nōmen, nōminis, n.: name

salus, salūtis, f.: safety

CIC IN CAT 4.3

6. **cum cīvibus tuīs** quasi **cum līberīs parens vīvis.**

quasi: as though

PLINY PANEG 21.4

CHAPTER 15: ENGLISH TO LATIN SENTENCES

1. The fates rule human beings.
2. We are not able to speak without tears.
3. I do not seek the joys of life.
4. Wars will leave nothing.
5. The good esteem the good (people).

JUV 9.32

CIC DE DIVIN 2.22

VERG A 11.180

SEN HERC 365

CIC DE AMIC 50

CHAPTER 15: PASSAGES

AENEAS TO HIS SON

disce, puer, **virtūtem ex mē vērumque** labōrem, **fortūnam ex aliīs.**

VERG A 12.435-6

puer, puerī, m.: boy
labor, labōris, m.: labor

16

Adverbs of the First and Second Declensions

Adverbs are an unusual part of speech because they can modify verbs, adjectives, and other adverbs. An adjective, on the other hand, can modify only a noun. (These rules also apply to English adverbs and adjectives.) In English, adverbs are often formed from adjectives by a simple addition of the suffix **-ly**. (However, this rule will not cover every English adverb.) In Latin, the procedure is equally straightforward:

▼ **For adjectives of the first and second declensions, add -ē to the stem.**

Thus,

stultus, a, um	"foolish"	→	**stultē**	"foolishly"
laetus, a, um	"happy"	→	**laetē**	"happily"
lentus, a, um	"slow"	→	**lentē**	"slowly"
pulcher, a, um	"beautiful"	→	**pulchrē**	"beautifully"

(In fact, you have already learned the adverbs **certē** in chapter 7, **valdē** in chapter 9, and **bene** in chapter 15.)

The unwary should be advised, however, that some adverbs add -**o**, thus yielding adverbs like **cito** and **tūtō**; others add -**um**, yielding adverbs like **multum** and **paulum**. The safest conclusion is that many—but not all—adverbs will end in -**ē**.

CHAPTER 16: VOCABULARY

clārus, a, um	*loud; clear; famous*
honestus, a, um	*honorable*
plānus, a, um	*plain, flat*
secūrus, a, um	*secure*
*mare, maris, n.	*sea*
puer, puerī, m.	*boy*

CHAPTER 16: PRACTICE SENTENCES (ANSWERS FOLLOW CHAPTER 66)

1. **valdē tuās litterās nunc exspectō.** CIC ATT 9.18.4
2. I shall speak truly. CIC LEG AGR 2.10
3. You think rightly. CIC ATT 14.11.2

CHAPTER 16: LATIN TO ENGLISH SENTENCES

1. **consilium nēmō clārē dat.** SEN E 38.1
2. **ita sunt hominēs miserē miserī.** PLAUT CIST 689
3. **nunc eram plānē in mediō marī.** CIC ATT 5.12.3
4. **valdē enim hominem dēsīderō.** CIC ATT 13.2B
5. **rectē dicis; negāre nōn possum.** CIC DE FIN 4.54
6. **nihil est aliud bene et beātē vivere nisi honestē et rectē vivere.** CIC PARADOX 15
7. **sed est plānē puer.** CIC ATT 16.11.6

CHAPTER 16: GLOSSED LATIN TO ENGLISH SENTENCES

1. **certē** dea **carmine digna est.** dea, ae, f.: goddess OV M 5.345
2. genus **est mortis male vivere.** genus, generis, n.: type, kind OV PONT 3.4.75
3. **nēmō potest valdē dolēre et** diū. diū: (adverb) for a long time SEN E 78.7
4. aurea **sunt vērē nunc** saecula. aureus, a, um: golden OV AA 2.277
   saeculum, i, n.: age, time
5. lentē currite, **noctis** equī. lentus, a, um: slow OV A 1.13.40
   currō (3): run
   equus, equī, m.: horse
6. **nunc,** spectātōrēs, **Iovis summī** causā **clārē** plaudite. spectātor, tōris, m.: spectator PLAUT AMPH 1146
   causā: (prep. + gen.) for the sake of
   plaudō (3): applaud

CHAPTER 16: ENGLISH TO LATIN SENTENCES

1. Speak (plural) well.   PLAUT ASIN 745
2. I will say clearly to you, father.   PHAEDR APP 18.3
3. I am wretchedly wretched.   PLAUT PSEUD 13
4. You are able to say nothing truly.   CIC ROSCAM 54
5. I will plainly be able to be secure.   [QUINT] DECL 6.13

17

Demonstratives **hic** and **ille**

Two of the most common words in Latin are **hic** meaning "this" and **ille** meaning "that." Unfortunately for the beginner, these common words have peculiarities of declension that make them unlike any other noun or adjective yet encountered. The redeeming quality is that several other common words decline similarly. That means if you learn **hic** and **ille** well, other common words will be easier.

Here is the declension of **hic**:

Case	Singular			Plural		
	masc	*fem*	*neut*	*masc*	*fem*	*neut*
nominative	hic	haec	hoc	hī	hae	haec
genitive	huius	huius	huius	hōrum	hārum	hōrum
dative	huic	huic	huic	hīs	hīs	hīs
accusative	hunc	hanc	hoc	hōs	hās	haec
ablative	hōc	hāc	hōc	hīs	hīs	hīs

Notice that some endings are familiar, especially in the plural, while others are unprecedented.

Here is the declension of **ille**:

Case	Singular			Plural		
	masc	*fem*	*neut*	*masc*	*fem*	*neut*
nominative	ille	illa	illud	illī	illae	illa
genitive	illīus	illīus	illīus	illōrum	illārum	illōrum
dative	illī	illī	illī	illīs	illīs	illīs
accusative	illum	illam	illud	illōs	illās	illa
ablative	illō	illā	illō	illīs	illīs	illīs

In most English grammar books, the words "this" and "that" are referred to as "demonstrative pronouns," but for Latin that title is misleading. I prefer to call them simply "demonstratives" because both **hic** and **ille** can be used equally as adjectives or as pronouns.

DEMONSTRATIVES AS ADJECTIVES

To qualify as an adjective, the demonstrative must be modifying a noun. When used as an adjective, **hic** means "this" ("these" in the plural) and **ille** means "that" ("those" in the plural). The following examples illustrate:

hic homō nōn sānus est.	This fellow is not sane.	PLAUT MERC 951
vidēsne tū puerum hunc?	Do you see this boy?	LIVY 1.39.3
hoc magnum est perīculum.	This danger is great.	PLAUT AUL 235
Neptūnō hās agō gratiās.	I give these thanks to Neptune.	PLAUT RUD 906

DEMONSTRATIVES AS PRONOUNS

However, when a demonstrative is not modifying a noun—that is, when it is acting as a substantive—the situation is more fluid. By themselves, forms of **hic** and **ille** can mean "this man/woman/thing" or "that man/woman/thing," as you would expect. But they often appear in contexts where English would use a third-person pronoun like "he," "she," "it," or "they." Only the context will determine which translation is better; sometimes either one is fine.

hic nihil habet.	This man has nothing.	PLAUT AUL 657
	He has nothing.	
sānane haec est?	Is this woman sane?	PLAUT EPID 649
	Is she sane?	
amōrem huic narrābō meum.	I will relate my love to this man.	TER AND 312
	I will relate my love to him.	

In particular, the genitive case is often used as a substantive to show possession. A preferable translation would be "his," "her," "its," or "their," depending on the context.

huius dicta intellegō.	I understand the remarks of this man.	PLAUT BACC 449
	I understand his remarks.	
nihil dē mōribus huius dicō.	I say nothing about the character of this man.	QUINT DECL 322
	I say nothing about his character.	
ego sum illīus māter.	I am the mother of that man.	PLAUT CIST 745
	I am his mother.	
tē hōrum lacrimae movent?	Do the tears of these men move you?	SENR C 7.8.2
	Do their tears move you?	

CHAPTER 17: VOCABULARY

hic, haec, hoc	*this, these*
ille, illa, illud	*that, those*
dēbeō, dēbēre, dēbuī, dēbitus	*ought*
servō , servāre, servāvī, servātus	*save, preserve*
iucundus, a, um	*pleasant*
nam	*for (explanatory)*
sapiens, sapientis, m.	*wise man*
sōlus, a, um	*alone; only*

CHAPTER 17: PRACTICE SENTENCES (ANSWERS FOLLOW CHAPTER 66)

1.	**pater hic meus est.**	PLAUT PERS 741
2.	**hōrum nihil negat.**	CIC PRO TULL 24
3.	**quis hoc potest vidēre?**	CATULLUS 29.1
4.	**haec mea est sententia.**	PLAUT PSEUD 379
5.	**tū illīus servus es?**	PLAUT PSEUD 1169
6.	This is my duty.	PLAUT PSEUD 377
7.	I am able to say this (thing).	CIC PRO SULLA 27
8.	This man is good.	TER AND 915

CHAPTER 17: LATIN TO ENGLISH SENTENCES

1.	**sōlus servāre hunc potes.**	TER PHOR 539
2.	**magna in illō ingeniī vīs est.**	SEN E 29.4
3.	**quid illīs respondēre possum?**	CIC FAM 5.10A.2
4.	**ego hanc amō et haec mē amat.**	PLAUT ASIN 631
5.	**salvus sum sī haec vēra sunt.**	TER AND 973
6.	**nam haec quidem vīta mors est.**	CIC TD 1.75
7.	**cēteri enim sine ratiōne, hī sine mente sunt.**	SEN E 13.9
8.	**patria mea tōtus hic mundus est.**	SEN E 28.4
9.	**sānus nōn est ex amōre illīus.**	PLAUT MERC 443
10.	**illud iter iūcundum esse dēbet.**	CIC TD 1.96
11.	**sī mihi nōn datis arma, huic date.**	OV M 13.380-1

CHAPTER 17: GLOSSED LATIN TO ENGLISH SENTENCES

1.	**illa** dīvīna **mens summa lex est.**	dīvīnus, a, um: divine	CIC DE LEG 2.11
2.	uxōrem **ille tuus pulcher** amātor **habet!**	uxor, uxōris, f.: wife amātor, amātōris, m.: lover	PROP 2.21.4
3.	**nam corpus hoc animī** pondus **et** poena **est.**	pondus, ponderis, n.: weight poena, ae, f.: punishment	SEN E 65.16
4.	**haec virtute** militum **vestrōrum, haec Rōmānō** nōmine **sunt digna.**	mīles, mīlitis, m.: soldier nōmen, nōminis, n.: name	LIVY 5.6.6

CHAPTER 17: ENGLISH TO LATIN SENTENCES

1. I will often praise that wise man.   CIC PARADOX 8
2. Concerning your son I answer this.   SENR C 7.1.2
3. We will be able to live without them.   SENR C 7.PR.7
4. Therefore this is now our life.   CIC FAM 9.20.3
5. Philosophy will give you this road.   SEN E 37.3

CHAPTER 17: PASSAGES

THERE'S SOMETHING ABOUT SABIDIUS

nōn amō tē, Sabidī, nec possum dīcere quāre;
   hoc tantum **possum dīcere — nōn amō tē.**

MART 1.32

---

quāre: why   tantum: only

18

Personal Pronouns: ego/nōs and tū/vōs

U p to now you have managed without knowing all forms of the personal pronouns, that is, the words for "I" and "we" and "you" (singular) and "you" (plural). You have worked with **ego** and **mē**, and **mihi** and **tibi**, and **tū** and **tē**, but there is more to the story. Following are the complete tables for the personal pronouns; they can exist in all cases except the vocative.

Case	Singular	
nominative	**ego**	**tū**
genitive	**meī**	**tuī**
dative	**mihi**	**tibi**
accusative	**mē**	**tē**
ablative	**mē**	**tē**

Case	Plural	
nominative	**nōs**	**vōs**
genitive	**nostrum / nostrī**	**vestrum / vestrī**
dative	**nōbīs**	**vōbīs**
accusative	**nōs**	**vōs**
ablative	**nōbīs**	**vōbīs**

Watch out for the genitive plural of each pronoun. There are two forms—one ending in -**um** and one ending in -**i**. Be prepared to see either one. The other problem with these genitive forms is that they are identical to certain forms of your old friends **noster** and

vester. However, the pronoun **nostrum/nostrī** means "of us" and the adjective **nostrum/nostrī** means "our."

nēmō nostrum crēdēbat.	No one of us was believing.	CIC DE FIN 2.55
nulla pars manet nostrī?	Does no part of us remain?	SEN TROAD 378-9

By the same token, the genitive singular of each pronoun—**meī** and **tuī**—will be identical to forms of **meus, -a, -um** and **tuus, -a, -um**. However, those adjectives mean "mine" and "yours"; the pronouns mean "of me" and "of you."

animus meī pars est.	The mind is part of me.	SEN E 113.5
pars est tuī.	He is part of you.	SEN PHAED 1267

REFLEXIVE USE OF PRONOUNS

Most of these forms also function as what are called "reflexive" pronouns, that is, those that reflect the subject. In English, we must use the suffix "-self" or "-selves" to form a reflexive, but in Latin, no special form is necessary for the first- and second-person pronouns. Thus,

cūrā tē.	Take care of yourself.	PLAUT CIST 113
nōbīs illud damus.	We give that to ourselves.	SEN BEN 4.13.3
nihil enim dīcam dē mē.	For I will say nothing about myself.	CIC PRO FLACC 103

WHEN USED WITH PREPOSITION *CUM*

There is one other peculiarity about the personal pronouns: when they are governed by the preposition **cum** "with," they naturally appear in the ablative case, since **cum** requires the ablative. The difference is that the **cum** is attached to the pronoun as one word, as in the following examples:

semper eris mecum.	You will always be with me.	OV M 10.204
vīvēs nōbīscum.	You will live with us.	CIC FAM 6.11.2
dominus vōbīscum.	The Lord [be] with you.	CATHOLIC MASS

CHAPTER 18: VOCABULARY

ego	*I*
nōs	*we*
tū	*you (singular)*
vōs	*you (plural)*
audeō, audēre, ausus sum	*dare*
gerō, gerere, gessī, gestus	*wage, manage, conduct*
dux, ducis, m.	*leader*
ferrum, ī, n.	*iron, sword*
fīlia, ae, f.	*daughter*
molestus, a, um	*annoying*
neuter, neutra, neutrum	*neither*
tamen	*nevertheless, however*

CHAPTER 18: PRACTICE SENTENCES (ANSWERS FOLLOW CHAPTER 66)

1. **nōs sumus Rōmānī.**   CIC DE ORAT 3.168
2. **gratiās nōbīs agit.**   CIC ATT 6.1.2
3. **gratiās mihi agō.**   SEN BEN 5.7.2
4. **tēcum bella geram.**   OV IBIS 137
5. **vōs vestrum cūrāte officium.**   PLAUT BACC 760
6. Hurry to me.   SEN E 35.4
7. I was thinking about you.   CIC ATT 5.10.1
8. The gods love us.   LIVY 1.23.9
9. I love you (plural).   PLAUT CIST 7
10. We have Trebatius with us.   CIC ATT 13.9.1

CHAPTER 18: LATIN TO ENGLISH SENTENCES

1. nōn ad bellum vōs nec ad perīculum vocō.   TAC HIST 1.38
2. tū tibi molestus es.   SEN E 21.1
3. dē vōbīs ac dē vestrīs līberīs cōgitāte.   CIC IN CAT 4.1
4. ferrum, Lucretia, mēcum est.   OV F 2.795
5. consiliī satis est in mē mihi.   OV M 6.40
6. nam ego nunc tibi sum summus Iuppiter.   PLAUT CAPT 863
7. neuter vestrum dīcere potest.   QUINT DECL 318
8. bellum gerere contrā nōs nōn audent.   QUINT DECL 255
9. fīliam ex tē tū habēs.   PLAUT AUL 781
10. caecī tamen ducem quaerunt, nōs sine duce errāmus.   SEN E 50.3
11. nam sine tē nostrum nōn valet ingenium.   PROP 2.30B.40

CHAPTER 18: GLOSSED LATIN TO ENGLISH SENTENCES

1. spērāre **nōs amīcī iubent.**   spērō (1): hope   CIC FAM 14.1.2
2. **vītae nōs** odium **tenet, timor mortis.**   odium, iī, n: hatred   SEN E 74.11
3. commendō **vōbīs parvum meum fīlium.**   commendō (1): entrust   CIC IN CAT 4.23
4. "**tū mē,**" **inquis** "vītāre turbam **iubēs?**"   vītō (1): avoid
turba, ae, f.: crowd   SEN E 8.1
5. **sed** quōniam **dī nōn sumus, nātūra nōs regit.**   quōniam: since   SENR C 1.6.3

CHAPTER 18: ENGLISH TO LATIN SENTENCES

1. Fortune wages war with me.   SEN E 51.8
2. Philosophy alone, you see, will rouse us.   SEN E 53.8
3. There is a god in us.   OV F 6.5
4. If you (plural) are well, we are well.   CIC FAM 14.14
5. I can live neither with you nor without you.   MART 12.46.2
6. Ought I to defend myself?   SENR C 1.4.8

Verbs of the Fourth Conjugation: Present System

As you might expect by analogy with the -e- and -a- conjugations, verbs of this family have an -i- as a connecting vowel. However, the picture is not as tidy as with the earlier families, as the following table will show:

Fourth Conjugation

dorm-i-ō	I sleep
dorm-ī-s	you sleep
dorm-i-t	he/she/it sleeps
dorm-ī-mus	we sleep
dorm-ī-tis	you sleep
dorm-iu-nt	they sleep

The third-person plural contains -**iu**- instead of -**i**- for the connecting vowel. Apart from that anomaly, the imperatives and the infinitive are what you would expect:

dorm-ī	sleep!	**dorm-īte**	sleep!
	dorm-īre	to sleep	

The imperfect tense has regular endings but a slight addition: -**iē**- instead of -**i**- for the connecting vowel.

Imperfect

dorm-iē-ba-m	I was sleeping	I slept
dorm-iē-bā-s	you were sleeping	you slept
dorm-iē-ba-t	he/she/it was sleeping	he/she/it slept
dorm-iē-bā-mus	we were sleeping	we slept
dorm-iē-bā-tis	you were sleeping	you slept
dorm-iē-ba-nt	they were sleeping	they slept

The future is like that of the third conjugation, with the addition of the characteristic -**i**-.

Future

dorm-i-am	I will sleep
dorm-i-ēs	you will sleep
dorm-i-et	he/she/it will sleep
dorm-iē-mus	we will sleep
dorm-iē-tis	you will sleep
dorm-ie-nt	they will sleep

CHAPTER 19: VOCABULARY

audiō, audīre, audī(v)ī, audītus	*hear, listen to*
impediō, impedīre, impedī(v)ī, impedītus	*hinder*
inveniō, invenīre, invēnī, inventus	*find*
nesciō, nescīre, nescī(v)ī, nescītus	*do not know; do not know how*
sciō, scīre, scī(v)ī, scītus	*know; know how (+ infinitve)*
sentiō, sentīre, sensī, sensus	*feel; express an opinion*
veniō, venīre, vēnī, ventus	*come*
ā/ab	*from (prep. + abl.)*
nōmen, nōminis, n.	*name*
paucī, ae, a	*(a) few*
senectus, senectūtis, f.	*old age*

CHAPTER 19: PRACTICE SENTENCES (ANSWERS FOLLOW CHAPTER 66)

1. **scīs iam meam sententiam.** PLAUT AUL 444
2. **ō Iuppiter, quid ego audiō?** TER AND 464-5
3. **atque hoc scītis vōs.** PLAUT STICH 591
4. You will find nothing. SEN E 57.6
5. You do not know the names of the gods. PLAUT BACC 124
6. You will hear the truth. SEN E 46.3
7. Who does not know this? CIC PRO FLACC 83
8. We heard nothing about Coelius. CIC ATT 6.4.1

CHAPTER 19: LATIN TO ENGLISH SENTENCES

1. **sentīs mea vulnera, sentīs.** OV HER 16.237
2. **audī, Iuppiter, haec scelera.** LIVY 8.5.8
3. **dē aurō nil sciō nisi nesciō.** PLAUT BACC 324
4. **itaque paucī veniunt ad senectūtem.** CIC DE SENEC 67
5. **nēmō cōgitātiōnem meam impediet.** SEN E 80.1
6. **amat et nōn sentit amōrem.** OV M 10.637

7. **venī igitur, sī vir es, et disce ā mē.** CIC FAM 9.18.3
8. **veniēs ad summa per plānum.** SEN E 84.13
9. **sōlus ferrum mortemque timēre aurī nescit amor.** LUCAN 3.118-9
10. **saepe veniēbat Autrōnius multīs cum lacrimīs.** CIC PRO SULLA 18

CHAPTER 19: GLOSSED LATIN TO ENGLISH SENTENCES

1.	**nātūram mutāre** pecūnia **nescit.**	pecūnia, ae, f.: money	HOR E 1.12.10
2.	**nescit Amor magnīs** cēdere **divitiīs.**	cēdō (3): yield	PROP 1.14.8
3.	tot **mē impediunt** cūrae.	tot: so many	TER AND 260
		cūra, ae, f.: care	

CHAPTER 19: ENGLISH TO LATIN SENTENCES

1. He fears to hear the truth. SEN E 29.1
2. For pleasure hinders counsel. CIC DE SENEC 42
3. The wise man alone knows how to love. SEN E 81.12
4. The fates will find a way. VERG A 10.113
5. I don't know the name of that fellow. TER ADEL 571-2

20

Verbs of the Third Conjugation in –iō: Present System

The class of third conjugation verbs, commonly called "third-io," is a blend of the third and fourth conjugations.

cap-i-ō	I take
cap-i-s	you take
cap-i-t	he/she/it takes
cap-i-mus	we take
cap-i-tis	you take
cap-i-unt	they take

A table containing a third conjugation and a fourth conjugation verb with a "third-io" in the middle will show what I mean. (Note the short **i** characteristic of the third conjugation):

Third conjugation	Third-io conjugation	Fourth conjugation
dīc-ō	cap-i-ō	dorm-i-ō
dīc-i-s	cap-i-s	dorm-ī-s
dīc-i-t	cap-i-t	dorm-i-t
dīc-i-mus	cap-i-mus	dorm-ī-mus
dīc-i-tis	cap-i-tis	dorm-ī-tis
dīc-u-nt	cap-i-unt	dorm-iu-nt

The imperatives and the infinitive are what you would expect of a third conjugation verb:

cap-e	take!	cap-ite	take!

cap-ere	to take

The imperfect tense looks exactly like that of the fourth conjugation:

Imperfect

cap-iē-ba-m	I was taking	I took
cap-iē-bā-s	you were taking	you took
cap-iē-ba-t	he/she/it was taking	he/she/it took
cap-iē-bā-mus	we were taking	we took
cap-iē-bā-tis	you were taking	you took
cap-iē-ba-nt	they were taking	they took

As does the future:

Future

cap-i-am	I will take
cap-i-ēs	you will take
cap-i-et	he/she/it will take
cap-iē-mus	we will take
cap-iē-tis	you will take
cap-ie-nt	they will take

CHAPTER 20: VOCABULARY

accipiō, accipere, accēpī, acceptus	*receive; accept*
capiō, capere, cēpī, captus	*take; capture; contain*
cupiō, cupere, cupī(v)ī, cupītus	*desire*
faciō, facere, fēcī, factus	*make; do; act*
fugiō, fugere, fūgī, fugitūrus	*flee*
incipiō, incipere, incēpī, inceptus	*begin*
scrībō, scrībere, scripsī, scriptus	*write*
vincō, vincere, vīcī, victus	*conquer*
*auris, auris, f.	*ear*
auxilium, iī, n.	*aid*
exiguus, a, um	*tiny*
forma, ae, f.	*beauty; form*
prīmum	*(adverb) first, for the first time*
ut	*as*

CHAPTER 20: PRACTICE SENTENCES (ANSWERS FOLLOW CHAPTER 66)

1.	**faciam ut iubēs.**	PLAUT MOST 928
2.	**tēcum esse cupiēbam.**	CIC ATT 8.11D.6
3.	**nōs patriam fugimus.**	VERG E 1.4
4.	**quid enim facere poterāmus?**	CIC IN PIS 13
5.	**nunc ratiōnēs cēterās accipite.**	PLAUT POEN 55-6
6.	**beneficium dominus ā servō accipit?**	SEN BEN 3.22.3
7.	They take arms.	LIVY 2.45.14
8.	Your joys are fleeing.	OV HER 15.109
9.	Do you desire to know the name?	MART 11.8.13
10.	Flee great things.	HOR E 1.10.32

CHAPTER 20: LATIN TO ENGLISH SENTENCES

1. **nam magna nōn capit exigua mens.** — SENR C 2.1.13
2. **litterās tuās iam exspectāre incipiēbam.** — CIC FAM 4.10.1
3. **vōs vincētis, illī fugient.** — LIVY 6.7.6
4. **nunc prīmum hoc aurēs tuae crīmen accipiunt?** — CIC VER 2.24
5. **quid enim ratiōne timēmus aut cupimus?** — JUV 10.4–5
6. **beneficia nec dare scīmus nec accipere.** — SEN BEN 1.1.1
7. **facere docet philosophia, nōn dīcere.** — SEN E 20.2
8. **ita faciam igitur ut scrībis.** — CIC ATT 11.7.1
9. **nostra sine auxiliō fugiunt bona.** — OV AA 3.79
10. **ne forma quidem et vīrēs beātum tē facere possunt.** — SEN E 31.10
11. **amābit sapiens, cupient cēterī.** — AFRANIUS FR 221

CHAPTER 20: GLOSSED LATIN TO ENGLISH SENTENCES

1. **nihil** invītus **facit sapiens.** — invītus, a, um: unwilling — SEN E 54.7
2. **tōtam** hodiē **Rōmam Circus capit.** — hodiē: today; Circus, i, m.: Circus Maximus — JUV 11.197
3. **multa tamen capiēs oscula, multa dabis.** — osculum, ī, n.: kiss — OV HER 13.120
4. **ubi** sōlitūdinem **faciunt, pācem** appellant. — sōlitūdo, sōlitūdinis, f.: desolation; appellō (1): call — TAC AGRIC 30.4

CHAPTER 20: ENGLISH TO LATIN SENTENCES

1. I desire you to come to me, but I fear the road. — CIC FAM 16.10.1
2. He does nothing except according to my advice. — PLINY E 4.17.8
3. They make (a) way by force. — LIVY 4.38.4
4. Your beauty captures me. — OV HER 4.64
5. Pain begins to conquer fear. — CIC ATT 2.18.2

21

Demonstrative **is**

The demonstrative **is, ea, id** functions much like the other two demonstratives **hic** and **ille**. Like them, it is often used as a third-person pronoun, where it can be translated with forms of "he," "she," "it," or "they."

The strange thing about this word is that it can be translated either as "this" or "that" depending on the context. Thus, it stands midway between **hic**, which is definitely a "this," and **ille**, which is definitely a "that."

Case	Singular			Plural		
	masc	*fem*	*neut*	*masc*	*fem*	*neut*
nominative	is	ea	id	eī / iī	eae	ea
genitive	eius	eius	eius	eōrum	eārum	eōrum
dative	eī	eī	eī	eīs / iīs	eīs / iīs	eīs / iīs
accusative	eum	eam	id	eōs	eās	ea
ablative	eō	eā	eō	eīs / iīs	eīs / iīs	eīs / iīs

IS, EA, ID AS ADJECTIVE

Just like the demonstratives **hic** and **ille**, forms of **is** can be used both as adjectives and as pronouns. The rules are the same: When modifying a noun, the form of **is** can be translated as "this" or "that" depending on the context. See the following examples:

ubi is homō est?	Where is this/that fellow?	PLAUT ASIN 338
ubi sunt eī hominēs?	Where are these/those fellows?	PLAUT RUD 156
nostrum est id malum.	This/that evil is ours.	CIC BRUTUS 5

IS, EA, ID AS PRONOUN

More commonly, forms of **is** appear as pronouns. You will know them as such when they do not modify a noun. (In effect, they are now substantives.) Here are examples:

ubi is nunc est?	Where is he now?	PLAUT CAPT 640
ubi ea nunc est?	Where is she now?	PLAUT CIST 742
eī nunc timeō.	I fear for him/her now.	TER PHOR 188
id grātum est mihi.	It is welcome to me.	CATULLUS 68.9
iīs igitur respondēbō.	Therefore I will respond to them.	CIC ATT 6.1.1

The genitive forms of **is, ea, id**—**eius, eōrum,** and **eārum**—are often used to show possession. This usage may present problems at first. Literally, these words mean "of him," "of her," "of it," and "of them." However, it is preferable to translate them with the English possessives "his," "her," "its," and "their." They do not modify the noun possessed, but technically exist as substantives. Here are some examples:

eius exspectāmus mortem.	We await his/her death.	PLAUT ASIN 531
laudābam eius ingenium.	I was praising his/her character.	PLINY E 1.16.1
hoc est eōrum officium.	This is their duty.	PLAUT PSEUD 139

In these examples, the literal rendering "death of him/her," "character of him/her," and "duty of them" would be such poor English that I advise you to translate them idiomatically.

CHAPTER 21: VOCABULARY

is, ea, id	*this, that*
amīcus, a, um	*friendly*
cūr	*why*
duo, duae, duo	*two*
grātus, a, um	*welcome*
voluntās, voluntātis, f.	*willingness, will*

CHAPTER 21: PRACTICE SENTENCES (ANSWERS FOLLOW CHAPTER 66)

1. **eius servōs habētis.**   CIC ROSCAM 77
2. **vīvitne is homō?**   PLAUT CAPT 989
3. **id autem facere nōn poterat.**   CIC RAB POST 28
4. **dī eam potestātem dabunt.**   PLAUT CAPT 934
5. **is quidem huius est pater.**   PLAUT CAPT 974
6. I will save his son.   SEN BEN 7.20.2
7. He will always be in that opinion.   AUCHER 4.54

CHAPTER 21: LATIN TO ENGLISH SENTENCES

1. **voluntās tamen eius mihi grāta est.**   CIC ATT 12.26.2
2. **exspectābō tuum consilium et eās litterās.**   CIC ATT 10.1.2
3. **nōn possum eī nōn amīcus esse.**   CIC FAM 9.24.1
4. **ea cum virō bellum gerit.**   CIC ATT 2.1.5
5. **sine scelere eum accūsāre nōn potes.**   CIC CAEC DIV 60
6. **id duae nōs sōlae scīmus.**   PLAUT CIST 145
7. **dat eam puellam eī servō.**   PLAUT CIST 166
8. **cūr eōrum verba nōn audīmus?**   CIC PRO FONT 11
9. **quis nōn factum eius laudābat?**   SALL C 51.32
10. **idque mihi valdē molestum est.**   CIC ATT 11.17A.3

CHAPTER 21: ENGLISH TO LATIN SENTENCES

1. Where are they (feminine)?   PLAUT POEN 1248
2. Soon you will hear his words.   TER AND 579
3. I will help you in this.   CIC ATT 7.1.9
4. He loves her wretchedly.   TER HT 190
5. Where is that gold?   PLAUT AUL 823

22

Third-Person Reflexive Pronoun and Adjective

This reflexive pronoun is carefully named to remind you that (1) it only affects third-person pronouns and (2) it reflects the subject of its clause. You have already encountered the reflexive concept in chapter 18 when you learned the first- and second-person pronouns **ego**, **nōs**, **tū** and **vōs**. However, in that chapter, there was no special form to be learned. Instead, the first- and second-person forms can all be reflexive as needed.

This chapter presents the reflexive of the third person. Latin is peculiar in that, unlike the first and second persons, there is no standard third-person pronoun. Sometimes it is bundled into the ending of the verb; sometimes it is expressed by forms of **hic**, **haec**, **hoc** or **ille**, **illa**, **illud** or **is**, **ea**, **id**. But no matter how it is expressed, whenever the third person needs a reflexive form, it uses one of the following:

Reflexive Pronoun: Third Person

nominative	—
genitive	**suī**
dative	**sibi**
accusative	**sē / sēsē**
ablative	**sē / sēsē**

This table will strike you as somehow lacking. You suspect a trick. There is no nominative form, you observe, and the singular and plural forms are identical. And how can the thing mean "himself," "herself," "itself," and "themselves"? The answer is that the reflexive pronoun has no intrinsic meaning of its own, but simply reflects the third-person subject of the clause. If that subject is "he"—no matter how it is expressed—the reflexive will mean "himself"; if it is "they," it will mean "themselves." The reason there is no nominative is because the reflexive always *reflects* the nominative and thus can never *be* the nominative. Some examples will help:

nēmō enim sibi beneficium dat.	For no one gives a favor to himself.	SEN BEN 5.9.1
sē honestē gerunt.	They conduct themselves honorably.	CIC ATT 6.1.13
suī amor est.	There is a love of one's self.	SEN E 82.15
habēbat enim vēra sēcum bona.	For he had true goods with himself.	SEN CONS SAP 5.7

(Note in the last example the **cum** joined with the ablative of the reflexive.)

THIRD-PERSON REFLEXIVE ADJECTIVE

There is also a third-person reflexive adjective **suus, -a, -um**. It too reflects whatever the subject is and thus can be translated, depending on the context, "his (own)", "her (own)", "its (own)", "their (own)." (The "own" is often unnecessary when the context makes it clear.) Consider the following:

suum officium facit.	He does his (own) duty.	TER ADEL 69
dant sua corpora somnō.	They give their bodies to sleep.	OV F 2.327
habent scelera lēgēs suās.	Crimes have their (own) laws.	SEN BEN 7.17.2

This form also has hazards for the beginning student. Although it reflects the subject, it must still agree with the noun it modifies in case, number, and gender, as in the following examples:

parentēs facient officium suum. Parents will do their (own) duty.   PLAUT PERS 618

Here **suum** reflects the subject **parentēs**, and thus means "their (own)," but it modifies **officium** and thus is neuter, accusative, and singular. (So do not be misled into translating it "its".)

Similarly:

amat virum suum.   She loves her (own) husband.   PLAUT STICH 284

Here the **suum** reflects the unexpressed subject "she" and hence means "her (own)"; however, it is also accusative singular and masculine to modify its noun, **virum**. (So do not be misled into translating it "his.")

And again:

suīs agit grātiās.   He gives thanks to his (own) men.   CAES BC 3.82.1

Here **suīs** reflects the unexpressed subject "he" and hence means "his (own)"; however, it is acting as a substantive in the dative plural and thus means "to his men."

One more:

agunt opus suum fāta.   The fates do their (own) job.   SEN AD MARC 21.7

Here **suum** reflects the subject **fata** and hence means "their (own)"; however, it is also accusative <u>singular</u> and neuter to modify its noun, **opus**. (So do not be misled into translating it "its.")

CHAPTER 22: VOCABULARY

–, suī, sibi, sē / sēsē, sē / sēsē	–self, –selves
suus, a, um	his/her/its (own); their (own)
Caesar, Caesaris, m.	Caesar
emō, emere, ēmī, emptus	buy
iūs, iūris, n.	law, right
metuō, metuere, metuī, —	fear
nimis	(adverb) too much
numquam	never
ostendō, ostendere, ostendī, ostentus	show, reveal
***urbs, urbis, f.**	city
vendō, vendere, vendidī, venditus	sell

CHAPTER 22: PRACTICE SENTENCES (ANSWERS FOLLOW CHAPTER 66)

1. Fortune has its (own) reason. PETR 82.6
2. They were defending their (own) opinion. CIC DE FIN 2.2

CHAPTER 22: LATIN TO ENGLISH SENTENCES

1. **sē ex deōrum nātūrā gerit.** SEN CLEM 1.19.9
2. **mea pugnat sententia sēcum.** HOR E 1.1.97
3. **habet sua iūra nātūra.** SENR C 9.5.7
4. **sōla virtūs in suā potestāte est.** AUCHER 4.24
5. **nec voluptātēs sibi emit sed sē voluptātibus vendit.** SEN VIT BEAT 14.3
6. **ubi sē adiuvat, ibi mē adiuvat.** PLAUT PERS 304
7. **numquam enim nimis cūrāre possunt suum parentem fīliae.** PLAUT STICH 96
8. **sapiens sē contentus est.** SEN E 9.5
9. **haec iam mē suam voluptātem vocat.** PLAUT RUD 437

CHAPTER 22: GLOSSED LATIN TO ENGLISH SENTENCES

1. **nātūrae autem sē sapiens** accommodat.

   accomodō (1): adapt

   SEN E 17.9

2. **Iuppiter aut in** avēs **aut sē** transformat **in aurum.**

   avis, is, m. or f.: bird
   transformō (1): transform

   OV A 3.12.33

3. **multī sē ā** gladiātōrum **vulneribus** āvertunt.

   gladiātor, tōris, m.: gladiator
   avertō (3): turn away

   QUINT DECL 279

4. **habet suōs vīta** terminōs.

   terminus, ī, m.: boundary

   QUINT DECL 335

5. **animus mala sua** proximīs tradit.

   proximus, ī, m.: neighbor
   tradō (3): pass on

   SEN IRA 3.8.1

CHAPTER 22: ENGLISH TO LATIN SENTENCES

1. Caesar is a god in his (own) city.

   OV M 15.746

2. Antonius fears his (own) shadow.

   QCIC COMM PET 9

3. By now he shows his (own) opinion.

   PLAUT STICH 56

4. Glory has nothing in itself.

   CIC TD 1.109

23

Perfect Tense

So far, you have learned three of the six Latin verb tenses: present, imperfect, and future. These three go together in many ways—similar endings and, above all, similar stems. In order to learn the final three tenses—perfect, pluperfect, and future perfect—you must learn a new concept, one that also applies to many English verbs:

▼ **Latin verbs have a present stem and a perfect stem.**

When you formed the first three tenses, you used the present stem; when you form the perfect tenses, you must start from the perfect stem. Unfortunately, there is no necessary connection between the present and the perfect stems, so they must be learned and memorized. The good news is that the endings of the perfect tense apply to **all** the conjugations—one pattern fits all verbs. Here, for example, is a verb of the fourth conjugation:

Perfect

audīv-ī	I have heard	I heard
audīv-istī	you have heard	you heard
audīv-it	he/she/it has heard	he/she/it heard
audīv-imus	we have heard	we heard
audīv-istis	you have heard	you heard
audīv-ērunt	they have heard	they heard

Now for a verb of the first conjugation:

Perfect

amāv-ī	I have loved	I loved
amāv-istī	you have loved	you loved
amāv-it	he/she/it has loved	he/she/it loved
amāv-imus	we have loved	we loved
amāv-istis	you have loved	you loved
amāv-ērunt	they have loved	they loved

Note that two translations are possible for the perfect: (1) a translation using "have/has" (corresponding to the English present perfect) or (2) the simple past. Only the context will help determine which is better. For example, after an unusually quick victory, Caesar is said to have remarked,

vēnī, vīdī, vīcī.   I came, I saw, I conquered.   SUET DJ 37.2

Here, the context shows this to be the proper translation. In the absence of a context, either translation is possible.

You might assume from these two examples that the perfect stem simply adds a -**v**- to the present stem. Unfortunately, it is not so simple. There really is no accurate way to predict the relation. Consider **habeō**:

Perfect

habu-ī	I have had	I had
habu-istī	you have had	you had
habu-it	he/she/it has had	he/she/it had
habu-imus	we have had	we had
habu-istis	you have had	you had
habu-ērunt	they have had	they had

Or **dīcō**:

Perfect

dix-ī	I have said	I said
dix-istī	you have said	you said
dix-it	he/she/it has said	he/she/it said
dix-imus	we have said	we said
dix-istis	you have said	you said
dix-ērunt	they have said	they said

The change from present stem to perfect stem is often only one or two letters, but some verbs change radically. The situation is similar to the so-called "strong" verbs in English, like "bring," which in the past becomes "brought" (not "bringed"). Those who learn English as a second language simply have to memorize such verbs. There is no way to predict when they will occur. It is the same with Latin.

Some conjugations are more user-friendly than others. The first conjugation is one of those. Almost every verb in the first conjugation follows the same pattern for all the principal parts. Here are the principal parts of three representative verbs of the first conjugation (including the perfect passive participle, to be learned in chapter 34):

amō	**amāre**	**amāvī**	**amātus**
negō	**negāre**	**negāvī**	**negātus**
rogō	**rogāre**	**rogāvī**	**rogātus**

Exceptions to this predictability are **dō** and **adiuvō**:

dō	**dare**	**dedī**	**datus**
adiuvō	**adiuvāre**	**adiūvī**	**adiutus**

The second conjugation shows several patterns:

habeō	**habēre**	**habuī**	**habitus**
debeō	**debēre**	**debuī**	**debitus**

But the pattern shifts slightly with these common second conjugation verbs:

videō	**vidēre**	**vīdī**	**vīsus**
moveō	**movēre**	**mōvī**	**mōtus**

Verbs of the fourth conjugation have a fairly common pattern:

audiō	**audīre**	**audīvī**	**audītus**
dormiō	**dormīre**	**dormīvī**	**dormītus**
sciō	**scīre**	**scīvī**	**scītus**

But many common fourth conjugation verbs depart from that pattern:

veniō	**venīre**	**vēnī**	**ventus**
sentiō	**sentīre**	**sensī**	**sensus**

Finally, the third conjugation is the most unpredictable of all:

vīvō	**vīvere**	**vixī**	**victus**
agō	**agere**	**ēgī**	**actus**
quaerō	**quaerere**	**quaesīvī**	**quaesītus**

Don't forget the **-iō** variety of the third conjugation:

capiō	**capere**	**cēpī**	**captus**
cupiō	**cupere**	**cupīvī**	**cupītus**
faciō	**facere**	**fēcī**	**factus**

In addition, the perfect stem of some third conjugation verbs is identical to the present stem:

defend-ō	**defendere**	**defend-ī**	**defensus**
ostend-ō	**ostendere**	**ostend-ī**	**ostensus**

What this means is that the third-person singular and the first-person plural of both tenses is identical. Thus, **defendit** could mean either "he defends" or "he (has) defended," and **ostendimus** could mean either "we show" or "we (have) showed," Only a context will settle the matter:

orbem Rōmānum ūnus Augustus tenuit et defendit. AUG CD 5.25

Augustus alone held and defended the Roman sphere.

(A related issue concerns verbs whose perfect stem differs from the present stem by having a long vowel. Here are some examples:

veniō	**venīre**	**vēnī**	**ventus**
fugiō	**fugere**	**fūgī**	**—**
em-ō	**emere**	**ēm-ī**	**emptus**

Here the presence of a long or short owel will determine whether the form is present or perfect. For example, **venit** is present but **vēnit** is perfect.)

Here are some examples of sentences using the perfect tense:

mutavimus consilium.	We changed/have changed the plan.	CIC FAM 14.15
vīdistis hominem.	You saw/have seen the fellow.	CIC VER 4.92
servī mē relīquērunt.	The slaves left/have left me.	SEN E 107.5
vixistī nōbīscum.	You lived/have lived with us.	PLINY PANEG 44.1
mē multa mōvērunt.	Many things moved/have moved me.	CIC ATT 6.4.1
magnam cēpī voluptātem.	I took/have taken great pleasure.	PLINY E 4.23.1
vīcit amor.	Love conquered/has conquered.	OV M 10.26

PERFECT ACTIVE INFINITIVE

Latin, like English, has a perfect active infinitive, formed from the perfect stem by adding **-isse**. It is translated "to have ... ." Although you may not often use it yourself, you may have heard

Tis better <u>to have loved</u> and lost than never <u>to have loved</u> at all.

Here are some Latin examples:

haec dixisse satis erat.	It was enough to have said these things.	QUINT DECL 268
potuī fūgisse puellam.	I was able to have fled the girl.	PROP 1.17.1
nōn satis est tuum tē officium fēcisse.		TER PHOR 724
	It is not enough for you to have done your duty.	

All verbs with their principal parts are contained in the vocabulary at the back of the book.

CHAPTER 23: VOCABULARY

adhuc	*so far, still*
causā	*for the sake of (with preceding genitive)*
et	*(adverb) also, as well*
imperium, iī, n.	*command; empire*
lībertās, lībertātis, f.	*liberty*
miseria, ae, f.	*misery, woe*
prō	*(prep. + abl.) in return for; on behalf of*

quantus, a, um	*how great, how much*
salūs, salūtis, f.	*safety; greeting*
tempus, temporis, n.	*time*

CHAPTER 23: PRACTICE SENTENCES (ANSWERS FOLLOW CHAPTER 66)

1. **arma dedī vōbīs.** — OV AA 2.741
2. A. **fuistīne līber?** B. **fuī.** — PLAUT CAPT 628
3. **quis enim sēcūrus amāvit?** — OV HER 19.109
4. **quid eae dixērunt tibi?** — PLAUT MG 60
5. **fēcit officium hic suum.** — PLAUT CAPT 297
6. **ferrum in vulnere relīquit.** — [QUINT] DECL 1.11
7. **ad mē dē eō nihil scripsistī.** — CIC ATT 1.3.2
8. **tacuī adhuc; nunc nōn tacēbō.** — PLAUT TRUC 817
9. **līberē potuimus sententiam dīcere?** — CIC ATT 14.14.2
10. We took arms. — CIC PHIL 12.16
11. He gave liberty to the slave. — SENR C 7.6.7
12. I have never heard the name. — CIC ATT 5.20.1
13. He lived, while he lived, well. — TER HEC 461
14. Did the Roman people accept this law? — CIC PHIL 5.7
15. Your fortune has defeated my fortune. — SEN CONS SAP 6.6

CHAPTER 23: LATIN TO ENGLISH SENTENCES

1. **ingenium mōvit sōla Corinna meum.** — OV A 3.12.16
2. **sed dē cēterīs et diximus multa et saepe dīcēmus.** — CIC DE SENEC 3
3. **tibi mē virtūs tua fēcit amīcum.** — HOR S 2.5.33
4. A. **malum vōbīs dabō.** B. **at tibi nōs dedimus dabimusque.** — PLAUT PERS 847
5. **quantus in exiguō tempore fūgit amor!** — PROP 1.12.12
6. **itaque habuī noctem plēnam timōris ac miseriae.** — CIC FAM 16.14.1
7. **respondit mihi paucīs verbīs.** — PLAUT CURC 333
8. **dē tōtā meā cōgitātiōne scripsī ad tē.** — CIC ATT 10.5.1
9. **dī tibi formam, dī tibi dīvitiās dedērunt.** — HOR E 1.4.6-7
10. A. **tū tuum negōtium gessistī bene.** B. **gere et tuum bene.** — CIC ROSCC 32

11. **Cynthia prīma fuit, Cynthia fīnis erit.**   PROP 1.12.20
12. **nōn prō meā adhuc sed prō patriae lībertāte pugnāvī.**   SEN E 24.7
13. **amō autem et semper amāvī ingenium, studium, mōrēs tuōs.**   CIC OR BRUT 33
14. **prō populī Rōmānī lībertāte arma cēpērunt.**   CIC PHIL 10.15
15. **vestrae salutis causā suum perīculum neglexērunt.**   CAES BG 7.77.9

CHAPTER 23: GLOSSED LATIN TO ENGLISH SENTENCES

1. **quō fūgit Venus**, heu?   heu!: alas!   HOR O 4.13.17

2. oscula **nulla dedī. at lacrimās sine fīne dedī.**   osculum, ī, n.: kiss   OV HER 3.14-15

3. reliquōs **enim deōs accēpimus, Caesarēs dedimus.**   reliquus, a, um: the remaining, other   VALMAX 1.PRAEF

4. **quis autem Rōmulum deum nisi Rōma** crēdidit?   crēdō, 3, crēdidī: believe   AUG CD 22.6

5. dīvisērunt **nātūram hominis in animum et corpus.**   dīvidō, 3, dīvīsī: divide   CIC DE FIN 4.16

6. **nōn** adversus **patriam sed inimīcōs suōs bellum gessit.**   adversus: (prep. + acc.) against   NEPOS 7.4.6

7. leōnem **in** amphitheātrō **spectāvimus.**   leo, leōnis, m.: lion
                                                            amphitheātrum, ī, n.: amphitheater   SEN BEN 2.19.1

CHAPTER 23: ENGLISH TO LATIN SENTENCES

1. Our love has been the cause of love for many.   OV A 3.11.20
2. For the gods have always been.   CIC ND 1.90
3. No one has seen the truth about the nature of the gods. CIC ND 1.94
4. I have given an empire without end.   VERG A 1.279
5. He lived to the highest old age.   CIC BRUTUS 179

CHAPTER 23: PASSAGES

NO PRESSURE

saepe pater dixit "generum **mihi, fīlia,** dēbēs".
saepe pater dixit "dēbēs mihi, nata, nepōtēs".

OV M 1.481–2

---

gener, erī, m.: son-in-law	dēbeō (2): owe
nata, ae, f.: daughter	nepos, nepōtis, m.: grandson

24

Pluperfect and Future Perfect Tenses/Dative of the Possessor

The two tenses introduced in this chapter are both common in Latin but little used in popular speech today. In addition, the future perfect is hardly seen at all except in specimens of older English. Thus, you may simply have to learn the formulas for translating them and wait for deeper understanding to develop.

PLUPERFECT TENSE

The pluperfect tense describes a time in the past that occurs before another time in the past; it is translated by the English auxiliary verb "had." For example, "I had forgotten to set the clock back before I went to bed on Saturday." Although this is a perfectly correct sentence, most people today avoid using the English pluperfect and would probably just say "I forgot to set the clock before I went to bed" since the time relation is self-evident. However, the Romans were sensitive to this relation and observed it much more often than we do. As a result, the pluperfect is common in all forms of Latin.

In forming its pluperfect tense, Latin gives you a gift—you already know the endings! Just take the perfect stem of any verb, in any conjugation, and add the imperfect of **sum**:

Pluperfect

audīv-eram	I had heard
audīv-erās	you had heard
audīv-erat	he/she/it had heard
audīv-erāmus	we had heard
audīv-erātis	you had heard
audīv-erant	they had heard

Here are some examples of sentences using the pluperfect:

rēgēs gesserant bella.	Kings had waged wars.	LIVY 9.17.11
dux fuerat bellī.	He had been a leader of war.	OV TRIST 4.2.28
quid vīderās, quid senserās, quid audīerās?		CIC PHIL 2.83

What had you seen, what had you felt, what had you heard?

FUTURE PERFECT TENSE

The future perfect is not much found in modern American speech and may be foreign to you. However, like the pluperfect, it too is common in Latin and has a very specific meaning, one that we tend to ignore in speaking English. Just as the pluperfect describes a time completed before a past time, so the future perfect describes a time completed before a future time. In normal English we usually ignore this distinction. For example, we say "After I go home, I will eat dinner" using the present, then the future. But in Latin, the first clause would have the future perfect, and the second the future because the act of going home occurs before the act of eating, both in the future.

The simplest way to render the future perfect is with the old-fashioned English future perfect: "will have." Although you may not realize it, these words convey exactly the same time relation as the Latin future perfect tense. They describe an action to be completed in the future that occurs before a later future act. For example, "By the time you come home, I will have cleaned the house" means that the act of cleaning the house will be completed before you get home. (However, most people would probably just say "I will clean the house before you get home.")

In forming the future perfect, you get a gift similar to that of the pluperfect, but not quite as tidy. Five out of six endings of the future perfect are formed from the future of **sum**, the exception being the third-person plural, which has -**erint** instead of -**erunt**:

Future Perfect

audīv-erō	I will have heard
audīv-eris	you will have heard
audīv-erit	he/she/it will have heard
audīv-erimus	we will have heard
audīv-eritis	you will have heard
audīv-erint	they will have heard

Here are some examples of sentences using the future perfect:

faciam ut iusseris.	I will do as you will have ordered.	PLAUT CURC 707
cum vīderō tē, sciēs.	When I will have seen you, you will know.	CIC ATT 13.22.3

Notice how, in each example, the action of the future perfect verb occurs before the action of the future verb.

DATIVE OF THE POSSESSOR

So far possession has been restricted to the genitive case; however, Latin also uses the dative case with the verb **sum** to show possession. It is called, fittingly, "dative of possession" or "dative of the possessor," since the possessor is usually a person. In this construction, the person possessing goes in the dative, the thing possessed in the nominative, and some form of the verb **sum** is used. For example, "I do not have time" would be recast as "There is not time to me" and appear in Latin as

nōn est mihi tempus.	I do not have time.	HOR S 2.4.1

Or, "He had two daughters" would be recast as "There were two daughters to him" and become in Latin

eī fīliae duae erant.	He had two daughters.	PLAUT STICH 539–40

Here are some more examples:

huic fīlia una est.	This (person) has one daughter.	PLAUT AUL 23
eī est fīlius.	He/She has a son.	PLAUT CAS 35
est tibi mater?	Do you have a mother?	HOR S 1.9.26
trēs illī fratrēs fuērunt.	He/She had three brothers.	CIC FAM 9.21.3

This construction is also used with the noun **nomen** "name." The person possessing the name goes in the dative, the word **nomen** is in the nominative, and the verb **sum** appears. Thus, the sentence "This is my name," would be recast as "This is the name to me" and become in Latin

id est nōmen mihi.	This is my name.	PLAUT PSEUD 637

Here are some more examples:

quid est eī hominī nōmen?	What is this fellow's name?	PLAUT PSEUD 977
quid erat eī nōmen?	What was his name?	PLAUT CAPT 983

CHAPTER 24: VOCABULARY

dormiō, dormīre, dormī(v)ī, dormītus	*sleep*
castra, ōrum, n. pl.	*camp (for soldiers)*
cum	*when*
imperātor, imperātōris, m.	*general; emperor*
insānus, a, um	*insane, unsound*
māter, matris, f.	*mother*
miles, militis, m.	*soldier*
***pars, partis, f.**	*part; side*
post	*after, behind (prep. + acc.)*
reliquus, a, um	*remaining, rest (of)*
remedium, īī, n.	*cure*
rex, rēgis, m.	*king*
umquam	*ever*
uxor, uxōris, f.	*wife*

CHAPTER 24: PRACTICE SENTENCES (ANSWERS FOLLOW CHAPTER 66)

1.	**numquam illum pater timuerat.**	[QUINT] DECL 1.3
2.	**cūr nōn vēnistī, ut iusseram?**	PLAUT ASIN 413
3.	**Epicūrī sententiam vīderimus.**	CIC TD 3.32
4.	**scrībam ad tē cum Caesarem vīderō.**	CIC ATT 2.1.9
5.	**mihi sunt vīrēs.**	OV HER 16.352
6.	He had waged great wars.	CIC DE FIN 2.65
7.	I have business.	PLAUT AMPH 1035
8.	He had never seen his (own) father.	CIC RAB POST 4
9.	We will know when you will have come.	CIC ATT 2.3.1
10.	I have wounds as well, citizens.	OV M 13.262-3

CHAPTER 24: LATIN TO ENGLISH SENTENCES

1. **tibi uxōrem fīliam dederō meam.**   PLAUT CIST 499
2. **nec senectūs mōrēs mūtāverat.**   CIC DE SENEC 10
3. **nōs, cum salvī vēnerimus, reliqua per nōs agēmus.**   CIC FAM 14.5.2
4. **vīdistī igitur virum, ut scripserās?**   CIC ATT 9.18.3
5. **et fueram patriae pars ego magna meae.**   OV HER 3.46
6. **bellum tibi fuit, imperātor, cum homine clārō.**   [SALL] CAES 1.2.2
7. **quid nōmen tibi est?**   PLAUT MEN 498
8. **sine remediō timor stultīs est.**   SEN QN 6.2.1
9. **nōn erit illī plānum iter.**   SEN PROV 5.9
10. **nam dē Italiā quidem nihil mihi umquam ostenderās.**   CIC ATT 8.11D.6
11. **dominum suum nōn defenderat, nōn servāverat.**   QUINT DECL 328
12. **tūne insānus eris sī accēperis?**   HOR S 2.3.67
13. **contrā iūra castrōrum fēcerat mīles.**   [QUINT] DECL 3.15
14. **certē dormiēbās, certē nihil senserās.**   [QUINT] DECL 1.9

CHAPTER 24: GLOSSED LATIN TO ENGLISH SENTENCES

1. **Magnum Claudius, Crassum Nero** interfēcerant.   interficiō, interficere, interfēcī, interfectus: kill   TAC HIST 1.48

2. **Publius Scīpio Africānus Aemiliānus** Carthāginem dēlēverat.   Carthāgo, Carthāginis, f.: Carthage | dēleō, dēlēre, dēlēvī, dēlētus: destroy   VP 2.4.2

3. **noctis erat medium, cūrās**que **et corpora somnus** solverat.   cūra, ae, f.: care | solvō, solvere, solvī, solūtus: loosen   OV M 10.368-9

CHAPTER 24: ENGLISH TO LATIN SENTENCES

1. I had seen that man after a long time.   SENR C 9.5.12
2. If I will have saved your son, will you not have my kindness?   SEN BEN 5.18
3. You have a mind.   HOR O 4.9.34
4. What is his name?   PLAUT TRIN 906
5. My father had been a king.   SEN MED 168
6. What was our mother's name?   PLAUT MEN 1131
7. She had given the highest favor of life.   QUINT DECL 251

CHAPTER 25

Adjectives of the Third Declension

I n addition to adjectives of the first and second declensions, learned in chapter 6, there are also adjectives in the third declension. (After this, there are no more adjective declensions.) As a general rule, third declension adjectives are declined like third declension i-stem nouns (learned in chapter 12), as the following table shows:

Case	Singular			Plural		
	masc	*fem*	*neut*	*masc*	*fem*	*neut*
nominative	brev-is	brev-is	brev-e	brev-ēs	brev-ēs	<u>brev-ia</u>
genitive	brev-is	brev-is	brev-is	<u>brev-ium</u>	<u>brev-ium</u>	<u>brev-ium</u>
dative	brev-ī	brev-ī	brev-ī	brev-ibus	brev-ibus	brev-ibus
accusative	brev-em	brev-em	brev-e	brev-ēs	brev-ēs	<u>brev-ia</u>
ablative	<u>brev-ī</u>	<u>brev-ī</u>	<u>brev-ī</u>	brev-ibus	brev-ibus	brev-ibus
vocative	brev-is	brev-is	brev-e	brev-ēs	brev-ēs	<u>brev-ia</u>

The relation to i-stem nouns is seen in the -**i** in the ablative singular and in the -**i**- in the genitive plurals and nominative and accusative plurals. I have underlined those forms.

Notice that the masculine and feminine forms are identical. Whenever this occurs, the tables will be written with only two columns—the masculine/feminine in one and the neuter in the other—as follows:

Case	Singular		Plural	
	masc/fem	*neut*	*masc/fem*	*neut*
nominative	**brev-is**	**brev-e**	**brev-ēs**	**brev-ia**
genitive	**brev-is**	**brev-is**	**brev-ium**	**brev-ium**
dative	**brev-ī**	**brev-ī**	**brev-ibus**	**brev-ibus**
accusative	**brev-em**	**brev-e**	**brev-ēs**	**brev-ia**
ablative	**brev-ī**	**brev-ī**	**brev-ibus**	**brev-ibus**
vocative	**brev-is**	**brev-e**	**brev-ēs**	**brev-ia**

Because of this feature, such third declension adjectives are often referred to as "adjectives of two terminations."

Another family of third declension adjectives declines as follows:

Case	Singular		Plural	
	masc/fem	*neut*	*masc/fem*	*neut*
nominative	**pār**	**pār**	**par-ēs**	**par-ia**
genitive	**par-is**	**par-is**	**par-ium**	**par-ium**
dative	**par-ī**	**par-ī**	**par-ibus**	**par-ibus**
accusative	**par-em**	**pār**	**par-ēs**	**par-ia**
ablative	**par-ī**	**par-ī**	**par-ibus**	**par-ibus**
vocative	**pār**	**pār**	**par-ēs**	**par-ia**

This family is referred to as "adjectives of one termination" since the nominative singular is the same for all three genders. Otherwise, it is declined exactly like the first pattern.

For completeness, here is a table of a very common type of third declension adjective, a "one-termination" kind. You will be seeing more of this pattern in chapter 36 when you learn about present active participles. The adjective **sapiens** means "wise":

Case	Singular		Plural	
	masc/fem	*neut*	*masc/fem*	*neut*
nominative	**sapiens**	**sapiens**	**sapient-ēs**	**sapient-ia**
genitive	**sapient-is**	**sapient-is**	**sapient-ium**	**sapient-ium**
dative	**sapient-ī**	**sapient-ī**	**sapient-ibus**	**sapient-ibus**
accusative	**sapient-em**	**sapiens**	**sapient-ēs**	**sapient-ia**
ablative	**sapient-ī**	**sapient-ī**	**sapient-ibus**	**sapient-ibus**
vocative	**sapiens**	**sapiens**	**sapient-ēs**	**sapient-ia**

The advent of third declension adjectives brings up an old problem, but in reverse. Back in chapters 10–12, when you first encountered third declension nouns, you learned that adjectives of the first and second declensions had to stay fixed in their declensions when modifying third declension nouns. The tables for **amor vērus** and **virtūs vēra** and **vulnus magnum** made this clear. The same principle now applies to third declension adjectives. No matter what kind of noun they modify—first, second, or third declension (or fourth or fifth later)—they must stay locked in their own declension and not borrow endings from other declensions. Here are some examples:

dī dīvitēs sunt.   The gods are wealthy.   PLAUT TRIN 490

(**dīvitēs** modifies **dī**; both are nominative, masculine, plural.)

valēte, cūrae mortālēs.   Farewell, mortal cares.   PETR 79.8.4-5

(**mortālēs** modifies **cūrae**; both are vocative, feminine, plural.)

grave est hoc crīmen.   This crime is serious.   CIC CAEC DIV 32

(**grave** modifies **crīmen**; both are nominative, singular, neuter.)

Here are some more examples:

pater vīrī fortis eram.   I was the father of a brave man.   QUINT DECL 278

omnēs malī sumus.   We are all bad.   SEN IRA 3.26.4

dī immortālēs!   Immortal gods!   PLAUT EPID 196

Even though the noun and its adjective are grammatically identical, their endings never match!

Note: Anything an adjective of first and second declensions can do or be, so can an adjective of the third declension. They can be used as substantives:

miser est dīvitis servus.	Wretched is the slave of a rich person.	PLAUT AMPH 167
fortēs Fortūna adiuvat.	Fortune helps the brave (people).	TER PHOR 203
sēsē omnēs amant.	All (people) love themselves.	PLAUT CAPT 104
omnia timeō.	I fear all (things).	CIC ATT 3.8.2

And they can modify infinitives:

nōn facile est scrībere.	It is not easy to write.	CIC FAM 1.8.1
ūtile est amīcōs vērōs habēre.	It is useful to have true friends.	AUCHER 2.37

In each example, the adjectives **facile** and **ūtile** are neuter singular nominative because they modify the infinitives **scrībere** and **habēre**; for grammatical purposes, infinitives are neuter nouns.

CHAPTER 25: VOCABULARY

brevis, breve	*short, brief*
dīves, dīvitis	*rich*
facilis, facile	*easy*
fēlix, fēlīcis	*fortunate, happy*
fortis, forte	*brave*
gravis, grave	*heavy, serious*
immortālis, immortale	*immortal*
mortālis, mortale	*mortal*
omnis, omne	*all, every*
pār, paris	*equal, equal to (+ dat)*
sapiens, sapientis	*wise*
apud	*with, at (prep. + acc)*
grātiās agō	*give thanks*
Latīnus, a, um	*Latin*
pecūnia, ae, f.	*money*
servitūs, servitūtis, f.	*slavery*

CHAPTER 25: PRACTICE SENTENCES (ANSWERS FOLLOW CHAPTER 66)

1. **inimīcum dīvitem habeō.**   QUINT DECL 337
2. **movet animus omnēs fortis.**   SEN TROAD 1146
3. **nēmō mortālium est fēlix.**   PLINY NH 7.130
4. **nēminem pecūnia dīvitem fēcit.**   SEN E 119.9
5. **sum fēlix fēlixque manēbō.**   OV M 6.193
6. **dī immortālēs mihi līberōs dedērunt.**   CIC RED POP 5
7. Love conquers all things.   VERG E 10.69
8. Every life is brief.   PUBLSYR
9. Fortune fears the brave.   SEN MED 159
10. I feel heavy pain.   SEN E 78.17
11. I have given myself to wise men.   SEN AD HELV 5.2
12. But all things will be easy if you will be well.   CIC FAM 16.11.1

CHAPTER 25: LATIN TO ENGLISH SENTENCES

1. **quam multīs dīvitiae gravēs sunt!**   SEN BREV VIT 2.4
2. **immortālēs agō tibi gratiās agamque dum vivam.**   CIC FAM 10.11.1
3. **dux atque imperātor vītae mortālium animus est.**   SALL BJ 1.3
4. **amor ingeniī nēminem umquam dīvitem fēcit.**   PETR 83.9
5. **cupiō enim Caesaris mortem omnibus esse acerbam.** CIC FAM 11.28.4
6. **saepe quaerimus verbum Latīnum pār Graecō.**   CIC DE FIN 2.13
7. **ō vīta miserō longa, fēlīcī brevis!**   PUBLSYR O3
8. **parem autem tē deō pecunia nōn faciet – deus nihil habet.** SEN E 31.10
9. **facilis est ad beātam vītam via.**   SEN IRA 2.13.2
10. **dīvitiae enim apud sapientem virum in servitūte sunt, apud stultum in imperiō.** SEN VIT BEAT 26.1

CHAPTER 25: GLOSSED LATIN TO ENGLISH SENTENCES

1. **nil sine magnō vita** labōre **dedit mortālibus.**

   labor, laboris, m.: labor

   HOR S 1.9.59-60

2. **omnēs uxōrēs dīvitēs servitūtem** exigunt.

   exigo, exigere: demand

   SENR C 1.6.5

3. **nam sine amōre gravī** fēmina **nulla dolet.**

   femina, ae, f.: woman

   PROP 3.8.10

CHAPTER 25: ENGLISH TO LATIN SENTENCES

1. However, the laws of philosophy are short.

   SEN E 94.15

2. The anger of kings is always heavy.

   SEN MED 494

3. The highest good is immortal.

   SEN VIT BEAT 7.4

4. All faults fight against nature.

   SEN E 122.5

5. All your citizens fear you.

   CIC IN CAT 1.17

26

Third Declension Adverbs

Adverbs of the third declension generally are formed by adding **-ter** to the stems of third declension adjectives, sometimes joined by an **–i**, sometimes not. There is no way to predict. So, for example, from **fortis** "brave" we get **fortiter** "bravely," and from **gravis** "heavy" we get **graviter** "heavily," and from **par** "equal" we get **pariter** "equally." However, the adverb form of **audax** "bold" is **audacter** "boldly," and the adverb form of **sapiens** "wise" is **sapienter** "wisely," and that of **vehemens** "strong" is **vehementer** "strongly." Here are some examples:

pugnāvī fortiter.	I fought bravely.	PLAUT MEN 129
tuum consilium vehementer laudō.	I strongly praise your advice.	CIC AD BRUT 1.2.2
vērum, Gallice, nōn libenter audīs.	Gallicus, you do not gladly hear the truth.	MART 8.76.8

In addition, a few third declension adjectives simply use the neuter accusative singular form as the adverb. Thus, we find **facile** "easily" from **facilis** "easy" and **dulce** "sweetly" from **dulcis** "sweet."

superās facile.	You win easily.	PLAUT MEN 192
dulce Venus rīsit.	Venus laughed sweetly.	OV HER 16.83

Adverbs like **facile** and **dulce** pose problems for the beginner. Are they adverbs or neuter adjectives in the nominative or accusative singular? The key is to look for a neuter nominative or accusative singular noun; if there is none, you are dealing with an adverb.

As before, adverbs do not decline, so the ending does not change.

CHAPTER 26: VOCABULARY

audax, audācis	*bold*
libens, libentis	*glad*
vehemens, vehementis	*strong*
suscipiō, suscipere, suscēpī, susceptus	*take up, undertake*

facile	*(adverb) easily*
invītus, a, um	*unwilling(ly)*
tam	*so*

CHAPTER 26: LATIN TO ENGLISH SENTENCES

1. **id tam audacter dīcere audēs?** PLAUT CAPT 630
2. **errābās, Verres, et vehementer errābās.** CIC VER 5.121
3. **dīc mihi – quid fēcī, nisi nōn sapienter amāvī?** OV HER 2.27
4. **suscēpī causam, Torquāte, suscēpī, et fēcī libenter.** CIC PRO SULLA 20

CHAPTER 26: GLOSSED LATIN TO ENGLISH SENTENCES

1. **facile omnēs, cum valēmus, recta consilia** aegrōtīs **damus.** TER AND 309

   aegrōtus, a, um: sick

CHAPTER 26: ENGLISH TO LATIN SENTENCES

1. How easily we humans err. SENR C 7.1.5
2. A bold life, full of crimes! PLINY NH 19.4
3. He said many things strongly and seriously. QUINT DECL 279
4. For no one gives gladly to the unwilling. SEN BEN 3.13.2

27

Ablative of Means and Cause

In chapter 3, you learned that certain prepositions like **in** require the ablative. In this and subsequent chapters, you will learn that the ablative can be used without a preposition in certain carefully defined situations. The first of these is called "ablative of means." When a noun is used as the instrument or means by which something is accomplished, it appears in the ablative—with no preposition. See these examples:

pugnābant armīs.	They were fighting with arms.	HOR S 1.3.102
clārē oculīs videō.	I see clearly with (my) eyes.	PLAUT MG 630
morte patriam servāvērunt.	They saved the homeland by death.	SEN BEN 6.36.2

In fact, you have already encountered this construction (without realizing it). In chapter 5 you found the sentence **verbīs laudō**, which you properly translated "I praise with words." Then in chapter 20 you encountered "They make (a) way by force," which you doubtless translated **vī viam faciunt**. You were successful because in chapter 3 you were told to translate the ablative with "by," "with," or "from." Now the full story can be told: Both were ablatives of means.

ABLATIVE OF CAUSE

Another common ablative use is ablative of cause: A noun in the ablative gives the cause or reason for something. A generally reliable translation is "because of" or "from." Here are some examples:

caeca amōre est.	She is blind because of/from love.	PLAUT MG 1259
animī vitiō miser est.	He is wretched because of a fault of mind.	[QUINT] DECL 6.16

You will notice that the same words—"with" and "from"—can be used to translate these new ablatives. There may be times, however, when they do not work as translations. Whatever English words are used to translate the ablative with no preposition, you must still be prepared to say what type of ablative the word is (means, cause, etc.).

CHAPTER 27: VOCABULARY

cerno, cernere, crēvī, crētus — *observe, perceive*

corrumpō, corrumpere, corrūpī, corruptus — *corrupt, bribe*

dēlectō, dēlectāre, dēlectāvī, dēlectātus — *delight*

furor, furōris, m. — *madness*

gladius, gladiī, m. — *sword*

liber, librī, m. — *book*

mūnus, mūneris, n. — *gift*

signum, ī, n. — *sign; seal*

CHAPTER 27: PRACTICE SENTENCES (ANSWERS FOLLOW CHAPTER 66)

1. **satisne ego oculīs cernō?** — PLAUT POEN 1299
2. **nōn facit hoc verbīs.** — TIB 1.5.43
3. **mē oculīs vīdistī tuīs.** — PLAUT RUD 1166
4. **nihil enim animō vidēre poterant.** — CIC TD 1.37
5. He conquered by strength. — CIC DE AMIC 55
6. You will help us with counsels. — CIC ATT 10.2.2
7. He was seeking (his) mother with (his) eyes. — [QUINT] DECL 2.23
8. You have lived because of our gift. — OV M 8.503

CHAPTER 27: LATIN TO ENGLISH SENTENCES

1. **nōn enim iam satis est consiliō pugnāre.** — CIC FAM 9.16.2
2. **sapiens quidem vincit virtūte Fortūnam.** — SEN E 71.30
3. **mūneribus servōs corrumpam.** — HOR S 1.9.57
4. **oculīs mihi signum dedit.** — PLAUT MG 123
5. **librīs mē dēlectō.** — CIC ATT 2.6.1
6. **nostrā miseriā tū es magnus.** — CIC ATT 2.19.3
7. **ita ille et salvus est et beneficiō meō vivit.** — QUINT DECL 335
8. **nēmō nisi vitiō suō miser est.** — SEN E 70.15
9. **animō autem vidēmus, animō cernimus.** — PLINY NH 11.146
10. **ratiōne furōrem vincere nōn poterat.** — OV M 7.10-11

CHAPTER 27: GLOSSED LATIN TO ENGLISH SENTENCES

1. **auribus teneō** lupum.

   lupus, ī, m.: wolf

   TER PHOR 506

2. **Cynthia prīma suīs miserum mē cēpit** ocellīs.

   ocellus, ī, m.: eye

   PROP 1.1.1

3. **corporis** gravitātem **et dolōrem animō** iūdicāmus.

   gravitas, tātis, f.: weight

   iūdicō (1): judge

   CIC TD 3.1

4. **natūram oculīs, nōn ratiōne,** comprehendimus.

   comprehendō, 3: grasp

   SEN QN 6.3.2

CHAPTER 27: ENGLISH TO LATIN SENTENCES

1. Help us with your opinion.

   CIC FAM 11.4.2

2. Now we hold all things with arms.

   CIC PHIL 12.13

3. I live because of the death of my son.

   [QUINT] DECL 6.1

4. He wages wars with swords.

   LUCAN 8.386

28 Relative Pronoun

The relative pronoun has been carefully named to remind you that (a) it is a kind of noun, and therefore has inflectional endings, and (b) it always "relates" to another noun, called the "antecedent." You would naturally expect the antecedent to "come before" (**ante+cedo**) the relative pronoun, and in English, this is practically always true. In Latin, with its freer word order, the antecedent usually precedes the relative pronoun, but may come afterward or be left out entirely.

The Latin relative pronoun can be translated into English by several words—"who," "which," or "that"—depending on the circumstances of the sentence. Here are its forms:

Case	Singular			Plural		
	masc	*fem*	*neut*	*masc*	*fem*	*neut*
nominative	**quī**	**quae**	**quod**	**quī**	**quae**	**quae**
genitive	**cuius**	**cuius**	**cuius**	**quōrum**	**quārum**	**quōrum**
dative	**cui**	**cui**	**cui**	**quibus**	**quibus**	**quibus**
accusative	**quem**	**quam**	**quod**	**quōs**	**quās**	**quae**
ablative	**quō**	**quā**	**quō**	**quibus**	**quibus**	**quibus**

Notice that the endings appear to be drawn from various declensions: **quō, quā, quō** from the first and second and **quibus** from the third. The genitive singular form **cuius** is related to the genitive singular form of **hic**.

MAIN AND SUBORDINATE CLAUSES

The relative pronoun brings you a new concept in grammar—the clause. For now, a working description of a clause is this: a group of words containing a subject and a conjugated verb predicate. A sentence containing the relative pronoun typically has two clauses, one main and one subordinate. Main clauses contain both a subject and a predicate and can "stand alone." Subordinate clauses also have subject and predicate but in addition have a word that makes the whole clause subordinate, that is, unable to stand alone. In this case, the subordinating word is the relative pronoun itself. Some examples will make this clearer:

omnia fēcī quae potuī.   I have done everything that I could.   CIC ATT 6.2.7

Here, the main clause is "I have done everything," and the subordinate clause is "that I could." The main clause could be a sentence on its own; the subordinate clause could not.

hunc amant quem timēbant.   They love him whom they feared.   CIC ATT 8.13.2

Here, the man clause is "They love him" and the subordinate clause is "whom they feared." The main clause could be a sentence on its own; the subordinate clause could not.

RULE FOR USING THE RELATIVE PRONOUN

As you saw in the previous table, the relative pronoun has various forms. In order to select the proper one, you must memorize the following rule:

▼   **The relative pronoun agrees with its antecedent in number and gender, but its case is determined by its use in its own clause.**

Take this sentence:

quis est senex quem videō?   Who is the old man whom I see?   TER PHOR 215

The antecedent of the relative pronoun **quem** is **senex**; it agrees with it in number (singular) and gender (masculine). However, its case is dictated by its use in the subordinate clause, where it is the direct object of **videō**, thus accusative **quem**.

Here's another example:

ubi est illa pax dē quā Balbus scripserat?   CIC ATT 9.14.2
Where is that peace about which Balbus had written?

The antecedent of the relative pronoun **quā** is **pax**; it agrees with it in number (singular) and gender (feminine). However, its case is generated by its use in the subordinate clause, where it is the object of the preposition **dē**, which requires the ablative **quā**.

RELATIVE PRONOUN WITH ANTECEDENT OMITTED

Sometimes the antecedent is left out, as in this sentence:

ego dīcam quod sentiō.   I will say (that) which I feel.   CIC BRUTUS 151

"I will say (that)" is the main clause; "which I feel" is the subordinate clause; the antecedent, had it been expressed, could have been **id** – "that (thing)." Here are some more with omitted antecedents:

miser est quī amat.	Wretched is (he) who loves.	PLAUT PERS 179
ubi sunt quae iussī?	Where are (the things) which I ordered?	PLAUT CIST 289
quī est sapiens stultus nōn est.	(He) who is wise is not stupid.	QUINT 5.10.74

RELATIVE PRONOUN WITH PRECEDING ANTECEDENT

Sometimes, contrary to what you might think possible, the antecedent even follows the relative pronoun, as in this sentence:

quī videt, is peccat.   He makes a mistake who sees.   PROP 2.32.1

I have deliberately translated this sentence in an unnatural way to bring out the reversed feeling of the Latin sentence. (It would have been perfectly acceptable Latin to write **is quī videt peccat** or **is peccat quī videt**. Each has a slightly different emphasis.)

CHAPTER 28: VOCABULARY

quī, quae, quod	*who, which, that*
dēbeō, dēbēre, dēbuī, dēbitus	*owe*
mittō, mittere, mīsī, missus	*send; let fall*
reddō, reddere, redidī, reditus	*give back; deliver*
crās	*tomorrow*
epistula, ae, f.	*letter*
exemplum, ī, n.	*copy; model*
hodiē	*today*

CHAPTER 28: PRACTICE SENTENCES (ANSWERS FOLLOW CHAPTER 66)

1. hoc quod rogō respondē.   PLAUT ASIN 578
2. haec quae vēra sunt dīcam.   CIC VER 3.158
3. multum est dē quō timet.   SENR C 7.8.5
4. A. quid ego audiō? B. id quod vērum est.   PLAUT AMPH 792-3
5. sunt enim multa vitia dē quibus dīxī.   QUINT 11.3.31
6. illī, quod nēmō fēcerat, fēcērunt.   CIC PHIL 2.114
7. quōs amor vērus tenuit, tenēbit.   SEN THY 551
8. quod meum erit, id erit tuum.   PLAUT TRIN 714
9. Wretched is the fellow who loves!   PLAUT ASIN 616
10. By now I see that man whom I was awaiting.   CIC REPUB 2.69
11. The mind receives (the things) which we see.   CIC TD 5.111

CHAPTER 28: LATIN TO ENGLISH SENTENCES

1. pater esse disce ab aliīs quī vērē sciunt.   TER ADEL 125
2. dīves sum sī nōn reddō eīs quibus dēbeō.   PLAUT CURC 373
3. ferrum est quod amant.   JUV 6.112
4. quod hodiē nōn est, crās erit.   PETR 45.2
5. magna pars ex iīs quōs amāvimus apud nōs manet.   SEN E 99.4
6. hoc erit post mē quod ante mē fuit.   SEN E 54.4
7. male vīvunt quī semper vīvere incipiunt.   SEN E 23.9
8. haec quae nōn vīdistis oculīs, animīs cernere potestis.   QUINT 9.2.41
9. ab Caesare epistulam accēpī cuius exemplum tibi mīsī.   CIC ATT 9.7B.1
10. nam quod tuum est meum est, omne meum est autem tuum.   PLAUT TRIN 329
11. multōs timēre dēbet, quem multī timent.   PUBLSYR

CHAPTER 28: GLOSSED LATIN TO ENGLISH SENTENCES

1. dīcam quod dignum est et senātōre et Romānō homine.   senātor, tōris, m.: senator   CIC PHIL 7.14

2. venit ad nōs ex iīs quōs amāmus etiam absentibus gaudium.   etiam: (adverb) even   SEN E 35.3
   absens, absentis: absent

3. **Ovidius nēscit quod bene** cessit **relinquere.**

cedō, (3), cessī, — : (here) turn out   SENR C 9.5.17

CHAPTER 28: ENGLISH TO LATIN SENTENCES

1. You will hear that which I have heard.   PLAUT EPID 507
2. I fear many things which I do not dare to write.   CIC ATT 7.4.3
3. The things which I say are great.   CIC CAEC DIV 39
4. We respond to those whom we have not heard.   CIC BRUTUS 208
5. This, at any rate, is my father whom I see.   PLAUT MERC 366

CHAPTER 28: PASSAGES

TO A PLAGIARIZER

quem recitās **meus est, o Fidentine,** libellus,
   sed male cum recitās, **incipit esse tuus.**

MART 1.38

---

recitō (1): recite   libellus, i, m.: book

THE UNIVERSALITY OF THE STOIC GOD

quid est deus? mens universī. **quid est deus?**
quod vidēs totum et quod nōn vidēs totum.

SEN QN 1.PR.13

---

universum, ī, n.: universe

CAESAR'S SOLDIERS ROAST HIM IN HIS TRIUMPH

Galliās **Caesar** subēgit, **Nīcomēdes Caesarem.**
ecce **Caesar nunc** triumphat, **quī** subēgit Galliās.
Nīcomēdes nōn triumphat, **quī** subēgit **Caesarem.**

SUET DJ 49.4

Gallia, ae, f.: Gaul	subigō, 3, subēgī: subdue
ecce: look!	triumphō (1): have victory parade

HUMAN NATURE

tum denique **hominēs nostra** intellegimus **bona**
cum quae in potestāte habuimus ea amīsimus.

PLAUT CAPT 142-3

denique: finally	amittō, 3, amīsī: lose
intellegō, 3, intellexī: understand	

JUVENAL LAMENTS THE DECLINE OF ROMAN FORMAL ATTIRE

pars magna Ītaliae est, sī vērum admittimus, **in quā**
nēmo togam sūmit **nisi** mortuus.

JUV 3.171-2

admittō (3): admit	sūmō (3): put on
toga, ae, f.: toga	mortuus, a, um: dead

29

First and Second Conjugations, Present Passive System/ Ablative of Agent

So far, all your sentences have been in the active voice; now it is time to learn the passive voice. Most of us were taught to avoid the passive voice in our writing. The usual reason given is that the passive is less "direct" or less "assertive" than the active voice. This is generally a good rule, but nobody told the Romans about it. The passive voice is common in all forms of Latin, far more than in English. Thus, it will confront you on every page.

There are various ways to describe the difference grammatically. Consider the following sentences:

(1) **The Romans used the passive voice often.**
(2) **The passive voice was often used by the Romans.**

The first sentence is cast in the active voice, the second in the passive. In sentence 1, the subject ("Romans") acts through the verb ("used") onto a direct object ("passive voice"). In sentence 2, the subject ("passive voice") is acted upon by the verb ("was used"). There is no direct object, and in fact there can be no true direct object of a passive verb.

Another way to describe passive voice, at least in English, is to say that a passive verb is always made up of some form of the verb "to be" and the perfect passive participle. This is how your computer is programed to spot passive and issue its warning. However, it may be a little early to expect you to be as systematic as a computer, especially since you have not yet learned the perfect passive participle in Latin. In my experience, English speakers learn more about the passive voice from studying Latin than they did in their English classes. Perhaps this will be true for you.

The passive endings that follow will apply to **all** tenses of the present system—present, imperfect, and future—of **all** verbs!

-r	**-mur**
-ris	**-minī**
-tur	**-ntur**

And here are the present passive forms of first and second conjugations:

Present Passive: First conjugation

am-o-r	I am (being) loved
am-ā-ris	you are (being) loved
am-ā-tur	he/she/it is (being) loved
am-ā-mur	we are (being) loved
am-ā-minī	you are (being) loved
am-ā-ntur	they are (being) loved

Present Passive: Second conjugation

move-o-r	I am (being) moved
mov-ē-ris	you are (being) moved
mov-ē-tur	he/she/it is (being) moved
mov-ē-mur	we are (being) moved
mov-ē-minī	you are (being) moved
mov-ē-ntur	they are (being) moved

Here is the imperfect passive of the first conjugation:

Imperfect passive: First conjugation

am-ā-ba-r	I was (being) loved
am-ā-bā-ris	you were (being) loved
am-ā-bā-tur	he/she/it was (being) loved

Imperfect passive: First conjugation

am-ā-bā-mur	we were (being) loved
am-ā-bā-minī	you were (being) loved
am-ā-bā-ntur	they were (being) loved

Ditto for the second conjugation:

Imperfect Passive: Second Conjugation

mov-ē-bā-r	I was (being) moved
mov-ē-bā-ris	you were (being) moved
mov-ē-bā-tur	he/she/it was (being) moved

mov-ē-bā-mur	we were (being) moved
mov-ē-bā-minī	you were (being) moved
mov-ē-bā-ntur	they were (being) moved

And the future passive of the first conjugation:

Future Passive: First Conjugation

am-ā-bo-r	I will be loved
am-ā-be-ris	you will be loved
am-ā-bi-tur	he/she/it will be loved

am-ā-bi-mur	we will be loved
am-ā-bi-minī	you will be loved
am-ā-bu-ntur	they will be loved

Ditto for the second conjugation:

Future Passive: Second Conjugation

mov-ē-bo-r	I will be moved
mov-ē-be-ris	you will be moved
mov-ē-bi-tur	he/she/it will be moved
mov-ē-bi-mur	we will be moved
mov-ē-bi-minī	you will be moved
mov-ē-bu-ntur	they will be moved

There is also a present passive infinitive; it is formed by changing the **-e** of the active infinitive to an **-ī** as follows:

amāre	to love	versus	**amārī**	to be loved
movēre	to move	versus	**movērī**	to be moved

Here are some straightforward Latin sentences written in the passive voice with very literal translations. I urge you to be very literal in translating the passive until you become used to it:

mūtārī enim fāta nōn possunt.	For the fates are not able to be changed.	CIC DE DIVIN 2.21
pecūnia dēbēbātur.	Money was (being) owed.	CIC PRO QUINCT 60
iubēmur pugnāre.	We are (being) ordered to fight.	QUINT DECL 271
nōn torquēberis.	You will not be tortured.	SEN E 119.2
corporī omne tempus datur.	All time is (being) given to the body.	CIC FAM 9.20.3
neuter timet, neuter timētur.	Neither one fears, neither one is (being) feared.	PLINY E 9.33.6

ABLATIVE OF AGENT

In order to show who is performing the action of a passive verb, the ablative with the preposition **ab** is used. The formal title is "ablative of personal agent with the passive voice" or "ablative of agent" for short. See the following examples:

ab aliīs laudābimur.	We will be praised by others.	QUINT 11.1.22
amāmur ā fratre et ā fīliā.	We are loved by (our) brother and by (our) daughter.	CIC ATT 4.2.7
quī ā multīs timētur, multōs timet.	(He) who is feared by many (people), fears many (people).	PUBLSYR

If the agent is not a person, the ablative of means is used, as you learned in chapter 27:

nōn movētur pecūniā.	He is not moved by money.	CIC VER 4.18
vōce Metellī servantur lēgēs.	The laws are preserved by the voice of Metellus.	LUCAN 3.139-40
dēlectābātur laudibus suīs Claudius.	Claudius was delighted by his (own) praises.	SEN APOCO 13.1

CHAPTER 29: VOCABULARY

habeō, habēre, habuī, habitus	*consider*
intellegō, intellegere, intellexī, intellectus	*understand*
parō, parāre, parāvī, parātus	*prepare, provide*
torqueō, torquēre, torsī, tortus	*torture*
vetō, vetāre, vetuī, vetitus	*forbid*
videor, vidērī, visus sum	*seem*
ā/ab	*(with passive forms) by*
cīvitas, cīvitātis, f.	*state*
memoria, ae, f.	*memory*

VOCABULARY NOTE The verb **videō** in the passive often acquires the meaning "seem." Thus, the form **vidētur,** which theoretically could mean "he/she/it is seen," more often means "he/she/it seems." As in English, there is usually a dative and an infinitive. Here are some examples:

ego tibi videor stultus.	I seem stupid to you.	PLAUT TRUC 922
timōris esse signum vidēbitur.	It will seem to be a sign of fear.	CIC PHIL 5.26
vidētur semper sapiens beātus.	The wise man always seems supremely happy.	CIC TD 5.31
possunt quia posse videntur.	They are able because they seem to be able.	VERG A 5.231

VOCABULARY NOTE   The verb **habeō** often bears the meaning "consider." It is similar to the English "hold," as in "We hold these truths to be self-evident." Note that when **habeō** "consider" appears in the passive, it acts like **sum** and takes no direct object. Here are some examples:

Cato clārus atque magnus habētur.	Cato is considered famous and also great.	SALL C 53.1
natūra animī mortālis habētur.	The nature of the soul is considered mortal.	LUCR 3.831

CHAPTER 29: PRACTICE SENTENCES (ANSWERS FOLLOW CHAPTER 66)

1.	**ego nam videor mihi sānus.**	HOR S 2.3.302
2.	**mens in factīs spectātur.**	QUINT DECL 369
3.	**dēlectāmur cum scrībimus.**	CIC DE FIN 1.3
4.	**sine causā ā tē accūsor.**	CIC ATT 1.5.3
5.	**nihil tibi dēbēbitur prō hōc?**	SEN BEN 6.18.2
6.	**quod semper movētur, aeternum est.**	CIC TD 1.53
7.	**eī virō autem mors parabātur.**	CIC PRO MIL 19
8.	**quī hoc dīcunt videntur mihi errāre.**	SEN E 57.7
9.	All things are owed to you (plural).	OV M 10.32
10.	No one can be held in life.	SEN E 12.10
11.	(He) who is feared fears.	SEN E 105.4
12.	Your letter was being awaited.	CIC FAM 1.8.7
13.	All things are (being) changed.	OV M 15.165
14.	You will be saved by our gift.	OV M 7.93

CHAPTER 29: LATIN TO ENGLISH SENTENCES

1. **bellum summā vī parabātur.** — LIVY 3.4.2
2. **nōn potes tūtus esse in eā cīvitāte in quā timēris.** — QUINT DECL 288
3. **rogor enim ab eius uxōre et fīliō.** — CIC ATT 10.10.4
4. **vōs dormītis nec haec adhuc mihi vidēminī intellegere.** — CIC FAM 8.17.2
5. **virtūs clāra aeternaque habētur.** — SALL C 1.4
6. **stultī autem malōrum memoriā torquentur.** — CIC DE FIN 1.57
7. **at quam pulchrē dīcere vidēbāris.** — CIC DE FIN 2.63
8. **dēbēmur mortī nōs nostraque.** — HOR AP 63
9. **numquam igitur dignē satis laudārī philosophia poterit.** — CIC DE SENEC 2
10. **et quid erat quod mē dēlectābat nisi amāre et amārī?** — AUG CONF 2.1.2

CHAPTER 29: GLOSSED LATIN TO ENGLISH SENTENCES

1. **sed dēbēbātur fātīs** tantae orīgo **urbis.** — tantus, a, um: so great; orīgo, orīginis, f.: origin — LIVY 1.4.1
2. **laudātur ab hīs,** culpātur **ab illīs.** — culpō (1): blame — HOR S 1.2.11
3. **nōn potest amor cum timōre** miscērī. — misceō (2): mix — SEN E 47.18
4. fortūnātus **sibi Dāmoclēs vidēbātur.** — fortūnātus, a, um: fortunate — CIC TD 5.62

CHAPTER 29: ENGLISH TO LATIN SENTENCES

1. I am delighted by his character and studies. — CIC PRO LIG 8
2. They are neither invited nor do they invite. — PLAUT MEN 458
3. Often what is given is tiny. — SEN E 81.14
4. Bad is the plan which cannot be changed. — PUBLSYR M54
5. Nothing of these (things) can be forbidden. — SEN E 11.6
6. The law, he says, forbids a free person to be tortured. — [QUINT] DECL 7.4

CHAPTER 29: PASSAGES

CICERO'S MEDITATION ON ETERNITY

longum illud tempus cum nōn erō magis **mē movet
quam hoc exiguum, quod mihi tamen** nimium **longum vidētur.**

CIC ATT 12.18.1

---

magis: more   nimium: too

THE RICH GET RICHER

semper pauper **eris, sī** pauper **es, Aemiliāne.
dantur** opēs **nullīs nunc nisi dīvitibus.**

MART 5.81

---

pauper, is: poor   opes, um, f. pl.: riches

NO NEED TO WORRY ABOUT THIS RIVAL POET

versiculōs **in mē narrātur scrībere Cinna.
nōn scrībit, cuius carmina nēmo** legit.

MART 3.9

---

versiculus, i, m.: paltry verse   legō, 3, lēgi: read

---

30 Nouns of the Fourth Declension/Ablative of Separation

The fourth declension is another quite regular declension. The nouns are overwhelmingly feminine and masculine, with a few neuters that can be learned later. Fourth declension nouns look somewhat like second declension nouns, with an admixture of the third declension:

Case	Singular		Plural	
nominative	**man-us**	hand	**man-ūs**	hands
genitive	**man-ūs**	of hand	**man-uum**	of hands
dative	**man-uī**	to/for hand	**man-ibus**	to/for hands
accusative	**man-um**	hand	**man-ūs**	hands
ablative	**man-us**	by/with/from hand	**man-ibus**	by/with/from hands
vocative	**man-us**	hand	**man-ūs**	hands

For completeness, I give a table for neuter nouns of the fourth declension; however, no such words will be used in this book:

Case	Singular		Plural	
nominative	**gen-ū**	knee	**gen-ua**	knees
genitive	**gen-ūs**	of knee	**gen-uum**	of knees
dative	**gen-ū**	to/for knee	**gen-ibus**	to/for knees
accusative	**gen-ū**	knee	**gen-ua**	knees
ablative	**gen-ū**	by/with/from knee	**gen-ibus**	by/with/from knees
vocative	**gen-ū**	knee	**gen-ua**	knees

Here are some sample sentences using the fourth declension:

alius exercitum regit.	Another (man) rules an army.	PLINY E 4.24.3
senātum etiam rēgēs habēbant.	Even the kings had a senate.	CIC PHIL 3.9
meās spectant manūs.	They are looking at my hands.	SENR C 1.8.6

ABLATIVE OF SEPARATION

The ablative can also be used by itself to show separation; it is called, appropriately, the "ablative of separation" and can usually be translated with "from." This type of ablative is often found with verbs or adjectives, which imply "separation from" or "freedom from," as in the following examples:

tū labōre līberās tē.	You free yourself from labor.	PLAUT ASIN 659
omnī aliā servitūte līber est.	He is free from all other slavery.	SENR C 7.4.4

CHAPTER 30: VOCABULARY

domus, domūs, f.	*house*
exercitus, exercitūs, m.	*army*
manus, manūs, f.	*hand; handwriting*
metus, metūs, m.	*fear*
senātus, senātūs, m.	*senate*
existimō, existimāre, existimāvī, existimātus	*think*
liberō, liberāre, liberāvī, liberātus	*free*
consul, consulis, m.	*consul*
equidem	*in fact*
iniuria, ae, f.	*injury*
poena, ae, f.	*punishment*

CHAPTER 30: PRACTICE SENTENCES (ANSWERS FOLLOW CHAPTER 66)

1.	**līberā patriam metū.**	SEN PHOEN 642-3
2.	**in senātum nōn vocābāmur.**	CIC PHIL 5.1

3. **nōs tē tuumque exercitum exspectāmus.** CIC AD BRUT 1.9.3
4. The senate is (being) called. CIC ATT 1.14.5
5. Move (your) hands; hurry! PLAUT PERS 772
6. He was fearing the anger of the senate. SALL BJ 25.7

CHAPTER 30: LATIN TO ENGLISH SENTENCES

1. **senātus lībertātem iīs cīvitātibus dedit.** LIVY 33.34.10
2. **manibus meīs iniūriam Fortūna fēcerat.** QUINT DECL 256
3. **senātūs auctoritātem numquam impedīvit.** CIC PRO SULLA 65
4. **semper equidem magnō cum metū incipiō dīcere.** CIC CLUENT 51
5. **mundum deōrum domum existimāre dēbēmus.** CIC ND 3.26
6. **gratiās agimus et ducibus vestris et exercitibus.** LIVY 6.26.5
7. **senātus haec intellegit, consul videt, hic tamen vīvit.** CIC IN CAT 1.2
8. **quid enim immortāle manūs mortālēs fēcērunt?** SEN AD POLY 1.1
9. **multōs Fortūna līberat poenā, metū nēminem.** SEN E 97.16
10. **tacē, Lucretia, inquit, Sextus Tarquinius sum; ferrum in manū est.** LIVY 1.58.2

CHAPTER 30: GLOSSED LATIN TO ENGLISH SENTENCES

1. **senātus autem**, mi **Brute, fortis est et habet fortēs ducēs.** mi: vocative of **meus** CIC FAM 11.18.1

2. **exercitūs populī Rōmānī** sub iugum **mīserant.** sub: (prep. + acc.) under
iugum, ī, n.: yoke VEG 1.15

CHAPTER 30: ENGLISH TO LATIN SENTENCES

1. Is not all fear slavery? CIC PARADOX 41
2. If you and the army are well, it is well. CIC FAM 5.2.1
3. I say nothing about the fate of our house. QUINT DECL 288
4. This part of Italy is without an army. CIC FAM 11.10.4
5. We can be freed from the fear of death. CIC TD 1.23

31

Third and Fourth Conjugations, Present Passive System

The passive forms of the third, fourth, and third-io conjugations are analogous to those of the first and second. The passive endings are identical. The only difficulties will be (1) knowing what the connecting vowel is in each form, and (2) remembering that the future tense is formed in the special way you learned in chapters 15, 19, and 20.

Tables for each conjugation follow:

Third Conjugation

cōg-o-r	I am (being) forced	**cōg-i-mur**	we are (being) forced
cōg-ĕ-ris	you are (being) forced	**cōg-i-minī**	you are (being) forced
cōg-i-tur	he/she/it is (being) forced	**cōg-u-ntur**	they are (being) forced

cōg-ē-ba-r	I was (being) forced	**cōg-ē-bā-mur**	we were (being) forced
cōg-ē-bā-ris	you were (being) forced	**cōg-ē-bā-minī**	you were (being) forced
cōg-ē-bā-tur	he/she/it was (being) forced	**cōg-ē-ba-ntur**	they were (being) forced

cōg-a-r	I will be forced	**cōg-ē-mur**	we will be forced
cōg-ē-ris	you will be forced	**cōg-ē-minī**	you will be forced
cōg-ē-tur	they will be forced	**cōg-e-ntur**	they will be forced

Fourth Conjugation

aud-io-r	I am (being) heard	**aud-ī-mur**	we are (being) heard
aud-ī-ris	you are (being) heard	**aud-ī-minī**	you are (being) heard
aud-ī-tur	he/she/it is (being) heard	**aud-iu-ntur**	they are (being) heard
aud-iē-ba-r	I was (being) heard	**aud-iē-bā-mur**	we were (being) heard
aud-iē-bā-ris	you were (being) heard	**aud-iē-bā-minī**	you were (being) heard
aud-iē-bā-tur	he/she/it was (being) heard	**aud-iē-ba-ntur**	they were (being) heard
aud-ia-r	I will be heard	**aud-iē-mur**	we will be heard
aud-iē-ris	you will be heard	**aud-iē-minī**	you will be heard
aud-iē-tur	he/she/it will be heard	**aud-ie-ntur**	they will be heard

Third-io Conjugation

cap-io-r	I am (being) taken	**cap-i-mur**	we are (being) taken
cap-ĕ-ris	you are (being) taken	**cap-i-minī**	you are (being) taken
cap-i-tur	he/she/it is (being) taken	**cap-iu-ntur**	they are (being) taken
cap-iē-ba-r	I was (being) taken	**cap-iē-bā-mur**	we were (being) taken
cap-iē-bā-ris	you were (being) taken	**cap-iē-bā-minī**	you were (being) taken
cap-iē-bā-tur	he/she/it was (being) taken	**cap-iē-ba-ntur**	they were (being) taken
cap-ia-r	I will be taken	**cap-iē-mur**	we will be taken
cap-iē-ris	you will be taken	**cap-iē-minī**	you will be taken
cap-iē-tur	he/she/it will be taken	**cap-ie-ntur**	they will be taken

You would expect these conjugations to form the passive infinitive analogously to the first and second conjugations, as shown in chapter 29. And indeed, the fourth conjugation does exactly that:

audīre	to hear	versus	**audīrī**	to be heard

However, the third and third-io conjugations do something unexpected. Instead of changing the **-e** to **-i**, as the other conjugations do, the entire active infinitive ending is replaced with an **-ī**:

cōgere	to force	versus	**cōgī**	to be forced
capere	to take	versus	**capī**	to be taken

This anomaly will be a constant thorn in your side when you read Latin. You will look at **capī** ("to be taken") and see the present imperative **cape** ("take!"), that is, unless you mistake both forms for **cēpī**, the perfect active ("I took"). The third conjugation is filled with forms that cause problems for beginning students. Consider these examples:

bellum gerī nōn potest.	War is not able to be waged.	CIC PHIL 5.45
āmittī nōn potest virtūs.	Virtue is not able to be lost.	CIC TD 2.32
tū illum corrumpī sinis.	You allow him to be corrupted.	TER ADEL 97

And then, there is the crowning indignity—with a few verbs, like **occīdō** and **ostendō**, the present passive infinitive is <u>identical</u> to the third principal part. Enjoy!

occīdī nōn potest pater.	A father is not able to be killed.	[QUINT] DECL 4.19

CHAPTER 31: VOCABULARY

āmittō, āmittere, āmīsī, āmissus	*lose*
cognoscō, cognoscere, cognōvī, cognitus	*get to know, recognize*
cōgō, cōgere, coēgī, coactus	*force; gather*
contemnō, contemnere, contempsī, contemptus	*scorn*
petō, petere, petī(v)ī, petītus	*seek; beg*
tangō, tangere, tetigī, tactus	*touch*
trahō, trahere, traxī, tractus	*drag, draw (out)*
certus, a, um	*certain, sure*
dubius, a, um	*doubtful*
laus, laudis, f.	*praise*
opera, ae, f.	*effort, help*
vel ... vel	*either ... or*
vox, vōcis, f.	*voice; remark*

CHAPTER 31: PRACTICE SENTENCES (ANSWERS FOLLOW CHAPTER 66)

1. **bellī causa quaeritur.**   LIVY 35.16.6
2. **dīcuntur sententiae gravēs.**   CAES BC 1.2.8
3. **dē Caesare quid audītur?**   CIC ATT 13.16.2
4. **nullō corrumperis aurō.**   OV F 2.661
5. **liber tibi mittētur.**   CIC ATT 1.13.5
6. **contemne contemnī.**   PUBLSYR
7. **nisi properāmus, relinquēmur.**   SEN E 108.24
8. **contemnar ā tē.**   CIC REPUB 1.31
9. **corrumpī nōn potuērunt.**   NEPOS 6.3.3
10. We are (being) driven by the fates.   SEN OED 980
11. They will be defeated by virtue.   CIC PRO SULLA 24
12. Can the truth be found?   CIC PRO MIL 59
13. They are not (being) dragged by Fortune.   SEN PROV 5.4
14. Messius was (being) defended by us.   CIC ATT 4.15.9
15. Danger is never conquered without danger.   PUBLSYR N7

CHAPTER 31: LATIN TO ENGLISH SENTENCES

1. **certa exspectantur, dubia metuuntur.**   SEN E 30.10
2. **capī Rōma nōn potuerat.**   LIVY 5.33.1
3. **trahimur omnēs studiō laudis.**   CIC PRO ARCH 26
4. **operam dā, opera reddētur tibi.**   PLAUT EPID 24
5. **nec vōce nec arte vincēmur.**   OV M 5.310-1
6. **sapiens autem ā nullō contemnitur.**   SEN CONS SAP 10.3
7. **audācēs cōgimur esse metū.**   OV TRIST 1.4.4
8. **sī āmittī vīta beāta potest, beāta esse nōn potest.**   CIC DE FIN 2.86
9. **carmina laudantur sed mūnera magna petuntur.**   OV AA 2.275
10. **numquam nimis dīcitur quod numquam satis discitur.**   SEN E 27.9
11. **nunc prīmum longās sōlus cognoscere noctēs cōgor.**   PROP 1.12.13-4
12. **nam virtus in animī bonīs et in corporis cernitur.**   CIC ACADPOS 21

CHAPTER 31: GLOSSED LATIN TO ENGLISH SENTENCES

1. iterum **ad Troiam magnus mittētur Achilles**.

   iterum: again

   VERG E 4.36

2. **vinceris aut vincis — haec in amōre** rota **est**.

   rota, ae, f.: wheel

   PROP 2.8.8

3. **sine** magistrō **vitia discuntur**.

   magister, trī, m.: teacher

   SEN QN 3.30.8

4. **regitur** providentiā **mundus**.

   providentia, ae, f.: providence

   QUINT 12.2.21

CHAPTER 31: ENGLISH TO LATIN SENTENCES

1. By now you will not be able to be scorned.

   CIC DE FIN 2.84

2. Now I am being dragged to wars.

   TIB 1.10.13

3. Either I will conquer you or I will be conquered by you.

   CIC FAM 7.31.1

4. A favor cannot be touched by the hand.

   SEN BEN 1.5.2

CHAPTER 31: PASSAGES

THE DIVINITY OF FORTUNE

totō quippe **mundō et omnibus locīs omnibusque** hōrīs **omnium vōcibus Fortūna sōla** invocātur **ac** nōminātur, **ūna accusātur**, rea **ūna agitur, ūna cōgitātur, sōla laudātur, sōla** arguitur **et cum** conviciīs colitur.

PLINY NH 2.22

quippe: for	hōra, ae, f.: hour
invocō (1): call upon	nōminō (1): name
ream agō: indict	arguō (3): charge
convicium, iī, n.: abuse	colō (3): worship

NO TEETOTALER POETS

nulla placēre diū **nec vīvere carmina possunt**
quae scrībuntur aquae pōtōribus.

HOR E 1.19.2-3

---

placeō (2): please   diū: for a long time
aqua, ae, f.: water   pōtor, ōris, m.: drinker

A SHAMELESS EXHIBITIONIST

nōn est, Tucca, satis quod **es** gulōsus;
et dīcī cupis et cupis vidērī.

MART 12.41

---

quod: (the fact) that   gulōsus, a, um: gluttonous

CHAPTER 32

Nouns of the Fifth Declension/Ablative of Time When/Accusative of Extent of Time

Once again, the traditional numbering of declensions may give a misleading impression. This family of nouns is in no sense "later than" or "harder than" the other declensions. It could be just as well called the **-ē-** declension since the stem of its nouns ends in -ē. It has perhaps the fewest nouns of the five declensions, but some of them are among the most used words in the language. The word **rēs** "thing" is indeed the most common noun in Latin, with a multiplicity of meanings and idiomatic uses.

Practically every noun in the fifth declension is feminine. A notable exception is the word **diēs**, which can be either masculine or feminine, with no apparent difference in meaning.

Case	Singular		Plural	
nominative	**di-ēs**	day	**di-ēs**	days
genitive	**di-ēī**	of day	**di-ērum**	of days
dative	**di-ēī**	to/for day	**di-ēbus**	to/for days
accusative	**di-em**	day	**di-ēs**	days
ablative	**di-ē**	by/with/from day	**di-ēbus**	by/with/from days
vocative	**di-ēs**	day	**di-ēs**	days

For completeness, here is the declension of **res**:

Case	Singular		Plural	
nominative	**rēs**	thing	**rēs**	things
genitive	**rēī**	of thing	**rērum**	of things
dative	**rēī**	to/for thing	**rēbus**	to/for things
accusative	**rem**	thing	**rēs**	things
ablative	**rē**	by/with/from thing	**rēbus**	by/with/from things
vocative	**rēs**	thing	**rēs**	things

Here are some sample sentences involving the fifth declension:

magna mē spēs tenet.	Great hope holds me.	CIC CLUENT 7
vīcerat noctem diēs.	Day had conquered night.	SEN TROAD 171
causās rērum videt.	He sees the causes of things.	CIC DE OFF 1.11
suscēpī causam reī publicae.	I have undertaken the cause of the republic.	CIC VER 2.1

ABLATIVE OF TIME WHEN

Another common use of the ablative is the "ablative of time when." A noun, usually a word relating to time like **diēs** "day," or **tempus** "time," or **hōra** "hour," or **annus** "year," appears in the ablative to show the point at which something happened. (This ablative is still with us: **annō Dominī** "in the year of the Lord.") Here are some more examples:

eō tempore mēcum esse nōn potuistī.	At that time you were not able to be with me.	CIC FAM 16.12.6
hōc annō Publius Lentulus consul populī Rōmānī fuit.	In this year Publius Lentulus was consul of the Roman people.	CIC RED SEN 9

ACCUSATIVE OF EXTENT OF TIME

Another way of expressing time uses the accusative; it is called "accusative of extent of time" because it describes the length of time something takes. Here are some examples:

diēs noctēsque bibite.	Drink (for) days and nights.	PLAUT MOST 22
tot annōs bella gerō.	For so many years I wage wars.	VERG A 1.47-48
caecus annōs multōs fuit.	He was blind for many years.	CIC TD 5.112
fuī enim apud illum multās horās.	For I was with him for many hours.	CIC ATT 16.2.3

CHAPTER 32: VOCABULARY

diēs, diēī, m. or f.	*day; time*
rēs, reī, f.	*thing; affair; net worth*
rēs publica, reī publicae, f.	*republic*
spēs, speī, f.	*hope*

perdō, perdere, perdidī, perditus	*ruin, waste; lose*
vītō, vītāre, vītāvī, vītātus	*avoid*
difficilis, difficile	*difficult*
hōra, ae, f.	*hour*
incertus, a, um	*uncertain*
iudex, iudicis, m.	*juror*

CHAPTER 32: PRACTICE SENTENCES (ANSWERS FOLLOW CHAPTER 66)

1. **aliās rēs agunt.**   PLAUT PSEUD 152
2. **spem autem pācis habeō nullam.**   CIC ATT 9.13A
3. **moveor hīs rēbus omnibus.**   CIC IN CAT 4.3
4. **eī rēī operam dabo.**   PLAUT PSEUD 1115
5. **rēī publicae fēcistī iniuriam.**   CIC VER 3.161
6. All hope is in you (plural).   CIC FAM 12.1.1
7. Do you not see the time of day?   PLAUT TRIN 811
8. Do you seek the cause of this thing?   SEN E 49.3
9. On this day there was not a senate.   CIC FAM 12.25.1
10. Many things are (being) done.   PLINY E 9.39.2

CHAPTER 32: LATIN TO ENGLISH SENTENCES

1. **spē trahor exiguā.**   OV TRIST 3.5.25
2. **nōn fuī, iūdicēs, dubius eō tempore.**   QUINT DECL 267
3. **amīcus certus in rē incertā cernitur.**   CIC DE AMIC 64
4. **equidem diēs noctēsque torqueor.**   CIC ATT 7.9.4
5. **sapiens nullum prō rē publicā perīculum vītābit.**   AUCHER 4.57
6. **spem reliquam nullam videō salūtis.**   CIC FAM 11.5.2
7. **fēlix [est] quī potuit rērum cognoscere causās.**   VERG G 2.490
8. **erat enim ars difficilis rectē rem publicam regere.**   CIC ATT 7.25
9. **omnis diēs, omnis hōra tē mūtat.**   SEN E 104.12
10. **sunt lacrimae rērum et mentem mortālia tangunt.**   VERG A 1.462

CHAPTER 32: GLOSSED LATIN TO ENGLISH SENTENCES

1. **nōn sentiunt virī fortēs in** aciē **vulnera.**

   aciēs, aciēī, f.: battle line

   CIC TD 2.58

2. **vērum gaudium rēs** sevēra **est.**

   sevērus, a, um: severe

   SEN E 23.4

3. crēdula **rēs amor est.**

   crēdulus, a, um: overly trusting

   OV M 7.826

4. **dēfendī rem publi- cam** adulescens, **nōn** dēseram senex.

   adulescens, centis, m.: young man

   dēserō (3): desert

   senex, senis, m.: old man

   CIC PHIL 2.118

CHAPTER 32: ENGLISH TO LATIN SENTENCES

1. Friends, I have wasted the day.

   SUET TIT. 8.1

2. For he said few good things.

   SENR C 7.PR.9

3. You are not able to be with yourself for an hour.

   HOR S 2.7.112

4. They had taken arms on behalf of the republic.

   CIC PHIL 11.20

5. For there is tiny hope for the republic.

   CIC FAM 12.9.2

6. For hope is the name of an uncertain good.

   SEN E 10.2

CHAPTER 32: PASSAGES

LAWYER JOKES IN ROME

cōgit mē Titus actitāre **causās et dīcit mihi saepe "magna rēs est." rēs magna est, Tite, quam facit** colōnus.

MART 1.17

actitō (1): conduct   colōnus, ī, m.: farmer

THE ONCE MIGHTY ROMAN PEOPLE

nam [populus] quī dabat ōlim
imperium, fasces, legiōnēs, omnia, nunc sē
continet atque duās tantum rēs anxius optat –
pānem et circensēs.

JUV 10.78-81

ōlim: once	fascis, is, m: general's baton
legiō, iōnis, f.: legion	contineō (2): restrain
anxius, a, um; anxious	tantum: (adverb) only
pānis, is, m.: bread	circensēs, ium, m. pl.: games in the Circus Maximus

33 ipse

The adjective **ipse** is called the "intensifier" because it makes a noun more emphatic. The English equivalents are "himself," "herself," "itself," and "themselves." The majority of its forms show the regular endings of the first and second declensions. The anomalous forms are in the same places as the anomalies of **hic**, **ille** and **is**, namely the genitive and dative singular. The potentially difficult forms are underlined:

Case	Singular			Plural		
	masc	*fem*	*neut*	*masc*	*fem*	*neut*
nominative	**ipse**	ipsa	ipsum	ipsī	ipsae	ipsa
genitive	**ipsīus**	**ipsīus**	**ipsīus**	ipsōrum	ipsārum	ipsōrum
dative	**ipsī**	**ipsī**	**ipsī**	ipsīs	ipsīs	ipsīs
accusative	ipsum	ipsam	ipsum	ipsōs	ipsās	ipsa
ablative	ipsō	ipsā	ipsō	ipsīs	ipsīs	ipsīs

This word can cause confusion because in English both the intensifier and the reflexive forms are "himself," "herself," "itself," and "themselves"—identical! However, in Latin, the two are quite different: (1) **ipse** is an adjective which, like all adjectives, can either modify a noun or stand alone as a substantive; (2) the reflexive is a pronoun which will always "reflect" the subject of a clause (see chapter 22).

Here are some examples of **ipse**:

hoc ipse quoque faciō.	I myself do this too.	SEN E 2.5
tē ipsum quaerō.	I am looking for you yourself.	TER ADEL 266
habēmus hominem ipsum.	We have the fellow himself.	TER EUN 835
nōn est enim in rēbus vitium sed in ipsō animō.		SEN E 17.12
	For the fault is not in things but in the mind itself.	

Sometimes, the force of **ipse** is best caught by the English word "very":

saepe faciēbat hoc ipsum.	He often used to do this very thing.	QUINT DECL 295
sed mē id ipsum dēlectāvit in tuīs litterīs.	But this very thing delighted me in your letter.	CIC ATT 6.1.17

You will occasionally find both the intensifier **ipse** and a reflexive pronoun used together in the same sentence. For now, translate each as a separate entity, even though the result sounds bizarre in English:

scrībam ipse dē mē.	I myself will write about myself.	CIC FAM 5.12.8
tē ipse vicistī.	You yourself have conquered yourself.	CIC FAM 12.13.1
rēs enim sē ipsa dēfendit.	For the thing itself defends itself.	CIC CLUENT 167

CHAPTER 33: VOCABULARY

ipse, ipsa, ipsum	–self, –selves; "very"
legō, legere, lēgī, lectus	read
Athēnae, Athēnārum, f. pl.	Athens

CHAPTER 33: PRACTICE SENTENCES (ANSWERS FOLLOW CHAPTER 66)

1. **sēcum ipse pugnat.** — CIC TD 3.47
2. **ipsa sē contemnit.** — PLAUT MG 1236
3. **nōn populum metuis, sed ipsōs deōs.** — CIC ND 1.85
4. The girl herself is good. — TIB 2.6.44
5. We will defend the case itself. — QUINT DECL 326
6. Pleasures themselves are feared. — SEN CLEM 1.26.2

CHAPTER 33: LATIN TO ENGLISH SENTENCES

1. **in eā quidem ipse sententiā sum.** — SEN VIT BEAT 13.1
2. **A. tē ipsum quaerēbam. B. et ego tē.** — TER AND 533
3. **equidem valdē ipsās Athēnās amō.** — CIC ATT 6.1.26
4. **itaque suōs librōs ipsī legunt cum suīs.** — CIC TD 1.6
5. **ipsum diem memoriā teneō.** — CIC FAM 7.3.1
6. **ingenium nōbīs ipsa puella facit.** — PROP 2.1.4

7. **voluptās summa in tē ipsō est.**   HOR S 2.2.19-20
8. **nōbīs ipsī molestī sumus.**   SEN QN 4A.PR.2
9. **ipse tē spectā, ipse tē laudā.**   SEN E 78.21
10. **factō torqueor ipse meō.**   OV PONT 1.1.60

CHAPTER 33: GLOSSED LATIN TO ENGLISH SENTENCES

1. avārus **ipse miseriae causa est suae.**   avārus, a, um: miserly   PUBLSYR A14

2. **senectūs ipsa est** morbus.   morbus, ī, m.: disease   TER PHOR 575

3. **sed quis** custōdiet **ipsōs** custōdēs?   custōdiō (4): guard   JUV 6.347-8
custōs, custōdis, m.: guard(ian)

CHAPTER 33: ENGLISH TO LATIN SENTENCES

1. Venus herself helps the brave.   TIB 1.2.16
2. Virtue itself will speak on behalf of me.   CIC DE FIN 2.65
3. I myself gave myself into slavery.   PETR 57.4
4. And so I will send you the very books.   SEN E 6.5
5. The thing itself is small, but the pain of my mind is great.   CIC FAM 13.77.3

CHAPTER 33: PASSAGES

ROME ENDURES ANOTHER CIVIL WAR

altera **iam** teritur **bellīs** cīvilibus aetās,
suīs et ipsa Rōma vīribus ruit.

HOR EPO 16.1-2

---

alter, a, um: a second   terō (3): grind
cīvilis, e: civil   aetās, aetātis, f.: age
ruō (3): collapse

NARCISSUS ADMIRES HIMSELF IN THE MIRROR POOL

sē cupit imprūdens **et quī probat, ipse probātur,**
dumque petit, petitur, pariterque accendit **et** ardet.

OV M 3.425-6

---

imprūdens, ntis: heedless   accendō (3): set a fire
ardeō (2): burn

ROLE REVERSAL IN A ROMAN MARRIAGE

custōdēs **das, Polla, virō, nōn accipis ipsa.**
    hoc est uxōrem dūcere, Polla, virum.

MART 10.69

---

custōs, custōdis, m.: guard

34

Participles: Perfect Passive

A participle is a verb-adjective; that is, it has the properties of both a verb and an adjective combined. In fact, the name "participle" was chosen because the form "participates" in the properties of both verb and adjective. This gives it a power that surpasses other grammatical forms. It also renders the participle a difficult concept to absorb, even though the English participle has the same properties.

There are four participles in Latin; in this chapter we will deal with one: the perfect passive participle. (Practice uttering this name aloud and do not be reluctant to use the big words you learn in Latin. They will set you apart.) As usual, the name gives a clue to its nature—it is perfect and it is passive. Later you will encounter participles that are present and future and active. This participle is in fact perfect—that is, it refers to past time—and passive. It is also the last of the four principal parts a standard Latin verb possesses (exceptions later). Like all the Latin participles, this one has "verb-ness" and "adjective-ness" wrapped into its nature. In other words, it has (a) tense and voice like a verb and (b) case, number, and gender like an adjective. This combination is what gives participles superpowers.

You will be glad to hear that this participle is declined like **bonus, -a, -um**:

Case	Singular			Plural		
	masc	*fem*	*neut*	*masc*	*fem*	*neut*
nominative	amāt-us	amāt-a	amāt-um	amāt-ī	amāt-ae	amāt-a
genitive	amāt-ī	amāt-ae	amāt-ī	amāt-ōrum	amāt-ārum	amāt-ōrum
dative	amāt-ō	amāt-ae	amāt-ō	amāt-īs	amāt-īs	amāt-īs
accusative	amāt-um	amāt-am	amāt-um	amāt-ōs	amāt-ās	amāt-a
ablative	amāt-ō	amāt-ā	amāt-ō	amāt-īs	amāt-īs	amāt-īs
vocative	amāt-e	amāt-a	amāt-um	amāt-ī	amāt-ae	amāt-a

Until you become more familiar with the perfect passive participle, translate it with the phrase "having been …" Thus **amātus** will mean "having been loved," **vīsus** will mean "having been seen," and **dictus** will mean "having been said." (For the more adventurous, try dropping the "having been" and see what happens. However, be warned: This may not work in every case.)

Here are some sample sentences:

iacet post āmissum Scaurus exercitum.	Scaurus lies behind the having-been-lost army.	[QUINT] DECL 3.13
coactus legibus eam uxōrem dūcet.	Having-been-forced by laws he will take her (as) wife.	TER AND 780-1
ō quam contempta rēs est homō!	O what a having-been-scorned thing is a human!	SEN QN 1.PR.5
cupīte atque exspectāte pater, salvē.	Having-been-desired and having-been-waited-for father, hello.	PLAUT POEN 1260-1

My translations are deliberately cumbersome; in every case, the "having been" could be omitted. However, for now I urge you to adopt this formula for translating the perfect passive participle. Later you can drop it.

CHAPTER 34: VOCABULARY

dēcipiō, dēcipere, dēcēpī, dēceptus	*deceive*
dūcō, dūcere, duxī, ductus	*bring, lead; marry; hire*
spērō, spērāre, spērāvī, spērātus	*hope (for)*
iuvenis, iuvenis, m.	*young man*
regnum, ī, n.	*(royal) rule; realm*
statim	*immediately*

CHAPTER 34: PRACTICE SENTENCES (ANSWERS FOLLOW CHAPTER 66)

1.	**vēnī exspectātus.**	CIC DOMO SUA 16
2.	**petīta relinquimus.**	SEN DE OTIO 1.2
3.	**dixit Marcellus ā mē rogātus.**	CIC Q FR 2.3.1
4.	**numquam pugnāvī nisi coactus.**	SENR C 1.8.6
5.	He sees the arms (having been) left.	OV M 12.144
6.	(Having been) defeated, I fled from (my) homeland.	OV TRIST 1.5.66

CHAPTER 34: LATIN TO ENGLISH SENTENCES

1. **quam multa nōn expectāta vēnērunt!**   SEN E 13.10
2. **contemptus amor vīrēs habet.**   PETR 108.14.5
3. **dūcentur captī iuvenēs captaeque puellae.**   OV A 1.2.27
4. **dēcepta dēcipit omnes.**   OV M 14.81
5. **homō doctus in sē semper dīvitiās habet.**   PHAEDR 4.22.1
6. A. **dī mē servātum cupiunt.** B. **at mē perditum.**   PLAUT RUD 1164
7. **spērāte Pamphilippe, ō spēs mea, ō mea vīta, ō mea   PLAUT STICH 583-4
    voluptās, salvē.**
8. **parātus igitur veniēbat Crassus, exspectabātur,   CIC BRUTUS 158
    audiēbātur.**
9. **nōn regnō sed rēge līberātī vidēmur.**   CIC FAM 12.1.1
10. **ad tē statim meā manū scriptās litterās mīsī.**   CIC FAM 3.6.2
11. **parātus miles arma nōn habuī.**   PETR 130.4

CHAPTER 34: GLOSSED LATIN TO ENGLISH SENTENCES

1. **Graecia capta** ferum victōrem   ferus, a, um: wild   HOR E 2.1.156
    cēpit.   victor, ōris, m.: victor

2. **suscipiō** inimīcitiās   inimīcitia, ae, f.: enmity CIC IN CAT 2.11
    hominum **perditōrum.**

3. **ad mea, dēceptī iuvenēs,**   praeceptum, ī, n.: teaching OV RA 41
    praecepta **venīte.**

CHAPTER 34: ENGLISH TO LATIN SENTENCES

1. Having been ordered by the emperor, I married a wife.   TAC ANN 2.37
2. Having been asked, I changed my plan.   CIC FAM 4.4.4
3. By now having been conquered, we have conquered.   PLAUT CAS 510
4. I gave the (having been) received money to mother.   QUINT DECL 330

CHAPTER 34: PASSAGES

UPSET VICTORY FOR CAESAR

an vērō **in Hispaniā rēs gestās Caesaris nōn audistis?** **duōs** pulsōs **exercitūs, duōs** superātōs **ducēs, duās** receptās prōvinciās?

CAES BC 2.32.5

---

an vērō: can it really be that	pellō, 3, pepulī, pulsus: beat
superō (1): defeat	recipiō, 3, recēpī, receptus: recapture
provincia, ae, f.: province	

OLD AGE CREEPS UP ON YOU

dum bibimus, **dum** serta, unguenta, **puellās** poscimus, obrēpit **nōn intellecta senectūs.**

JUV 9.128-9

---

bibō (3): drink	sertum, ī, n.: garland
unguentum, ī, n.: perfumed oil	poscō (3): call for
obrēpō (3): creep up	

---

35 Perfect Passive System of All Conjugations

In the previous chapter, you made the acquaintance of the perfect passive participle; now you are ready to learn the remaining three passive tenses—the perfect, pluperfect, and future perfect. Here Latin gives you another gift: All verbs, no matter what conjugation, employ the following formula:

(1) perfect passive participle + present tense of **sum** = perfect passive
(2) perfect passive participle + imperfect tense of **sum** = pluperfect passive
(3) perfect passive participle + future tense of **sum** = future perfect passive

A table makes this clearer:

Perfect Passive: Masculine Subject

amātus sum	I was loved	I have been loved
amātus es	you were loved	you have been loved
amātus est	he was loved	he has been loved
amātī sumus	we were loved	we have been loved
amātī estis	you were loved	you have been loved
amātī sunt	they were loved	they have been loved

There are few things to notice:

(1) As usual, the perfect tense is capable of two different translations, which only a context can establish.
(2) The ending of the participle changes with the change from singular to plural.
(3) The ending of the participle can denote gender as well.

Thus, for completeness, here is the same table with a feminine subject implied:

Perfect Passive: Feminine Subject

amāta sum	I was loved	I have been loved
amāta es	you were loved	you have been loved
amāta est	she was loved	she has been loved
amātae sumus	we were loved	we have been loved
amātae estis	you were loved	you have been loved
amātae sunt	they were loved	they have been loved

And with a neuter subject implied:

Perfect Passive: Neuter Subject

amātum sum	I was loved	I have been loved
amātum es	you were loved	you have been loved
amātum est	it was loved	it has been loved
amāta sumus	we were loved	we have been loved
amāta estis	you were loved	you have been loved
amāta sunt	they were loved	they have been loved

The pluperfect passive looks like this:

Pluperfect Passive

iussus,-a,-um eram	I had been ordered
iussus,-a,-um erās	you had been ordered
iussus,-a,-um erat	he/she/it had been ordered
iussī,-ae,-a erāmus	we had been ordered
iussī,-ae,-a erātis	you had been ordered
iussī,-ae,-a erant	they had been ordered

And the future perfect like this:

Future Perfect

victus,-a,-um erō	I will have been conquered
victus,-a,-um eris	you will have been conquered
victus,-a,-um erit	he/she/it will have been conquered
victī,-ae,-a erimus	we will have been conquered
victī,-ae,-a eritis	you will have been conquered
victī,-ae,-a erunt	they will have been conquered

As with the perfect active, there is also a perfect passive infinitive. It is formed from the perfect passive participle and **esse** (two words). You will not have to deal with it until we reach Chapter 41 on indirect statement.

Here are some sample sentences:

hoc scriptum est.	This was/has been written.	PLAUT BACC 739
dīvitiae parātae sunt.	Riches were/have been prepared.	SEN E 25.4
redditus mihi est animus.	(My) mind has been returned to me.	[QUINT] DECL 15.7
mōtus eram dictīs.	I had been moved by the remarks.	OV TRIST 4.10.23

CHAPTER 35: VOCABULARY

crēdō, crēdere, crēdidī, crēditus	*believe*
damnō, damnāre, damnāvī, damnātus	*condemn*
reperiō, reperīre, repperī, repertus	*discover*
antīquus, a, um	*ancient*
dīligens, dīligentis	*diligent*
ergō	*therefore*
etiam	*(adverb) also; even*
forum, ī, n.	*forum*
Graecia, ae, f.	*Greece*

CHAPTER 35: PRACTICE SENTENCES (ANSWERS FOLLOW CHAPTER 66)

1. **inventa vītae via est.**   CIC DE FIN 5.15
2. **male gesta rēs erat.**   LIVY 1.37.6
3. **numquam dicta erunt omnia.**   QUINT 2.13.17
4. **perditus sum miser.**   PLAUT CURC 133
5. **ingeniō est poena reperta meō.**   OV TRIST 2.12
6. **Terentia dēlectāta est tuīs litterīs.**   CIC ATT 2.12.4
7. He has been/was praised by all.   CIC OR BRUT 31
8. Now life has been given to me.   OV TRIST 3.3.36
9. Fortune has been changed.   LUCAN 3.21
10. (He) who conquered has been conquered.   SEN IRA 2.34.5

CHAPTER 35: LATIN TO ENGLISH SENTENCES

1. **audīre vōcem vīsa sum.**   PLAUT CIST 543
2. **animī remedia inventa sunt ab antīquīs.**   SEN E 64.8
3. **liber tuus et lectus est et legitur ā mē dīligenter.**   CIC FAM 6.5.1
4. A. **dīc ergō.** B. **at vetita sum.**   PLAUT PERS 239
5. **armīs vīcit, vitiīs victus est.**   SEN E 51.5
6. **mūneribus meus est captus puer.**   TIB 1.9.11
7. **at omnēs quī missī erant ā Graeciā fūgērunt.**   SENR S 2.17
8. **duae dictae sunt sententiae quārum neutram probō.**   CIC PHIL 11.16
9. **illa quae ā sapientibus virīs reperta sunt nōn satis crēdimus.**   SEN E 59.9
10. **accūsātī damnātīque [sunt] multī cum līberīs atque etiam ā līberīs suīs.**   SUET T 61.2

CHAPTER 35: GLOSSED LATIN TO ENGLISH SENTENCES

1. **nēmō ab aliō contemnitur nisi ā sē** ante **contemptus est.**

   ante: (adverb) before, previously

   SEN AD HELV 13.6

2. iacta alea **est.**

   iacio, 3, iēcī, iactus: throw

   alea, ae, f.: die

   SUET DJ 33

CHAPTER 35: ENGLISH TO LATIN SENTENCES

1. For this state has always been defended by me.   CIC FAM 14.3.4
2. The sign will have been given by me.   PLAUT BACC 758
3. For this name alone has been left to me.   SEN HERC 1-2
4. A brief life has been given to us by Nature.   CIC PHIL 14.32
5. Never had (your) voice been heard in the forum.   CIC IN PIS 1
6. The thing will have been managed according to (my) opinion.   SEN BEN 4.11.1

CHAPTER 35: PASSAGES

OVID'S GIRLFRIEND PLAYS A DIRTY TRICK ON HIM

dicta erat aegra mihi; praeceps āmens**que** cucurrī.
   vēnī, et rīvālī **nōn erat aegra meō.**

OV A 3.11.25-6

---

praeceps, cipitis: headlong
currō, 3, cucurrī, cursus: run, race

āmens, āmentis: frantic
rīvālis, is, m: rival

36

Participles: Present Active

Chapter 34 introduced you to the participle, the verbal adjective that can do so many things. Here is the second of the four Latin participles: the present active participle. As usual, the name gives a clue to its nature—it is present and it is active. The best way to translate the present active participle is with the English present active participle, the form of the verb ending in -ing. Unfortunately, many people have been taught that the verb forms ending in -ing are gerunds, and this will cause confusion. It is true that they <u>can</u> be gerunds—in English!—but they are definitely <u>not</u> gerunds in Latin. So at this stage in your Latin learning, think of the English -ing forms as present active participles. Gerunds in both languages will come later.

The Latin present active participle is formed from the present stem of the verb and is declined like a third declension adjective. (In fact, it is declined exactly like the adjective **sapiens**, presented in a special table in chapter 25.) Here is the pattern for the first conjugation; the masculine and feminine forms are identical and thus are written in one column:

Case	Singular		Plural	
	masc/fem	*neut*	*masc/fem*	*neut*
nominative	ama-ns	ama-ns	ama-ntēs	ama-ntia
genitive	ama-ntis	ama-ntis	ama-ntium	ama-ntium
dative	ama-ntī	ama-ntī	ama-ntibus	ama-ntibus
accusative	ama-ntem	ama-ns	ama-ntēs	ama-ntia
ablative	ama-nte/ī	ama-nte/ī	ama-ntibus	ama-ntibus
vocative	ama-ns	ama-ns	ama-ntēs	ama-ntia

(Note the two endings for the ablative singular—an -**e** if the participle is being used as a noun, and an -**ī** if it is being used as an adjective.)

For completeness, here are the corresponding forms for all conjugations:

Case	Singular		Plural	
	masc/fem	*neut*	*masc/fem*	*neut*
nominative	move-ns	move-ns	move-ntēs	move-ntia
genitive	move-ntis	move-ntis	move-ntium	move-ntium
dative	move-ntī	move-ntī	move-ntibus	move-ntibus
accusative	move-ntem	move-ns	move-ntēs	move-ntia
ablative	move-nte/ī	move-nte/ī	move-ntibus	move-ntibus
vocative	move-ns	move-ns	move-ntēs	move-ntia

Case	Singular		Plural	
	masc/fem	*neut*	*masc/fem*	*neut*
nominative	age-ns	age-ns	age-ntēs	age-ntia
genitive	age-ntis	age-ntis	age-ntium	age-ntium
dative	age-ntī	age-ntī	age-ntibus	age-ntibus
accusative	age-ntem	age-ns	age-ntēs	age-ntia
ablative	age-nte/ī	age-nte/ī	age-ntibus	age-ntibus
vocative	age-ns	age-ns	age-ntēs	age-ntia

Case	Singular		Plural	
	masc/fem	*neut*	*masc/fem*	*neut*
nominative	scie-ns	scie-ns	scie-ntēs	scie-ntia
genitive	scie-ntis	scie-ntis	scie-ntium	scie-ntium
dative	scie-ntī	scie-ntī	scie-ntibus	scie-ntibus
accusative	scie-ntem	scie-ns	scie-ntēs	scie-ntia
ablative	scie-nte/ī	scie-nte/ī	scie-ntibus	scie-ntibus
vocative	scie-ns	scie-ns	scie-ntēs	scie-ntia

Case	Singular		Plural	
	masc/fem	*neut*	*masc/fem*	*neut*
nominative	**capie-ns**	**capie-ns**	**capie-ntēs**	**capie-ntia**
genitive	**capie-ntis**	**capie-ntis**	**capie-ntium**	**capie-ntium**
dative	**capie-ntī**	**capie-ntī**	**capie-ntibus**	**capie-ntibus**
accusative	**capie-ntem**	**capie-ns**	**capie-ntēs**	**capie-ntia**
ablative	**capie-nte/ī**	**capie-nte/ī**	**capie-ntibus**	**capie-ntibus**
vocative	**capie-ns**	**capie-ns**	**capie-ntēs**	**capie-ntia**

(There is no present active participle for **sum**.)

Because the participle is a verb-adjective blend, it has the properties of both latent within it. For now, that means it can (a) modify a noun (like an adjective); (b) stand alone (like a substantive); or (c) take a direct object (like a verb). Here are some examples of the participle modifying a noun:

incipiens omnia sentit amor.   Beginning love feels all things.   OV AĀ 2.648

iterum scrībō mittōque rogantia verba!   OV HER 20.33

                                        Again I write and send begging words!

Sometimes a participle can modify an "understood" noun, like the unexpressed subject of a verb:

haec properantēs scrīpsimus.   Hurrying, we wrote these things.   CIC ATT 4.4

And here are some participles standing alone; you can call them "substantive participles" if you like. Generally you will need the word "one" or "ones" for proper English translation:

audentēs Fortūna iuvat.   Fortune helps the daring (ones).   SEN E 94.28

cupientem fugis.   You flee one desiring.   SEN TROAD 1175

spectā pugnantem.   Look at the one fighting.   [QUINT] DECL 3.19

audī vocēs petentium.   Hear the voices of the ones seeking.   SEN BEN 3.5.2

Participles can also display their verb powers; here are some taking a direct object:

ego vitam dedī mortem timentī.   I gave life to one fearing death.   SEN BEN 3.31.2

currēbat fugiens hostem.   He was running (while) fleeing the enemy.   HOR S 1.3.10

vidēbis deōs omnia dantēs, nihil habentēs.   SEN TRANQ AN 8.5

                        You will see the gods giving all things, having nothing.

A participle can also be modified by an adverb, as in this line from Horace:

dulce rīdentem Lalagēn amābō.   I will love sweetly laughing Lalage.   HOR O 1.22.23

CHAPTER 36: VOCABULARY

cadō, cadere, cecidī, cāsūrus	*fall*
cēdō, cēdere, cessī, cessus	*yield*
cēnō, cēnāre, cēnāvī, cēnātus	*dine*
regnō, regnāre, regnāvī, regnātus	*reign*
rīdeō, rīdēre, rīsī, rīsus	*laugh (at)*
sedeō, sedēre, sēdī, sessus	*sit*
amātor, amātōris, m.	*lover*
dulcis, dulce	*sweet*
magis	*more*
sīc	*thus, so*

CHAPTER 36: PRACTICE SENTENCES (ANSWERS FOLLOW CHAPTER 66)

1. **petentī respondē.**   HOR S 2.5.1-2
2. **ibi sedens haec ad tē scrībēbam.**   CIC ATT 1.10.3
3. I will respond to one asking.   PLAUT MERC 515
4. Hurrying he seeks the city.   LUCR 3.1067

CHAPTER 36: LATIN TO ENGLISH SENTENCES

1. **illum audiens tē vidēbar vidēre.**   CIC FAM 10.3.1
2. **illam inveniēs dulcī cum matre sedentem.**   OV TRIST 3.7.3
3. **ut oculus sīc animus sē nōn videns alia cernit.**   CIC TD 1.67
4. **umbra es amantis magis quam amātor.**   PLAUT MG 625
5. **quī metuens vīvet, līber mihi nōn erit umquam.**   HOR E 1.16.66
6. **cēnantī mihi, sī cum uxōre vel paucīs, liber legitur.**   PLINY E 9.36.4
7. **rīdentem dīcere vērum quid vetat?**   HOR S 1.1.24-25
8. **pugnantēs prō patriae lībertāte cecidērunt.**   CIC ND 3.49
9. **haec spectans a tē spectābar.**   OV HER 21.103
10. **verum dīcentibus facile cēdam.**   CIC TD 3.51

CHAPTER 36: GLOSSED LATIN TO ENGLISH SENTENCES

1. **sed** cuncta **timēmus amantēs.**

   cunctus, a, um: all

   OV M 7.719

2. **vīdimus patriam** ruentem.

   ruō (3): collapse

   SEN AGAM 611

3. **urbem** trēs portās **habentem Rōmulus reliquit.**

   trēs, tria: three

   porta, ae, f.: gate

   PLINY NH 3.66

4. mīlitat **omnis amans, et habet sua castra** Cupīdo.

   mīlitō (1): be a soldier

   Cupīdo, Cupīdinis, m: Cupid

   OV A 1.9.1

5. **hominēs sōlī** animālium nōn sitientēs bibimus.

   animal, animālis, n.: animal

   sitiō (4): be thirsty

   bibō (3): drink

   PLINY NH 23.42

CHAPTER 36: ENGLISH TO LATIN SENTENCES

1. We had seen Caesar reigning.

   CIC PHIL 2.108

2. All things will be clear and certain to one not hurrying.

   LIVY 22.39.22

3. They showed the way to the wandering ones.

   PETR 79.4

4. You flee and fear laughing girls.

   PETR 109.10.5

CHAPTER 36: PASSAGES

TO A TEASE

das numquam, semper prōmittis, **Galla, rogantī.**
   sī semper fallis, **iam rogo, Galla – negā.**

MART 2.25

prōmittō (3): promise   fallō (3): disappoint

VIVISECTION VERSUS DISSECTION

incīdere **autem** vīvōrum **corpora et** crūdēle **et** supervacuum **est,** mortuōrum **discentibus** necessarium.

CELS 1.PR.P.12.35-36

---

incīdō (3): cut into   vīvus, a, um: living
crūdēlis, e: cruel   supervacuus, a, um: unnecessary
mortuus, a, um: dead   necessārius, a, um: necessary

37

Ablative Absolute

The construction called ablative absolute introduces another use for the ablative, this time in conjunction with a participle, usually one of the two participles you have had: perfect passive or present active. English has a similar construction, but since we don't have an ablative case, it is simply called an "absolute" or "participial absolute." Here are some common English examples; notice they are encountered quite often in speech and writing:

> All things being equal, ...
> Time having been called, ...
> That having been said, ...

Each example contains a noun—"things" and "Time" and "That"—and a participle—"being" and "having been called" and "having been said." Notice that these are not complete sentences; you cannot make a sentence out of a mere participle. "All things are equal" and "Time has been called" and "That has been said" are complete sentences, but they are no longer absolutes in either English or Latin. (The term "absolute" is used because the construction is "cut off" [**absolūtus**] grammatically from the rest of the sentence.)

As in English, the Latin ablative absolute contains both a participle and a noun, with the additional factor that both are in the ablative, the participle modifying the noun. A serviceable translation for now is to use the word "with" and proceed literally:

Pompeiō fugiente, timent.	With Pompeius fleeing, they fear.	LUCAN 1.522
sene sciente, hoc fēcī.		PLAUT MG 144
	With the old man knowing, I did this (thing).	
interfectō rēge, līberī nōn sumus?		CIC ATT 14.11.1
	With the king having been killed, are we not free?	

The following sentences appear to violate the formula for ablative absolute of noun plus a participle in the ablative. However, classical Latin had no present participle for the verb **sum**; in other words, there is no word corresponding to the English participle "being." Many Latin ablative absolutes require you to supply the participle "being" mentally, although it is not present in the Latin construction. Here are some examples:

mē duce, tūtus eris.	With me (being) leader, you will be safe.	OV AA 2.58
quam bene Sāturnō vīvēbant rēge!	How well they lived with Saturn (being) king!	TIB 1.3.35

CHAPTER 37: VOCABULARY

augeō, augēre, auxī, auctus	*increase, enlarge*
iaceō, iacēre, iacuī, —	*lie, lie down, lie in ruins*
lateō, latēre, latuī, —	*lie hidden*
fābula, ae, f.	*story, tale; play*
***hostis, hostis, m.**	*enemy (national)*
hūmānus, a, um	*human*
īrātus, a, um	*angry*
iustus, a, um	*just; proper*
vīnum, ī, n.	*wine*

CHAPTER 37: PRACTICE SENTENCES (ANSWERS FOLLOW CHAPTER 66)

1. **Pansa fūgerat, vulneribus acceptīs.**   CIC AD BRUT 1.3A
2. **Hortensius ad mē vēnit, scriptā epistulā.**   CIC ATT 10.17.1

CHAPTER 37: LATIN TO ENGLISH SENTENCES

1. **iam cum hoste, nullō impediente, bellum iustum gerēmus.**   CIC IN CAT 2.1
2. **relinquit animus Sextium, gravibus acceptīs vulneribus.**   CAES BG 6.38.4
3. **patrēs enim veniunt, āmissīs fīliīs, īrātī.**   CIC VER 5.120
4. **quid rīdēs? mutātō nōmine, dē tē fābula narrātur.**   HOR S 1.1.69-70
5. **nam lacrimae, causā saepe latente, cadunt.**   OV HER 21.194
6. **contempsit omnia et, damnātīs hūmānae vitae furōribus, fūgit.**   SEN E 68.8
7. **multīs iam sententiīs dictīs, rogātus sum sententiam.**   CIC DOMO SUA 16
8. **nox erat et, vīnō somnum faciente, iacēbant.**   OV F 1.421
9. **magnum animum et semper habuistī et nunc, Fortūnā adiuvante, augēre potes.**   CIC FAM 11.23.1

CHAPTER 37: GLOSSED LATIN TO ENGLISH SENTENCES

1. gladiātor **igitur est quī in** harēnā, **populō spectante, pugnāvit.** QUINT DECL 302

   gladiātor: gladiator   harēna, ae, f.: sand

CHAPTER 37: ENGLISH TO LATIN SENTENCES

1. With this (man) as leader, we took the camp.   CIC PRO MUR 38
2. The highest general fled, with the army having been lost.   CIC DE DIVIN 1.24

CHAPTER 37: PASSAGES

ORPHEUS MOURNS EURYDICE DEAD

tē, dulcis cōniunx, **tē,** sōlō **in** lītore **sēcum,**
tē, veniente diē, tē, dēcēdente canēbat.

VERG G 4.465-6

cōniunx, cōniugis, f.: spouse	lītus, lītoris, n.: shore
sōlus, a, um: lonely	dēcēdō (3): withdraw
canō (3): sing	

Participles: Future Passive/Passive Periphrastic/Dative of Agent

There are two more participles to learn, the future passive and future active. This chapter contains only the former; the latter will be explained in chapter 40. The future passive participle indicates both futurity and passivity; possible translations are "to be …" or "about to be …" It is formed from the present stem of the verb with the distinguishing infix -**nd**- and uses the familiar endings of the first and second declensions:

Case	Singular		
	masc	*fem*	*neut*
nom	**amand-us**	**amand-a**	**amand-um**
gen	**amand-ī**	**amand-ae**	**amand-ī**
dat	**amand-ō**	**amand-ae**	**amand-ō**
acc	**amand-um**	**amand-am**	**amand-um**
abl	**amand-ō**	**amand-ā**	**amand-ō**
voc	**amand-e**	**amand-a**	**amand-um**

Case	Plural		
	masc	*fem*	*neut*
nom	**amand-ī**	**amand-ae**	**amand-a**
gen	**amand-ōrum**	**amand-ārum**	**amand-ōrum**
dat	**amand-īs**	**amand-īs**	**amand-īs**
acc	**amand-ōs**	**amand-ās**	**amand-a**
abl	**amand-īs**	**amand-īs**	**amand-īs**
voc	**amand-ī**	**amand-ae**	**amand-a**

The corresponding forms from the other conjugations are as follows:

move-nd-us	move-nd-a	move-nd-um
move-nd-ī	move-nd-ae	move-nd-ī
etc.	etc.	etc.
scribe-nd-us	scribe-nd-a	scribe-nd-um
scribe-nd-ī	scribe-nd-ae	scribe-nd-ī
etc.	etc.	etc.
audie-nd-us	audie-nd-a	audie-nd-um
audie-nd-ī	audie-nd-ae	audie-nd-ī
etc.	etc.	etc.
capie-nd-us	capie-nd-a	capie-nd-um
capie-nd-ī	capie-nd-ae	capie-nd-ī
etc.	etc.	etc.

Be careful to distinguish this participle from the present active participle, which has third declension endings, and the -nt- infix, like **amans, amantis. amandus, -a, -um** is translated "to be loved" or "about to be loved" while **amans, amantis** is translated "loving." For comparison, both participles are used in the following phrase:

... metuens magis quam metuendus ...   SALL BJ 20.2

... fearing more than to be feared ...

Here are some sentences containing the future passive participle:

rēs nōn amandās amant. They love things not to be loved.   AUG CD 8.8

fugienda petimus. We seek things to be avoided.   SEN PHAED 699

dedit mihi epistulam legendam tuam.   CIC Q FR 3.1.19

He gave me your letter to be read.

populus Rōmānus consulī bellum gerendum dedit.   CIC PHIL 11.18

The Roman people gave the war to be waged to the consul.

THE PASSIVE PERIPHRASTIC

The future passive participle is frequently combined with a form of the verb **sum** in the construction, called the "passive periphrastic." (Let it roll off your tongue and prepare yourself for the "active periphrastic.") Thus, you would expect **amandus sum** to mean "I am to be loved," and sometimes it does. More often, however, the idea of worth or obligation was imported into the construction and the result is that **amandus sum** usually should be translated "I am worthy to be loved" or "I must be loved" or "I have to be loved." I recommend the last as your default translation until you become comfortable with the construction.

Here it is in the present tense:

Present Tense

amandus sum	I have to be loved	**amandī sumus**	we have to be loved
amandus es	you have to be loved	**amandī estis**	you have to be loved
amandus est	he has to be loved ˙	**amandī sunt**	they have to be loved

And in the imperfect tense:

Imperfect Tense

movenda eram	I had to be moved	**movendae erāmus**	we had to be moved
movenda erās	you had to be moved	**movendae erātis**	you had to be moved
movenda erat	she had to be moved	**movendae erant**	they had to be moved

And in the future tense:

Future Tense

audiendus erō	I will have to be heard	**audiendī erimus**	we will have to be heard
audiendus eris	you will have to be heard	**audiendī eritis**	you will have to be heard
audiendus erit	he will have to be heard	**audiendī erunt**	they will have to be heard

(The passive periphrastic also occurs in the perfect system—perfect, pluperfect, and future perfect—but I am not providing tables for those tenses.)

Here are some examples:

Rōma relinquenda est.	Rome has to be left.	OV TRIST 1.3.62
docendus est.	He has to be taught.	SEN QN 2.38.2
dīcenda haec fuerunt.	These things had to be said.	SEN BEN 3.29.1
duo occidendī erunt.	Two (men) will have to be killed.	[QUINT] DECL 3.9
imperium dandum fuit.	Command had to be given.	CIC PHIL 11.20

(For now, avoid using "must" to translate the passive periphrastic. The problem with "must" is that it only works in the present tense; try forming the future or past tenses of it and see what happens.)

DATIVE OF AGENT WITH THE PASSIVE PERIPHRASTIC

In all other passive constructions, personal agency has been shown by **ab/ā** plus the ablative case. However, with the passive periphrastic you will find a new use for the dative case: "dative of agent with the passive periphrastic." (Practice saying that aloud to your friends.) Here are some examples:

frāter est exspectandus mihi.	My brother has to be waited for by me. (I have to wait for my brother.)	TER PHOR 460
nunc hoc tibi cūrandum est.	Now this must be taken care of by you. (You have to take care of this.)	PLAUT BACC 691
quid igitur nōbīs faciendum est?	Therefore, what has to be done by us? (Therefore, what do we have to do?)	CIC VER 4.11
laudandus erit tibi Antōnius.	Antony will have to be praised by you. (You will have to praise Antony.)	SENR S 6.1

You will discover that the Romans used the passive periphrastic, with and without the dative of agent, far more often that they used the verb **dēbeō** "ought" to indicate obligation. So, instead of saying, "I must do my duty" they were just as likely to say, "My duty must be done by me" and use the passive periphrastic with the dative of agent. The result when translated literally into English is cumbersome and wordy. Your computers would never let you get away with it. However, I advise you to use the literal translation for a while until you become familiar with the construction.

█ CHAPTER 38: VOCABULARY

mora, ae, f.	*delay*
perpetuus, a, um	*perpetual*
ultimus, a, um	*last, final*
ūnus, a, um	*one, alone*

CHAPTER 38: PRACTICE SENTENCES (ANSWERS FOLLOW CHAPTER 66)

1. **vulnera cūranda sunt.**   QUINT DECL 268
2. **gratiae sunt agendae.**   CIC FAM 8.11.2
3. **puer didicit quod discendum fuit.**   CIC DE ORAT 3.87
4. **igitur cōgendus fuistī.**   PLINY PANEG 5.6
5. **exercitūs habent nōn contemnendōs.**   CIC FAM 10.24.6
6. **mihi Munātius eās litterās legendās dedit.**   CIC FAM 10.12.2
7. **facta fugis; facienda petis.**   OV HER 7.13
8. Peace has to be sought.   LIVY 7.40.5
9. The truth has to be said.   SENR C 1.8.6
10. But it will have to be done.   SEN TRANQ AN 5.5
11. War has to be waged.   CIC PHIL 11.16

CHAPTER 38: LATIN TO ENGLISH SENTENCES

1. **omnia armīs agenda erunt.**   SUET DJ 31.2
2. **nihil in vitā nisi laudandum aut fēcit aut dixit.**   VP 1.12.3
3. **dīvitī hominī id aurum servandum dedit.**   PLAUT BACC 338
4. **senātūs auctōritās mihi dēfendenda fuit.**   CIC ATT 1.16.1
5. **nox est perpetua ūna dormienda.**   CATULLUS 5.6
6. **omnia, inquit, hominī, dum vīvit, speranda sunt.**   SEN E 70.6
7. **arte meā capta est, arte tenenda meā est.**   OV AA 2.12
8. **ultima semper exspectanda diēs hominī.**   OV M 3.135-6
9. **rēs mihi Rōmānās dederās, Fortūna, regendās.**   LUCAN 7.110
10. **mors ultima poena est nec metuenda virīs.**   LUCAN 8.395-6

CHAPTER 38: ENGLISH TO LATIN SENTENCES

1. For nothing must be done without reason.   SEN BEN 4.10.2
2. I see nothing to be feared, but nevertheless I fear.   SEN THY 435
3. The pleasure of Venus must not be hurried.   OV AA 2.717
4. All delay will have to be avoided.   CELS 8.9.P.344.4
5. But it had to be done.   CIC ATT 13.11.1

CHAPTER 38: PASSAGES

IN THE GOOD OLD DAYS, THE SENATE SIMPLY DECLARED MARTIAL LAW

Gāiō Mariō, Lūciō Valeriō consulibus senātus rem publicam dēfendendam dedit; Lūcius **Sāturnīnus** tribūnus plēbis, **Gāius Glaucia** praetor **est** interfectus. **omnēs illō diē Scaurī, Metellī, Claudiī, Catulī, Scaevolae, Crassī arma** sumpsērunt.

CIC PHIL 8.15

tribūnus, ī, m.: tribune	praetor, ōris, m.: praetor
plebs, plēbis, f.: common people	interficiō, 3, interfēcī, interfectus: kill
sūmō, 3, sumpsī: take up	

39

īdem

The common word **īdem** "(the) same" is formed from the demonstrative **is, ea, id** (which you learned in chapter 21) plus the suffix **-dem**. Review chapter 21 and notice how some forms of **īdem** differ slightly from those of **is, ea, id**:

Case	Singular			Plural		
	masc	*fem*	*neut*	*masc*	*fem*	*neut*
nominative	ī-dem	ea-dem	i-dem	ī-dem	eae-dem	ea-dem
genitive	eius-dem	eius-dem	eius-dem	eōrun-dem	eārun-dem	eōrun-dem
dative	eī-dem	eī-dem	eī-dem	īs-dem	īs-dem	īs-dem
accusative	eun-dem	ean-dem	i-dem	eōs-dem	eās-dem	ea-dem
ablative	eō-dem	eā-dem	eō-dem	īs-dem	īs-dem	īs-dem

(In general, when the letter **-m** precedes the **-dem**, it changes to **-n**.)

Here are some examples of **īdem**:

īdem enim fīnis omnium est.	For the end of all (people) is the same.	SEN E 66.44
omnes idem sentiebatis.	You all were feeling the same (thing).	CIC RED SEN 29
eadem reī natura est.	The nature of the thing is the same.	QUINT DECL 332

Note that in order to say, "the same as," the Romans often used a form of the relative pronoun (**quī, quae, quod**) to do the work of "as." Consider these examples:

īdem sum quī semper fuī.	I am the same as I always was.	PLAUT AMPH 447
īdem erant quī fuerant.	They were the same as they had been.	CIC ATT 4.5.1
idem fecī quod Cato.	I did the same (thing) as Cato.	QUINT DECL 377

CHAPTER 39: VOCABULARY

īdem, eadem, idem	*(the) same*
amīcitia, ae, f.	*friendship*
meretrix, meretrīcis, f.	*prostitute*
mulier, mulieris, f.	*woman*
opīnio, opīniōnis, f.	*opinion*
quoque	*also*

CHAPTER 39: PRACTICE SENTENCES (ANSWERS FOLLOW CHAPTER 66)

1. **nōn eadem rēs est.** — MART 12.96.9
2. **eadem enim ipse didicistī.** — CIC ACADPOS 5
3. **eadem faciēmus quae cēterī?** — SEN E 5.6
4. **idem nōbīs faciendum est.** — SEN BEN 7.29.2
5. I was in the same arms. — CIC PRO LIG 9
6. For the same things are said by many. — CIC TD 2.6

CHAPTER 39: LATIN TO ENGLISH SENTENCES

1. **tamen in eādem sum voluntāte.** — CIC ATT 11.13.4
2. **nōbīs quoque idem existimandum est.** — CIC TD 1.35
3. **līberōs āmīsī et eōdem tempore āmīsī.** — QUINT DECL 337
4. **eandem meretrīcem amāvērunt duo iuvenēs, fīliī nostrī.** — QUINT DECL 344
5. **hīs ego litterīs lectīs, in eādem opīniōne fuī quā reliquī omnēs.** — CIC ATT 8.11D.3
6. **multās ā tē accēpī epistulās eōdem diē, omnēs dīligenter scriptās.** — CIC ATT 10.4.1
7. **"Nātūram" vocā, "Fātum", "Fortūnam"; omnia eiusdem deī nōmina sunt.** — SEN BEN 4.8.3

CHAPTER 39: GLOSSED LATIN TO ENGLISH SENTENCES

1. **ego tamen īdem sum quī et** infans **fuī et puer et** adulescens. — infans, infantis, m.: baby adulescens, adulescentis, m.: young man — SEN E 121.16

CHAPTER 39: ENGLISH TO LATIN SENTENCES

1. A letter about the same things was delivered to me.   CIC FAM 15.1.2
2. In men and women there is not the same danger.   CELS 6.11.P.249.16
3. The same (things) must be said about friendship.   CIC DE FIN 1.68
4. No one of us is the same in old age as he was as a youth.   SEN E 58.22

CHAPTER 39: PASSAGES

CAN'T LIVE WITH YOU OR WITHOUT YOU

difficilis, facilis, **iucundus, acerbus es īdem –**
    nec tēcum possum vīvere nec sine tē.

MART 12.46

---

facilis, e: easy

OVID'S ADVERTISEMENT FOR HIS WORK "CURES FOR LOVE"

Nāso **legendus erat tum cum didicistis amāre;**
    īdem nunc vōbīs Nāso **legendus erit.**

OV RA 71-2

Naso, Nasōnis, m.: Ovid's last name

I DIDN'T KILL MY BROTHER

fratrem **nōn occīdī – nōn potuī** fratrem **occīdere. idem timuimus, idem doluimus, idem**
flevimus, **eundem patrem habuimus, eandem matrem, eandem** novercam.

SENR C 7.1.12

---

frater, fratris, m.: brother   fleō, 2, flēvī, flētus: weep for
noverca, ae, f.: stepmother

Participles: Future Active/Active Periphrastic

The fourth and final participle in Latin is the future active participle. We have nothing like it in English, so to render it we must use a phrase like "about to …" or "going to …" It is formed from the perfect passive participle, that is the fourth principal part of a verb, with the addition of the infix **-ūr-**:

Case	Singular		
	masc	*fem*	*neut*
nominative	**amāt-ūr-us**	**amāt-ūr-a**	**amāt-ūr-um**
genitive	**amāt-ūr-ī**	**amāt-ūr-ae**	**amāt-ūr-ī**
dative	**amāt-ūr-ō**	**amāt-ūr-ae**	**amāt-ūr-ō**
accusative	**amāt-ūr-um**	**amāt-ūr-am**	**amāt-ūr-um**
ablative	**amāt-ūr-ō**	**amāt-ūr-ā**	**amāt-ūr-ō**
vocative	**amāt-ūr-e**	**amāt-ūr-a**	**amāt-ūr-um**

Case	Plural		
	masc	*fem*	*neut*
nominative	**amāt-ūr-ī**	**amāt-ūr-ae**	**amāt-ūr-a**
genitive	**amāt-ūr-ōrum**	**amāt-ūr-ārum**	**amāt-ūr-ōrum**
dative	**amāt-ūr-īs**	**amāt-ūr-īs**	**amāt-ūr-īs**
accusative	**amāt-ūr-ōs**	**amāt-ūr-ās**	**amāt-ūr-a**
ablative	**amāt-ūr-īs**	**amāt-ūr-īs**	**amāt-ūr-īs**
vocative	**amāt-ūr-ī**	**amāt-ūr-ae**	**amāt-ūr-a**

The corresponding forms from the other conjugations are as follows:

mōt-ūr-us	mōt-ūr-a	mōt-ūr-um
mōt-ūr-ī	mōt-ūr-ae	mōt-ūr-ī
etc.	etc.	etc.
script-ūr-us	script-ūr-a	script-ūr-um
script-ūr-ī	script-ūr-ae	script-ūr-ī
etc.	etc.	etc.
audit-ūr-us	audit-ūr-a	audit-ūr-um
audit-ūr-ī	audit-ūr-ae	audit-ūr-ī
etc.	etc.	etc.
capt-ūr-us	capt-ūr-a	capt-ūr-um
capt-ūr-ī	capt-ūr-ae	capt-ūr-ī
etc.	etc.	etc.

The verb **sum** also has a future active participle, its only participle:

fut-ūr-us	fut-ūr-a	fut-ūr-um
fut-ūr-ī	fut-ūr-ae	fut-ūr-ī
etc.	etc.	etc.

Here are some examples of the future active participle:

vōbīs dedī bona certa mansūra.   SEN PROV 6.5

I have given you certain goods, about to last.

vēnī ad vōs victōriam pulchram petītūrus.   SENR C 7.1.9

I came/have come to you (plural) about to seek a beautiful victory.

THE ACTIVE PERIPHRASTIC

In chapter 38 you encountered the future passive participle and its use in the passive periphrastic. Latin has an analogous combination for the future active participle called (appropriately) the "active periphrastic." However, there is an important difference. The active periphrastic is simply the sum of its parts; it has no imported idea of obligation or anything else. Thus, **amātūrus sum** means "I am about to/going to love," and **futūrum est** means "it is about to/going to be." Here are some examples:

quid agis? quid actūrus es?	What are you doing? What are you going to do?	PLINY E 9.32
dictūra es quod rogō?	Are you going to say what I ask?	TER AND 751
vērī amīcī futūrī sumus.	We are going to be true friends.	CIC DE FIN 2.85
et quid futūrum erat?	And what was going to be?	QUINT DECL 287
nec lectūra fuī.	And was I not going to read.	OV HER 21.5

Latin also has a future active infinitive formed from the future active participle and **esse**. It will not be used until the next chapter on indirect statement.

CHAPTER 40: VOCABULARY

incrēdibilis, incrēdibile	*incredible*
tālis, tāle	*such*
tamquam	*as though*
tristis, triste	*sad*

CHAPTER 40: PRACTICE SENTENCES (ANSWERS FOLLOW CHAPTER 66)

1.	**omne futūrum incertum est.**	SEN AD MARC 23.1
2.	**quaerō – quid factūrī fuistis?**	CIC PRO LIG 24
3.	**tū dedistī iam; hic datūrus est.**	PLAUT TRUC 960
4.	**clāra rēs est quam dictūrus sum.**	CIC VER 3.61
5.	You are always going to live.	SENR S 6.4
6.	Are you (plural) not about to dine?	PLAUT MERC 750
7.	I was going to ask the father of the girl.	SENR C2.3.6
8.	After death we are going to be wretched.	CIC TD 1.13

CHAPTER 40: LATIN TO ENGLISH SENTENCES

1.	**incrēdibile est quod dictūrus sum, sed tamen vērum.**	SEN QN 4A.PR.4
2.	**tristēs erant amīcī tālem āmissūrī virum.**	SEN TRANQ AN 14.8
3.	A. **tua uxor, quid agit?** B. **immortālis est, vīvit victūraque est.**	PLAUT TRIN 55-6

4. **omnia quae ventūra sunt in incertō iacent.** SEN BREV VIT 9.1
5. **munera multa dedī, multa datūra fuī.** OV HER 2.110
6. **signa ostenduntur ā dīs rērum futūrārum.** CIC ND 2.12
7. **nōn accusātūrus patrem sed mē dēfensūrus sum.** SENR C 2.6.9
8. **nostrum nōn mortāle futūrum est carmen.** OV PONT 2.6.33-4
9. **bellum scriptūrus sum quod populus Rōmānus cum lugurthā, rēge Numidārum, gessit.** SALL BJ 5.1

CHAPTER 40: GLOSSED LATIN TO ENGLISH SENTENCES

1. **nōn enim doceō sed** admoneō **doctūrōs.**   admoneō: prompt   QUINT 1.4.17
2. **effugere enim nēmō id potest quod futūrum est.**   effugiō (3-io): escape   CIC ND 3.14

CHAPTER 40: ENGLISH TO LATIN SENTENCES

1. He was not about to see (his) friend. [QUINT] DECL 9.22
2. There is going to be war in Italy. CIC ATT 11.18.1
3. You (plural) live as though always about to live. SEN BREV VIT 3.4
4. Are you going to send your wife to me? PLAUT CAS 610

CHAPTER 40: PASSAGES

THE NATURE OF WISDOM

ō Dēmea,
istuc **est** sapere – **nōn quod ante** pedēs modo **est**
vidēre **sed etiam illa quae futūra sunt** prospicere.

TER ADEL 385-88

---

istuc (=istud+ce): this here   sapiō (3): be prudent
pēs, pedis, m.: foot   nōn ... modo: not just
prospiciō (3): foresee

PAST, PRESENT, FUTURE

in tria **tempora** vīta dīviditur – **quod fuit, quod est, quod futūrum est. ex iīs quod agimus breve est, quod actūrī sumus dubium, quod ēgimus certum.**

SEN BREV VIT 10.2

---

trēs, tria: three   dīvido (3): divide

41

Indirect Statement

So far, every Latin sentence you have encountered has been in the form called "direct statement." You were unaware of this fact, and with good reason. There was no point in calling attention to the concept of direct statement until you were ready to learn about indirect statement. Now you are. (For the same reason, you were not told that all your verbs were in the active voice until you were ready for the passive voice. The same will be true for the concepts of "indicative" and "subjunctive," but that is for another chapter.)

As a rule of thumb, English indirect statement is characterized by the word "that" used as a subordinating conjunction. For example, "You are in love" is a direct statement; "I know" is also a direct statement; but "I know that you are in love" contains an indirect statement. The formerly direct statement "You are in love" becomes indirect by subordinating it using "that" as the conjunction. In English it is as simple as "that"; in Latin, not so simple. To convert direct to indirect statement in Latin, you must perform an operation on the grammar of the direct statement, as follows:

tū amās.   You are in love.   PLAUT CAS 725

To make it indirect, one simply joins it to a verb of reporting (more on this below) and voilá:

sciō tē amāre.   I know that you are in love.   PLAUT MERC 577

The former subject **tū** has become the accusative **tē**; the former conjugated verb **amās** has become the infinitive **amāre**. The result seems to say something like "I know you to be in love," but that is not the way to translate indirect statement. Instead, reverse the operation described: (1) Find the accusative; (2) put "that" before it; (3) find the infinitive; and (4) convert it to a conjugated verb.

Here are some more examples:

(1) **cōgitā tē mortālem esse.**   Think that you are mortal.   SEN E 35.3
(2) **sē putant vincere.**   They think that they conquer.   LIVY 2.64.6
(3) **vidēs ipsam mortem nec malum esse nec bonum.**   You see that death itself is neither a good nor a bad thing.   Sen E 82.13

Notice the kind of verbs that introduce indirect statement—"think," "see," "know," "hear," "believe," and many others like them typically signal an indirect statement. Some books refer to them as "verbs of the head." Up to this point, such verbs have usually governed a simple accusative, a direct object. Now look for an accusative and an infinitive, a sign of indirect statement.

All the examples so far have involved the present infinitive, but in fact, any of Latin's six infinitives can confront you in this construction, active or passive, present, perfect, or future! You have been introduced to almost all the infinitives in earlier chapters. Now it will be useful to have a table of the infinitives handy, say from the verb **amō**:

	Active	**Passive**
present	amāre	amārī
perfect	amāvisse	amātus esse
future	amātūrus esse	amātum īrī

Or the verb **scrībō**:

	Active	**Passive**
present	scrībere	scrībī
perfect	scripsisse	scriptus esse
future	scriptūrus esse	scriptum īrī

(Note that there is also a future passive infinitive, which always ends in **-um īrī**.)

Let us not forget the infintives of **sum**. (Can you explain why there are only three?):

	Active
present	esse
perfect	fuisse
future	futūrus esse

Previously, there was not much use for the perfect and future infinitives; now be prepared to see any of them appear in indirect statement:

(4) **putō mē ita esse factūrum.** I think that I will do thus.   CIC ATT 3.8.3

(5) **ōrātiōnem spērat invēnisse sē.**   TER AND 407

   He hopes that he found/has found the speech.

(6) **vīdī nostrōs amīcōs cupere bellum.**   CIC FAM 9.6.2

   I saw that our friends were desiring war.

(7) **negābās datūrum esse tē mihi.**   PLAUT PSEUD 1314

   You denied that you would/were going to give to me.

(8) **vēnisse eās salvās audīvī.** I heard that they had come safe.   TER PHOR 575-6

There are several things to notice here. One is that the introductory verb can come at the beginning, middle, or end of the sentence. Another is that when an infinitive contains a participle (future active and perfect passive) that participle must agree with the accusative subject, hence **factūrum** (to agree with **mē**) and **datūrum** (to agree with **tē**). And the participle can come before or after the **esse**, contrary to the impression you may have formed.

When the infinitive appears in indirect statement, you do not translate it as an infinitive in English. Instead, it will be translated as a conjugated verb. There is no mechanical formula for doing this because, in indirect statement, the infinitive has no absolute time value, as before, but only relative time value according to the following rule:

▼ **present infinitive** shows **same time as the main verb**

▼ **future infinitive** shows **time after the main verb**

▼ **perfect infinitive** shows **time before the main verb**

Let's return to the examples:

(1) **putō mē ita esse factūrum.**   I think that I will do thus.   CIC ATT 3.8.3

The introductory verb **putō** is present; the infinitive **esse factūrum** is future; thus the "doing" happens after the "thinking," captured in English by writing "will do."

(2) **ōrātiōnem spērat invēnisse sē.**   TER AND 407

   He hopes that he found/has found the speech.

The introductory verb **spērat** is present; the infinitive **invēnisse** is perfect; thus the "finding" happened before the "hoping," captured in English by writing "found" or "has found" (depending on the context).

(3) **vīdī nostrōs amīcōs cupere bellum.**   CIC FAM 9.6.2

   I saw that our friends were desiring war.

The introductory verb **vīdī** is in past tense; the infinitive **cupere** is present; thus the "desiring" happened at the same time as the "seeing." Here, the English is a little more complicated: In order to make the "desiring" be contemporaneous with the "seeing," we must say "were desiring" even though the underlying Latin infinitive is <u>present</u>.

(4) **negābās datūrum esse tē mihi.**   PLAUT PSEUD 1314
    You denied that you would/were going to give to me.

The introductory verb **negābās** is in a past tense; the infinitive **datūrum esse** is future; thus the "giving" happened after the "denying." Here, instead of "will," proper English requires "would" or "were going to" (depending on the context) since the introductory verb is in the past.

(5) **vēnisse eās salvās audīvī.**   I heard that they had come safe.   TER PHOR 575-6

The introductory verb **audīvī** is in a past tense; the infinitive **vēnisse** is perfect; thus the "coming" happened before the "hearing." To capture this relation, English uses "had come," a pluperfect, even though the underlying infinitive is <u>perfect</u>.

Here are some more examples of indirect statement:

sānum tē crēdis esse?	Do you believe that you are sane?	TER ADEL 748
timēre sē dīcunt.	They say that they are afraid.	CIC PHIL 10.15
mē videō vīvere.	I see that I live.	PLAUT MEN 461
scīre sē nesciunt.	They do not know that they know.	SEN E 75.9
sapientiam bonum esse dīcunt.	They say that wisdom is a good thing.	SEN E 117.2
perdidisse mē omnem pecuniam dīcō.	I say that I (have) lost all the money.	QUINT DECL 269

There is one more problem that can arise in indirect statement: Is the accusative the <u>subject</u> of the infinitive or the <u>direct object</u> of the infinitive? You have seen that word order has less of a role in Latin than in English. However, as a general rule, when dealing with indirect statement, you will find that the first accusative is usually the subject, the second usually the object. Take the following sentence:

dīc mē illam amāre.   PLAUT PERS 303

In theory, this sentence could mean either (a) "Say that I love her" or (b) "Say that she loves me." However, since the **mē** precedes the **illam**, it is probably the subject of the infinitive and means "Say that I love her." However, it is possible that **illam** could be the subject of the infinitive and **mē** is its object; then the sentence would mean "Say that she loves me." In its original context, it actually does mean the former, but with no context to work from, the sentence is potentially ambiguous.

Here are some examples in which the context helps determine the meaning:

mē putātis manūs nōn habēre. You think that I do not have hands.   SENR C 1.4.10

(Not: You think that hands do not have me.)

mortem mē timuisse dīcis.   You say that I feared death.   CIC PRO PLANC 90

(Not: You say that death feared me.)

crēdō hunc mē nōn amāre.   I believe that this man does not love me.   CIC ATT 9.18.1

(Not: I believe that I do not love this man.)

But in one famous case, an indirect statement was deliberately ambiguous. Pyrrhus, king of Epirus, asked the Delphic oracle if he should make war against the Romans and received the following answer:

dīcō tē, Pyrrhe, vincere posse Rōmānōs.   AUG CD 3.17

Pyrrhus, overconfident, understood this to mean "I say that you, Pyrrhus, are able to conquer the Romans." After all, the **tē** comes before the **Rōmānōs**, thus prompting him to take the **tē** as the subject of the infinitive and **Rōmānōs** as its object. However, after he lost the war, he realized that it could equally, and in fact did, mean "I say that the Romans, Pyrrhus, are able to conquer you." **Rōmānōs** was the subject of the infinitive and **tē** the object. (Even though the oracle was originally given in Greek, the same rules for indirect statement apply in Greek as in Latin, making the oracular utterance ambiguous in Greek as well.)

CHAPTER 41: VOCABULARY

accidō, accidere, accidī, —	*happen*
clāmō, clāmāre, clāmāvī, clāmātus	*shout*
perveniō, pervenīre, pervēnī, perventus	*reach*
aetas, aetātis, f.	*age*
innocens, innocentis	*innocent*

CHAPTER 41: PRACTICE SENTENCES (ANSWERS FOLLOW CHAPTER 66)

1.	**tū esse mē tristem putās?**	PLAUT ASIN 837
2.	**tē ā mē amārī scīs.**	CIC ATT 1.20.7
3.	**consulem tū tē fuisse putās?**	CIC IN PIS 29
4.	**videō tē bona perdidisse.**	CIC FAM 9.18.4
5.	**dormīre sē dormiens cōgitat.**	SEN E 53.7

6. **videō mūtāta esse omnia.**   CIC ATT 11.11.1
7. **nōn dixī esse hoc futūrum?**   TER AND 621
8. **ipse rēgem sē esse dīcēbat.**   SEN E 108.13
9. **servum esse audīvī meum apud tē.**   PLAUT POEN 761-2
10. **Brūtum vīsum īrī ā mē putō.**   CIC ATT 15.25
11. I denied that I knew.   CIC FAM 8.16.4
12. He says that the universe is a god.   CIC ND 1.39
13. You know that many people say many things.   MART 6.56.5
14. Do you deny that you received a kindness?   SEN BEN 4.6.1
15. We know that death is not a bad thing.   SEN CONS SAP 8.3

CHAPTER 41: LATIN TO ENGLISH SENTENCES

1. **deōs putās hūmāna neglegere.**   CIC ND 3.89
2. **sciō equidem mē tē esse nunc et tē esse mē.**   PLAUT CAPT 249
3. **sentit igitur animus sē movērī.**   CIC TD 1.55
4. **clāmābat ille miser sē cīvem esse Rōmānum.**   CIC VER 5.161
5. **maneō in sententiā et gaudeō tē mansisse.**   CIC ATT 9.10.8
6. **dixit enim mihi tē esse in Ītaliā.**   CIC ATT 4.4
7. **pervenisse tē ad ultimum aetātis hūmānae vidēmus.** SEN BREV VIT 3.2
8. **quid tū accidere in mediō marī crēdis?**   SEN E 14.15
9. **iuvenem nostrum nōn possum nōn amāre, sed ab eō nōs nōn amārī plāne intellegō.**   CIC ATT 10.10.6

CHAPTER 41: ENGLISH TO LATIN SENTENCES

1. We believe that pleasure is a fault.   SEN E 59.1
2. You (plural) knew that I had conquered with these arms. QUINT DECL 369
3. They say that the senate has been corrupted.   CIC RAB POST 6
4. She does not know that she is blind.   SEN E 50.2
5. He was shouting that he was innocent.   SENR C 7.8.6

CHAPTER 41: PASSAGES

inter **spem cūramque, timōrēs** inter **et īrās,
omnem crēde diem tibi** dīluxisse suprēmum.

HOR E 1.4.12-13

---

inter: (prep. + acc.) among	dīlūceō, 2, dīluxī: shine
suprēmus, a, um: final	

---

iurant **autem mīlitēs omnia sē** strēnuē **factūrōs [esse] quae** praeceperit **imperātor, numquam** dēsertūrōs **[esse]** militiam **nec mortem** recusātūrōs **[esse] prō Rōmānā rē publicā.**

VEG 2.5

---

iurō (1): swear	strēnuus, a, um: prompt
praecipiō, 3, praecēpī: instruct	dēserō, 3, dēseruī, dēsertus: desert
mīlitia, ae, f.: military service	recūsō (1): refuse

42

Comparative and Superlative of Adjectives/Idiomatic Uses/Ablative of Comparison

U p to now, all the adjectives you have seen have been expressed in what is called the "positive" degree. There are two other degrees: comparative and superlative. In English we have two ways of doing this: (1) with the suffixes -er and -est; or (2) with the words "more" and "most." Thus we say "easier" (comparative degree) and "easiest" (superlative degree), but for longer words, like "beautiful," we usually say "more beautiful" and "most beautiful."

Although Latin does have words for "more" and "most," the normal way of forming the comparative and superlative is with a special infix. For the comparative this infix is (generally) **-ior-** and for the superlative it is (generally) **-issim-**. Here are the comparative forms of **vērus, -a, -um**:

Case	Singular		Plural	
	masc/fem	*neut*	*masc/fem*	*neut*
nominative	**vēr-ior**	**vēr-ius**	**vēr-ior-ēs**	**vēr-ior-a**
genitive	**vēr-iōr-is**	**vēr-iōr-is**	**vēr-iōr-um**	**vēr-iōr-um**
dative	**vēr-iōr-ī**	**vēr-iōr-ī**	**vēr-iōr-ibus**	**vēr-iōr-ibus**
accusative	**vēr-iōr-em**	**vēr-ius**	**vēr-iōr-ēs**	**vēr-iōr-a**
ablative	**vēr-iōr-e**	**vēr-iōr-e**	**vēr-iōr-ibus**	**vēr-iōr-ibus**
vocative	**vēr-ior**	**vēr-ius**	**vēr-iōr-ēs**	**vēr-iōr-a**

And the superlative:

Case	Singular		
	masc	*fem*	*neut*
nominative	**vēr-issim-us**	**vēr-issim-a**	**vēr-issim-um**
genitive	**vēr-issim-ī**	**vēr-issim-ae**	**vēr-issim-ī**
dative	**vēr-issim-ō**	**vēr-issim-ae**	**vēr-issim-ō**
accusative	**vēr-issim-um**	**vēr-issim-am**	**vēr-issim-um**
ablative	**vēr-issim-ō**	**vēr-issim-ā**	**vēr-issim-ō**
vocative	**vēr-issim-e**	**vēr-issim-a**	**vēr-issim-um**

Case	Plural		
	masc	*fem*	*neut*
nominative	**vēr-issim-ī**	**vēr-issim-ae**	**vēr-issim-a**
genitive	**vēr-issim-ōrum**	**vēr-issim-ārum**	**vēr-issim-ōrum**
dative	**vēr-issim-īs**	**vēr-issim-īs**	**vēr-issim-īs**
accusative	**vēr-issim-ōs**	**vēr -issim-ās**	**vēr-issim-a**
ablative	**vēr-issim-īs**	**vēr-issim-īs**	**vēr-issim-īs**
vocative	**vēr-issim-ī**	**vēr-issim-ae**	**vēr-issim-a**

Adjectives of the third declension have a similar comparative:

Case	Singular		Plural	
	masc/fem	*neut*	*masc/fem*	*neut*
nominative	**brev-ior**	**brev-ius**	**brev-iōr-ēs**	**brev-iōr-a**
genitive	**brev-iōr-is**	**brev-iōr-is**	**brev-iōr-um**	**brev-iōr-um**
dative	**brev-iōr-ī**	**brev-iōr-ī**	**brev-iōr-ibus**	**brev-iōr-ibus**
accusative	**brev-iōr-em**	**brev-ius**	**brev-iōr-ēs**	**brev-iōr-a**
ablative	**brev-iōr-e**	**brev-iōr-e**	**brev-iōr-ibus**	**brev-iōr-ibus**
vocative	**brev-ior**	**brev-ius**	**brev-iōr-ēs**	**brev-iōr-a**

And the superlative:

Case	Singular		
	masc	*fem*	*neut*
nominative	**brev-issim-us**	**brev-issim-a**	**brev-issim-um**
genitive	**brev-issim-ī**	**brev-issim-ae**	**brev-issim-ī**
dative	**brev-issim-ō**	**brev-issim-ae**	**brev-issim-ō**
accusative	**brev-issim-um**	**brev-issim-am**	**brev-issim-um**
ablative	**brev-issim-ō**	**brev-issim-ā**	**brev-issim-ō**
vocative	**brev-issim-e**	**brev-issim-a**	**brev-issim-um**

Case	Plural		
	masc	*fem*	*neut*
nominative	**brev-issim-ī**	**brev-issim-ae**	**brev-issim-a**
genitive	**brev-issim-ōrum**	**brev-issim-ārum**	**brev-issim-ōrum**
dative	**brev-issim-īs**	**brev-issim-īs**	**brev-issim-īs**
accusative	**brev-issim-ōs**	**brev-issim-ās**	**brev-issim-a**
ablative	**brev-issim-īs**	**brev-issim-īs**	**brev-issim-īs**
vocative	**brev-issim-ī**	**brev-issim-ae**	**brev-issim-a**

Here are some sentences containing comparative and superlative adjectives:

aliōs fēliciōrēs vidēre nōn potuit.	He was not able to see others happier.	SEN E 55.5
gladiōs longiōrēs fēcit.	He made the swords longer.	NEPOS 11.1.4
timēre quid gravius potest?	What more serious (thing) can he fear?	SEN TROAD 612
nōn potuit vōtum plēnius esse meum.	My vow could not be more full.	OV TRIST 5.9.22
dīcī enim nihil potest vērius.	For nothing more true can be said.	CIC DE FIN 2.9

Note: The superlative forms of adjectives ending in **–er**, like **līber**, **miser**, and **pulcher**, are **līberrimus**, **miserrimus**, and **pulcherrimus**.

IDIOMATIC USES

The comparative degree can often be translated with "rather" instead of "more." This occurs when the context suggests no obvious object of comparison, as in the following example:

sunt illīus scripta leviōra.	His writings are rather trivial.	CIC DE FIN 1.7

By the same token, the superlative degree can often be translated with "very" instead of "most." This happens when the context suggests no obvious candidates for comparison, as in the following examples:

ūnum verbum dixistī vērissimum.	You have said one very true word.	PLAUT MERC 206
id tūtissimum est.	This is a very safe thing.	TER ADEL 552
grātissimae mihi tuae litterae fuērunt.		CIC FAM 10.4.1
	Your letter was very welcome to me.	

ABLATIVE OF COMPARISON

A frequent companion to the comparative adjective is another type of ablative: the "ablative of comparison." That is, if you want to claim that some noun is "more true" than some other noun, the second noun can be put in the ablative. I say "can" because you have already learned a word for "than," **quam**, back in chapter 10. (This word has many manifestations: (1) "how" in chapter 7; (2) "than" in chapter 10; (3) a form of the relative pronoun in chapter 28; and soon (4) a form of the interrogative adjective in chapter 49.) Here is an example of the ablative of comparison:

> **nōn sum līberior Brūtō?**   Am I not freer than Brutus?   PERS 5.84-5

This sentence could have been expressed by using **quam** as follows:

> **nōn sum līberior quam Brūtus?**

Here, **quam** is a coordinator, which means that the two compared nouns, "I" and "Brutus" are both put into the same case, here, nominative.

Here is another example:

> **hōc mihi nihil potest esse grātius.**   CIC ATT 2.1.12
> Nothing can be more welcome to me than this.

(This sentence could have been expressed **nihil potest esse gratius mihi quam hoc.**)

Here are some more examples of the ablative of comparison:

> **nēmō est miserior mē.**   No one is more wretched than me.   TER HT 263
> **nihil autem est levius aquā.**   Nothing you see is lighter than water.   SEN QN 1.3.7

▌ CHAPTER 42: VOCABULARY

cārus, a, um	*dear*
levis, leve	*light, trivial*
lux, lūcis, f.	*light*
poēta, ae, m.	*poet*
vērō	*in fact; however*

CHAPTER 42: PRACTICE SENTENCES (ANSWERS FOLLOW CHAPTER 66)

1.	**est lūce clārius.**	CIC TD 1.90
2.	**breviōrēs litterās ad tē mittō.**	CIC ATT 5.7
3.	**vērō vērius nihil est.**	SEN QN 2.34.2
4.	**cārissimum virum āmīserat.**	SEN AD HELV 19.4
5.	**nihil mihi gratius facere potes.**	CIC ATT 5.14.3
6.	**quis mē miserior umquam fuit?**	CIC ATT 11.2.3
7.	You were stupider than a stupid person.	PLAUT CURC 551
8.	What are you saying, most dear friend?	PETR 71.5
9.	Never have I seen a more stupid person.	TER EUN 1009

CHAPTER 42: LATIN TO ENGLISH SENTENCES

1.	**nēmō est mihi tē amīcus antīquior.**	CIC FAM 11.27.2
2.	**sed tū ex amīcīs certīs mihi es certissimus.**	PLAUT TRIN 94
3.	**sed sunt haec leviōra, illa vērō graviōra.**	CIC PRO PLANC 86
4.	**ō matre pulchrā fīlia pulchrior.**	HOR O 1.16.1
5.	**nīl sēcūrius est malō poētā.**	MART 12.63.13
6.	**accēpit gravissimum parens vulnus morte fīlii.**	NEPOS 10.6.2
7.	**bona opīniō hominum tūtior pecūniā est.**	PUBLSYR B19
8.	**nihil inveniēs rectius rectō, nōn magis quam vērius vērō.**	SEN E 66.8
9.	**vale, iūcundissime Tiberī, et fēlīciter rem gere.**	SUET T 21.4
10.	**ita sunt omnia omnium miseriārum plēnissima.**	CIC ATT 2.24.4

CHAPTER 42: GLOSSED LATIN TO ENGLISH SENTENCES

1.	gladiātōrēs **graviōribus armīs discunt quam pugnant.**	gladiātor, tōris, m.: gladiator	SENR C 9.PRAEF.4
2.	**brevissima ad dīvitiās per** contemptum **dīvitiārum via est.**	contemptus, ūs, m.: scorn	SEN E 62.3

CHAPTER 42: ENGLISH TO LATIN SENTENCES

1. Nothing can be more wretched than this.   CIC ATT 9.13A
2. What more serious was able to happen to me?   QUINT DECL 246
3. For nothing can be more pleasant nor more dear to me than your life.   CIC FAM 11.20.2
4. All your plans are clearer than light to us.   CIC IN CAT 1.6
5. My wife or son are not dearer to me than (my) father and the republic.   TAC ANN 1.42

CHAPTER 42: PASSAGES

STOOD UP BY AN OLD GIRLFRIEND

ego mendācem **stultissimus** usque **puellam
ad mediam noctem exspectō.**

HOR S 1.5.82-3

---

mendax, mendācis: lying   usque: all the way

A PARASITE'S LAMENT

miser homō est quī ipse sibi quod edit **quaerit et id** aegrē **invenit,
sed ille est miserior quī et** aegrē **quaerit et nihil invenit;
ille miserrimus est, quī cum** esse **cupit, tum quod** edit **nōn habet.**

PLAUT CAPT 461-3

---

edō, esse: eat aegrē: barely

43

Special and Irregular Comparison of Adjectives/Idiomatic Uses

In both English and Latin, certain adjectives have irregular comparative and superlative forms. In English, "good" becomes "better" and "best" (not "gooder" and "goodest"); "bad" becomes "worse" and "worst" (not "badder" and "baddest," not yet anyway). There are more of these in Latin, and they are among the most common words. Here is a table:

Positive	Comparative	Superlative
bonus, -a, -um	melior, melius	optimus, -a, -um
malus, -a, -um	pēior, pēius	pessimus, -a, -um
magnus, -a, um	maior, maius	maximus, -a, um
parvus, -a, -um	minor, minus	minimus, -a, -um
–	plūrēs, plūra	plūrimus, -a, -um

The saving thing about these words is that they all have common English derivatives, which will help you memorize or recognize them.

Here are some sample sentences:

plūra scrībere nōn possum.	I am not able to write more (things).	CIC ATT 3.2.1
causam habent optimam.	They have the best cause.	CIC FAM 11.19.2
dux causae meliōris eris.	You will be the leader of the better cause.	LUCAN 4.259
maximum remedium īrae mora est.	The greatest cure for anger is delay.	SEN IRA 2.29.1
cūrātur ā multīs, timētur ā plūribus.	He is cared for by many; he is feared by more.	PLINY E 1.5.15
quis plūrimum habet? is quī minimum cupit.	Who has the most? He who desires the least.	PUBLSYR

IDIOMATIC USES

Note that the comparative degree can again often be translated with "rather" instead of "more." The context will guide you.

nulla res maior sine eo gerebatur.   NEPOS 2.1.3

        No rather large thing was done without him.

nobis enim scribuntur saepe maiora.   CIC ATT 5.8.3

        For to us are often written rather large matters.

And the superlative degree can again often be translated with "very" instead of "most."

dēfendī plūrimōs.   I have defended very many.   CIC RAB POST 9

natūra minimum petit.   Nature seeks very little.   SEN E 17.9

CHAPTER 43: VOCABULARY

maior, maius	*bigger, greater*
maximus, a, um	*biggest, largest*
melior, melius	*better*
minimus, a, um	*smallest, least*
minor, minus	*smaller, less*
optimus, a, um	*best*
pēior, pēius	*worse*
pessimus, a, um	*worst*
plūs	*more*
plūrēs, plūra	*more*
plūrimus, a, um	*very many, most*
possideō, possidēre, possēdī, possessus	*possess, own*
tormentum, ī, n.	*torture*

CHAPTER 43: PRACTICE SENTENCES (ANSWERS FOLLOW CHAPTER 66)

1. **pessimae estis.**   PLAUT TRUC 295
2. **potest melior vincere.**   SEN E 14.13
3. **māiōra discenda sunt.**   QUINT 1.3.15
4. **nōs optimōs esse crēdimus.**   SEN E 59.11
5. **Terentia tibi maximās gratiās agit.**   CIC ATT 3.8.4
6. Friendship is the greatest good.   CIC INVENT 1.95
7. You will have less money.   SEN E 42.9
8. The universe has nothing greater than Jupiter.   OV TRIST 2.38
9. Nothing is better than reason and wisdom.   CIC ND 2.18
10. You have given back more than you had received.   CIC FAM 3.13.1

CHAPTER 43: LATIN TO ENGLISH SENTENCES

1. **minus habeō quam spērāvī.**   SEN IRA 3.30.3
2. **hominī plūrima ex homine sunt mala.**   PLINY NH 7.5
3. **maxima pars mundī – deus – latet.**   SEN QN 7.30.4
4. **māiōre tormentō pecūnia possidētur quam quaeritur.**   SEN E 115.16
5. **vincuntur enim meliōra pēiōribus.**   SEN QN 6.28.2
6. **pēior est bellō timor ipse bellī.**   SEN THY 572
7. **quid hominī potest darī māius quam glōria et laus?**   PLINY E 3.21.6
8. **plūra bella gessit quam cēterī lēgērunt.**   CIC IMP POMP 28
9. **maximīs minimīsque corporibus pār est dolor vulneris.** SEN TRANQ AN 8.2.

CHAPTER 43: GLOSSED LATIN TO ENGLISH SENTENCES

1. **optimus est post malum principem diēs prīmus.**   princeps, principis, m.: emperor   TAC HIST 4.42

CHAPTER 43: ENGLISH TO LATIN SENTENCES

1. I am not able to write to you without the greatest pain.   CIC ATT 11.5.1
2. To conquer was worse.   LUCAN 7.706
3. I give you more than I received.   PETR 45.13
4. And so I gave thanks to Caesar with more words.   CIC FAM 4.4.4
5. The gods ignore smaller things.   CIC ND 3.86
6. You can give me no greater kindness.   CIC FAM 13.8.3

CHAPTER 43: PASSAGES

TRAGEDY AND COMEDY AGREE ON THIS

antīquum poētam audīvī scripsisse in tragoediā
mulieres duās pēiōres esse quam ūnam. rēs ita est.

PLAUT CURC 591-2

---

tragoedia, ae, f.: tragedy

THE POET CATULLUS THANKS THE LAWYER CICERO

disertissime **Rōmulī** nepōtum,
quot **sunt** quot**que** fuēre, **Marce Tullī,**
quot**que** post **aliīs erunt in** annīs,
gratiās tibi maximās Catullus
agit pessimus omnium poēta,
tantō **pessimus omnium poēta,**
quantō **tū optimus omnium** patrōnus.

CATULLUS 49

---

disertus, a, um: eloquent   nepōs, nepōtis, m.: descendant
quot: as many as   post (adverb): later
tantō ... quantō: as much ... as   fuēre = fuērunt
annus, ī, m.: year   patrōnus, ī, m.: lawyer

Comparative and Superlative of Adverbs/Idiomatic Uses

Like adjectives, adverbs also appear in comparative and superlative degrees; these are built from the corresponding adjective forms. Thus, once you know the comparative and superlative of an adjective, there is a very mechanical process for determining the adverb. And another good thing is that the adverb has only one form; it does not decline. In chapter 42, you learned how the comparative and superlative degrees of adjectives were formed from the positive as follows:

positive	**stultus, -a, -um**	stupid
comparative	**stultior, -ius**	stupider
superlative	**stultissimus, -a, -um**	stupidest

positive	**gravis, e**	heavy
comparative	**gravior, -ius**	heavier
superlative	**gravissimus, -a, -um**	heaviest

You already know that the positive adverb is formed by adding -**ē** or -**ter** to the adjective:

| **stultus** | stupid | → | **stultē** | stupidly |
| **gravis** | heavy | → | **graviter** | heavily |

Now for the mechanical process: (1) The comparative adverb has the same form as the neuter singular accusative of the adjective; (2) the superlative adverb is formed by adding -**ē** to stem of the adjective. The results are as follows:

| **stultior** | stupider | → | **stultius** | more stupidly |
| **stultissimus** | stupidest | → | **stultissimē** | most stupidly |

| **gravior** | heavier | → | **gravius** | more heavily |
| **gravissimus** | heaviest | → | **gravissimē** | most heavily |

Here are some examples of comparative and superlative adverbs in sentences:

dīc, orō tē, clārius.	Speak, I beg you, more clearly.	CIC ATT 4.8A.1
rectissimē fēcit.	He (has) acted most rightly.	PLINY E 5.9.6
pulcherrimē ēgī aetātem.	I have led (my) life most beautifully.	PLAUT MG 1312
tuās litterās semper maximē exspectō.	I always await your letter(s) very greatly.	CIC ATT 3.17.3

You may be getting nervous about the comparative adverb. It ends in **-ius**, and thus is identical to the neuter comparative adjective. How is one to distinguish between the comparative adverb and the comparative adjective in the neuter? Answer: If there is a neuter noun in the sentence, the form in question is assuredly the adjective. Otherwise, even a Roman would have trouble deciding. When there is no neuter noun in the grammatical vicinity, you are dealing with the comparative adverb. Here are a few examples:

ipsā rē publicā nihil mihi est cārius.	CIC FAM 2.15.3
Nothing is dearer to me than the republic itself.	
quid Iove māius habēmus?	OV M 2.62
What do we have greater than Jupiter?	

In the first example, the comparative form **cārius** modifies the neuter noun **nihil**; in the second, the comparative form **maius** modifies the neuter pronoun **quid**. Both are adjectives.

IDIOMATIC USES

The comparative forms in Latin, both adjective and adverb, often allow the translation "rather," "quite," or even "too" instead of "more." This is usually the case if there is no obvious object of comparison. Here are some examples:

līberius vīvēbat.	He was living too freely.	NEPOS 2.1.2
dixit audācius.	He spoke rather boldly.	CIC TD 3.20
in umbrā voluptātis diūtius lūsī.	For too long I have played in the shade of pleasure.	PETR 129.4
pugnantem illum saepius vīdī.	I have seen him fighting quite often.	QUINT DECL 271

In addition, there are some idiomatic uses of a couple of the comparative and superlative adverbs. The adverb form of the superlative adjective **plūrimus** is not **plūrimē**, but **plūrimum** and means "most" or "very much." The superlative adverb **maximē** often means "especially," and the superlative adverb **minimē** can mean "not at all" in addition to "least."

plūrimum cum eō vīxit.	He lived with him very much.	QUINT DECL 259
id enim est maximē vītandum.	For this is especially to be avoided.	CIC DE ORAT 1.132
consilium nōbīs minimē iūcundum est.	The plan is not at all pleasant to us.	CIC FAM 4.4.5

CHAPTER 44: VOCABULARY

diū	(adverb) for a long time, long
prior, prius	sooner; before
tantus, a, um	so great, so much
turpis, turpe	shameful
ūtilis, utile	useful
serviō, servīre, servī(v)i, servītus	be a slave

CHAPTER 44: PRACTICE SENTENCES (ANSWERS FOLLOW CHAPTER 66)

1. **potuit diūtius vīvere.**   SEN AD MARC 21.6
2. **ad tē minus multa scrībō.**   CIC ATT 3.10.3
3. **libentissimē lēgi tuās litterās.**   CIC FAM 12.19.1
4. **multa sunt pulcherrimē dicta.**   SENR C 1.4.10
5. I esteem you most strongly.   CIC FAM 13.4.1
6. I am not able to speak more plainly.   CIC VER 4.27
7. He is especially to be praised.   CIC BRUTUS 250

CHAPTER 44: LATIN TO ENGLISH SENTENCES

1. **servīre diūtius nōn potest cīvitās.**   CIC PHIL 10.19
2. **hominēs hominibus maximē ūtilēs esse possunt.**   CIC DE OFF 2.11
3. **dīcam brevius quam rēs tanta dīcī potest.**   CIC PARADOX 6
4. **prius tū emis quam vendō, pater.**   PLAUT MERC 456
5. **saepe ad nōs īra venit, saepius nōs ad illam.**   SEN IRA 3.12.1
6. **melius inveniam viam quam quaerō sōlus.**   SEN PHOEN 5-6

7. **victus turpissimē, āmissīs etiam castrīs, sōlus fūgit.** CIC FAM 7.3.2
8. **valet autem auctōritās eius apud illum plūrimum.** CIC ATT 5.11.3

CHAPTER 44: GLOSSED LATIN TO ENGLISH SENTENCES

1. **mē** benignius **omnēs** salūtant **quam** salūtābant **prius.** PLAUT AUL 114-5
      benignus, a, um: kindly   salūtō (1): greet
2. interfectus **est etiam fortissimē pugnans Crastinus.** CAES BC 3.99.2
      interficiō, 3, interfēcī, interfectus: kill

CHAPTER 44: ENGLISH TO LATIN SENTENCES

1. You answer sooner than I ask. PLAUT MERC 456
2. Humans are taught better by models. PLINY PANEG 45.6
3. But their opinions moved me less. CIC ATT 8.9A.1

CHAPTER 44: PASSAGES

ROMAN CHAUVINISM

meum semper iudicium fuit omnia nostrōs aut invēnisse per sē sapientius quam Graecōs aut accepta ab illīs fēcisse meliōra.

CIC TD 1.1

45

Present Subjunctive/ Jussive, Hortatory, and Deliberative

It is now time to learn the subjunctive mood. The English subjunctive is practically extinct in the speech of modern Americans, though it can still be found in the mouths of those who say "If I were you" and "Whether it be now or later." If you have studied Spanish or French or Italian, or other Romance languages, where it is still much used, you have come to grips with the subjunctive.

Since the subjunctive is found so infrequently in our speech, it is natural to wonder what it is. Long ago I learned that whatever formulation a teacher gives to this question, the student will inevitably cling to it and regurgitate it when asked to explain the subjunctive at hand. Hence the cryptic answer: I could tell you, but then I would have to flunk you.

It is better to think of the subjunctive in the way you have come to understand the case system, as one of the distinctive structures that Latin speakers evolved, and not try to delve too deeply into its essence. As you will see, the path to mastery involves, as always, following grammatical rules. Instead of trying to determine just how "subjunctive" an action is, you will be asked to state whether the structure is a purpose clause, a result clause, an indirect question, or something similar.

The tables that follow contain the present tense of the subjunctive, both active and passive, for all conjugations, plus **sum** and **possum**. You will be happy to learn that the endings are your old friends from earlier days. To better bring out this feature of the subjunctive, I have put dashes in every form. Notice that no English translations are offered. That is because there is no baseline translation for a subjunctive verb. All depends on the structure in which it appears.

Present Subjunctive

Active		Passive	
am-e-m	am-ē-mus	am-e-r	am-ē-mur
am-ē-s	am-ē-tis	am-ē-ris	am-ē-minī
am-e-t	am-e-nt	am-ē-tur	am-e-ntur

Present Subjunctive

Active		Passive	
mov-ea-m	mov-eā-mus	mov-ea-r	mov-eā-mur
mov-eā-s	mov-eā-tis	mov-eā-ris	mov-eā-minī
mov-ea-t	mov-ea-nt	mov-eā-tur	mov-ea-ntur
duc-a-m	duc-ā-mus	duc-a-r	duc-ā-mur
duc-ā-s	duc-ā-tis	duc-ā-ris	duc-ā-minī
duc-a-t	duc-a-nt	duc-ā-tur	duc-a-ntur
aud-ia-m	aud-iā-mus	aud-ia-r	aud-iā-mur
aud-iā-s	aud-iā-tis	aud-iā-ris	aud-iā-minī
aud-ia-t	aud-ia-nt	aud-iā-tur	aud-ia-ntur
cap-ia-m	cap-iā-mus	cap-ia-r	cap-iā-mur
cap-iā-s	cap-iā-tis	cap-iā-ris	cap-iā-minī
cap-ia-t	cap-ia-nt	cap-iā-tur	cap-ia-ntur

And of course **sum** and **possum**, which are quite regular on their own terms:

Present Subjunctive

sim	sīmus	pos-sim	pos-sīmus
sīs	sītis	pos-sīs	pos-sītis
sit	sint	pos-sit	pos-sint

(If you are wondering about the passive forms of **sum**, there are none. As with the English verb "to be," **sum** can never be passive.)

As you study these tables, you will see the familiar active and passive endings. In addition, observe the pattern involved in forming the present subjunctive: the first conjugation, normally distinguished by the vowel -**a**-, receives an -**e**-; the second conjugation, normally distinguished by an -**e**-, receives an -**ea**-; the third conjugation receives an -**a**; and the fourth and third-io receive an -**ia**. Once again, it is a vowel that carries crucial information.

This chapter will contain two uses of the subjunctive: the jussive (which includes the hortatory) and the deliberative subjunctive.

JUSSIVE AND HORTATORY SUBJUNCTIVE

The jussive subjunctive is used to urge someone to do something, but not by giving a direct order. (The term is derived from the fourth principal part of **iubeō, iussus,** meaning "having been ordered.") The jussive construction, whether in English or Latin, is more indirect than the imperative. We also have a jussive construction in English whose distinguishing mark is the helping verb "let." For example, "Let the buyer beware" (in Latin, **caveat emptor**) is an exhortation addressed indirectly to the buyer. A direct command would require the imperative, "Buyer, beware" (in Latin, **cave, emptor**). It is important to remember that the word "let" in this construction does not mean "allow." Marie Antoinette did not mean "Allow them to eat cake" but something like "Why don't they all just eat cake?" Here are some examples:

negent, sī possunt.	Let them deny, if they can.	CIC VER 4.19
exercitus mittātur.	Let the army be sent.	CIC FAM 10.23.6
cēna dētur.	Let a dinner be given.	PLAUT BACC 537
veniat Caesar cum copiīs quās habet.	Let Caesar come with the forces which he has.	CIC FAM 10.23.6

One can also address a jussive to the first person, as in "Let me count the ways" or "Let us now praise famous men." In this case, the subjunctive is usually referred to as "hortatory subjunctive." (The jussive is rarely used with the second person.)

dīcāmus bona verba.	Let us speak good words.	TIB 2.2.1
nunc, nunc pugnēmus.	Now, now let us fight.	SEN R S 2.4
Rōmānī omnēs vocēmur.	Let us all be called Romans.	LIVY 8.5.6

The negative of both the jussive and the hortatory subjunctive requires the word **nē**:

nē nimis amēmus vītam.	Let us not love life too much.	SEN E 24.24
nē damnent quae nōn intellegunt.	Let them not condemn (things) which they do not understand.	QUINT 10.1.26

DELIBERATIVE SUBJUNCTIVE

The deliberative subjunctive is used when a speaker is trying to come to a decision and expresses the difficulty of deciding in the form of a question:

quid dīcam?	What am I to say?	CIC ATT 1.17.6
quo fugiam?	Where am I to flee?	PLAUT MOST 513
a fratre vincar?	Am I to be conquered by (my) brother?	SEN AGAM 26

These are not requests for information; they express the difficulty of deciding. (Note also that the present subjunctive in the first-person singular often is identical to a future indicative; beware!) You will also find the deliberative subjunctive used with the second and third person as well:

sed quid agās?	What are you to do?	CIC FAM 2.15.2
quid crēdat?	What is he to believe?	CATULLUS 106.2

The negative in a deliberative subjunctive is **nōn**:

quid nōn metuam ab eo?	What am I not to fear from him?	PLAUT PSEUD 1087
quō curram? quō nōn curram?	Where am I to run? Where am I not to run?	PLAUT AUL 713

As the examples show, a dependable way to translate a deliberative subjunctive is with "am I to" or "are you to" or "is he/she to" in the form of a question. Later you can be more creative.

CHAPTER 45: VOCABULARY

nē	*not (with negative jussive)*
quōmodo	*how*
toga, ae, f.	*toga (worn in peace)*
triumphus, ī, m.	*triumph (victory parade)*
vōtum, ī, n.	*vow, wish*

CHAPTER 45: PRACTICE SENTENCES (ANSWERS FOLLOW CHAPTER 66)

1. **sed quid spērem?**   TER PHOR 1022
2. **agāmus deō gratiās.**   SEN E 12.10
3. **idem nōs faciāmus.**   SEN E 59.13
4. **bella gerant aliī.**   OV HER 13.84
5. **mortis via quaerātur.**   SEN OED 1031-2
6. **spēs bona det virēs.**   OV HER 11.61
7. **quid tē vocem?**   SEN OED 1009
8. **vocētur mulier.**   CIC VER 1.66
9. **ab aliīs ergō laudēmur.**   QUINT 11.1.22
10. **ubi inveniam Pamphilum?**   TER AND 338
11. **tē ratiō dūcat, nōn fortūna.**   LIVY 22.39.21
12. Let us love the homeland.   CIC PRO SEST 143
13. Let them prepare arms.   VERG A 4.290
14. What am I to do now?   PLAUT CAS 549

CHAPTER 45: LATIN TO ENGLISH SENTENCES

1. **vīvāmus, mea Lesbia, atque amēmus.**   CATULLUS 5.1
2. **tam magnās spēs relinquam?**   SEN E 22.9
3. **mors mea nē careat lacrimīs.**   CIC TD 1.117
4. **quid faciāmus hominēs miserrimī?**   PETR 73.1
5. **imperātor in bellō summam habeat potestātem.**   QUINT DECL 348
6. **cēdant carminibus rēgēs rēgumque triumphī.**   OV A 1.15.33
7. **ad illa mittāmus animum quae aeterna sunt.**   SEN E 58.27
8. **id esse optimum putēmus quod erit rectissimum.**   CIC PRO SEST 143
9. **omnia vincit Amor – et nōs cēdāmus Amōrī.**   VERG E 10.69
10. A. **scribe.** B. **quid scribam?** A. **salūtem tuō patrī verbīs tuīs.**   PLAUT BACC 731
11. **sibi sua habeant regna rēgēs, sibi dīvitiās dīvitēs.**   PLAUT CURC 178

CHAPTER 45: ENGLISH TO LATIN SENTENCES

1. Let us remain therefore in that same wretched opinion. CIC ATT 9.13A
2. How am I to live without you? PLAUT MG 1206
3. Let my vows be changed. SEN HERC 112
4. Let arms yield to the toga. CIC PHIL 2.20
5. What am I to say to (my) father now? TER AND 612
6. Let us therefore give the command to Caesar. CIC PHIL 5.45

CHAPTER 45: PASSAGES

THE SOUL IS IMMORTAL

cōgitēmus dēnique **corpus virōrum fortium magnōrumque hominum esse mortāle,
animī vērō** mōtūs **et virtūtis glōriam** sempiternam.

CIC PRO SEST 143

---

dēnique (adverb): finally   mōtus, ūs, m.: movement
sempiternus, a, um: everlasting

46 Imperfect Subjunctive/Purpose Clauses

The imperfect subjunctive is the easiest subjunctive to form and therefore to recognize. You simply take the present active infinitive of any verb—no matter what conjugation—and add the appropriate endings, both active and passive:

Imperfect Subjunctive

Active		Passive	
amāre-m	amārē-mus	amāre-r	amārē-mur
amārē-s	amārē-tis	amārē-ris	amārē-minī
amāre-t	amāre-nt	amārē-tur	amāre-ntur
movēre-m	movērē-mus	movēre-r	movērē-mur
movērē-s	movērē-tis	movērē-ris	movērē-minī
movēre-t	movēre-nt	movērē-tur	movēre-ntur
dūcere-m	dūcerē-mus	dūcere-r	dūcerē-mur
dūcerē-s	dūcerē-tis	dūcerē-ris	dūcerē-minī
dūcere-t	dūcere-nt	dūcerē-tur	dūcere-ntur
audīre-m	audīrē-mus	audīre-r	audīrē-mur
audīrē-s	audīrē-tis	audīrē-ris	audīrē-minī
audīre-t	audīre-nt	audīrē-tur	audīre-ntur
capere-m	caperē-mus	capere-r	caperē-mur
caperē-s	caperē-tis	caperē-ris	caperē-minī
capere-t	capere-nt	caperē-tur	capere-ntur

Even the normally irregular verbs **sum** and **possum** form the imperfect subjunctive like all the other verbs, from the present infinitive. (There is of course no passive of **sum** or **possum**).

Imperfect Subjunctive

esse-m	essē-mus	posse-m	possē-mus
essē-s	essē-tis	possē-s	possē-tis
esse-t	esse-nt	posse-t	posse-nt

Notice that again no translations are offered; there is no "basic" or "default" translation of any subjunctive until it is used in a particular structure. Please do not assign one mentally; it will just get you in trouble.

In the last chapter you learned independent uses of the subjunctive: jussive, hortatory and deliberative. "Independent" means the main verb of a sentence is subjunctive. More commonly, the subjunctive is found in a dependent clause. The term "dependent" means that the subjunctive is contained in a subordinate clause attached to a main clause. Subordinate clauses cannot exist independently; they need to be joined to a main clause. Thus, the majority of subjunctives in Latin are found in sentences consisting of at least two clauses—a main and a subordinate.

PURPOSE CLAUSE: PRESENT SUBJUNCTIVE

The first such use is the purpose clause. Here the subjunctive is introduced by the conjunction **ut**, a word you first met in chapter 20 that means "as." You will now see it used in various subjunctive constructions; in a purpose clause, **ut** has the meaning "in order that" and the subjunctive is translated with a "may" or a "might":

hoc agit ut doleās.	He does this in order that you may hurt.	JUV 5.157
dīcō ego tibi iam ut sciās.	I tell you now in order that you may know.	PLAUT EPID 668

Notice that each sentence consists of two clauses—an independent clause and a dependent clause. The independent (or main clause) can stand alone, the dependent (or subordinate clause) cannot. That is because it is introduced by a subordinating conjunction, in this case the word **ut**. Thus, **hoc agit** and **dīcō ego tibi iam** are the main clauses; **ut doleās** and **ut sciās** are the subordinate clauses.

The negative form of a purpose clause uses **nē** instead of **ut**:

tacē nē audiat.	Be quiet in order that he may not hear.	PLAUT MG 1254
nē cadam, amābō, tenē mē.	Hold me, please, in order that I may not fall.	PLAUT CAS 634

For now, I urge you to use the cumbersome phrase "in order that" to translate purpose clauses. The clever student may see that "so that" (or "lest" for negatives) would work equally well. This is true, but it will confuse the issue when we come to result clauses.

PURPOSE CLAUSE: IMPERFECT SUBJUNCTIVE

These examples all involved present subjunctive. That is because the introductory verbs were all in the present tense. However, under certain conditions, a purpose clause may contain an imperfect subjunctive. Here are some examples:

occīsus est ut tacērem.	He was killed in order that I might be silent.	[QUINT] DECL 19.1
fūgimus nē servīrēmus.	We fled in order that we might not be slaves.	SENR C 7.6.7
pecūniam dedistī ut praemium acciperēs.	You gave money in order that you might receive a reward.	QUINT DECL 345
omnia fēcit ut beneficium redderet.	He did all things in order that he might return the kindness.	SEN BEN 7.14.4

In these examples, all the verbs of the main clauses are in the perfect tense, while all the verbs of the subordinate clauses are imperfect subjunctive and are translated using the modal verb "might." The key to this puzzle is contained in the following rule for determining the tense of subjunctive in a purpose clause:

▼ **If the verb of the main clause is in a past tense, use imperfect subjunctive.**

▼ **If the verb of the main clause is in any other tense, use present subjunctive.**

In practical terms, this means that when you have a purpose clause containing a present subjunctive, translate it with "may"; when the subjunctive is imperfect, translate it with a "might." Note: This translation tip applies only to purpose clauses!

CHAPTER 46: VOCABULARY

ut	*(in purpose clause) in order that*
nē	*(in purpose clause) in order that ... not*
edō, esse, ēdī, ēsus	*eat*
hūc	*hither, to here*
tandem	*finally, at last*
*testis, testis, m.	*witness*

CHAPTER 46: LATIN TO ENGLISH SENTENCES

1. **dīcō, Venus, ut tū audiās.** PLAUT RUD 1343
2. **veniunt ut audiant, nōn ut discant.** SEN E 108.6
3. **ante senectūtem cūrāvī ut bene vīverem.** SEN E 61.2
4. **lēgum omnēs servī sumus ut līberī esse possīmus.** CIC CLUENT 146
5. **vērum nōn dīcimus, nē audiāmus.** PUBLSYR
6. **omnia fēcī — sunt mihi dī testēs — ut tandem sānior essem.** OV M 9.541-2
7. **nōn ut edam vīvō, sed ut vīvam edō.** QUINT 9.3.85
8. **dēmus operam nē accipiāmus iniūriam.** SEN IRA 3.8.1

CHAPTER 46: GLOSSED LATIN TO ENGLISH SENTENCES

1. A. **cūr mē miseram** verberās?
   B. **ut misera sīs.** — verberō (1): beat — PLAUT AUL 42
2. vomunt **ut edant, edunt ut** vomant. — vomō (3): vomit — SEN AD HELV 10.3
3. **puerōs in** lūdum **mittunt ut discant quae nesciunt verba.** — lūdus, ī, m.: school — VARRO LL 9.15

CHAPTER 46: ENGLISH TO LATIN SENTENCES

1. Listen, woman, in order that you may know my opinion. PLAUT CIST 521
2. Be quiet therefore in order that you may hear. PLAUT EPID 241
3. For you leave all (things) in order that you may have this (thing). SEN E 76.27
4. I was sent hither in order that I might speak to you. PLAUT CAS 680-1

CHAPTER 46: PASSAGES

WISHY WASHY

nē laudet dignōs, laudat Callistratus omnēs.
   cuī malus est nēmō, quis bonus esse potest?

MART 12.80

NOTHING PERSONAL

cūr nōn mittō meōs tibi, Pontiliāne, libellōs?
   nē mihi tū mittās, Pontiliāne, tuōs.

MART 7.3

---

libellus, ī, m.: book

POORER BUT HAPPIER

ut puerōs **emeret, Labiēnus vendidit** hortōs.
   nīl nisi fīcētum **nunc Labiēnus habet.**

MART 12.33

---

puer, puerī, m.: (here) beautiful slave boy
hortī, ōrum, m. pl.: estate with gardens
fīcētum, ī, n.: fig farm (= a major case of hemorrhoids)

LIFE COACH

aliquis **vir bonus nōbīs** dīligendus **est ac semper ante oculōs habendus, ut sīc, tamquam illō spectante, vīvāmus et omnia, tamquam illō vidente, faciāmus.**

SEN E 11.8

---

aliquis, aliquid: some   dīligō, 3: select

ūnus nauta: Genitive/Dative Singular Only

A special group of adjectives receive their own chapter because they appear to act like old friends from the first and second declension (like **bonus, -a, -um**), and for the most part they do, except in the genitive and dative singular. Here, with no warning, they have the endings **-īus** and **-ī**. There are only ten of these adjectives in all of Latin, but they are very useful words that appear often. In fact, all of them, except for **ullus**, **uter**, and **uterque**, have appeared often in previous chapters. For completeness, the ten adjectives are as follows:

alius, alia, aliud	*(an)other*
alter, altera, alterum	*another (of two), a second*
neuter, neutra, neutrum	*neither (of two)*
nullus, nulla, nullum	*no, none*
sōlus, sōla, sōlum	*only, alone*
tōtus, tōta, tōtum	*whole*
ullus, ulla, ullum	*any*
ūnus, ūna, ūnum	*one*
uter, utra, utrum	*which (of two)*
uterque, utraque, utrumque	*each (of two)*

They can be remembered by the acrostic **ūnus nauta** (nine out of the ten at least). And their full declension goes like this:

Case	Singular			Plural		
	masc	*fem*	*neut*	*masc*	*fem*	*neut*
nominative	sōl-us	sōl-a	sōl-um	sōl-ī	sōl-ae	sōl-a
genitive	<u>sōl-īus</u>	<u>sōl-īus</u>	<u>sōl-īus</u>	sōl-ōrum	sōl-ārum	sōl-ōrum
dative	<u>sōl-ī</u>	<u>sōl-ī</u>	<u>sōl-ī</u>	sōl-īs	sōl-īs	sōl-īs
accusative	sōl-um	sōl-am	sōl-um	sōl-ōs	sōl-ās	sōl-a
ablative	sōl-ō	sōl-ā	sōl-ō	sōl-īs	sōl-īs	sōl-īs

Only the six underlined forms are unexpected, but they will cause problems. For one thing, the genitive singular in -**īus** may look like a second declension noun such as **filius** (nominative singular), and the dative singular in -**ī** can cause all sorts of problems.

Here are some examples using the genitive and dative:

ūnī gratiās agēbant.	They were giving thanks to one (man).	CIC PHIL 14.13
nullī dēbēre tē iūdicās?	Do you judge that you owe to no one?	SEN BEN 4.6.3
dat nēmō nisi alterī.	No one gives except to another.	SEN BEN 5.9.4
nōn dabō ullī quod accipere nōn poterit.	I will not give to anyone what he will not be able to receive.	SEN BEN 7.18.2

CHAPTER 47: VOCABULARY

alius, a, ud	(an)other
alius ... alius	one ... another; some ... other; different ... different
alter, altera, alterum	another (of two), a second
neuter, neutra, neutrum	neither (of two)
nullus, a, um	no, none
sōlus, a, um	only, alone
tōtus, a, um	whole
ullus, a, um	any
ūnus, a, um	one, alone
uter, utra, utrum	which (of two)
uterque, utraque, utrumque	each (of two)
postulō, postulāre, postulāvī, postulātus	demand
consulātus, ūs, m.	consulship
praemium, iī, n.	reward
prūdentia, ae, f.	wisdom

VOCABULARY NOTE The word **alius** is often used in combination with itself to form a very idiomatic pairing. There are various ways to translate this idiom:

---

aliud respondet, aliud putat.	He answers one thing; he thinks another.	SEN E 82.19
homō semper aliud, Fortūna aliud cōgitat.	A human always thinks one thing, Fortune another.	PUBLSYR H14
numquam aliud natūra, aliud sapientia dīcit.	Never does nature say one thing, wisdom another.	JUV 14.321
alia minōra, alia māiōra erunt.	Some (things) will be smaller, other (things) greater.	SEN E 71.33
aliud aliōs movet.	Different things move different people.	PLINY E 1.20.12

CHAPTER 47: LATIN TO ENGLISH SENTENCES

1. **nullī est hominī perpetuum bonum.** — PLAUT CURC 189
2. **nēmō sibi grātus est quī alterī nōn fuit.** — SEN E 81.21
3. **hoc nullīus praemiī spē faciam.** — CIC FAM 8.17.2
4. **sīc ūnīus virī prūdentiā Graecia līberata est.** — NEPOS 2.5.3
5. **omnia sunt excitanda tibi, Gaī Caesar, ūnī.** — CIC PRO MARC 23
6. **nullī aliī in hōc pectore locus fuit.** — QUINT DECL 332
7. **uterque suō studiō dēlectātus contempsit alterum.** — CIC DE OFF 1.4
8. **aliud aliī natura iter ostendit.** — SALL C 2.9
9. **nihil ā vōbīs nisi huius temporis tōtīusque meī consulātūs memoriam postulō.** — CIC IN CAT 4.23

CHAPTER 47: GLOSSED LATIN TO ENGLISH SENTENCES

1. **omnia utrīusque consilia ad concordiam spectāvērunt.** concordia, ae, f.: civic harmony CIC FAM 4.2.3

CHAPTER 47: ENGLISH TO LATIN SENTENCES

1. I praise each one (of two). — CIC ATT 13.3.1
2. Which side will conquer? — SEN TROAD 644
3. All things were in the power of one. — CIC FAM 13.19.1

CHAPTER 47: PASSAGES

FORTUNE FAVORS THE RICH TOO

habet Africānus mīliens, **tamen** captat.
Fortūna multīs dat nimis, satis nullī.

MART 12.10

---

mīliens: millions
captō (1): butter up rich, childless old people to change their wills

---

SEVEN BRIDES FOR PHILEROS

septima **iam, Phileros, tibi** conditur **uxor in** agrō.
    plūs nullī, Phileros, quam tibi reddit ager.

MART 10.43

---

septimus, a, um: seventh   condō (3): bury
ager, agrī, m.: (here) farm

DEPENDS ON WHAT YOU MEAN BY "OF"

librōs dīcimus esse Cicerōnis; eōsdem Dōrus librārius **suōs vocat, et utrumque vērum est — alter illōs tamquam** auctor **sibi, alter tamquam** emptor adserit; **ac rectē utrīusque dīcuntur esse; utrīusque enim sunt, sed nōn eōdem** modō. **sīc potest Titus Līvius a Dōrō accipere aut emere librōs suōs.**

SEN BEN 7.6.1

---

librārius, iī, m.: bookseller   auctor, auctōris, m.: author
emptor, emptōris, m.: buyer   adserō (3): claim
modus, ī, m.: manner

48

Result Clauses

Another very common use of the subjunctive is in the result clause. Like the purpose clause, result employs the subordinator **ut** with the subjunctive, either present or imperfect, in the subordinate clause. Thus, a result clause will often look much like a purpose clause. However, there are two differences: (1) The main clause of result will generally contain a "tip-off" word like "so" (**ita**, **tam**, or **sīc**), "such" (**tālis**), "so much" (**tantus**), or several others; and (2) the negative of a result clause is **nōn**, not **nē**.

Here are some examples; notice that the subjunctive can show either the potential result or, more unexpectedly, the actual result of an action:

nōn sum tam dēmens ut aegrotāre cupiam.　　　　　SEN E 67.4

　　　I am not so crazy that I (would) desire to be sick.

ita sum perturbātus ut omnia timērem.　　　　　CIC CLUENT 51

　　　I was so disturbed that I was (actually) fearing everything.

sunt ita multī ut eōs carcer capere nōn possit.　　　　　CIC IN CAT 2.22

　　　There are so many that the jail is not (actually) able to hold them.

Like the purpose clause construction, the result subjunctive can have either present or imperfect subjunctive depending on the tense of the introductory verb. In fact, the rule for result clauses is the same as that for purpose clauses:

▼　**If the verb of the main clause is in a past tense, use imperfect subjunctive.**

▼　**If the verb of the main clause is in any other tense, use present subjunctive.**

Note that the verbs **efficiō** and **accidō** and can take a result clause:

eādem nocte accidit ut esset lūna plēna.　　　　　CAES BG 4.29.1

　　　On the same night it happened that the moon was full.

effice ut ab omnibus et laudēmur et amēmur.　　　　　CIC ATT 1.15.1

　　　Bring about that we are both praised and loved by all.

CHAPTER 48: VOCABULARY

efficiō, efficere, effēcī, effectus	*render, bring about*
occīdō, occīdere, occīdī, occīsus	*kill*
dēterior, ius	*worse*
rūmor, rūmōris, m.	*rumor*
victōria, ae, f.	*victory*

CHAPTER 48: LATIN TO ENGLISH SENTENCES

1. **dīlige sīc aliōs ut sīs tibi cārus amīcus.**   CATO DISTICHS 1.11
2. **tālēs enim nōs esse putāmus ut iūre laudēmur.**   CIC DE OFF 1.91
3. **id mihi sīc erit grātum ut nulla rēs grātior esse possit.**   CIC ATT 16.16E.2
4. **bellum autem ita suscipiātur ut nihil aliud nisi pax quaesīta videātur.**   CIC DE OFF 1.80
5. **nōn ego effēcī ut occīderentur līberī tuī.**   [QUINT] DECL 11.7
6. **victōria autem ita incerta est ut dēterior causa parātior mihi esse videātur.**   CIC ATT 8.15.2
7. **illa sīc scripta sunt ut nē legantur quidem.**   CIC DE LEG 1.8

CHAPTER 48: GLOSSED LATIN TO ENGLISH SENTENCES

1. **nōn valet** tantum **animus ut sē ipse videat.**   tantum (adverb): so much   CIC TD 1.67
2. **habuī fīlium tam bonum ut illum amāre posset etiam** noverca.   noverca, ae, f.: step-mother   SENR C 9.6.6

CHAPTER 48: ENGLISH TO LATIN SENTENCES

1. Am I so great that I am able to rouse a rumor?   SEN E 43.1
2. In them there was so much authority that there was great hope.   NEPOS 13.3.2

49

Interrogative Pronoun and Adjective: **aliquis/ aliquī**

Although you may not realize it, you have been using the interrogative pronoun ever since chapter 1 when you learned the word **quid** and chapter 2 when you learned the word **quis**. Now it is time to learn the whole paradigm. The interrogative pronoun and adjective look a lot like the relative pronoun; in some cases, they are identical. However, the interrogative forms, as their name indicates, are used for questions. They usually occur at the beginning of a direct question, as in English, but may sometimes be delayed for emphasis. (This will change when we get to <u>indirect</u> questions, in chapter 50, which involve the subjunctive.)

The interrogative pronoun is usually translated with forms of "who?" in the masculine and feminine and "what?" in the neuter. The following table will show its forms. (Note that the masculine and feminine forms are identical; in most grammar books, they are written in one column.)

Case	Singular			Plural		
	masc	*fem*	*neut*	*masc*	*fem*	*neut*
nominative	quis	quis	quid	quī	quī	quae
genitive	cuius	cuius	cuius	quōrum	quōrum	quōrum
dative	cui	cui	cui	quibus	quibus	quibus
accusative	quem	quem	quid	quōs	quōs	quae
ablative	quō	quō	quō	quibus	quibus	quibus

Here are some examples, not using **quis** or **quid**:

cuius dūcit fīliam?	Whose daughter is he marrying?	PLAUT AUL 289
cuī mē reliquistī?	To whom have you left me?	[QUINT] DECL 6.7
quem fugis?	Whom do you flee?	VERG A 6.466
ā quibus ergō accipiēmus?	From whom therefore shall we receive?	SEN BEN 2.18.3

INTERROGATIVE ADJECTIVE

The interrogative adjective, as its name indicates, is an adjective, and as such will always modify a noun. It is translated "what?" and its forms are identical to those of the relative pronoun:

Case	Singular			Plural		
	masc	*fem*	*neut*	*masc*	*fem*	*neut*
nominative	qui(s)	quae	quod	quī	quae	quae
genitive	cuius	cuius	cuius	quōrum	quārum	quōrum
dative	cui	cui	cui	quibus	quibus	quibus
accusative	quem	quam	quod	quōs	quās	quae
ablative	quō	quā	quō	quibus	quibus	quibus

You might be wondering how to distinguish the relative pronoun from the interrogative adjective, since the forms are identical. In practice, this is not usually a problem: The interrogative adjective is generally the first word of a sentence, its noun tends to be nearby, and the sentence will either be a question or an exclamation. The relative pronoun scarcely ever meets all three of those conditions.

Here are some reassuring examples of the interrogative adjective:

quod verbum audiō?	What word do I hear?	TER AND 240
quem ego hominem accūsō?	What person am I accusing?	CIC VER 4.104
quae haec est miseria?	What misery is this?	TER ADEL 555
quō iūre prohibētur?	By what right is it prohibited?	QUINT DECL 344

ALIQUIS/ALIQUI

Closely related to the interrogative pronoun and its adjective form are the indefinite pronoun **aliquis** and its adjective **aliquī**. The pronoun means "someone" or "something" and the adjective means "some." They are formed from the interrogative pronoun and adjective with the prefix **ali-**, which indicates "some." First the pronoun forms:

Case	Singular			Plural		
	masc	*fem*	*neut*	*masc*	*fem*	*neut*
nominative	ali-quis	ali-qua	ali-quid	ali-quī	ali-quae	ali-qua
genitive	ali-cuius	ali-cuius	ali-cuius	ali-quōrum	ali-quārum	ali-quōrum
dative	ali-cui	ali-cui	ali-cui	ali-quibus	ali-quibus	ali-quibus
accusative	ali-quem	ali-quam	ali-quid	ali-quōs	ali-quās	ali-qua
ablative	ali-quō	ali-quā	ali-quō	ali-quibus	ali-quibus	ali-quibus

Now the adjective forms:

Case	Singular			Plural		
	masc	*fem*	*neut*	*masc*	*fem*	*neut*
nominative	ali-quī	ali-qua	ali-quod	ali-quī	ali-quae	ali-qua
genitive	ali-cuius	ali-cuius	ali-cuius	ali-quōrum	ali-quārum	ali-quōrum
dative	ali-cui	ali-cui	ali-cui	ali-quibus	ali-quibus	ali-quibus
accusative	ali-quem	ali-quam	ali-quod	ali-quōs	ali-quās	ali-qua
ablative	ali-quō	ali-quā	ali-quō	ali-quibus	ali-quibus	ali-quibus

Here are some examples of each:

scribe aliquid magnum.	Write something great.	MART 1.107.2
aliquis ūnō teste contentus est.	Someone is content with one witness.	SENR C 7.5.1
nōn omnēs hominēs aliquō errōre dūcuntur?	Are not all human beings led by some error?	PLINY E 9.12.1

CHAPTER 49: VOCABULARY

quis, quis, quid	*(pronoun) who? what?*
qui(s), quae, quod	*(adjective) what?*
aliquis, aliquid	*(pronoun) someone, something*
aliquī, aliqua, aliquod	*(adjective) some*

cēna, ae, f.	*dinner*
frater, fratris, m.	*brother*
princeps, principis, m.	*emperor*
sub	*(prep. + abl.) under*

CHAPTER 49: PRACTICE SENTENCES (ANSWERS FOLLOW CHAPTER 66)

1. **aliquid dīcendum est.** QUINT 7.1.37
2. **quae tibi manet vīta?** CATULLUS 8.15
3. **quae causa lacrimārum est?** QUINT DECL 267
4. **quō nōs vocābis nōmine?** PLAUT ASIN 652
5. **mē esse aliquid putāvī.** PLINY E 1.23.2
6. **quis tenet mentem furor?** SEN PHOEN 557
7. To whom is life not torture? SEN QN 5.18.15
8. Anger has some pleasure. SEN IRA 2.32.1
9. I believe that you heard something. CIC FAM 2.13.2

CHAPTER 49: LATIN TO ENGLISH SENTENCES

1. **cuī nōn est mors ūna satis?** PETR 108.14.7
2. **sub quō lībertās principe tanta fuit?** MART 5.19.6
3. **fratrem suum potuit aliquis occīdere?** QUINT DECL 321
4. **quod verbum aurēs meās tetigit?** PLAUT POEN1375-6
5. **damnātus est aliquis, accusante tē.** QUINT DECL 268
6. **ō fīlī, in quibus tē malīs reliquī?** [QUINT] DECL 6.17
7. **quam hic nōn amāvit meretrīcem?** TER ADEL 149
8. **aliquid gaudeō discere ut doceam.** SEN E 6.4
9. **nēmō contrā sē dīcit nisi aliquō cōgente.** QUINT DECL 314
10. **quam rem publicam habēmus? in quā urbe vīvimus?** CIC IN CAT 1.9

CHAPTER 49: ENGLISH TO LATIN SENTENCES

1. What cause drove the fellow into crime?   QUINT DECL 312
2. Whom, he says, shall I invite to the dinner?   TER AND 453
3. Therefore, they are worthy of some punishment.   QUINT DECL 339
4. However, what place will be safe for us?   CIC ATT 8.3.5

CHAPTER 49: PASSAGES

SNOWY WHITES

Thāis habet nigrōs, niveōs **Laecānia** dentēs.
    quae ratiō est? emptōs haec **habet,** illa **suōs.**

MART 5.43

---

niger, gra, grum: black	niveus, a, um: snowy-white
dens, dentis, m.: tooth	haec ... illa: the latter ... the former

---

HOW ARE THE MIGHTY FALLEN!

Seiānus ducitur uncō **spectandus; gaudent omnēs.** "**quae** labra, **quis illī**
vultus **erat! numquam,** sī quid **mihi crēdis, amāvī
hunc hominem. sed quō cecidit** sub **crīmine?**"

JUV 10.66-9

---

uncus, ī, m.: hook	labrum, ī, n.: lip
vultus, ūs, m.: face, look	sī quid: if at all
sub: (prep. + abl.) under	

---

50 Perfect/Pluperfect Subjunctive/Indirect Questions

The last two tenses of the subjunctive are the perfect and pluperfect. This brings the total number of subjunctive tenses to four versus six for indicative. Latin has no subjunctive in the future or future perfect. (You can amuse yourself by speculating why "future" and "subjunctive" are inimical to each other as long as you don't get confused.) This is a good thing—only four tenses of subjunctive to remember.

Here is another good thing: Like the imperfect subjunctive, the perfect and pluperfect subjunctive have the same formation for all verbs, regardless of conjugation. The following formula will fit all verbs, even irregular verbs like **sum**:

▼ **To form the perfect active subjunctive, add the endings**

-erim	-erīmus
-erīs	-erītis
-erit	-erint

to the perfect stem.

Here is the table; as always, no translation is offered for any subjunctive:

Perfect Active Subjunctive

amāverim	habuerim	dixerim	cēperim	audīverim	fuerim
amāverīs	habuerīs	dixerīs	cēperis	audīverīs	fueris
amāverit	habuerit	dixerit	cēperit	audīverit	fuerit
amāverimus	habuerīmus	dixerīmus	cēperīmus	audīverimus	fuerīmus
amāveritis	habuerītis	dixerītis	cēperītis	audīveritis	fuerītis
amāverint	habuerint	dixerint	cēperint	audīverint	fuerint

(You are probably noticing that the perfect active subjunctive is nearly identical to the future perfect indicative, except for the first-person singular. This is a distressing fact of Latin grammar; from now on, you must scrutinize the context to see if a perfect subjunctive is called for or if the form could be future perfect. It is sometimes a difficult call.)

The pluperfect active subjunctive is distinguished by the infix -**isse**-. This makes it easy to recognize, although to translate it will require further analysis:

▼ **To form the pluperfect active subjunctive, add the endings**

–issem	–issēmus
–issēs	–issētis
–isset	–issent

to the perfect stem.

Here is the table:

Pluperfect Active Subjunctive

amāvissem	habuissem	dixissem	cēpissem	audīvissem	fuissem
amāvissēs	habuissēs	dixissēs	cēpissēs	audīvissēs	fuissēs
amāvisset	habuisset	dixisset	cēpisset	audīvisset	fuisset
amāvissēmus	habuissēmus	dixissēmus	cēpissēmus	audīvissēmus	fuissēmus
amāvissētis	habuissētis	dixissētis	cēpissētis	audīvissētis	fuissētis
amāvissent	habuissent	dixissent	cēpissent	audīvissent	fuissent

The perfect passive subjunctive is also formed the same for all verbs according to the following formula:

▼ **To form the perfect passive subjunctive,**
   combine the present subjunctive of sum

sim	sīmus
sis	sītis
sit	sint

with the perfect passive participle.

Here is the table:

Perfect Passive Subjunctive

amātus sim	habitus sim	dictus sim	captus sim	audītus sim
amātus sīs	habitus sīs	dictus sīs	captus sīs	audītus sīs
amātus sit	habitus sit	dictus sit	captus sit	audītus sit
amātī sīmus	habitī sīmus	dictī sīmus	captī sīmus	audītī sīmus
amātī sītis	habitī sītis	dictī sītis	captī sītis	audītī sītis
amātī sint	habitī sint	dictī sint	captī sint	audītī sint

(There is of course no passive of the verb **sum**.)

The pluperfect passive subjunctive is also formed the same for all verbs according to the following formula:

▼ **To form the pluperfect passive subjunctive, combine the imperfect subjunctive of sum**

> essem essēmus
> essēs essētis
> esset essent

with the perfect passive participle.

Here is the table:

Pluperfect Passive Subjunctive

amātus essem	habitus essem	dictus essem	captus essem	audītus essem
amātus essēs	habitus essēs	dictus essēs	captus essēs	audītus essēs
amātus esset	habitus esset	dictus esset	captus esset	audītus esset
amātī essēmus	habitī essēmus	dictī essēmus	captī essēmus	audītī essēmus
amātī essētis	habitī essētis	dictī essētis	captī essētis	audītī essētis
amātī essent	habitī essent	dictī essent	captī essent	audītī essent

INDIRECT QUESTION

So far you have dealt exclusively with _direct_ questions; you have been carefully shielded from any <u>indirect</u> questions. That is, all questions so far have begun with an interrogative word—like **ubi** or **quid** or **quis**—and required a question mark such as these:

ubi est?	Where is he?	PLAUT STICH 326
quid dīcis?	What are you saying?	QUINT DECL 286
quid ēgistī?	What have you done?	TER PHOR 682

Now that you have been presented with all tenses of the subjunctive, you are ready for the indirect forms of such questions, namely the following:

dic ubi sit.	Say where he is.	OV M 8.861
sciō quid dīcas.	I know what you are saying.	SEN AD MARC 16.1
quid ēgeris nesciō.	I do not know what you have done.	CIC FAM 14.4.4

In this construction there are similarities between Latin and English. Both contain introductory verbs, like "Say," "I know," and "I do not know"; both have interrogative words in mid-sentence; and both drop the question mark at the end, thus making the designation "indirect <u>question</u>" somewhat puzzling. However, the examples show clearly enough why the terminology is appropriate. An indirect question is simply a direct question that has been recast to follow an introductory verb or clause. The difference is that in English—but <u>not</u> in Latin—we invert the subject and predicate: The direct question "Where is he?" (predicate precedes subject) becomes "Say where he is" (subject precedes predicate). In Latin, the verb becomes subjunctive, as you can see in the examples.

The subjunctive in an indirect question is <u>not</u> to be translated with "let" or "may" or "might" or any sort of subjunctive marker. Instead it is properly rendered in English with a simple indicative. In the examples, the subjunctive **sit** is translated "is," the subjunctive **dicās** is translated "you are saying," and the subjunctive **ēgeris** is translated "you have done." In fact, here is a valuable tip for translating the subjunctive part of an indirect question:

▼ **The subjunctive verb in an indirect question can be translated as if it were indicative.**

Examine the three examples; in each one the subjunctive is properly translated as though the verb were indicative. Here are some more examples of indirect questions; notice how in every case the subjunctive can be translated as if it were indicative:

nōn scīs quis ego sim?	Do you not know who I am?	PLAUT MEN 302
nesciō quid scrīpserim.	I do not know what I wrote/have written.	SENR C 1.7.16
dīcam tamen quid sentiam.	Nevertheless, I will say what I feel.	SEN E 16.2

sciēbam quid meruissem.	I knew what I had deserved.	PETR 132.4
quaerunt ā mē ubi sit pecūnia.	They inquire of me where the money is.	CIC CLUENT 72
quīn dīcis quid factūrus sīs?	Why don't you say what you are going to do?	PLAUT PERS 144

BEWARE: This translation tip applies only to indirect questions, not to any other uses of the subjunctive!

CHAPTER 50: VOCABULARY

utrum ... an — ... or (signals two-pronged question)

CHAPTER 50: PRACTICE SENTENCES (ANSWERS FOLLOW CHAPTER 66)

1.	**sciō enim cuī scrībam.**	CIC FAM 11.10.2
2.	**rogābis mē ubi sit.**	PLAUT BACC 189
3.	**videō quid ēgerim.**	CIC VER 1.35
4.	**quid fēcerim narrābō.**	CIC DE ORAT 2.198
5.	**disce quid sit vīvere.**	TER HT 971
6.	**cūr ego nōn timuerim quaeris?**	CIC DOMO SUA 8
7.	**nōn sentit quam male dormiat.**	PUBLSYR
8.	I do not know where I am.	PLAUT CAS 413
9.	You know well to whom I am speaking.	OV TRIST 1.5.7
10.	Let us inquire what the good is.	SEN E 118.8
11.	We see what happened to Marcus Crassus.	CIC DE DIVIN 1.29

CHAPTER 50: LATIN TO ENGLISH SENTENCES

1.	**quid dīceret nēmō intellēgebat.**	SEN APOCO 6.2
2.	**audī quid mē in épistulā tuā dēlectāverit.**	SEN E 59.4
3.	**nescīs, insāne, nescīs quantās vīrēs virtus habeat.**	CIC PARADOX 17
4.	**nōn quī fuerīmus sed quī nunc sīmus vidē.**	PHAEDR APP 29.10
5.	**omnis diēs, omnis hōra quam nihil sīmus ostendit.**	SEN E 101.1
6.	**dīc nōbīs ubi sīs futurus.**	CATULLUS 55.15
7.	**nēmō quam bene vīvat sed quam diu cūrat.**	SEN E 22.17

8. **ad tē statim mittēmus ut sciās ubi sīmus.**   CIC ATT 3.22.1

9. **nēmō tamen scīit utrum servus essem an līber.**   PETR 57.9

10. **videāmus quid sit causa mortis.**   QUINT DECL 270

CHAPTER 50: GLOSSED LATIN TO ENGLISH SENTENCES

1. **cōgitō mēcum quam multī corpora** exerceant, **ingenia quam paucī.**   SEN E 80.2

   exerceō, 2, exercuī, exercitus: exercise

CHAPTER 50: ENGLISH TO LATIN SENTENCES

1. Now I know what love is.   VERG E 8.43

2. Do you not know what has been done?   TER AND 791

3. I will say what ruined you (plural).   OV AA 3.41

4. He did not know who had killed his master.   QUINT DECL 328

5. I will teach what faults have to be avoided.   AUCHER 1.11

CHAPTER 50: PASSAGES

PEN PAL

nesciō tam multīs quid **scrībās, Fauste, puellīs:**
   hoc sciō, quod **scrībit nulla puella tibi.**

MART 11.64

---

quid: (here) why   quod: (here) that

THEY WERE ALWAYS CLOSE

quārē **nōn habeat, Fabulle, quaeris**
uxōrem Themisōn? habet sorōrem.

MART 12.20

---

quārē: why   soror, sorōris, m.: sister

WHY I LOVE MY FARM

quid mihi reddat ager **quaeris, Line,** Nōmentānus?
    hoc mihi reddit ager – **tē, Line, nōn videō.**

MART 2.38

---

ager, agrī, m.: farm   Nōmentānus, a, um: near Nomentum

NEW FIELDS TO PLOW

Artemidōrus habet puerum sed vendidit agrum;
    agrum **prō puerō Calliodōrus habet.**
dīc uter ex istīs melius rem gesserit, Aucte –
    Artemidōrus amat, Calliodōrus arat.

MART 9.21

---

ager, agrī, m.: farm   arō (1): plow

You were first introduced to the word **cum** in chapter 5; it was a preposition meaning "with." Later, in chapter 24, you discovered the same word can also be a conjunction meaning "when." In this chapter, you will learn that as a conjunction **cum** can govern the subjunctive, and when it does, it may bear the meaning "when," "since," or "although," depending on the context. See these examples:

etiam cum valērent, lēgēs vincēbantur.	Even when they were strong, the laws were being conquered.	TAC ANN 2.51
cum dare nōn possem mūnera, verba dabam.	Since I was not able to give gifts, I was giving words.	OV AA 2.166
cum timēret Othō, timēbātur.	Although Otho was fearing, he was feared.	TAC HIST 1.81

(A tip for translating the subjunctive in a **cum** clause: Treat the subjunctive as though it were indicative and proceed accordingly.)

Note: **cum** can still govern the indicative, as it has since chapter 24, but with this difference in nuance—**cum** with the indicative indicates an exact time "when"; **cum** with the subjunctive indicates the circumstances surrounding an event. Here are some examples:

cum tū es līber, gaudeō.	When you are free, I rejoice.	PLAUT MEN 1148
cum haec legēs, habēbimus consulēs.	When you will read these things, we will have consuls.	CIC ATT 5.12.2
cum vidēbis, tum sciēs.	When you will see, then you will know.	PLAUT BACC 145

CHAPTER 51: VOCABULARY

cum	*(+ subjunctive) when, since, although*

CHAPTER 51: LATIN TO ENGLISH SENTENCES

1. **id faciō quod pater meus fēcit cum iuvenis esset.**   SENR C 2.6.11
2. **miserrimum est timēre cum spērēs nihil.**   SEN TROAD 425
3. **cum possideant plūrima, plūra petunt.**   OV F 1.212
4. **cum tē tam multī peterent, tū mē ūna petistī.**   PROP 2.20.27
5. **nōn sumus in ullīus potestāte, cum mors in nostrā**   SEN E 91.21
   potestāte sit.
6. **multa, cum essem consul, dē summīs reī publicae**   CIC PRO SULLA 14
   perīculīs audīvī.
7. **cūr, cum inimīcī nōs essēmus, vōs amīcī fuistis?**   [QUINT] DECL 9.15
8. **nōn sentiō in animō aetātis iniūriam, cum sentiam**   SEN E 26.2
   in corpore.
9. **cum accūsātus esset, facile eō iūdiciō līberātus est.**   CIC VER 2.68

CHAPTER 51: ENGLISH TO LATIN SENTENCES

1. For it is difficult to be silent when you are hurting.   CIC PRO SULLA 31
2. I came to you although I had a rich father.   SENR C 1.1.2
3. I was in so great tortures when I was writing these things.   PLINY E 8.23.8
4. Although Hannibal is in Italy, you are preparing to leave Italy? LIVY 28.42.20

CHAPTER 51: PASSAGES

NOT SO DUMB AFTER ALL

cum faciās versūs nullā nōn **lūce** ducēnōs,
    Vāre, nihil recitās. nōn sapis, **atque** sapis.

MART 8.20

---

versus, ūs, m.: verse   nullus nōn: (idiom) every
ducēnī, ae, a: 200 at a time   sapiō (3): have sense
recitō (1): recite

---

52 ferō

One of the most common verbs in Latin is the slightly irregular **ferō**, which means "carry," "bring," or "bear." It is found not only in the simple form, but also compounded with many prepositions such as **adferō, conferō, deferō, inferō, perferō, proferō**, and more. Sometimes the translation of these compounds is quite straightforward. **adferō** can mean "bring to," **perferō** can mean "carry through," **proferō** can mean "carry forward," and so forth. Sometimes, however, they acquire other meanings that seem to have wandered away from what you would expect. Since **ferō** and its compounds are so ubiquitous, the subject requires a special chapter.

The following tables will show the various forms of **ferō**. Most of them are what you would expect of a regular third conjugation verb. For example, the imperfect and future forms have no irregularities. The anomalous forms are only in the present tense; they are underlined for clarity:

Present Indicative

Active		Passive	
ferō	ferimus	feror	ferimur
fers	fertis	ferris	feriminī
fert	ferunt	fertur	feruntur

Present Imperative

fer	ferte	–	–

Present Infinitive

ferre		ferrī	

In the rest of its conjugation, **ferō** is perfectly regular. It acts just like a normal third conjugation verb. For completeness, here are the remaining forms of **ferō**:

Imperfect Indicative

Active		Passive	
ferēbam	ferēbāmus	ferēbar	ferēbāmur
ferēbās	ferēbātis	ferēbāris	ferēbāminī
ferēbat	ferēbant	ferēbātur	ferēbāntur

Future Indicative

feram	ferēmus	ferar	ferēmur
ferēs	ferētis	ferēris	ferēminī
feret	ferent	ferētur	ferentur

Present Subjunctive

Active		Passive	
feram	ferāmus	ferar	ferāmur
ferās	ferātis	ferāris	ferāminī
ferat	ferant	ferātur	ferantur

Imperfect Subjunctive

ferrem	ferrēmus	ferrer	ferrēmur
ferrēs	ferrētis	ferrēris	ferrēminī
ferret	ferrent	ferrētur	ferrentur

I omit the perfect system of **ferō** since it too is perfectly regular; the only odd thing is that its perfect form is **tulī** and the perfect passive participle is **lātus**.

In all types of Latin, **ferō** and its compounds are very common. Here are some examples:

pācem ad vōs ferō.	I bring peace to you.	PLAUT AMPH 32
quid fers? dīc mihi.	What are you bringing? Tell me.	PLAUT MERC 161
quō ferimur?	Where are we being carried?	SENR S 1.15
ferte fortiter.	Bear (it) bravely.	SEN PROV 6.6
nōn poterō ferre hoc.	I will not be able to bear this (thing).	TER HEC 133

ferendum hoc quidem nōn est.   This (thing) is not to be borne.   CIC VER 1.66

CHAPTER 52: VOCABULARY

ferō, ferre, tulī, lātus   *carry, bring, bear*

cubiculum, ī, n.   *bedroom*
praeter   *(prep. + acc.) except for, beyond*

CHAPTER 52: PRACTICE SENTENCES (ANSWERS FOLLOW CHAPTER 66)

1. **tulit dolōrem ut vir.**   CIC TD 2.53
2. **quod dī dant ferō.**   PLAUT AUL 88
3. **bene ferre magnam disce fortūnam.**   HOR O 3.27.74-5
4. **ferimus quae possumus arma.**   OV F 2.9
5. **stultī timent Fortūnam, sapientēs ferunt.**   PUBLSYR S6
6. (My) father was bearing arms.   OV HER 8.89
7. I am not able to bear love.   [QUINT] DECL 14.8
8. I am not able to bear these things nor will I bear (them).   CIC ATT 7.2.7

CHAPTER 52: LATIN TO ENGLISH SENTENCES

1. **ferte miserō atque innocentī auxilium.**   TER ADEL 155
2. **quis tē feret praeter mē, quī omnia ferre possum?**   CIC FAM 7.13.1
3. **vēnī ut auxilium feram.**   PLAUT AMPH 870
4. **ut tū Fortūnam, sīc nōs tē, Celse, ferēmus.**   HOR E 1.8.17
5. **eius avāritiam cīvēs Rōmānī ferre nōn potuērunt.**   CIC VER 1.70
6. **haec ferenda nōn erant.**   CIC ATT 8.14.2
7. **contrā mē arma tulit et eum bellō cēpī.**   CIC FAM 5.10A.1
8. **quod acerbum fuit ferre, tulisse iūcundum est.**   SEN E 78.14
9. **quō feror insānus?**   OV AA 3.667
10. **sed tamen ferēs hoc ipsum quod scrībō ut omnia mea fers ac tulistī.**   CIC ATT 12.41.2

CHAPTER 52: GLOSSED LATIN TO ENGLISH SENTENCES

1. **nōn possum ferre,** Quirītēs, **Graecam urbem.**   Quirītēs, ium: Romans   JUV 3.60-1
2. **vitium uxōris aut** tollendum **aut ferendum est.** tollō, 3: remove   AG 1.17
3. **omnēs** nātiōnēs **servitūtem ferre possunt; nostra cīvitās nōn potest.**   CIC PHIL 10.20

   nātio, nātiōnis, f.: nation

CHAPTER 52: ENGLISH TO LATIN SENTENCES

1. (Your) father ordered us to bring this silver to you.   PLAUT ASIN 732-3
2. I will bravely bear my fortune.   SENR C 2.1.16
3. A good soldier will bear wounds.   SEN VIT BEAT 15.5
4. He was carried into the bedroom from the dinner.   SEN E 12.8
5. Roman citizens had borne arms against the Roman people.   [CAES] BEL AFR 97.1

53

volō/nōlō/mālō

As often happens, words for common things are irregular. This is true of the very common words **volō**, "want," **nōlō**, "not want," and the less common **mālō**, "prefer." Although it is not immediately obvious, the three are in fact related. **nōlō** is a contraction of **nōn + volō** ("not want") and **mālō** is a contraction of **magis + volō** ("more want"). Thus, if you learn **volō** thoroughly, the other two will be easier to recognize.

As you can see from the following list, the principal parts of these verbs are connected:

volō	velle	voluī	–	*want*
nōlō	nolle	noluī	–	*not want*
mālō	malle	māluī	–	*want more, prefer*

Notice the lack of a fourth principal part; these verbs have no passive forms. (In fact, as a general rule, verbs that lack a fourth principal part do not have passive forms.)

In the tables that follow, the irregular forms are underlined. As you can see, these irregulars occur only in the present tense. Elsewhere, the verbs behave like regular third conjugation verbs:

volō		nōlō		mālō	
Present Tense					
volō	I want	nōlō	I don't want	mālō	I prefer
<u>vīs</u>	you want	<u>nōn vīs</u>	you don't want	<u>māvīs</u>	you prefer
<u>vult</u>	s/he wants	<u>nōn vult</u>	s/he doesn't want	<u>māvult</u>	s/he prefers
<u>volumus</u>	we want	<u>nōlumus</u>	we don't want	<u>mālumus</u>	we prefer
<u>vultis</u>	you want	<u>nōn vultis</u>	you don't want	<u>māvultis</u>	you prefer
volunt	they want	nōlunt	they don't want	mālunt	they prefer

volō		nōlō		mālō	
Imperfect Tense					
volēbam	I wanted	**nōlēbam**	I didn't want	**mālēbam**	I prefered
volēbās	you wanted	**nōlēbas**	you didn't want	**mālēbās**	you prefered
volēbat	s/he wanted	**nōlēbat**	s/he didn't want	**mālēbat**	s/he prefered
volēbāmus	we wanted	**nōlēbāmus**	we didn't want	**mālēbāmus**	we prefered
volēbātis	you wanted	**nōlēbātis**	you didn't want	**mālēbātis**	you prefered
volēbant	they wanted	**nōlēbant**	they didn't want	**malēbant**	they prefered
Future Tense					
volam	I will want	**nōlam**	I will not want	**mālam**	I will prefer
volēs	you will want	**nōlēs**	you will not want	**mālēs**	you will prefer
volet	s/he will want	**nōlet**	s/he will not want	**mālet**	s/he will prefer
volēmus	we will want	**nōlēmus**	we will not want	**mālēmus**	we will prefer
volētis	you will want	**nōlētis**	you will not want	**mālētis**	you will prefer
volent	they will want	**nōlent**	they will not want	**mālent**	they will prefer

The irregular present and imperfect subjunctive forms are as follows; as usual, no translation is offered:

Present Subjunctive Forms

velim	nōlim	mālim
velīs	nōlīs	mālīs
velit	nōlit	mālit
velīmus	nōlīmus	mālīmus
velītis	nōlītis	mālītis
velint	nōlint	mālint

Imperfect Subjunctive Forms

vellem	nollem	mallem
vellēs	nollēs	mallēs
vellet	nollet	mallet
vellēmus	nollēmus	mallēmus
vellētis	nollētis	mallētis
vellent	nollent	mallent

The perfect and pluperfect subjunctive forms are formed regularly:

Perfect Subjunctive Forms

voluerim	nōluerim	māluerim
voluerīs	nōluerīs	māluerīs
voluerit	nōluerit	māluerit
voluerīmus	nōluerīmus	māluerīmus
voluerītis	nōluerītis	māluerītis
voluerint	nōluerint	māluerint

Pluperfect Subjunctive Forms

voluissem	nōluissem	māluissem
voluissēs	nōluissēs	māluissēs
voluisset	nōluisset	māluisset
voluissēmus	nōluissēmus	māluissēmus
voluissētis	nōluissētis	māluissētis
voluissent	nōluissent	māluissent

Here are some examples of **volō** and **nōlō**:

ego tē facere hoc volō.	I want you to do this.	PLAUT BACC 93
amīcum habēre vult.	He wants to have a friend.	SEN E 9.3
frater, faciam ut tū volēs.	Brother, I will do as you will want.	PLAUT MEN 1152
nōs dēcipī nōluit.	He did not want us to be deceived.	SEN E 30.10

NŌLŌ IN NEGATIVE COMMANDS

So far in this book, all commands have been positive, using the imperative form of the verb. That was because negative commands are usually formed by using the imperative of **nōlō** with an infinitive. In effect, you are saying "Do not want to …" rather than "Do not …" Here are some examples:

nōlī timēre.	Do not fear.	SEN E 12.10
nōlīte mihi dare praemia.	Do not give me rewards.	QUINT DECL 315

HOW TO USE MĀLŌ

The verb **mālō** is a contraction from **magis volō**, meaning "want more." Thus, to the Roman, it naturally goes with the word **quam**, meaning "than." Here are some examples of **mālō** that show its use with **quam**. If you think of the two as meaning "want more … than" you can perhaps get from there to "prefer":

vincī quam vincere māluit.   SEN BEN 4.32.2
> He wanted more to be conquered than to conquer.

esse quam vidērī bonus mālēbat.   SALL C 54.6
> He wanted more to be than to seem good.

accipere tū nōn mavīs quam ego dare.   PLAUT POEN 706
> You do not want more to receive than I (want) to give.

(Notice that this is one Latin construction where the meaning depends on the word order.)

CHAPTER 53: VOCABULARY

volō, velle, voluī, —	*want*
nōlō, nolle, nōluī, —	*not want*
mālō, malle, māluī, —	*prefer*

CHAPTER 53: PRACTICE SENTENCES (ANSWERS FOLLOW CHAPTER 66)

1. **iam faciam quod vultis.** — HOR S 1.1.16
2. **dīcant quod volunt.** — AUG CD 9.23
3. **id tē scīre voluī.** — CIC ATT 1.6.1
4. **nōlī haec contemnere.** — CIC CAEC DIV 39
5. **crēde quod māvīs.** — SEN E 13.13
6. **ea quae tū vīs volō.** — PLAUT EPID 265
7. **dīcit sē velle dūcere uxōrem.** — PLINY E 4.2.6
8. **dominum mūtāre, nōn līber esse vult.** — CIC PARADOX 41
9. **servīre quam pugnāre māvult.** — CIC ATT 7.15.2
10. I don't want to say more (things). — AUCHER 4.67
11. I have said what I was wanting. — PLAUT POEN 1231
12. I did not want to give a favor. — SEN E 81.5
13. We want the Roman people to be free. — CIC PHIL 11.3
14. They can do these things but they don't want to. — SEN E 104.26

CHAPTER 53: LATIN TO ENGLISH SENTENCES

1. **libenter hominēs id quod volunt crēdunt.** — CAES BG 3.18.6
2. **dūcunt volentem fāta, nōlentem trahunt.** — SEN E 107.11
3. **sī vultis nihil timēre, cōgitāte omnia esse metuenda.** — SEN QN 6.2.3
4. **quid est sapientia? semper idem velle atque idem nolle.** — SEN E 20.5
5. **quid tibi vīs, insāne? meōs sentīre furōrēs?** — PROP 1.5.3
6. **sed, amīce magne, nōlī hanc epistulam Atticō ostendere.** — CIC FAM 7.29.2
7. **audiō tē dīcentem, "mālō glōriam quam vitam."** — SENR C 1.8.2
8. **utrum māvīs habēre multum an satis?** — SEN E 119.6
9. **incerta prō certīs, bellum quam pācem mālēbant.** — SALL C 17.6
10. **paucī lībertātem, pars magna iūstōs dominōs volunt.** — SALL HIST IV.69.18

CHAPTER 53: GLOSSED LATIN TO ENGLISH SENTENCES

1. dēsināmus **quod voluimus velle.**   dēsinō (3): cease   SEN E 61.1

2. propter **amōrem uxōrem nōlet dūcere.**   propter: (prep. + acc.) because of   TER AND 155

CHAPTER 53: ENGLISH TO LATIN SENTENCES

1. The gods want me unharmed and preserved.   PLAUT TRIN 1076
2. He preferred to be an enemy (rather) than a friend.   CIC PHIL 5.3
3. You don't know what you want.   SEN E 21.1
4. I do not want you to be deceived.   SEN E 37.1
5. He preferred to be under the Romans (rather) than under a king.   LIVY 42.30.5

CHAPTER 53: PASSAGES

IMAGE PROBLEM OR PRETTY PETTY

bellus **homō et magnus vīs īdem, Cotta, vidērī;**
    sed quī bellus **homō est, Cotta, pusillus homō est.**

MART 1.9

---

bellus, a, um: pretty   pusillus, a, um: petty

KEEP ME WAITING—BUT NOT TOO LONG

Galla, negā – satiātur **amor nisi gaudia torquent;**
    sed nōlī nimium, Galla, negāre diu.

MART 4.38

---

satiō (1): sate   nimium: too

TO A CRITIC

cum tua nōn ēdās, carpis **mea carmina, Laelī.**
  carpere **vel nōlī nostra vel** ēde **tua.**

MART 1.91

ēdō (3): publish   carpō (3): bash

YOU NEVER KNOW WHERE IT'S BEEN

bāsia **dās aliīs, aliīs dās, Postume,** dextram.
  dīcis **"utrum māvīs? ēlige." mālō manum.**

MART 2.21

---

bāsium, iī, n.: kiss   dextra, ae, f.: right hand
ēligō (3): choose

---

54 iste

As you near the end of this book, you are probably thinking that Latin had run out of words for "this" and "that." Regretfully, there is one more—a very common one, especially in spoken Latin. The demonstrative **iste** means "that" but with a twist. It imparts an emphasis that can either be positive or negative, depending on the context. For example, Cicero may refer to his opponent with forms of **iste**—in this case the word has a pejorative meaning (which I try to bring out in these idiomatic translations):

quid sibi iste vult?	What does that guy think he's doing?	CIC CAEC DIV 69
quandō iste sententiam dicere audēbit?	When will "our friend" dare to say an opinion?	CIC VER 2.76
nihil iam in istam mulierem dīcō.	I say nothing now against that woman.	CIC PRO CAEL 38

But the same word, in a different context, can show a proprietary interest in its object which conveys fondness or approval. For example:

istam amō.	I love that girl.	PLAUT ASIN 845
iste liber meus est.	That book is mine.	MART 11.2.8
laudant illa sed ista legunt.	They praise those things but they read those things.	MART 4.49.10

In the last example, Martial is contrasting the praised but unread books (**illa**) with the books people actually read—his (**ista**).

Here is the declension of **iste**:

case	singular			plural		
	masc	*fem*	*neut*	*masc*	*fem*	*neut*
nom	<u>iste</u>	ista	<u>istud</u>	istī	istae	ista
gen	<u>istīus</u>	<u>istīus</u>	<u>istīus</u>	istōrum	istārum	istōrum
dat	<u>istī</u>	<u>istī</u>	<u>istī</u>	istīs	istīs	istīs
acc	istum	istam	istud	istōs	istās	ista
abl	istō	istā	istō	istīs	istīs	istīs

The underlined forms show divergences from the **bonus, -a, -um** paradigm. Notice the genitive and dative singular in **-īus** and **-ī**; these mark **iste** as like the other demonstratives **hic, ille,** and **is.**

As a general rule, if you are asked to translate "that" into Latin, feel free to use a form of **ille, illa, illud** or of **is, ea, id.** Only when a context clearly dictates a pejorative tone (or its complete opposite!) should you use forms of **iste.**

CHAPTER 54: VOCABULARY

iste, ista, istud	*that*
commūnis, commune	*common, shared*
mereo, merēre, meruī, meritus	*deserve*

CHAPTER 54: LATIN TO ENGLISH SENTENCES

1. **nam ego istam domum vidēre nōn possum.**   CIC ATT 13.38.1
2. **Antōnī, ego istud scelus facere possum.**   SENR C 7.2.4
3. **vēnī nōn ut istum accūsārem sed ut mē defenderem.**   SENR C 9.5.11
4. **certē uterque istōrum est miserrimus.**   CIC ATT 10.4.4
5. **ista deī vox est, deus est in pectore nostrō.**   OV PONT 3.4.93
6. **perpetuōs meruit domus ista triumphōs.**   OV TRIST 3.1.41
7. **sī crīmen est istud, utrīque commūne est.**   QUINT DECL 335
8. **incrēdibile est quam ego ista nōn cūrem.**   CIC ATT 13.23.3

CHAPTER 54: GLOSSED LATIN TO ENGLISH SENTENCES

1. **nōn est ista mea** culpa.

   culpa, ae, f.: fault

   CIC IN CAT 2.3

2. **errāre** mehercule **mālō cum** Platōne ... **quam cum istīs vera sentīre.**

   mehercule: by Hercules!

   Plato, Platōnis, m.: Plato

   CIC TD 1.39

CHAPTER 54: ENGLISH TO LATIN SENTENCES

1. Is <u>that</u> (kind of) life not death?

   SEN E 77.18

2. Who is <u>that</u>? (exasperated)

   SEN E 12.3

3. What (kind of) friendship is <u>that</u>?

   CIC DE FIN 2.79

4. I am not going to listen to <u>that</u> guy.

   SENR S 6.27

CHAPTER 54: PASSAGES

HEAVENLY STOICISM

virtūs enim ista, quam affectāmus, magnifica **est, nōn quia per sē beātum est malō caruisse, sed quia animum** laxat **et** praeparat **ad** cognitiōnem caelestium.

SEN QN 1.PR.6

affectō (1): seek	praeparō (1): prepare
magnificus, a, um: magnificent	cognitio, iōnis, f.: knowledge
laxō (1): broaden	caelestis, e: heavenly

55 Conditions

A condition is simply a sentence that contains the word "if," that is, **sī** in Latin. The good news is that you have been translating conditions without knowing it ever since you learned the word **sī** in chapter 1. Congratulations! However, there is more to conditions than what you have seen. For one thing, a condition proper contains two clauses—a main or "if-clause" (called the **protasis**) and a subordinate or "then-clause" (called the **apodosis**). For another, Latin has a very definite classification of conditions. This chapter will present five, two with the indicative and three with the subjunctive.

FUTURE MORE VIVID

Latin has a condition that employs the future indicative in both protasis and apodosis. It is called a future more vivid condition because this form conveys the speaker's vivid sense of a future action. Here are some examples:

dīcam sī poterō.	I will say if I will be able.	HOR S 2.2.8
sī volēs, manēbō.	If you will want, I will remain.	PLAUT ASIN 597
tristis eris sī sōlus eris.	You will be sad if you will be alone.	OV RA 583

Although the translations sound unnatural in English, I advise you to stick with them for a while. It shows your teacher that you realize the form of the condition.

FUTURE MOST VIVID

A related condition is the future most vivid condition. The only difference is that the protasis, the if-clause, contains a future perfect instead of a future. The speaker is still imagining the action as vividly future, but the change from future to future perfect means that the action of the protasis must definitely occur before the action of the apodosis. I still advise you to translate both tenses literally into English, even though the result sounds strange to our ears:

dīcam sī potuerō.	I will say if I will have been able.	PETR 66.1
sciam sī dīxeris.	I will know if you will have spoken.	PLAUT PSEUD 657
vīnum sī biberis, nihil vidēbis.		MART 6.78.4
	If you will have drunk the wine, you will see nothing.	

The implication in these examples is that the action of the apodosis cannot take place until the action of the protasis has definitely occurred.

The following three conditions use the subjunctive to mean definite things. These must be learned and their implications pondered.

FUTURE LESS VIVID

The first type of subjunctive condition is called future less vivid. It has present subjunctive in both protasis and apodosis. The title points to the nature of the form: It supposes a future event whose possibility is dubious but not impossible, at least in the speaker's mind. The most effective way to capture this in English is to use "were to" for the protasis and "would" for the apodosis. Don't be alarmed if the translation sounds strange or stilted to you. At this stage, the goal is to display mastery over the subject. You can refine your translations in second-year Latin. Here are some examples:

meam rem nōn cūrēs, sī rectē faciās.	PLAUT CAPT 632
You would not care about my thing, if you were to act rightly.	
sī tū mē rogēs, dīcam ut sciās.	PLAUT CURC 12-3
If you were to ask me, I would say in order that you may know.	

PRESENT CONTRARY-TO-FACT

The second type is called present contrary-to-fact and employs the imperfect subjunctive in both protasis and apodosis. (Note the symmetry of the subjunctive conditions.) This form of condition presents a situation that is unreal or contrary to the facts as the speaker believes them. In English, such a sentence would be "If I were you (but I am not), I would not do that," or "If she were giving the orders (but she isn't), I would obey them." The best way to translate a present contrary-to-fact condition in English is to use "were" or "were … -ing" for the protasis and "would" for the apodosis. This too is passing away in the speech of many people, but it will communicate to your teacher that you know what type of condition you are dealing with. Here are some examples:

sī dīceret, nōn crēderētur.	If he were speaking, he would not be believed.	CIC ROSCAM 103
nōn audērēs accūsāre patrem sī timērēs.	You would not dare to accuse (your) father if you were afraid.	QUINT DECL 349
sī possem, sānior essem.	If I were able, I would be saner.	OV M 7.18

(In the last example, Medea struggles between love for Jason and duty to her father.)

PAST CONTRARY-TO-FACT

Finally we have the past contrary-to-fact condition; it presents an unreal situation as existing in the past and employs pluperfect subjunctive in both protasis and apodosis. An English example is "If we had known about it, we would have called you." Use "had" with the perfect participle for protasis and "would have" for the apodosis:

> **nōn mūtassem patrem sī nātūram mūtāre potuissem.**　　SENR C 1.1.4
> I would not have changed (my) father if I had been able to change (his) nature.

Before you start translating, there are several details about conditions you should know:

(1) The negative of **sī** is usually **nisi**, meaning "if … not" or "unless."
(2) The protasis (if-clause) may come after the apodosis (then-clause).
(3) Partial conditions are common, either just a protasis or just an apodosis standing by itself:

> **quid si hoc fecissem?**　　What if I had done this?　　CIC INVENT 2.140

(4) Sometimes conditions are mixed, especially the contrary-to-fact type—the protasis can be past contrary-to-fact (pluperfect subjunctive) and the apodosis can be present (imperfect subjunctive):

> **quid facerēs sī amīcum perdidissēs?**　　SEN E 99.2
> What would you do if you had lost a friend?

CHAPTER 55: PRACTICE SENTENCES (ANSWERS FOLLOW CHAPTER 66)

After translating, name the type of condition.

1. sī possim, velim.   PLAUT CIST 116
2. vincētur sī cesserit.   SEN E 78.15
3. quid sī hoc accidisset?   CIC INVENT 2.140
4. inveniēs, vērē sī reperīre volēs.   OV PONT 3.1.34
5. sī potuerō, faciam vōbīs satis.   CIC BRUTUS 21
6. movērent mē, sī essent fortiōrēs.   CIC ATT 9.13.6
7. sī fratrem reliquissem, omnia timērem.   CIC FAM 2.15.4
8. facerem idem quod Gāius Marius fēcit.   CIC PRO RAB 35
9. If he will have come, we will conquer.   SENR S 5.4
10. If he were living, you (plural) would hear his words.   CIC ROSCC 42

CHAPTER 55: LATIN TO ENGLISH SENTENCES

1. magis dīcās, sī sciās quod ego sciō.   PLAUT MG 1429
2. pater tuus, sī vīveret, prō patriā arma cēpisset.   QUINT DECL 352
3. sī ipse negōtium meum gererem, nihil gererem nisi
   consiliō tuō.   ATT 13.3.1
4. sī fēceris id quod ostendis, magnam habēbō grātiam.   CIC FAM 5.19.2
5. quid facere potuissem, nisi tum consul fuissem?   CIC REPUB 1.10
6. nōn accēpisset rēs publica hoc vulnus.   CIC FAM 10.33.1
7. id sī ita putārem, levius dolērem.   CIC ATT 11.6.1
8. quid sī tē rogāverō aliquid? nōnne respondēbis?   CIC TD 1.17
9. sī ratiōne dēfendī nōn possem, iūre dēfenderer.   QUINT DECL 348

CHAPTER 55: GLOSSED LATIN TO ENGLISH SENTENCES

1. possem vīvere, nisi in   litterae, ārum, f. pl.:
   litterīs vīverem?   (here) literature   CIC FAM 9.26.1

CHAPTER 55: ENGLISH TO LATIN SENTENCES

1. Therefore, you will see the fellow if you will want.   CIC ATT 4.12
2. You will rule many if reason will have ruled you.   SEN E 37.4
3. I would write more if I myself were able.   CIC ATT 8.15.3
4. If I had known that you were there, I would have come to you myself.   CIC DE FIN 3.8
5. You would know if you had been with me.   SENR C 2.4.7

CHAPTER 55: PASSAGES

READIN'S BELIEVIN'

hērēdem **tibi mē, Catulle, dīcis.**
nōn crēdam nisi lēgerō, Catulle.

MART 12.73

hērēs, hērēdis, m.: heir

CAESAR SURVEYS THE CARNAGE AT PHARSALIA

"hoc voluērunt; tantīs rēbus gestīs, Gāius Caesar condemnātus **essem, nisi ab exercitū auxilium petissem."**

SUET DJ 30.4

condemnō (1): find guilty

DUELIN' GENERALS

"meā operā, Quinte Fabī, Tarentum recēpistī." **"certē,"** inquit rīdens, **"nam nisi tū āmīsissēs, numquam** recēpissem."

CIC DE SENEC 11

meā operā: thanks to me   recipiō, 3, recepi: recover
rīdeō (2): laugh

56

Deponent Verbs

Deponents are an important and ubiquitous class of Latin verbs. They are easy to describe but take some getting used to.

▼ A deponent verb is passive in form but active in meaning.

This means that such apparently dependable passive forms as **amātur** or **habēbuntur** must now be constantly double-checked to make sure they are not really active in meaning. (I sympathized with the student who, by a Freudian slip, referred to them as "despondent" verbs.)

Deponents exist in all the conjugations. Thus, they will provide excellent practice for recognizing passive forms. The only thing is, these passive forms must be translated actively. Here are some common deponents:

magnō loquor cum dolōre.	I speak with great pain.	CIC PHIL 1.31
vērum fatērī volō.	I want to confess the truth.	SEN E 79.11
tē autem hortāmur omnēs.	However, we all exhort you.	CIC DE FIN 5.6
vitiīs nēmō sine nascitur.	No one is born without faults.	HOR S 1.3.68
fīlius nātus nōn est.	A son was not born.	CIC INVENT 2.122
mīlitēs cum gladiīs sequuntur consulem.		CIC PHIL 7.13
	Soldiers with swords follow the consul.	

The deponent often strikes the student as an unnecessarily cruel twist of Latin grammar. Why should there be such a thing as a verb that appears passive but is really active? What other fundamental concepts will turn out to have an evil twin? There are various theories to account for the phenomenon, but ultimately, as so often, the best recourse is simple acceptance, the fifth stage of Latin, which you should have reached by now. Such verbs exist and are common. Experience has shown that once the initial irritation wears off, students soon come to terms with deponents. You have already learned all the passive forms necessary; now you simply make a fundamental adjustment. In the long run, deponents prove to be an excellent way to cement your understanding of the difference between active and passive voice, both in Latin and in English.

(You may be wondering how a deponent can be used to indicate passive; for example, if **sequor** means "I follow," how would you say, "I am followed"? The answer is that you cannot use **sequor** to say, "I am followed." You would either have to find a non-deponent verb that means "follow" and make it passive or, if you insist on using **sequor**, recast the sentence entirely.)

THE THREE EXCEPTIONS

Then there are the three exceptions to the fundamental rule for deponents, that they are passive in form but active in meaning:

(1) The present active participle is **active** in form and **active** in meaning.
(2) The future active participle is **active** in form and **active** in meaning.
(3) The passive periphrastic is **passive** in form and **passive** in meaning.

Here are examples of (1), a deponent in the present active participle form; note that the forms are active in form and active in meaning:

occīdistī tū Cicerōnem loquentem.	You killed Cicero speaking.	SENR C 7.2.4
audī sequentia tempora.	Listen to the following times.	[QUINT] DECL 6.23

Here are examples of (2), a deponent in the future active participle form; note that they are active in form and active in meaning:

fīlia mea moritūra est.	My daughter is about to die.	SENR C 2.2.4
quae passūrus est hic puer?	What (things) is this boy about to suffer?	QUINT DECL 340

Here are examples of (3), the passive periphrastic used with deponents; note that the forms are passive in form and passive in meaning:

vērum fatendum est.	The truth must be confessed.	[QUINT] DECL 6.21
tōta alia sequenda via est.	A whole other road must be followed.	SEN BEN 2.7.3
hortandus es nobis, Luci?	Must you be urged by us, Lucius?	CIC DE FIN 5.6
	(Do we have to urge you, Lucius?)	

SEMI-DEPONENTS

With the introduction of deponents, a small mystery may at last be cleared up. A few verbs in Latin are called "semi-deponent" because they are non-deponent in the present system and deponent in the perfect system. You have already encountered the verb **audeō, audēre** meaning "dare"; now you can absorb the perfect **ausus sum**, a deponent meaning "I (have) dared." The same is true of **gaudeō, gaudēre, gāvīsus sum** "rejoice."

Here are examples of those two semi-deponents:

in iūdicium venīre ausus est.	He dared to come into the trial.	CIC PRO CAEC 2
līberōrum tuōrum bonīs plūrimum gāvīsa es.	You rejoiced very much in the good things of your children.	SEN AD HELV 14.3

IMPERATIVES OF DEPONENTS

Deponent verbs also have two imperatives, a singular and a plural. Consider the following table:

	Singular			Plural	
1st	**hortor, hortārī**	**hortāre**	"urge"	**hortāminī**	"urge"
2nd	**fateor, fatērī**	**fatēre**	"confess"	**fatēminī**	"confess"
3rd	**sequor, sequī**	**sequere**	"follow"	**sequiminī**	"follow"
3rd-io	**morior, morī**	**morere**	"die"	**moriminī**	"die"
4th	**mentior, mentīrī**	**mentīre**	"lie"	**mentīminī**	"lie"

These forms will present problems. The singular imperative looks like an active infinitive, and if you forget that you are dealing with a deponent verb, you may wrongly translate it as though it were an infinitive. Hopefully, the result will be so bizarre that it will jog your memory.

The plural imperative definitely does not look like an infinitive, but it is identical to the second-person plural of the present tense. Thus, you may be tempted to translate it as such. Usually, however, an imperative is set off by commas, which should bring you back to reality. Also, the context generally makes it clear that you are dealing with an imperative and not an indicative.

CHAPTER 56: VOCABULARY

fateor, fatērī, fassus sum	*confess*
hortor, hortārī, hortātus sum	*urge, exhort*
loquor, loquī, locūtus sum	*talk, speak*
morior, morī, mortuus sum	*die*
nascor, nascī, nātus sum	*be born*
patior, patī, passus sum	*suffer; allow*
sequor, sequī, secūtus sum	*follow*

CHAPTER 56: PRACTICE SENTENCES (ANSWERS FOLLOW CHAPTER 66)

1. lībera ego sum nāta. PLAUT CURC 607
2. sī taceās, loquar. PLAUT TRIN 148
3. prō rē publicā moriēris. SEN E 76.27
4. ego mē amāre hanc fateor. TER AND 896
5. plūs loquimur quam sat est. PLAUT CIST 122
6. bona nascī ex malō nōn possunt. SEN E 87.24
7. innocentem fuisse patrem fatētur. QUINT 7.1.56
8. id autem nec nascī potest nec morī. CIC REPUB 6.27
9. nōn trahuntur ā Fortūnā, sequuntur illam. SEN PROV 5.4
10. dixit nēminem nātum līberum esse, nēminem servum. SENR C 7.6.18
11. eum ad salūtem patriae hortābar. CIC ATT 8.9.1
12. I will confess true things. OV HER 8.97
13. He suffers the injuries of war. CIC PHIL 12.9
14. The law follows the gold. PROP 3.13.50
15. Talk (plural) with me. TER PHOR 549
16. You (feminine) have suffered force. SENR C 1.2.12
17. Let us die in liberty. CIC PRO RAB 16
18. You friend has talked with me. SEN E 11.1
19. You, however, will suffer nothing. SEN E 71.7
20. You understand what follows. CIC TD 5.50

CHAPTER 56: LATIN TO ENGLISH SENTENCES

1. amor fugiendus nōn est; nam ex eō vērissima nascitur amīcitia. AUCHER 2.35
2. nec vitia nostra nec remedia patī possumus. LIVY PRAEF 9
3. videō meliōra probōque, dēteriōra sequor. OV M 7.20-21
4. nunc patimur longae pācis mala. JUV 6.292
5. fatērisne eadem quae hic fassus est mihi? PLAUT CAPT 317
6. quō mē uocās aut quid hortāris? CIC DE LEG 1.14
7. sīc igitur prīmā moriēris aetāte, Propertī? sed morere. PROP 2.8.17-8
8. dī enim semper fuērunt, nātī numquam sunt. CIC ND 1.90
9. vel sequiminī mē vel, sī māvultis, dūcite. PETR 99.4
10. turpe est aliud loquī, aliud sentīre. SEN E 24.19

11. **fateātur id quod negārī nōn potest.**   CIC VER 1.12

12. **sciō quem animum, quod horter ingenium.**   PLINY E 1.3.5

CHAPTER 56: GLOSSED LATIN TO ENGLISH SENTENCES

1. **magnōs hominēs virtūte** mētimur,   mētior (4): measure   NEPOS 18.1.1
   nōn fortūnā.

2. **dum loquimur, fūgerit** invida **aetās.**   invidus, a, um: envious   HOR O 1.11.7–8

3. **in** convīviīs **loquebantur, sed in tormentīs tacēbant.**   SEN E 47.4

   convīvium, iī, n.: dinner-party

4. **ita** ferī **ut sē morī sentiat.**   feriō (4): strike   SUET CAL 30.1

CHAPTER 56: ENGLISH TO LATIN SENTENCES

1. I talk with you as though with myself.   CIC ATT 8.14.2

2. No one is born rich.   SEN E 20.13

3. "Fortune," he says, "has forced me to suffer these things."   SENR C 1.2.3

4. Tears followed the words.   OV M 9.781

5. He suffers perpetual punishments.   OV M 4.467

6. Caesar himself urges me toward peace.   CIC ATT 7.21.3

CHAPTER 56: PASSAGES

NOT SO WELL MATCHED

cum sītis similēs **parēsque vītā,**
uxor pessima, pessimus marītus,
mīror nōn bene convenīre **vōbīs.**

MART 8.35

---

similis, e: similar   marītus, ī, m.: husband
mīror (1): be amazed   convenit vōbīs: you get along

DEPENDS WHAT YOU MEAN BY "OWE"

Sexte, nihil dēbēs, nīl dēbēs, Sexte, fatēmur.
   dēbet enim, sī quis solvere, **Sexte, potest.**

MART 2.3

---

quis, quid: anyone, anything   solvō (3): pay

THE ROMAN WAY

"Rōmānus sum" inquit **"cīvis; Gāium Mūcium vocant. hostis hostem occīdere voluī, nec ad mortem minus animī est quam fuit ad** caedem; **et facere et patī fortia Rōmānum est."**

LIVY 2.12.9

---

caedēs, is, f.: killing

ROMAN PATRIOTISM

dulce et decōrum **est prō patriā morī;**
mors et fugācem persequitur **virum.**

HOR O 3.2.13-14

---

decōrus, a, um: honorable   fugax, fugācis: prone to flight
persequor (3): pursue

SLAVE VS. FREE VS. FREED

omnēs hominēs aut līberī sunt aut servī. rursus **līberōrum hominum aliī** ingenuī **sunt, aliī**
lībertīnī. ingenuī **sunt quī līberī nātī sunt;** lībertīnī **quī ex iustā** servitūte manumissī **sunt.**

GAIUS 1.9-11

---

rursus: again   ingenuus, a, um: free-born
lībertīnus, a, um: freed   manumittō (3): set free

57

Dative with Special Verbs

There is a small but significant group of Latin verbs that, for no obvious reason, govern the dative instead of the accusative. Though there are historical reasons for this phenomenon, the first-year student need not worry about them. You may, if you like, make up little stories to explain to yourself why, for example, "persuade" and "obey" and "harm" and "spare" and "please" should govern the dative, but only as mnemonic devices. A better idea is to open a new mental file and call it "verbs that take the dative." (And later a smaller file for verbs that take the ablative. And the genitive!) Here are some examples:

nōndum mihi crēdis?	Do you not yet believe me?	TER PHOR 492
ignosce mihi.	Forgive me.	CIC FAM 12.2.3
pārent auctōritātī vestrae.	They obey your (plural) authority.	CIC PHIL 7.13
tū mihi sōla placēs.	You alone please me.	PROP 2.7.19
nōbīs carmina nostra placent.	Our poems please us.	MART 6.60.4

Note that one of these verbs—**crēdō**—has appeared before with no hint that a dative might be involved. This is because **crēdō** takes a dative when a person is believed and may take an accusative when a thing is believed. Here are some examples:

tū haec nōn crēdis?	Do you not believe these things?	CIC TD 1.10
errās sī id crēdis.	You are wrong if you believe this.	TER HT 105

Verbs that govern the dative can also appear in the passive, but the result will strike you as bizarre:

mihi nōn crēditur.	I am not believed.	[QUINT] DECL 7.3
nullī ignoscitur.	No one is forgiven.	SEN CLEM 1.24.1

The explanation of this phenomenon can be deferred until you learn about the impersonal passive.

CHAPTER 57: VOCABULARY

crēdō , crēdere, crēdidī, crēditus	*believe, trust*
ignoscō, ignoscere, ignōvī, ignōtus	*forgive*
īrascor, īrascī, īrātus sum	*get mad (at)*
noceō, nocēre, nocuī, nocitūrus	*harm*
pāreō, pārēre, pāruī, ––	*obey*
placeō, placēre, placuī, placitus	*please, be pleasing to*
cito	*(adverb) quickly*

CHAPTER 57: PRACTICE SENTENCES (ANSWERS FOLLOW CHAPTER 66)

1. **nulla illī iniūria nocet.**   SEN CONS SAP 3.4
2. **īrascētur etiam sibi.**   SEN IRA 1.14.2
3. **sī invītus pārēs, servus es.**   PUBLSYR
4. **placent vōbīs hominum mōrēs?**   CIC VER 3.208
5. **māter īrāta est patrī vehementer.**   PLAUT MERC 923
6. **quis nōn ignoscit rem tantam timentī?**   QUINT DECL 348
7. **potest igitur testibus iūdex nōn crēdere?**   CIC PRO FONT 21
8. Does this please you?   CIC ATT 6.6.2
9. I obeyed my parents.   SEN BEN 3.38.2
10. Caesar's anger has harmed me.   OV PONT 1.4.29
11. I have never believed Fortune.   SEN AD HELV 5.4
12. I do not believe (my) eyes about the fellow.   SEN VIT BEAT 2.2
13. It is not enough if you (plural) have forgiven me.   QUINT DECL 266
14. Let us love the homeland; let us obey the senate.   CIC PRO SEST 143

CHAPTER 57: LATIN TO ENGLISH SENTENCES

1. **deō pārēre lībertās est.**   SEN VIT BEAT 15.7
2. **oculīs magis quam auribus crēdidērunt.**   LIVY 6.26.5
3. **ignoscētis mihi dīcentī "nōn possum."**   QUINT DECL 315
4. **nēmō autem nātūrae sānus īrascitur.**   SEN IRA 2.10.6

5. **malus malō nocet facitque pēiōrem.** SEN E 109.4
6. **ego autem nē īrascī possum quidem iīs quōs valdē amō.** CIC ATT 2.19.1
7. **multa bona nostra nōbīs nocent.** SEN E 5.9
8. **cito nōbīs placēmus.** SEN E 59.11
9. **utrumque enim vitium est – et omnibus crēdere et nullī.** SEN E 3.4
10. **nātūram optimam dūcem tamquam deum sequimur eīque pārēmus.** CIC DE SENEC 5
11. **plus mihi nocitūra est īra quam iniūria.** SEN IRA 3.25.4

CHAPTER 57: GLOSSED LATIN TO ENGLISH SENTENCES

1. **nōn** ignāra **malī, miserīs** succurrere **discō.** VERG A 1.630

   ignārus, a, um: ignorant of   succurrō (3): help (+ dative)

CHAPTER 57: ENGLISH TO LATIN SENTENCES

1. My consulate does not please Marcus Antonius. CIC PHIL 2.12
2. No one will be able to be mad at me. CIC IMP POMP 37
3. Let a great mind obey god. SEN E 71.16
4. Many have forgiven enemies. SEN IRA 3.24.2
5. You will obey the senate and the Roman people. CIC PHIL 13.14

CHAPTER 57: PASSAGES

SO MANY GIRLS, SO LITTLE TIME

pulchrior hāc illa est, haec est quoque pulchrior illā,
   et magis haec nōbīs et magis illa placet.

OV A 2.10.7-8

PAULA IS DESPERATE—FOR ME!

nūbere **Paula cupit nōbīs, ego dūcere Paulam**
    nōlō – anus **est. vellem, sī magis esset** anus.

MART 10.8

---

nūbō (3): marry (+ dative)   anus, ūs, f.: old woman

TUNNEL BUDDIES

moechus **es Aufidiae, quī vir, Scaevīne, fuistī;**
    rīvālis **fuerat quī tuus, ille vir est.**
cūr aliēna placet tibi, quae tua nōn placet, uxor?
    numquid **sēcūrus nōn potes** arrigere?

MART 3.70

---

moechus, ī, m.: adulterer   rīvālis, is, m.: rival
numquid: can it be that   arrigō (3): get it up

SULPICIA, ON MARRIED LOVE

omnēs Sulpiciam legant puellae
ūnī quae cupiunt virō placēre;
omnēs Sulpiciam legant marītī
ūnī quī cupiunt placēre nuptae.

MART 10.35.1-4

---

marītus, ī, m.: husband   nupta, ae, f.: bride

58

Dative with Compound Verbs

Many Latin verbs consist of a basic verb compounded with a preposition. Examples are **adferō** "bring to," **anteponō** "put before," and **imponō** "put on." Such verbs can take both an accusative (generated by the verb) and a dative (generated by the preposition). This may strike you as odd since no Latin preposition by itself governs the dative; still, such verbs are quite common. Here are some examples:

adfer mihi arma.	Bring arms to me.	PLAUT CIST 284
mortem servitūtī anteponāmus!	Let us put death before slavery!	CIC PHIL 3.29

A related group of compound verbs taking the dative consists of the verb **sum** compounded with the prepositions **dē** and **prō**. These verbs take only the dative with no accusative, logically enough, since the verb **sum** does not take a direct object. Consider the verbs **dēsum** "be lacking" and **prōsum** "benefit":

mihi dēest consilium.	I lack a plan. (A plan is lacking to me.)	CIC FAM 14.4.3
reī nullī prōdest mora nisi īracundiae.	Delay benefits no thing except anger.	PUBLSYR R2

An even odder subgroup of this kind of verb consists of compound verbs that mean "take away" or "remove." They too take an accusative (of the thing taken) and a dative (of the person from whom it was taken away). By this point in your development, you might think that an ablative (of separation) would have been more logical, but the Romans used another logic and employed the dative. Two such verbs are **adimō** "take away from" and **ēripiō** "snatch away from." The noun governed by "from" will appear in the dative, as in the following examples:

ēripite istī gladium.	Snatch the sword away from that one.	PLAUT CAS 629
hunc mihi timōrem ēripe.	Snatch this fear away from me.	CIC IN CAT 1.18
consulatum vōbīs ēripiēbant.	They snatched the consulship away from you.	CIC PRO SULLA 49

CHAPTER 58: VOCABULARY

adferō, adferre, attulī, allātus	*bring (accusative) to (dative)*
antepōnō, antepōnere, anteposuī, antepositus	*put (accusative) before (dative)*
dēsum, dēesse, dēfuī, dēfutūrus	*be lacking to (+ dative)*
ēripiō, ēripere, ēripuī, ēreptus	*snatch (accusative) away from (dative)*
impōnō, impōnere, imposuī, impositus	*put (accusative) in/on (dative)*
prōsum, prōdesse, prōfuī, prōfutūrus	*benefit (+ dative)*

CHAPTER 58: PRACTICE SENTENCES (ANSWERS FOLLOW CHAPTER 66)

1. **praemium ēripuī tibi.** SEN TROAD 998
2. **vim adferēbam senatuī.** CIC PHIL 2.16
3. **nihil huic ēripī potest.** CIC RAB POST 41
4. **eōs omnēs cēterīs antepōnimus.** AUG CD 8.9
5. **nunc mihi prōdest bona voluntās?** SEN BEN 4.21.6
6. **omne beātum est cuī nihil dēest.** CIC TD 5.39
7. A letter is brought to me. CIC ATT 9.12.1
8. But a plan is not lacking to you. CIC FAM 7.9.2
9. What name do we put on these (things)? SEN QN 1.11.2
10. Your letter brought sleep to me. CIC ATT 9.7.7

CHAPTER 58: LATIN TO ENGLISH SENTENCES

1. **adferunt laudem līberī parentibus.** QUINT 3.7.18
2. **iūs meum ēreptum est mihi.** PLAUT RUD 711
3. **lēgēs cīvitātī per vim imposuit.** CIC PHIL 7.15
4. **multa petentibus dēsunt multa.** HOR O 3.16.42-3
5. **ego tuīs neque dēsum neque dēerō.** CIC FAM 12.2.3
6. **nam vel prōdesse amīcō possum vel inimīcum perdere.** PLAUT CAPT 773
7. **sīc eadem prōdest causa nocetque mihi.** OV PONT 2.3.54
8. **hominum nostrōrum prūdentiam cēterīs omnibus et maximē Graecīs antepōnō.** CIC DE ORAT 1.197

CHAPTER 58: GLOSSED LATIN TO ENGLISH SENTENCES

1. **lēgēs omnium salūtem** singulōrum **salūtī antepōnunt.**   singulus, a, um: individual   CIC DE FIN 3.64

CHAPTER 58: ENGLISH TO LATIN SENTENCES

1. I put the memory of friendship before all the remaining virtues.   CIC RAB POST 44
2. No god will snatch you away from me.   SEN HERC 503-4
3. They brought great hope of better things to us.   CIC ATT 10.15.1
4. How will he be able to put an end on (his) life?   SEN E 58.37
5. Poets want either to benefit or to delight.   HOR AP 333
6. To harm is easy, to benefit difficult.   QUINT 8.5.6

CHAPTER 58: PASSAGES

DINNER AT CATULLUS'S

cēnābis bene, mī **Fabulle, apud mē**
paucīs, sī tibi dī favent, **diēbus,**
sī tēcum attuleris bonam atque magnam
cēnam, nōn sine candidā **puellā**
et vīnō et sale **et omnibus** cachinnīs.

CATULLUS 13.1-5

---

faveō (2): favor (+ dative)	mī: voc. masc. sing. of meus
candidus, a, um: luscious	sāl, salis, m.: salt, wit
cachinnus, ī, m.: laugh	

YOU WOULD CRY TOO IF IT HAPPENED TO YOU

ēripitur nōbīs iam prīdem **cāra puella,**
et tū mē lacrimās fundere, **amīce, vetās?**

PROP 2.8.1-2

---

prīdem: (adverb) for a long time   fundō, 3: pour

59

Indirect Commands

Another use of the subjunctive is found in the construction called indirect command (also called jussive noun clause in some books). The indirect command is a subset of the purpose clause and, like a purpose clause, it has **ut** for positive commands, **nē** for negative, and uses either present or imperfect subjunctive according to the rule given in chapters 46 and 48:

▼ **If the verb of the main clause is in a past tense, use imperfect subjunctive.**

▼ **If the verb of the main clause is in any other tense, use present subjunctive.**

What distinguishes indirect commands from purpose clauses is this: They will be introduced by a leading verb that implies ordering, asking, requesting, begging, demanding, or the like. A partial list of such verbs follows, many of which have appeared in previous chapters, as noted:

hortor	urge	(chapter 59)
moneō	warn	(chapter 59)
orō	beg	(chapter 59)
petō	seek	(chapter 31)
postulō	demand	(chapter 47)
rogō	ask	(chapter 2)

In English, we simply tack an infinitive onto such verbs; in Latin you will find a dependent subjunctive. We say, "I beg you to listen"; Latin says (roughly), "I beg that you may listen." Here are some examples with two translations; the first is a very literal but cumbersome rendering, the second a more fluent version. Observe that you can usually translate an indirect command by converting the Latin subjunctive to an English infinitive:

hortēmur ut properent.	Let us encourage in order that they may hurry. PLAUT CAS 422
	Let us encourage them to hurry.

nē properēs orō.	I beg that you may not hurry.	OV RA 277
	I beg you not to hurry.	
cūrā ut valeās.	Take care in order that you may be well.	CIC ATT 1.5.8
	Take care to be well.	
orāvit ut causam miserōrum cīvium susciperet.	He begged that he might take up the cause of the wretched citizens.	LIVY 7.41.1
	He begged him to take up the cause of the wretched citizens.	

Occasionally, the introductory verb requires a slightly different structure for an indirect command. The common verbs **petō** (beg) and **postulō** (demand), when used in an indirect command, employ the preposition **ā/ab**, as in the following examples:

petō ā tē ut mihi ignoscās.   CIC IN VAT 7

    I beg from you in order that you may forgive me.

    I beg you to forgive me.

ab eō petiī ut ad tē litterās mitteret.   CIC FAM 8.16.4

    I begged from him that he might send a letter to you.

    I begged him to send a letter to you.

postulō ā tē ut mihi illum reddās servum.   PLAUT CAPT 938

    I demand from you that you may return that slave to me.

    I demand that you return that slave to me.

Since the indirect command requires **ut** for positive and **nē** for negative, the only way to distinguish it from a purpose clause or result clause is the presence of the verb of requesting.

CHAPTER 59: VOCABULARY

moneō, monēre, monuī, monitus	*warn*
orō, orāre, orāvī, orātus	*beg (for)*

CHAPTER 59: PRACTICE SENTENCES (ANSWERS FOLLOW CHAPTER 66)

1. **sī nōs amātis, cūrāte ut valeātis.**   CIC FAM 14.5.2
2. **tē orō ut dē hāc miserā cōgitēs.**   CIC ATT 11.23.3
3. Lepidus begs me to come.   CIC ATT 13.42.3
4. I warn you (plural) not to do (it).   CIC RAB POST 18

CHAPTER 59: LATIN TO ENGLISH SENTENCES

1. **rogant mē ut cum Curiānō loquar.** PLINY E 5.1.8
2. **tē semper orāvimus nē contrā Caesarem pugnārēs.** CIC ATT 9.7A.1
3. **Antōnius petēbat ā mē per litterās ut sibi ignoscerem.** CIC ATT 11.7.2
4. **monendus es nē mē moneās.** PLAUT PSEUD 915
5. **orō ut illīus animum atque ingenium regās.** PLAUT BACC 494
6. **deōs rogā ut illī factō tuō ignoscant.** PETR 137.8
7. **hortātur ut commūnis libertātis causā arma capiant.** CAES BG 7.4.4

CHAPTER 59: GLOSSED LATIN TO ENGLISH SENTENCES

1. **meus mē orāvit fīlius ut tuam sorōrem poscerem uxōrem sibi.** soror, sorōris, f.: sister poscō (3): request PLAUT TRIN 449-50
2. **ego vōs hortārī** tantum **possum ut amīcitiam omnibus rēbus hūmānīs antepōnātis.** tantum (adverb): only CIC DE AMIC 17

CHAPTER 59: ENGLISH TO LATIN SENTENCES

1. They demand that the signal be given. LIVY 2.45.6
2. I beg you, Epidicus, to forgive me. PLAUT EPID 728-9
3. You urge me to write something. CIC ATT 2.12.3
4. I asked him to say what he had in mind. CIC ATT 8.10

CHAPTER 59: PASSAGES

PROFESSIONAL JEALOUSY

ut recitem **tibi nostra rogās** epigrammata. **nōlō.**
   nōn audīre, Celer, sed recitāre **cupis.**

MART 1.63

---

recitō (1): recite   epigrammata, n. pl.: epigrams

60 fīō

The verb **fīō, fierī, factus sum** functions as the passive for the verb **faciō**. In effect, this unique verb is a sort of reverse deponent—active in form, passive in meaning—at least in the present, imperfect, and future tenses. In the other three tenses (perfect, pluperfect, and future perfect) it shares the forms of **faciō**. In addition to its strictly passive meaning ("be made" or "be done") **fīō** can also have the meaning "happen" or "become" as well as several others. It is a very common verb; here are its forms:

Present Indicative		Present Subjunctive	
fīō	fīmus	fīam	fīāmus
fīs	fītis	fīās	fīātis
fit	fīunt	fīat	fīant

Imperative		Infinitive
fī	fīte	fierī

Imperfect Indicative		Imperfect Subjunctive	
fīēbam	fīēbāmus	fierem	fierēmus
fīēbās	fīēbātis	fierēs	fierētis
fīēbat	fīēbant	fieret	fierent

Future Indicative			
fīam	fīēmus		
fīēs	fīētis		
fīet	fīent		

Perfect Indicative		Perfect Subjunctive	
factus sum	factī sumus	factus sim	factī sīmus
factus es	factī estis	factus sīs	factī sītis
factus est	factī sunt	factus sit	factī sint

Pluperfect Indicative		Pluperfect Subjunctive	
factus eram	factī erāmus	factus essem	factī essēmus
factus erās	factī erātis	factus essēs	factī essētis
factus erat	factī erant	factus esset	factī essent

Future Perfect Indicative			
factus erō	factī erimus		
factus eris	factī eritis		
factus erit	factī erunt		

Some examples will show the range of meanings **fīō** can have. Its basic nature is to be the passive of **faciō** "do" or "make." Notice that **fīō** functions as a grammatical equals sign, like the verb **sum**, so that whatever case appears on one side also appears on the other:

omnia cito facta sunt.	All things were done quickly.	SENR C 2.3.17
consul sum factus.	I was made consul.	CIC DE AMIC 96
nox est facta longior.	The night was made longer.	PLAUT AMPH 113

From this, **fīō** easily acquires the meaning "become":

deus fierī vult?	Does he want to become a god?	SEN APOCO 8.3
mulier facta est iam ex virō.	She has now become a woman from a man.	PLAUT TRUC 134
homō enim sapiens fierī potest.	For a human being can become wise.	CIC ND 2.36

And the meaning "happen":

fātō omnia fīunt.	All things happen by fate.	CIC DE FATO 21
in bellō factum est.	It happened in war.	QUINT DECL 348
hoc cotīdiē fierī vidēmus.	We see that this happens every day.	CIC CLUENT 116

From the meaning "happen," **fīō** can generate a result clause as follows:

> **nātūrā fīt ut līberī ā parentibus amentur.** CIC DE FIN 3.62
> By nature, it happens that children are loved by (their) parents.

Sometimes, particularly in the form **fīt**, it seems to mean little more than **est**:

nulla ergō fīt mora.	Therefore, there is no delay.	PETR 105.4
ita fīt semper vīta beāta sapientis.	Thus, the life of the wise man is always supremely happy.	CIC TD 5.82

CHAPTER 60: VOCABULARY

fīō, fierī, factus sum   *be made, be done; become; happen*

CHAPTER 60: PRACTICE SENTENCES (ANSWERS FOLLOW CHAPTER 66)

1. **fierī nihil potest.** CIC ATT 2.14.2
2. **quid nunc fīet?** TER ADEL 288
3. **quid fierī possit sciō.** SEN E 88.17
4. **ex eā rē quid fīat vidē.** TER AND 385
5. **ego ita dīcō factum esse.** PLAUT EPID 207
6. **quid fierī posset nōn vidēbāmus.** CIC FAM 12.30.6
7. Peace was made. PLAUT AMPH 965
8. I myself am becoming better. CIC FAM 9.18.3
9. From a friend, he becomes an enemy. SEN E 91.5
10. He is a human being; he wants to become free. PLAUT TRIN 563-4

CHAPTER 60: LATIN TO ENGLISH SENTENCES

1. **cito fīt quod diī volunt.** PETR 76.8
2. **fīat quod vultis.** SENR C 1.PR.4
3. **quī invītus servit, fīt miser, servit tamen.** PUBLSYR Q64
4. **crās quoque fīet idem.** OV RA 104
5. **mundus deōrum hominumque causā factus est.** CIC ND 2.154
6. **dum cīvitās erit, iūdicia fīent.** CIC ROSCAM 91

7. **ita fīet ut animī virtūs corporis virtūtī antepōnātur.**   CIC DE FIN 5.38

8. **bonum ex malō nōn fīt; dīvitiae fīunt autem ex avāritiā; dīvitiae ergō nōn sunt bonum.**   SEN E 87.22

CHAPTER 60: GLOSSED LATIN TO ENGLISH SENTENCES

1. "vae," **inquit**, "**putō, deus fīō.**"   vae: alas!   SUET VES 23.4

2. **plānē Fortūnae fīlius, in manū illīus** plumbum **aurum fīēbat.**   plumbum, ī, n.: lead   PETR 43.7

3. **brevis esse** labōrō, obscūrus **fīō.**   labōrō (1): labor
   obscūrus, a, um: obscure   HOR AP 25-6

CHAPTER 60: ENGLISH TO LATIN SENTENCES

1. Now I want to become another (person).   PLAUT POEN 126

2. Brutus was made the first consul.   SUET DJ 80.3

3. We will see what is able to be done.   CIC ATT 12.38A.2

4. Now I will become a poet.   PLAUT PSEUD 404

CHAPTER 60: PASSAGES

MARTIAL ON MARRIAGE

uxorem quārē locuplētem **dūcere nōlim
   quaeritis? uxōrī** nūbere **nōlō meae.**
inferior mātrōna **suō sit, Prisce, marītō;
   nōn** aliter **fīunt fēmina virque parēs.**

MART 8.12

---

quārē: why   locuplēs, locuplētis: wealthy
nūbō (3): marry (+ dative)   inferior, ius: inferior
mātrōna, ae, f.: married woman   aliter (adverb): otherwise

IVORY TOWER

ego adulescentulōs **existimō in** scholīs **stultissimōs fierī, quia
nihil ex hīs quae in** ūsū **habēmus aut audiunt aut vident.**

PETR 1.3

---

adulescentulus, ī, m.: teenager   schola, ae, f.: school
ūsus, ūs, m.: experience

LOGICAL DISTINCTIONS

**"aut futūrum," inquit, "est aut nōn; sī futūrum est, fīet, etiam sī vōta
nōn suscipis. sī nōn est futūrum, etiam sī suscēperis vōta, nōn fīet."**

SEN QN 2.37.3

THE POWER OF FORTUNE

sī Fortūna volet, fīēs dē rhētore **consul;
sī volet haec eadem, fīet dē consule** rhētor.

JUV 7.197–8

---

rhētor, rhētoris, m.: speech teacher

61

eō

In Latin the verb "go," like the verb "be," is quite irregular. Like **sum**, it appears to change its stem from time to time. However, it is as common as the word "go" in English and has many compounds that pop up in all sorts of contexts. One good piece of news—there is no passive voice, which reduces the number of forms. In addition, most of the irregularities are contained in the present system.

Present Tense

eō	I go	**īmus**	we go
īs	you go	**ītis**	you go
it	he/she/it goes	**eunt**	they go

Imperative

ī	go	**īte**	go

Infinitive

īre	to go	

Imperfect Tense

ībam	I was going	**ībāmus**	we were going
ībās	you were going	**ībātis**	you were going
ībat	he/she/it was going	**ībant**	they were going

Future Tense			
ībō	I will go	**ībimus**	we will go
ībis	you will go	**ībitis**	you will go
ībit	he/she/it will go	**ībunt**	they will go

Present Subjunctive	
eam	eāmus
eās	eātis
eat	eant

All other tenses of **eō** are regular, both indicative and subjunctive.

The verb **eō** has a present active participle with perfectly predictable endings. The catch is that the stem changes from time to time as follows:

Case	Singular		Plural	
	masc/fem	*neut*	*masc/fem*	*neut*
nominative	**iens**	**iens**	**eunt-ēs**	**eunt-ia**
genitive	**eunt-is**	**eunt-is**	**eunt-ium**	**eunt-ium**
dative	**eunt-ī**	**eunt-ī**	**eunt-ibus**	**eunt-ibus**
accusative	**eunt-em**	**iens**	**eunt-ēs**	**eunt-ia**
ablative	**eunt-ī**	**eunt-ī**	**eunt-ibus**	**eunt-ibus**
vocative	**iens**	**iens**	**eunt-ēs**	**eunt-ia**

The verb **eō** is often compounded with a preposition. The result is usually just the sum of its parts. For example, **exeō** means "I go out," and **redeō** means "I go back." Occasionally, however, the compounded verb takes on a new meaning that seems to be more than the sum of its parts. In particular, the common verb **pereō** rarely means "I go through" and practically always means "I perish."

Here are some examples of **eō** by itself and in compounds:

iamne ītis?	(By) now are you going?	PLAUT POEN 678
īte mēcum.	Go (plural) with me.	AUCHER 4.63

ad forum ībō.	I will go to the forum.	PLAUT TRIN 727
manēte dum ego hūc redeō.	Remain while I return here.	PLAUT RUD 879
rediit ad mīlitēs.	He returned to the soldiers.	CIC PHIL 13.19
vēritās numquam perit.	Truth never perishes.	SEN TROAD 614
periit cum exercitū.	He perished with the army.	CIC DE DIVIN 2.71

CHAPTER 61: VOCABULARY

eō, īre, īī, itus	*go*
exeō, exīre, exīī, exitus	*go out*
pereō, perīre, perīī, peritus	*perish*
redeō , redīre, redīī, reditus	*go back, return*
senex, senis, m.	*old man*

CHAPTER 61: PRACTICE SENTENCES (ANSWERS FOLLOW CHAPTER 66)

1. **mē īre iussit ad eam.**   PLAUT BACC 575
2. **at nōs ad tē ībāmus.**   TER PHOR 899
3. **rogant mē servī quō eam.**   PLAUT CURC 362
4. **hoc peritūrum est.**   SEN E 42.9
5. **occīsus est ā cēnā rediens.**   CIC ROSCAM 97
6. **Pompeius et consulēs ex Italiā exiērunt.**   CIC ATT 9.6.4
7. Go, bring arms to me.   PLAUT CIST 284
8. We go, we come, we see.   TER PHOR 103-4
9. I went back into father's house.   QUINT DECL 377

CHAPTER 61: LATIN TO ENGLISH SENTENCES

1. **vōs cēterī īte hūc ad nōs.**   PLAUT AUL 330
2. **mortālia facta perībunt.**   HOR AP 68
3. **sī ītūra est, eat.**   PLAUT MG 1299
4. **prō multīs perīre mālunt quam cum multīs.**   AUCHER 4.57
5. **vir fortis ac sapiens nōn fugere dēbet ē vitā sed exīre.**   SEN E 24.25
6. **sed exeuntem fīlium videō meum.**   PLAUT MERC 961
7. **ībō ad forum atque haec facta narrābō senī.**   PLAUT TRUC 313
8. **redeuntem ā cenā senem saepe vidēbam puer.**   CIC DE SENEC 44
9. **accipimus peritūra peritūrī.**   SEN PROV 5.7

CHAPTER 61: GLOSSED LATIN TO ENGLISH SENTENCES

1. quālis artifex **pereō.**   quālis, e: what a(n)   artifex, artificis, m.: artist   SUET N 49.1

CHAPTER 61: ENGLISH TO LATIN SENTENCES

1. Go and goodbye.   PLAUT AUL 263
2. Go (plural) if you're going.   PLAUT POEN 1237
3. I will go and remain there.   PLAUT ASIN 126
4. I saw the woman going out.   PLAUT CIST 547
5. My friend has perished.   QUINT DECL 289
6. I return now to your letter.   CIC ATT 14.13.5

CHAPTER 61: PASSAGES

SOCRATES'S LAST WORDS TO THE COURT

"**sed tempus est,**" inquit, "**iam** hinc **abīre mē ut moriar, vōs ut vītam agātis. utrum autem sit melius, dī immortālēs sciunt, hominem quidem scīre** arbitror **nēminem.**"

CIC TD 1.99

hinc: from here   arbitror (1): think

THE PATH TO THE UNDERWORLD

ībant obscūrī sōlā **sub nocte per umbram**
perque domōs Dītis vacuās **et** inānia **regna.**

VERG A 6.268

obscūrus, a, um: dark   sōlus, a, um: lonely
Dīs, Dītis, m.: Hades   vacuus, a, um: empty
inānis, e: empty

62

Expressions of Place/Locative Case/ Cardinal Numbers

Latin has a special way of dealing with names of cities and towns when movement or location is involved. Contrary to what your instincts might tell you, no preposition is used. So if there is movement toward a named city, use the simple accusative; if there is movement away from a named city, use the simple ablative. Here are some examples:

mīserat etiam epistulās Rōmam.	He had even sent letters to Rome.	PLINY E 3.9.13
Spartam redīre nōlēbat.	He did not want to return to Sparta.	NEPOS 4.3.3
maximīs rēbus gestīs, Athēnās vēnērunt.		NEPOS 7.5.7

   With the greatest things having been done, they came to Athens.

in mē incurrit Rōmā veniens Curio.		CIC ATT 2.12.2

   Coming from Rome, Curio runs into me.

From the Roman point of view, a small island fell in this category since there would only be one city on it. Thus,

sextō diē Dēlum Athēnīs vēnimus.	CIC ATT 5.12.1

   On the sixth day we came to Delos from Athens.

(Larger islands like Sicily with more than one town or city do not fall under this rule.) In addition, the common word **domum** "home(ward)" needs no preposition:

nunc domum properō.	Now I am hurrying home(ward).	PLAUT PERS 272
A. **quō ergō īs nunc?** B. **domum.**		PLAUT PERS 191

   A. Where therefore are you going now? B. Home(ward).

LOCATIVE CASE

However, if you are not moving toward or away from, but are located in a named city (or small island), there is one final case to learn: the locative case. For most declensions, the locative is the same as the ablative. However, for singular nouns in the first and second declensions, the locative is the same as the genitive. Here are some examples:

Rōmae enim videor esse cum tuās litterās legō.   CIC ATT 2.15.1

　　　For I seem to be at Rome when I read your letters.

tē Athēnīs esse audiēbāmus.　　We heard that you were at Athens.　　CIC ATT 1.5.3

Ephesī sum nātus.　　　I was born at Ephesus.　　PLAUT MG 648

In addition, there is the irregular but common word **domī** "at home":

huius domī mortuus est.　　He died at his home.　　CIC CLUENT 165

multōs annōs nostrae domī vixit.　　CIC TD 5.113

　　　For many years he lived at our home.

CARDINAL NUMBERS

Some good news about the Latin cardinal numbers: Most of them below 100 do not decline, and most of them have well-known English derivatives. You could probably guess them at sight. The first three cardinals do decline and their forms are given at the end of this chapter:

ūnus, ūna, ūnum	*one*
duo, duae, duo	*two*
trēs, tria	*three*

Then come the indeclinables:

quattuor	*four*
quinque	*five*
sex	*six*
septem	*seven*
octo	*eight*
novem	*nine*
decem	*ten*

As in English, the higher numbers are formed from the lower numbers:

undecim	*eleven*
duodecim	*twelve*
tredecim	*thirteen*
quattuordecim	*fourteen*
quindecim	*fifteen*
sēdecim	*sixteen*

septemdecim	*seventeen*
duodēvīgintī	*eighteen*
undēvīgintī	*nineteen*
vīgintī	*twenty*

Finally, there are the multiples of ten:

trīgintā	*thirty*
quadrāgintā	*forty*
quīnquāgintā	*fifty*
sexāgintā	*sixty*
septuāgintā	*seventy*
octōgintā	*eighty*
nonāgintā	*ninety*
centum	*one hundred*

MILLE

The word for "thousand," **mille**, has special needs. In the singular it does not decline, but grammatically it behaves as though it were plural; thus, you will find examples like these:

nōn mihi mille placent.	A thousand [girls] do not please me.	OV A 1.3.15
"mille," inquit "nummōs invēnī."	He says, "I have found a thousand sesterces."	PETR 98.2

However, the plural **mīlia** does decline—like a neuter i-stem of the third declension:

mīlia
mīlium
mīlibus
mīlia
mīlibus

When the plural of "thousands" is used, it generates a genitive "thousands of ..." as follows:

novem mīlia hostium occīdit.	LIVY 35.21.7

He killed nine thousand(s) of the enemy.

quattuor mīlia librōrum Didymus grammaticus scrīpsit.	SEN E 88.37

Didymus the grammarian wrote four thousand(s) (of) books.

DECLENSIONS OF UNUS, DUO, AND TRES

For completeness, here are the forms of **unus**:

Case	Singular			Plural		
	masc	*fem*	*neut*	*masc*	*fem*	*Neut*
nominative	**ūn-us**	**ūn-a**	**ūn-um**	**ūn-ī**	**ūn-ae**	**ūn-a**
genitive	**ūn-īus**	**ūn-īus**	**ūn-īus**	**ūn-ōrum**	**ūn-ārum**	**ūn-ōrum**
dative	**ūn-ī**	**ūn –ī**	**ūn-ī**	**ūn-īs**	**ūn-īs**	**ūn-īs**
accusative	**ūn-um**	**ūn-am**	**ūn-um**	**ūn-ōs**	**ūn-ās**	**ūn-a**
ablative	**ūn-ō**	**ūn-ā**	**ūn-ō**	**ūn-īs**	**ūn-īs**	**ūn-īs**

You may be wondering why **ūnus** has a plural. The reason is that a small number of Latin nouns with singular meanings are grammatically plural. Consider the following:

ego ad Caesarem ūnās Capuā litterās dedī.

I gave (mailed) one letter to Caesar from Capua.

CIC ATT 8.2.1

Mercifully, **duo** and **trēs** exist only in the plural:

	masc	*fem*	*neut*
nominative	**du-o**	**du-ae**	**du-o**
genitive	**du-ōrum**	**du-ārum**	**du-ōrum**
dative	**du-ōbus**	**du-ābus**	**du-ōbus**
accusative	**du-ōs**	**du-ās**	**du-o**
ablative	**du-ōbus**	**du-ābus**	**du-ōbus**

	masc/fem	*neut*
nominative	**tr-ēs**	**tr-ia**
genitive	**tr-ium**	**tr-ium**
dative	**tr-ibus**	**tr-ibus**
accusative	**tr-ēs**	**tr-ia**
ablative	**tr-ibus**	**tr-ibus**

CHAPTER 62: VOCABULARY

annus, ī, m.	*year*
centuriō, centuriōnis, m.	*centurion*
domī	*at home*
domum	*home(ward)*
fortasse	*perhaps*
legiō, legiōnis, f.	*legion*
trēs, tria	*three*

CHAPTER 62: PRACTICE SENTENCES (ANSWERS FOLLOW CHAPTER 66)

1.	**ī domum.**	Plaut Asin 940
2.	**vīsne Rōmam īre?**	Livy 5.22.5
3.	**is eō tempore erat Ravennae.**	Caes BC 1.5.5
4.	**sī audērem, Athēnās peterem.**	Cic Att 3.7.1
5.	**māior annīs sum quinquāgintā.**	Livy 42.34.11
6.	**centum et novem vixit annōs.**	Quint 3.1.9
7.	**sex fīliī nōbīs, duae fīliae sunt.**	Livy 42.34.4
8.	Go (plural) to Rome to the senate.	Livy 6.26.2
9.	Are you about to go home?	Plaut Bacc 146
10.	I was not at Rome.	Pliny E 2.2.2
11.	Will I dine alone at home?	Plaut Stich 599
12.	Servius Tullius reigned for forty-four years.	Livy 1.48.8

CHAPTER 62: LATIN TO ENGLISH SENTENCES

1.	**vixit trēs et sexāgintā annōs.**	SEN R S 6.22
2.	**sī ante eam diem nōn vēneris, Rōmae tē fortasse vidēbō.**	CIC ATT 2.11.2
3.	**nam ego eram domī imperātor summus in patriā meā.**	PLAUT PSEUD 1171
4.	**diēs est tempus vīgintī et quattuor hōrārum.**	SEN E 12.7
5.	**ego vērō iam tē nec hortor nec rogō ut domum redeās.**	CIC FAM 7.30.1
6.	**negābant eum Rōmam esse reditūrum.**	CIC PRO MIL 62

7. **Rōmulus septem et trigintā regnāvit annōs, Numa trēs et quadrāgintā.** — LIVY 1.21.6

8. **in tōtā autem legiōne erant centuriōnēs quinquāgintā quinque.** — VEG 2.8

9. **per annōs centum cum populō Rōmānō bellum gessimus.** — LIVY 23.42.6

10. **quattuor reperiō causās cūr senectūs misera videātur.** — CIC DE SENEC 15

CHAPTER 62: GLOSSED LATIN TO ENGLISH SENTENCES

1. **centum** raucōrum **vocem habes.**   raucus, a, um: hoarse   — SENR C 1.7.18

2. **maximum** Thēbīs **scelus** māternus **amor est.**   — SEN OED 629-30

   Thēbae, ārum, f. pl.: Thebes   māternus, a, um: maternal

3. **Rōmae omnia** venālia **sunt.**   venālis, e: for sale   — SALL BJ 8.1

CHAPTER 62: ENGLISH TO LATIN SENTENCES

1. That man forbade me to come home.   — PLAUT EPID 67A
2. A poet does not want to dine at home.   — MART 11.24.15
3. The other consul remained at Rome.   — LIVY 2.33.4
4. He both was born and died at Athens.   — CIC BRUTUS 63
5. Hannibal was holding eight thousand people.   — CIC DE OFF 3.114

CHAPTER 62: PASSAGES

OUTNUMBERED OR TOO MUCH OF A GOOD THING

trigintā tibi sunt puerī totidemque **puellae;**
    ūna est nec surgit mentula. **quid faciēs?**

MART 12.86

---

totidem: just as many   surgō, 3: stand up
mentula, ae, f.: dick

63

Relative Clauses of Characteristic

In chapter 28, you learned about the relative pronoun and its clauses. At the time, there was no reason to suspect that a subjunctive might be involved because, of course, you had not learned the subjunctive. Now that you have, it is time to learn its use in connection with the relative pronoun. As you remember, the relative pronoun always functions with an antecedent, whether that word is expressed or merely implied. Up to this chapter, the antecedent was always a definite entity, even if it did not actually appear in the sentence. However, when Romans imagined an <u>indefinite</u> or <u>generalized</u> antecedent, they used a subjunctive in the relative clause.

Perfectly confused? Here is an English example: "I am the man who loaned you the money" would not, in Latin, require a subjunctive in the relative clause because the antecedent is definite; "I am a man who helps his needy friends" would require a subjunctive because the antecedent is being typed or characterized. Hence the name "relative clause of characteristic." Here are some examples:

est quī vincī possit.   He is (the kind of person) who can be conquered.   HOR S 1.9.55

stultum est dare alicuī quod accipere nōn possit.   SEN BEN 7.18.1

It is foolish to give to someone (the sort of thing) which he cannot receive.

sunt alia quae magis timeam.   CIC PHIL 5.29

There are other things (of the sort) which I fear more.

This use of the subjunctive is common and may occur even where you don't think it should. One such place is in negative expressions such as "There is no one who thinks that way" or "There is nothing which I like better." Here the verbs "thinks" and "like" would be subjunctive in Latin because the antecedents "no one" and "nothing," though apparently definite enough, strike the Roman mind as generalized classes. It is as though you are saying, "There is no one (of the sort) who thinks that way" or "There is nothing (of the sort) which I like better." Here are some examples:

nihil est quod ego mālim.   CIC ATT 13.29.1

There is nothing (of the sort) which I prefer.

sōlus est quem dīligant dī.   TER AND 973

He is the only one whom the gods esteem.

nihil est quod deus efficere nōn possit.   CIC DE DIVIN 2.86
There is nothing which (the) god is not able to bring about.

By a similar logic, questions taking the form "Who is there who … ?" or "What is there which … ?" also require a subjunctive in the relative clause:

quis est quī nōn probet?   Who is there who does not approve?   CIC PRO MIL 77
quid est quod metuās?   What is it which you fear?   PLAUT BACC 92

CHAPTER 63: PRACTICE SENTENCES (ANSWERS FOLLOW CHAPTER 66)

1. **quid habēs quod possīs dīcere?**   CIC CAEC DIV 59
2. **nihil est quod nōn emī possit.**   CIC LEG AGR 1.15
3. **res nulla est quae scrībenda sit.**   CIC ATT 11.11.1

CHAPTER 63: LATIN TO ENGLISH SENTENCES

1. **populus est quem timēre dēbeāmus.**   SEN E 14.7
2. **at nunc dīcam quod libenter audiās.**   TER PHOR 488
3. **nōn enim sumus iī quibus nihil vērum esse videātur.**   CIC ND 1.12
4. **quid tandem est quod nōn dīvitiae corrūperint?**   SENR C 2.1.11
5. **quī reī publicae sit hostis, fēlix esse nēmō potest.**   CIC PHIL 2.64
6. **nēmō est hominum quem ego nunc magis cuperem vidēre quam tē.**   TER EUN 561
7. **quid enim est quod contrā vim sine vī fierī possit?**   CIC FAM 12.3.1
8. **dē tē audiēbāmus ea quae maximē vellēmus.**   CIC FAM 12.25A.2
9. **multōs tibi dabō quī nōn amīcō sed amīcitiā caruerint.**   SEN E 6.3
10. **adhuc nēminem cognōvī poētam quī sibi nōn optimus vidērētur.**   CIC TD 5.63

CHAPTER 63: GLOSSED LATIN TO ENGLISH SENTENCES

1. **nulla est** celeritās **quae possit cum animī** celeritāte contendere.   CIC TD 1.43
celeritās, tātis, f.: swiftness   contendō (3): compete

CHAPTER 63: ENGLISH TO LATIN SENTENCES

1. There is no one who can understand you.   SEN E 7.9
2. There is nothing which must not be feared.   CIC ATT 2.17.1
3. No one loves us who does not esteem you.   CIC FAM 16.7
4. What is there which he does not immediately know?   PLINY E 1.22.3

CHAPTER 63: PASSAGES

TO MY PLAGIARIST, PAULUS

carmina Paulus emit, recitat sua carmina Paulus.
  nam quod emās possīs iūre vocāre tuum.

MART 2.20

---

recitō (1): recite

MODEL OF A SHORT LETTER

ōlim mihi nullās epistulās mittis. "nihil est," inquis, "quod scrībam." at hoc ipsum
scrībe – nihil esse quod scrībās, vel sōlum illud, unde incipere priōrēs solēbant: "sī
valēs, bene est; ego valeō." hoc mihi sufficit; est enim maximum.

PLINY E 1.11

ōlim: for some time   unde: from where
priorēs, priorum: men of old   soleō (2): be accustomed
sufficiō (3): be enough

64 Gerund and Gerundive

Back in chapter 36, you were sternly warned not to use the term "gerund" in dealing with the present active participle. In this chapter on the Latin gerund, you will see why. As for the gerundive, there is simply nothing like it in English, which makes it in some ways less dangerous than the gerund, but in others renders it almost inexplicable.

THE GERUND

The gerund, in both Latin and English, is a verbal noun, but that requires careful explaining. (Well, there's a gerund right there: "explaining.") Many students have been taught to call the -ing form in English the gerund, but this is inexact and misleading. True, all gerunds end in -ing, but not all -ing forms are gerunds. Everything depends on how it is used. Gerunds are nouns made out of verbs by adding -ing. Thus, "I am singing" does not contain a gerund, but "I love singing" does. In the first example, "singing" is part of the predicate, while in the second, "singing" is the direct object, thus a verbal noun. You can see how confusion would arise.

In Latin, you form a gerund by adding the infix **–nd-** to the present stem of the verb. Here is a table showing all the forms of the gerund for all the conjugations, including deponents (none for **sum**):

Case	Non-Deponents				
nominative	–	–	–	–	–
genitive	amandī	habendī	dicendī	capiendī	audiendī
dative	amandō	habendō	dicendō	capiendō	audiendō
accusative	amandum	habendum	dicendum	capiendum	audiendum
ablative	amandō	habendō	dicendō	capiendō	audiendō

Case	Deponents				
nominative	–	–	–	–	–
genitive	hortandī	fatendī	loquendī	patiendī	mentiendī
dative	hortandō	fatendō	loquendō	patiendō	mentiendō
accusative	hortandum	fatendum	loquendum	patiendum	mentiendum
ablative	hortandō	fatendō	loquendō	patiendō	mentiendō

Notice that, after all the repetitions have been allowed for, the gerund has only four forms, all singular. Where is the nominative, you ask? There is no nominative because whenever a gerund would appear in the nominative, the Romans used the infinitive. So instead of saying, "Seeing is believing," they would have said, "To see is to believe," as in the following:

vīvere est cōgitāre.	To live (living) is to think (thinking).	CIC TD 5.111
beneficium accipere lībertātem est vendere.	To accept (accepting) a favor is to sell (selling) liberty.	PUBLSYR B5

The other cases of the gerund are used like this:

ego vīvendō vīcī mea fāta.	By living, I have conquered my fates.	VERG A 11.160
nōn habēs gravēs causās moriendī?	Do you not have serious causes for (of) dying?	QUINT DECL 337
accipiendō dās; dandō accipis.	By (means of) receiving you give; by (means of) giving you receive.	SEN BEN 5.8.6

THE GERUNDIVE

The gerundive is the most difficult Latin form to explain. Though it acts like a gerund, it is an adjective, not a noun, which seems logically impossible. In fact, the gerundive has a logic of its own, but first the good news—you have already learned all of its forms in chapter 38:

Gerundive		
ama-nd-us	ama-nd-a	ama-nd-um
ama-nd-ī	ama-nd-ae	ama-nd-ī
ama-nd-ō	ama-nd-ae	ama-nd-ō
ama-nd-um	ama-nd-am	ama-nd-um
ama-nd-ō	ama-nd-ā	ama-nd-ō
ama-nd-e	ama-nd-a	ama-nd-um
ama-nd-ī	ama-nd-ae	ama-nd-a
ama-nd-ōrum	ama-nd-ārum	ama-nd-ōrum
ama-nd-īs	ama-nd-īs	ama-nd-īs
ama-nd-ōs	ama-nd-ās	ama-nd-a
ama-nd-īs	ama-nd-īs	ama-nd-īs
ama-nd-ī	ama-nd-ae	ama-nd-a

That's right. Back in chapter 38, you learned about the future passive participle. It just so happens that the gerundive is identical in form—**but not in behavior**—to the future passive participle. Although they are formed identically, please regard them as two utterly distinct and unrelated creatures. Tell yourself that despite having the same spelling, despite showing the same -**nd**- infix attached to the present stem of a verb, and despite being declined like a regular adjective of the first and second declensions, the gerundive constitutes one category, the future passive participle a totally different category. You will see why I so urge as you read on.

The experts disagree about the origin of the gerundive. Wherever it came from, it is best to treat the gerundive as an offshoot or outgrowth of the gerund. In a nutshell:

▼ **Whenever the gerund takes a direct object, the gerundive <u>may</u> be substituted.**

For example, the sentence "He will help us in writing letters" could be written in Latin with either the gerund or gerundive. This is because the gerund "writing" takes a direct object "letters." Using the gerund gives

nōs in scrībendō epistulās adiūvābit.

Here, **scrībendō** is a gerund in the ablative governed by **in**; **epistulās** is accusative, the direct object of the gerund **scrībendō**.

But since the gerund is taking an accusative here, the gerundive can also be used with no difference in meaning. The conversion from gerund to gerundive proceeds according to the following formula:

(1) Take the case of the gerund (in this example, ablative).
(2) Take the gender and number of its direct object (in this example, feminine plural).
(3) Combine the two so that both words agree in case, number, and gender.

Presto, the gerundive:

nōs in epistulīs scrībendīs adiūvābit.	He will help us in writing letters.	SUET VIT HORAT

Here are some more examples of the gerundive:

nōn videō causam mūtandī locī.	I do not see a cause for (of) changing place.	CIC PRO DEIOT 21
ūnus parandō dabitur exsiliō diēs.	One day will be given for preparing exile.	SEN MED 295
fīo miser quaerendō argentō.	I become wretched by seeking money.	PLAUT PERS 5

Rewriting these sentences with the gerund yields the following:

nōn videō causam mūtandī locum.

ūnus parandō dabitur exsilium diēs.

fīo miser quaerendō argentum.

In each case, the noun appears as the direct object of the gerund. There is no difference in meaning.

Note that both the gerund or gerundive, when used with the preposition **ad**, generally show purpose:

nōs ad audiendum parātī sumus. CIC TD 1.17
  We are ready for the purpose of hearing (to hear).

habēmus satis temporis ad cōgitandum. CIC ATT 12.27.3
  We have enough (of) time for the purpose of thinking (to think).

pecūnia coacta est ad agrōs emendōs. CIC LEG AGR 1.15
  Money was gathered for the purpose of buying (to buy) fields.

CHAPTER 64: VOCABULARY

imperō, imperāre, imperāvī, imperātus   *order, command*

CHAPTER 64: PRACTICE SENTENCES (ANSWERS FOLLOW CHAPTER 66)

After translating, say whether the form is a gerund or gerundive.

1. **est ista recta docendī via.**   CIC DE LEG 2.8
2. **ille amandō mē occīdit.**   SEN BEN 2.14.5
3. **nox tibi fīnem dīcendi fēcit.**   CIC PRO TULL 6
4. **sunt enim omnia dīcendō excitanda.**   CIC DE ORAT 2.187
5. **sē contentus est sapiens ad beātē vīvendum.**   SEN E 9.13
6. This is the time of (for) learning.   SEN E 36.4
7. You call me for the purpose of writing.   CIC OR BRUT 34

CHAPTER 64: REVIEW SENTENCES (ANSWERS FOLLOW CHAPTER 66)

The following sentences illustrate four Latin constructions that are easily confused: (1) the future passive participle, (2) the passive periphrastic, (3) the gerund, and (4) the gerundive. Some of these sentences have appeared in previous chapters.

FUTURE PASSIVE PARTICIPLE

1. **consulibus senātus rem publicam dēfendendam dedit.**   CIC PHIL 8.15
2. **dīvitī aurum servandum dedit.**   PLAUT BACC 338
3. **nihil timendum videō, sed timeō tamen.**   SEN THY 435
4. **fugienda petimus.**   SEN PHAED 699
5. **sed pars magis metuenda fatōrum manet.**   SEN OED 793

PASSIVE PERIPHRASTIC

6. **discenda virtūs est.**   SEN E 123.16

7. **malum audiendum est.** PLAUT MERC 178
8. **laudandus erit tibi Antōnius.** SENR S6.1
9. **omnia armīs agenda erunt.** SUET DJ 31.2
10. **senatūs auctōritās mihi defendenda fuit.** CIC ATT 1.16.1

GERUND

11. **sapientia ars vīvendī est.** CIC DE FIN 1.42
12. **agendī tamen viam nōn videō.** CIC ATT 5.4.1
13. currendō superābit **omnēs.**   currō, 3: run   superō, 1: surpass OV M 7.755

GERUNDIVE

14. princeps **vestrae lībertātis dēfendendae fuī.**   princeps: (here) chief CIC PHIL 4.1
15. **quam causam dandī** venēnī **fīliō meō habuī?**   venēnum, ī, n.: poison QUINT DECL 319

CHAPTER 64: LATIN TO ENGLISH SENTENCES

1. **nihil agendō hominēs male agere discunt.** CATO APUD COL 11.1.26
2. **ad omnia patienda parēs sumus.** SEN E 91.16
3. **pariter hōs perīre amandō videō.** PLAUT CURC 187
4. **omnēs enim vincendī studiō tenēbāmur.** CIC PRO LIG 28
5. **neque enim exeundī Rōmā potestās nōbīs fuit.** CIC ATT 1.3.2
6. **male imperandō summum imperium āmittitur.** PUBLSYR M31
7. **aliam ratiōnem huius bellī gerendī nullam videō.** CIC ATT 9.19.3
8. **ego in hāc sententiā dīcendā nōn pārēbō dolōrī meō.** CIC PROV CONS 2
9. **līberōrum quaerendōrum causā eī uxor data est.** PLAUT CAPT 889

CHAPTER 64: GLOSSED LATIN TO ENGLISH SENTENCES

1. rem **Rōmānam auxerant hostibus in cīvitātem accipiendīs.**   LIVY 1.33.1
   rēs, reī, f.: (here) state

2. **audendō atque agendō** rēs **Rōmāna** crēvit.   LIVY 22.14.14
   rēs, reī, f.: (here) state   crescō, 3, crēvī, crētus: grow

CHAPTER 64: ENGLISH TO LATIN SENTENCES

1. The hope of dining well deceives you (plural).   JUV 5.166
2. No one becomes braver by getting mad.   SEN IRA 1.13.5
3. Nevertheless, I will not make an end of asking.   CIC ATT 16.16E.2
4. (My) eyes hurt from watching.   PLAUT MEN 882

CHAPTER 64: PASSAGES

ROMAN FOREIGN POLICY ACCORDING TO SALLUST

Rōmānīs cum nātiōnibus, **populīs, rēgibus** cunctīs **una et ea** vetus **causa** bellandī **est –** cupīdo prōfunda **imperiī et dīvitiārum.**

SALL HIST IV.69.5

nātio, nātionis, f.: nation	cunctus, a, um: all
vetus, veteris: old	bellō (1): war
cupīdo, cupīdinis, f.: desire	prōfundus, a, um: profound

65

The Supine/Double Dative

Your final Latin hurdle (in this book) is the verb formation called **supine**, again a construction unlike anything in English. There are two forms of the supine—one in the accusative, the other in the ablative. The accusative form ends in -**um**; it is often found with a verb of motion and denotes purpose. This form is particularly tricky since it is identical to a perfect passive participle, and your first instinct will be to translate it accordingly. Unfortunately, the supine is active, not passive, and your translation will be off accordingly.

For example, **eō dormītum** means "I am going for the purpose of sleeping," or, in normal English, "I am going to sleep." **dormītum** is the accusative supine form indicating purpose. Here are some more:

rūs habitātum abiī.	I went off to the country to dwell.	TER HEC 224
eō lavātum.	I am going to wash.	PLAUT AUL 579

The supine in the ablative ends in –**ū** and specifies the relation of a noun to an adjective; a useful translation is "in respect to."

nōn difficile dictū est.	It is not difficult in respect to the saying (to say).	QUINT 7.1.5
grave dictū est sed dīcendum tamen.	It is serious in respect to the saying (to say) but nevertheless it has to be said.	CIC PHIL 9.8
ita māiōrēs nātū solent dīcere.	Thus, the elders in (respect to) birth are accustomed to say.	PLINY E 2.14.3

(Note that **dictū** and **nātū** appear to be forms of fourth declension nouns; however, these nouns do not exist. If you like, you can think of the supine as being a fourth declension noun formed from the fourth principal part of a verb, creating a noun that only exists in two forms—the accusative and the ablative.)

DOUBLE DATIVE

There is one more use of the dative to be learned, one which is quite common in Latin but quite unlike anything in English. The construction is called the double dative because you will find two nouns in the dative, and neither is an indirect object nor a dative of agent nor any of the other datives you have learned. The first dative normally refers to a person and will be translated like any normal dative, with "to" or "for." The second dative, however, can often be captured by using the phrase "as a." Several examples will illustrate this very Latin idiom; the cumbersome translation is designed to bring out the underlying construction:

mihi magnō dolōrī est.	It is (as a) great pain to me.	CIC ATT 6.9.2
est enim mihi magnae cūrae.	For it is (as a) great care to me.	CIC DE FIN 3.8
cum dī tē amant, voluptātī est mihi.		PLAUT RUD 1183
	When the gods love you, it is (as a) pleasure to me.	
cuī bonō fuit?	To whom was it (as a) good?	CIC ROSCAM 84

There is no mechanical way to identify the presence of a double dative. The verb **sum** is often involved but does not have to be. Be on the lookout for a plethora of datives. In general, one dative will refer to a person, the other to an abstract entity. A major problem is that the abstract noun often appears to be a genitive, and a clever student can appear to translate it that way successfully. For example, in the second sentence, **cūrae** could be mistaken for the genitive and forced into an incorrect translation.

CHAPTER 65: VOCABULARY

lūdō, lūdere, lūsī, lūsus	*play*
facilis, facile	*easy*

CHAPTER 65: PRACTICE SENTENCES (ANSWERS FOLLOW CHAPTER 66)

1.	**nīl est dictū facilius.**	TER PHOR 300
2.	**facile factū fuit.**	CIC PRO TULL 21
3.	**auxiliō iīs fuit.**	PLAUT AMPH 92
4.	**īmusne sessum?**	CIC DE ORAT 3.17
5.	He is going to sleep.	PLAUT AUL 302
6.	I will be a joy to you (plural).	PLAUT POEN 1217

CHAPTER 65: LATIN TO ENGLISH SENTENCES

1. **facile est inventū.**   PLAUT TRIN 679
2. **exemplō aliīs dēbētis esse.**   LIVY 3.21.6
3. **lūsum it Maecēnās, dormītum ego Vergiliusque.**   HOR S 1.5.48
4. **studia mihi nostra salūtī fuērunt.**   SEN E 78.3
5. **quaerāmus ergō quid optimum factū sit.**   SEN VIT BEAT 2.2
6. **incrēdibile dictū est, sed ā mē vērissimē dīcētur.**   CIC CLUENT 195
7. **rēs ista bonō nēminī praeter istum fuit.**   AUCHER 4.53
8. **ad Caesarem vēnit orātum ut sibi ignosceret.**   CAES BELL ALEX 67.1
9. **spectātum veniunt, veniunt spectentur ut ipsae.**   OV AA 1.99

CHAPTER 65: GLOSSED LATIN TO ENGLISH SENTENCES

1. **paucīs** temeritās **est bonō,**   temeritās, tātis, f.: rashness   PHAEDR 5.4.12
   multīs malō.

CHAPTER 65: ENGLISH TO LATIN SENTENCES

1. These things are bitter even to hear.   CIC FAM 7.30.1
2. I say that the book was a (source of) safety to me.   CIC BRUTUS 14
3. Greed is a great evil to humans.   AUCHER 2.37
4. "Nothing is easier to know," he said.   LIVY 23.13.1

CHAPTER 65: PASSAGES

WE TEACH OUR CHILDREN ALL TOO WELL

nōs docuimus, ex nōbīs audiunt, nostrās amicās, **nostrōs** concubīnōs **vident, omne** convivium obscaenīs canticīs strepit, pudenda **dictū spectantur. fit ex hīs** consuētūdo, inde **nātūra. discunt haec miserī** antequam **sciant vitia esse.**

QUINT 1.2.7-8

amīca, ae, f.: girl-friend	concubīnus, i, m.: boy-friend
convivium, ii, n.: dinner party	obscaenus, a, um: obscene
canticum, i, n.: song	strepō (3): resound
pudendus, a, um: shameful	consuētūdo, tūdinis, f.: habit
inde: from there	antequam: before

WHO BENEFITS?

Lūcius Cassius ille, quem populus Rōmānus vērissimum et sapientissimum iūdicem putābat, identidem **in causīs quaerere** solēbat **"cuī bonō"** fuisset.

CIC ROSCAM 84

identidem: over and over	soleō (2): be accustomed

66

Fear Clauses

Fear clauses are a subset of the purpose clause; as such they have **ut** and **nē** with a subjunctive in the dependent clause and are introduced by a verb of fearing in the main clause. They also follow sequence of tense. The tricky thing about them is that they appear to operate in reverse from a purpose clause. That is, if you fear that something <u>may</u> happen, you use **nē**; if you fear that something may <u>not</u> happen, you use **ut**. Here are some examples:

nunc metuō nē peccet.	Now I fear that he may do wrong.	PLAUT PERS 624
ferrum nē habēret metuī.	I feared that she might have a sword.	PLAUT CAS 908
nē malī fīant timēs?	Do you fear that they may become bad?	SEN THY 313
verēbar ut redderentur.	I was fearing that they might not be delivered.	CIC FAM 12.19.1

The explanation for this phenomenon is perhaps that fear clauses were originally two independent sentences: "I fear" and a jussive "let it not (**nē**) happen." These two were eventually combined to give the standard fear clause with **nē** for positive fears and **ut** for negative fears.

CHAPTER 66: VOCABULARY

vereor, verērī, veritus sum   *fear*

CHAPTER 66: PRACTICE SENTENCES (ANSWERS FOLLOW THIS CHAPTER)

1. **metuit nē illam vendās.**   PLAUT PSEUD 284
2. **timeō nē vērum sit quod audiō.**   SENR C 2.3.1
3. I fear that he may perish.   OV M 7.16

CHAPTER 66: LATIN TO ENGLISH SENTENCES

1. A. **quid? metuis nē tē vendam?** B. **nōn metuō, pater.**   PLAUT PERS 357
2. **nōn timeō nē mūtent tē, timeō nē impediant.**   SEN E 32.2
3. **vereor nē dēsīderēs officium meum.**   CIC FAM 6.6.1
4. **timeō nē innocentem damnāveris.**   SENR C 7.1.1
5. **vereor ut satis diligenter actum in senātū sit.**   CIC ATT 6.4.2
6. **timeō nē male facta antīqua mea sint inventa omnia.**   PLAUT TRUC 774

CHAPTER 66: ENGLISH TO LATIN SENTENCES

1. I feared that he would call me a poet.   PETR 90.2
2. I fear that they may be hindered.   CIC FAM 11.10.4

ANSWERS TO SCRAMBLED SENTENCES

See Introduction, pp. xi-xii

"She had changed clothes since the afternoon and now was wearing a handsome blue dress."

Plainsong, Kent Haruf, p. 119

"Then in the night she woke when she heard someone coughing in the next room."

Plainsong, Kent Haruf, p. 37

ANSWERS TO PRACTICE SENTENCES

CHAPTER 6

1. Your advice is true.   CIC ATT 10.10.2
2. **laudō consilium tuum.**   PLAUT PERS 548
3. **nullum habeō dominum.**   SEN E 47.12

CHAPTER 7

1. Is it enough for you?   TER PHOR 1047
2. For now you (fem.) are mine.   PLAUT EPID 648
3. You are able to fight.   OV M 13.364
4. **ubi estis, servī?**   PLAUT CIST 649
5. A. **malus es?** B. **malus sum.**   PLAUT POEN 866
6. **laudāre nōn possum.**   CIC PRO MIL 33

CHAPTER 8

1. He praises things belonging to another.   SEN HERC 341
2. You are able to give many things.   SEN BEN 5.4.1
3. You are not able to deny the rest.   CIC VER 3.132
4. **magna rogā.**   MART 11.68.2
5. **malum est avāritia.**   CIC INVENT 1.95
6. **sī potestis, bonōs laudāte.**   SEN VIT BEAT 27.1

CHAPTER 9

1. Watch, wretched ones!   SEN AGAM 758
2. You have our counsels.   CIC ATT 5.21.10
3. Take care of your (plural) duty.   PLAUT BACC 760
4. The fault is ours, not nature's.   SEN E 22.15
5. **miser sum.**   PLAUT PSEUD 80
6. **Balbus est aeger.**   CIC ATT 13.47A.1
7. **animus līber est.**   QUINT DECL 282
8. **vestrās litterās exspectō.**   CIC FAM 14.16

CHAPTER 10

1. No one is without a fault. — SENR C 2.4.4
2. He is able to love no one. — [QUINT] DECL 14.10
3. Therefore, no one is able to be supremely happy. — CIC DE FIN 2.87
4. Is philosophy not the law of life? — SEN E 94.39
5. Do you not now see the character of human beings? — PLAUT PERS 385
6. **ita vīta est hominum.** — TER ADEL 739
7. **es homō miser.** — CIC DE FIN 2.24
8. **lex est ratiō summa.** — CIC DE LEG 1.18
9. **lēgēs damus līberīs populīs.** — CIC DE LEG 3.4

CHAPTER 12

1. I see no end of evil. — CIC ATT 9.18.2
2. The body has great strength. — SEN E 15.1
3. He is in danger of death. — CELS 2.8.P.50.12
4. Death is neither a good thing nor a bad thing. — SEN AD MARC 19.5
5. **amās bonam mentem.** — PETR 3.1
6. **dē morte nōn cōgitāmus.** — SEN AD MARC 9.2
7. **vīs magna populī est.** — [SEN] OCT 185

CHAPTER 13

1. Will we have war? — SENR S5.5
2. I will give no kindness. — SEN BEN 2.15.2
3. He had a small son. — PHAEDR APP 3.3
4. The gods will love you. — PLAUT MEN 278
5. Love is a god of peace. — PROP 3.5.1
6. **tibi consilium dabimus.** — CIC ATT 9.7A.1
7. **pugnābat fīlius noster.** — QUINT DECL 278
8. **manet et semper manēbit.** — CIC DE LEG 1.1

CHAPTER 14

1. You will always be mine. — OV A 3.11B.17
2. None will be free. — PROP 2.23.24

3. And by now it was full night.   PETR 92.1
4. **nihil tūtum erat.**   SENR C2.5.2
5. **negāre nōn poterat.**   [QUINT] DECL 17.19

CHAPTER 15

1. I fear to say the truth to you.   OV HER 20.107
2. Now what will you (plural) do?   PLAUT PSEUD 504
3. Seek my father.   PLAUT MEN 736
4. For the mind seeks reason.   LUCR 2.1044
5. **animum rege.**   HOR E 1.2.62
6. **bella relinque virīs.**   OV M 12.476
7. **dīcam meam sententiam.**   PLAUT CURC 702
8. **causās dēfendere possum.**   HOR S 2.5.34
9. **quaerēbat argentum avāritia.**   PLINY NH 33.4

CHAPTER 16

1. I really await your letter now.   CIC ATT 9.18.4
2. **vērē dīcam.**   CIC LEG AGR 2.10
3. **tū rectē cōgitās.**   CIC ATT 14.11.2

CHAPTER 17

1. This is my father.   PLAUT PERS 741
2. He denies nothing of these (things).   CIC PRO TULL 24
3. Who is able to see this (thing)?   CATULLUS 29.1
4. This is my opinion.   PLAUT PSEUD 379
5. Are you that man's slave?   PLAUT PSEUD 1169
6. **hoc meum est officium.**   PLAUT PSEUD 377
7. **hoc possum dīcere.**   CIC PRO SULLA 27
8. **bonus est hic vir.**   TER AND 915

CHAPTER 18

1. We are Romans.   CIC DE ORAT 3.168
2. He gives thanks to us.   CIC ATT 6.1.2

3. I give thanks to myself.   SEN BEN 5.7.2
4. I will wage wars with you.   OV IBIS 137
5. Take care of your (plural) duty.   PLAUT BACC 760
6. **properā ad mē.**   SEN E 35.4
7. **dē tē cōgitābam.**   CIC ATT 5.10.1
8. **nōs dī amant.**   LIVY 1.23.9
9. **ego vōs amō.**   PLAUT CIST 7
10. **Trebātium nōbīscum habēmus.**   CIC ATT 13.9.1

CHAPTER 19

1. By now you know my opinion.   PLAUT AUL 444
2. O Jupiter, what do I hear?   TER AND 464-5
3. And also you (plural) know this.   PLAUT STICH 591
4. **nihil inveniēs.**   SEN E 57.6
5. **deōrum nescīs nōmina.**   PLAUT BACC 124
6. **vērum audiēs.**   SEN E 46.3
7. **quis hoc nescit?**   CIC PRO FLACC 83
8. **dē Coeliō nihil audiēbāmus.**   CIC ATT 6.4.1

CHAPTER 20

1. I will do as you bid.   PLAUT MOST 928
2. I desired to be with you.   CIC ATT 8.11D.6
3. We are fleeing (our) homeland.   VERG E 1.3-4
4. For what were we able to do?   CIC IN PIS 13
5. Now accept (plural) the other reasons.   PLAUT POEN 55-6
6. Does a master receive a favor from a slave?   SEN BEN 3.22.3
7. **arma capiunt.**   LIVY 2.45.14
8. **fugiunt tua gaudia.**   OV HER 15.109
9. **scīre cupis nōmen?**   MART 11.8.13
10. **fuge magna.**   HOR E 1.10.32

CHAPTER 21

1. You (plural) have his slaves.   CIC ROSCAM 77
2. Is this fellow living?   PLAUT CAPT 989

3. You see, he was not able to do this. CIC RAB POST 28

4. The gods will give this power. PLAUT CAPT 934

5. He at any rate is his father. PLAUT CAPT 974

6. **servābō fīlium eius.** SEN BEN 7.20.2

7. **erit in eā sententiā semper.** AUCHER 4.54

CHAPTER 22

1. **suam habet fortūna ratiōnem.** PETR 82.6

2. **dēfendēbant sententiam suam.** CIC DE FIN 2.2

CHAPTER 23

1. I have given arms to you (plural). OV AA 2.741

2. A. Were you free? B. I was. PLAUT CAPT 628

3. For who has loved secure? OV HER 19.109

4. What did they (feminine) say to you? PLAUT MG 60

5. This one/He did his duty. PLAUT CAPT 297

6. He left the sword in the wound. [QUINT] DECL 1.11

7. You wrote nothing about it to me. CIC ATT 1.3.2

8. I have been quiet so far; now I will not be quiet. PLAUT TRUC 817

9. Were we able to say (our) opinion freely? CIC ATT 14.14.2

10. **arma cēpimus.** CIC PHIL 12.16

11. **servō lībertātem dedit.** SENR C 7.6.7

12. **nōmen audīvī numquam.** CIC ATT 5.20.1

13. **vixit, dum vixit, bene.** TER HEC 461

14. **hanc lēgem populus Rōmānus accēpit?** CIC PHIL 5.7

15. **vīcit fortūna tua fortūnam meam.** SEN CONS SAP 6.6

CHAPTER 24

1. (His) father had never feared that man. [QUINT] DECL 1.3

2. Why did you not come, as I had ordered? PLAUT ASIN 413

3. We will have seen the opinion of Epicurus. CIC TD 3.32

4. I will write to you when I will have seen Caesar. CIC ATT 2.1.9

5. I have strength. OV HER 16.352

6. **bella magna gesserat.** CIC DE FIN 2.65

7. **mihi negōtium est.**   PLAUT AMPH 1035

8. **patrem suum numquam vīderat.**   CIC RAB POST 4

9. **scīēmus cum vēneris.**   CIC ATT 2.3.1

10. **sunt et mihi vulnera, cīvēs.**   OV M 13.262-3

CHAPTER 25

1. I have a rich enemy.   QUINT DECL 337

2. A brave mind moves all (people).   SEN TROAD 1146

3. No one of mortals (no mortal) is happy.   PLINY NH 7.130

4. Money has made no one rich.   SEN E 119.9

5. I am happy and I will remain happy.   OV M 6.193-5

6. The immortal gods have given me children.   CIC RED POP P 5

7. **omnia vincit Amor.**   VERG E 10.69

8. **vīta omnis brevis est.**   PUBLSYR

9. **fortūna fortēs metuit.**   SEN MED 159

10. **dolōrem gravem sentiō.**   SEN E 78.17

11. **sapientibus mē virīs dedī.**   SEN AD HELV 5.2

12. **sed erunt omnia facilia sī valēbis.**   CIC FAM 16.11.1

CHAPTER 27

1. Do I perceive enough with (my) eyes?   PLAUT POEN 1299

2. She does not do this with words.   TIB 1.5.43

3. You saw me with your eyes.   PLAUT RUD 1166

4. For they were able to see nothing with the mind.   CIC TD 1.37

5. **vīcit vīribus.**   CIC DE AMIC 55

6. **nōs consiliīs adiūvābis.**   CIC ATT 10.2.2

7. **matrem quaerēbat oculīs.**   [QUINT] DECL 2.23

8. **vixistī mūnere nostrō.**   OV M 8.503-4

CHAPTER 28

1. Answer this (thing) which I ask.   PLAUT ASIN 578

2. I will say these things which are true.   CIC VER 3.158

3. There is much about which he fears.   SENR C 7.8.5

4. A. What do I hear? B. That which is true.   PLAUT AMPH 792-3

5. For there are many faults about which I have spoken. — QUINT 11.3.31

6. Those men/They have done what no one had done. — CIC PHIL 2.114

7. (Those) whom true love has held, it will hold. — SEN THY 551

8. That (thing) will be yours, which will be mine. — PLAUT TRIN 714

9. **miser est homō quī amat!** — PLAUT ASIN 616

10. **videō iam illum quem exspectābam.** — CIC REPUB 2.69

11. **animus accipit quae vidēmus.** — CIC TD 5.111

CHAPTER 29

1. For to myself I seem sane. — HOR S 2.3.302

2. The mind is viewed in deeds. — QUINT DECL 369

3. We are delighted when we write. — CIC DE FIN 1.3

4. Without cause, I am accused by you. — CIC ATT 1.5.3

5. Will nothing be owed to you in return for this? — SEN BEN 6.18.2

6. (That) which is always moved is eternal. — CIC TD 1.53

7. For this man, however, death was (being) prepared. — CIC PRO MIL 19

8. (Those) who say this seem to me to be wrong. — SEN E 57.7

9. **omnia dēbentur vōbīs.** — OV M 10.32

10. **nēmō in vītā tenērī potest.** — SEN E 12.10

11. **quī timētur timet.** — SEN E 105.4

12. **exspectābantur litterae tuae.** — CIC FAM 1.8.7

13. **omnia mūtantur.** — OV M 15.165

14. **servāberis mūnere nostrō.** — OV M 7.93

CHAPTER 30

1. Free the homeland from fear. — SEN PHOEN 642-3

2. We were not being called into the senate. — CIC PHIL 5.1

3. We await you and your army. — CIC AD BRUT 1.9.3

4. **senātus vocātur.** — CIC ATT 1.14.5

5. **movē manūs; properā!** — PLAUT PERS 772

6. **timēbat īram senātūs.** — SALL BJ 25.7

CHAPTER 31

1. The cause of the war is (being) sought.   LIVY 35.16.6
2. Serious opinions are (being) said.   CAES BC 1.2.8
3. What is heard about Caesar?   CIC ATT 13.16.2
4. You are (being) bribed by no gold.   OV F 2.661
5. The book will be sent to you.   CIC ATT 1.13.5
6. Scorn to be scorned.   PUBLSYR
7. Unless we hurry, we will be left behind.   SEN E 108.24
8. I will be scorned by you.   CIC REPUB 1.31
9. They were not able to be bribed.   NEPOS 6.3.3
10. **fātīs agimur.**   SEN OED 980
11. **virtūte vincentur.**   CIC PRO SULLA 24
12. **vērum invenīrī potest?**   CIC PRO MIL 59
13. **nōn trahuntur ā Fortūnā.**   SEN PROV 5.4
14. **Messius dēfendēbātur ā nōbīs.**   CIC ATT 4.15.9
15. **numquam perīculum sine perīculō vincitur.**   PUBLSYR N7

CHAPTER 32

1. They are doing other things.   PLAUT PSEUD 152
2. You see, I have no hope of peace.   CIC ATT 9.13A.1
3. I am moved by all these things.   CIC IN CAT 4.3
4. I will give effort to this thing.   PLAUT PSEUD 1115
5. You have done an injury to the republic.   CIC VER 3. 161
6. **omnis spēs in vōbīs est.**   CIC FAM 12.1.1
7. **diēī tempus nōn vidēs?**   PLAUT TRIN 811
8. **causam huius reī quaeris?**   SEN E 49.3
9. **eō diē nōn fuit senātus.**   CIC FAM 12.25.1
10. **multae rēs aguntur.**   PLINY E 9.39.2

CHAPTER 33

1. He himself fights with himself.   CIC TD 3.47
2. She herself scorns herself.   PLAUT MG 1236
3. You do not fear the people, but the gods themselves.   CIC ND 1.85
4. **ipsa puella bona est.**   TIB 2.6.44
5. **causam ipsam dēfendēmus.**   QUINT DECL 326
6. **voluptātēs ipsae timentur.**   SEN CLEM 1.26.2

CHAPTER 34

1. I came (having been) awaited.   CIC DOMO SUA 16
2. We leave behind things (having been) sought.   SEN DE OTIO 1.2
3. (Having been) asked by me, Marcellus spoke.   CIC Q FR 2.3.1
4. I (have) never fought unless (having been) forced.   SENR C 1.8.6
5. **arma relicta videt.**   OV M 12.144
6. **ā patriā fūgī victus.**   OV TRIST 1.5.66

CHAPTER 35

1. The way of life has been/was found.   CIC DE FIN 5.15
2. The thing had been managed badly.   LIVY 1.37.6
3. Never will all (things) have been said.   QUINT 2.13.17
4. I wretched have been ruined.   PLAUT CURC 133
5. By my talent, punishment has been discovered.   OV TRIST 2.12
6. Terentia was delighted by your letter.   CIC ATT 2.12.4
7. **laudātus est ab omnibus.**   CIC OR BRUT 31
8. **nunc mihi vīta data est.**   OV TRIST 3.3.36
9. **fortūna est mūtāta.**   LUCAN 3.21
10. **victus est quī vīcit.**   SEN IRA 2.34.5

CHAPTER 36

1. Respond to one seeking.   HOR S 2.5.1-2
2. Sitting there I was writing these things to you.   CIC ATT 1.10.3
3. **rogantī respondēbō.**   PLAUT MERC 515
4. **properans urbem petit.**   LUCR 3.1067

CHAPTER 37

1. With wounds having been received, Pansa had fled.   CIC AD BRUT 1.3A
2. Hortensius came to me, with the letter having been written.   CIC ATT 10.17.1

CHAPTER 38

1. The wounds have to be cured.   QUINT DECL 268
2. Thanks have to be given.   `CIC FAM 8.11.2
3. The boy learned what had to be learned.   CIC DE ORAT 3.87
4. Therefore you had to be forced.   PLINY PANEG 5.6
5. They have armies not to be scorned.   CIC FAM 10.24.6
6. Munatius gave me this/that letter to be read.   CIC FAM 10.12.2
7. You flee having-been-done things; you seek
    things to-be-done.   OV HER 7.13
8. **pax petenda est.**   LIVY 7.40.5
9. **vērum dīcendum est.**   SENR C 1.8.6
10. **sed faciendum erit.**   SEN TRANQ AN 5.5
11. **bellum gerendum est.**   CIC PHIL 11.16

CHAPTER 39

1. It is not the same thing.   MART 12.96.9
2. For you yourself have learned the same things.   CIC ACADPOS 5
3. Shall we do the same (things) as the rest?   SEN E 5.6
4. We must do the same thing.   SEN BEN 7.29.2
5. **īsdem in armīs fuī.**   CIC PRO LIG 9
6. **eadem enim dīcuntur ā multīs.**   CIC TD 2.6

CHAPTER 40

1. Every thing about-to-be is uncertain.   SEN AD MARC 23.1
2. I ask—what were you (all) going to do?   CIC PRO LIG 24
3. You already gave; this one is about to give.   PLAUT TRUC 960
4. It is a famous thing which I am about to say.   CIC VER 3.61
5. **semper victūrus es.**   SENR S6.4
6. **nōn estis cēnātūrī?**   PLAUT MERC 750
7. **rogātūrus fuī puellae patrem.**   SENR C2.3.6
8. **post mortem miserī futūrī sumus.**   CIC TD 1.13

CHAPTER 41

1. Do you think that I am sad?   PLAUT ASIN 837
2. You know that you are loved by me.   CIC ATT 1.20.7
3. Do you think that you were consul?   CIC IN PIS 29
4. I see that you have lost (your) goods.   CIC FAM 9.18.4
5. Sleeping he thinks that he is sleeping.   SEN E 53.7
6. I see that all (things) have been changed.   CIC ATT 11.11.1
7. Did I not say that this (thing) would be?   TER AND 621
8. He himself was saying that he was a king.   SEN E 108.13
9. I heard that my slave was with you.   PLAUT POEN 761-2
10. I think that Brutus will be seen by me.   CIC ATT 15.25
11. **negāvī mē scīre.**   CIC FAM 8.16.4
12. **mundum deum dīcit esse.**   CIC ND 1.39
13. **scīs multōs dīcere multa.**   MART 6.56.5
14. **negās tē accēpisse beneficium?**   SEN BEN 4.6.1
15. **scīmus mortem malum nōn esse.**   SEN CONS SAP 8.3

CHAPTER 42

1. It is clearer than light.   CIC TD 1.90
2. I send shorter letters to you.   CIC ATT 5.7
3. Nothing is more true than truth.   SEN QN 2.34.2
4. She had lost a most dear husband.   SEN AD HELV 19.4
5. You can do nothing more welcome to me.   CIC ATT 5.14.3
6. Who was ever more wretched than me?   CIC ATT 11.2.3
7. **stultior stultō fuistī.**   PLAUT CURC 551
8. **quid dīcis, amīce cārissime?**   PETR 71.5
9. **numquam hominem stultiōrem vīdī.**   TER EUN 1009

CHAPTER 43

1. You (feminine plural) are very bad.   PLAUT TRUC 295
2. The better (person) is able to conquer.   SEN E 14.13
3. Greater things have to be learned.   QUINT 1.3.15
4. We believe that we are (the) best.   SEN E 59.11
5. Terentia gives the greatest thanks to you.   CIC ATT 3.8.4

6. **maximum bonum est amīcitia.**   CIC INVENT 1.95
7. **pecūniam minōrem habēbis.**   SEN E 42.9
8. **mundus nīl Iove māius habet.**   OV TRIST 2.38
9. **ratiōne et sapientiā nihil est melius.**   CIC ND 2.18
10. **plus quam accēperās reddidistī.**   CIC FAM 3.13.1

CHAPTER 44

1. He was able to live longer.   SEN AD MARC 21.6
2. I write less many things to you.   CIC ATT 3.10.3
3. I have read your letter most gladly.   CIC FAM 12.19.1
4. Many things were said most beautifully.   SENR C 1.4.10
5. **tē vehementissimē dīligō.**   CIC FAM 13.4.1
6. **nōn possum dīcere plānius.**   CIC VER 4.27
7. **maximē laudandus est.**   CIC BRUTUS 250

CHAPTER 45

1. But what am I to hope?   TER PHOR 1022
2. Let us give thanks to god.   SEN E 12.10
3. Let us do the same (thing).   SEN E 59.13
4. Let others wage wars.   OV HER 13.84
5. Let the way of death be sought.   SEN OED 1031–2
6. Let good hope give strength.   OV HER 11.61
7. What am I to call you?   SEN OED 1009
8. Let the woman be called.   CIC VER 1.66
9. Therefore, let us be praised by others.   QUINT 11.1.22
10. Where am I to find Pamphilus?   TER AND 338
11. Let reason lead you, not fortune.   LIVY 22.39.21
12. **amēmus patriam.**   CIC PRO SEST 143
13. **arma parent.**   VERG A 4.290
14. **quid ego nunc faciam?**   PLAUT CAS 549

CHAPTER 49

1. Something has to be said.   QUINT 7.1.37
2. What life remains for you?   CATULLUS 8.15

3. What cause is there of tears?   QUINT DECL 267

4. By what name will you call us?   PLAUT ASIN 652

5. I thought that I was something.   PLINY E 1.23.2

6. What madness holds (your) mind?   SEN PHOEN 557

7. **cuī nōn vīta tormentum est?**   SEN QN 5.18.15

8. **īra habet aliquam voluptātem.**   SEN IRA 2.32.1

9. **crēdō tē audisse aliquid.**   CIC FAM 2.13.2

CHAPTER 50

1. For I know to whom I am writing.   CIC FAM 11.10.2

2. You will ask me where he is.   PLAUT BACC 189

3. I see what I have done/did.   CIC VER 1.35

4. I will tell what I have done/did.   CIC DE ORAT 2.198

5. Learn what it is to live.   TER HT 971

6. You inquire why I did not fear?   CIC DOMO SUA 8

7. He does not feel how badly he sleeps.   PUBLSYR

8. **ubi sim nesciō.**   PLAUT CAS 413

9. **scīs bene cuī dīcam.**   OV TRIST 1.5.7

10. **quaerāmus quid sit bonum.**   SEN E 118.8

11. **Marcō Crassō quid acciderit vidēmus.**   CIC DE DIVIN 1.29

CHAPTER 52

1. He bore the pain as a man.   CIC TD 2.53

2. What the gods give I bear.   PLAUT AUL 88

3. Learn to bear great fortune well.   HOR O 3.27.74-5

4. We bring the arms which we are able.   OV F 2.9

5. The foolish fear Fortune; the wise bear (it).   PUBLSYR S6

6. **pater arma ferēbat.**   OV HER 8.89

7. **amōrem ferre nōn possum.**   [QUINT] DECL 14.8

8. **nōn possum haec ferre nec feram.**   CIC ATT 7.2.7

CHAPTER 53

1. Soon I will do what you (plural) want.   HOR S 1.1.16

2. Let them say what they want.   AUG CD 9.23

3. I wanted you to know it.   CIC ATT 1.6.1
4. Do not scorn these things.   CIC CAEC DIV 39
5. Believe what you prefer.   SEN E 13.13
6. These things which you want I want.   PLAUT EPID 265
7. He says that he wants to marry a wife.   PLINY E 4.2.6
8. He wants to change master, not to be free.   CIC PARADOX 41
9. He prefers to be a slave (rather) than to fight.   CIC ATT 7.15.2
10. **nōlō plūra dīcere.**   AUCHER 4.67
11. **dixī quod volēbam.**   PLAUT POEN 1231
12. **nōluī beneficium dare.**   SEN E 81.5
13. **populum Rōmānum līberum esse volumus.**   CIC PHIL 11.3
14. **haec possunt facere sed nōlunt.**   SEN E 104.26

CHAPTER 55

1. If I were to be able, I would want.   PLAUT CIST 116
   future less vivid
2. He will be conquered if he will have yielded.   SEN E 78.15
   future most vivid
3. What if this had happened?   CIC INVENT 2.140
   past contrary-to-fact; partial
4. You will find, if you truly (will) want to discover.   OV PONT 3.2.34
   future more vivid
5. If I will have been able, I will do enough for you (plural). CIC BRUTUS 21
   future most vivid
6. They would move me, if they were stronger.   CIC ATT 9.13.6
   present contrary-to-fact
7. If I had left (my) brother, I would be fearing all things. CIC FAM 2.15.4
   mixed contrary to fact
8. I would do the same thing which Gaius Marius did.   CIC PRO RAB 35
   mixed
9. **sī vēnerit, vincēmus.**   SENR S5.4
   future most vivid
10. **sī vīveret, verba eius audīrētis.**   CIC ROSCC 42
    present contrary-to-fact

CHAPTER 56

1.	I (feminine) was born free.	PLAUT CURC 607
2.	If you were to be quiet, I would talk.	PLAUT TRIN 148
3.	You will die on behalf of the republic.	SEN E 76.27
4.	I confess that I love her.	TER AND 896
5.	We talk more than is enough.	PLAUT CIST 122
6.	Good things are not able to be born from a bad thing.	SEN E 87.24
7.	He confesses that (his) father was innocent.	QUINT 7.1.56
8.	However, it can neither be born nor die.	CIC REPUB 6.27
9.	They are not dragged by Fortune; they follow her.	SEN PROV 5.4
10.	He said that no one had been born free, no one a slave.	SENR C 7.6.18
11.	I was exhorting him toward the safety of the homeland.	CIC ATT 8.9.1
12.	**vēra fatēbor.**	OV HER 8.97
13.	**bellī patitur iniūriās.**	CIC PHIL 12.9
14.	**aurum lex sequitur.**	PROP 3.13.50
15.	**loquiminī mēcum.**	TER PHOR 549
16.	**vim passa es.**	SENR C 1.2.12
17.	**in lībertāte moriāmur.**	CIC PRO RAB 16
18.	**locūtus est mēcum amīcus tuus.**	SEN E 11.1
19.	**tū tamen nihil patiēris.**	SEN E 71.7
20.	**intellegis quid sequātur.**	CIC TD 5.50

CHAPTER 57

1.	No injury harms him.	SEN CONS SAP 3.4
2.	He will even get mad at himself.	SEN IRA 1.14.2
3.	If you obey unwilling(ly), you are a slave.	PUBLSYR
4.	Does people's character please you (plural)?	CIC VER 3.208
5.	Mother got mad at father strongly.	PLAUT MERC 923
6.	Who does not forgive (one) fearing so great a thing?	QUINT DECL 348
7.	Therefore, is a juror not able to believe witnesses?	CIC PRO FONT 21
8.	**placet hoc tibi?**	CIC ATT 6.6.2

9. **parentibus meīs pāruī.**   SEN BEN 3.38.2
10. **Caesaris īra mihi nocuit.**   OV PONT 1.4.29-30
11. **numquam ego Fortūnae crēdidī.**   SEN AD HELV 5.4
12. **oculīs dē homine nōn crēdō.**   SEN VIT BEAT 2.2
13. **nōn est satis sī mihi ignōvistis.**   QUINT DECL 266
14. **amēmus patriam, pareāmus senātuī.**   CIC PRO SEST 143

CHAPTER 58

1. I snatched the reward away from you.   SEN TROAD 998
2. I was bringing force to the senate.   CIC PHIL 2.16
3. Nothing can be snatched away from him.   CIC RAB POST 41
4. We put them all before the rest.   AUG CD 8.9
5. Does a good will benefit me now?   SEN BEN 4.21.6
6. Everything is supremely happy to which nothing
    is lacking.   CIC TD 5.39
7. **mihi epistula adfertur.**   CIC ATT 9.12.1
8. **sed tibi consilium nōn dēest.**   CIC FAM 7.9.2
9. **hīs quod nōmen impōnimus?**   SEN QN 1.11.2
10. **litterae tuae mihi somnum attulērunt.**   CIC ATT 9.7.7

CHAPTER 59

1. If you (plural) love us, take care to be well.   CIC FAM 14.5.2
2. I beg you to think about this wretched woman.   CIC ATT 11.23.3
3. **orat Lepidus ut veniam.**   CIC ATT 13.42.3
4. **moneō nē faciātis.**   CIC RAB POST 18

CHAPTER 60

1. Nothing can be done.   CIC ATT 2.14.2
2. Now what will happen?   TER ADEL 288
3. I know what can happen.   SEN E 88.17
4. From this thing see what happens.   TER AND 385
5. I say that it happened thus.   PLAUT EPID 207
6. We did not see what was able to be done.   CIC FAM 12.30.6
7. **facta pax est.**   PLAUT AMPH 965

8. **ipse melior fīō.**   CIC FAM 9.18.3

9. **ex amīcō fīt inimīcus.**   SEN E 91.5

10. **homō est; vult fierī līber.**   PLAUT TRIN 563-4

CHAPTER 61

1. He ordered me to go to her.   PLAUT BACC 575

2. But we were going to you.   TER PHOR 899

3. The slaves ask me (to) where I am going.   PLAUT CURC 362

4. This (thing) is going to perish.   SEN E 42.9

5. He was killed returning from a dinner.   CIC ROSCAM 97

6. Pompeius and the consuls have gone out of Italy.   CIC ATT 9.6.4

7. **ī, adfer mihi arma.**   PLAUT CIST 284

8. **īmus, venīmus, vidēmus.**   TER PHOR 103-4

9. **rediī in domum patris.**   QUINT DECL 377

CHAPTER 62

1. Go home.   PLAUT ASIN 940

2. Do you want to go to Rome?   LIVY 5.22.5

3. At that time he was at Ravenna.   CAES BC 1.5.5

4. If I dared, I would seek Athens.   CIC ATT 3.7.1

5. I am greater (older) than fifty years.   LIVY 42.34.11

6. He lived for 109 years.   QUINT 3.1.9

7. We have six sons, two daughters.   LIVY 42.34.4

8. **īte Rōmam ad senātum.**   LIVY 6.26.2

9. **itūrus es domum?**   PLAUT BACC 146

10. **nōn eram Rōmae.**   PLINY E 2.2.2

11. **sōlus cēnābō domī?**   PLAUT STICH 599

12. **Servius Tullius regnāvit annōs quattuor
    et quadrāgintā.**   LIVY 1.48.8

CHAPTER 63

1. What do you have which you are able to say?   CIC CAEC DIV 59

2. There is nothing which cannot be bought.   CIC LEG AGR 1.15

3. There is no thing which must be written.   CIC ATT 11.11.1

CHAPTER 64

▎ REVIEW SENTENCES

FUTURE PASSIVE PARTICIPLE

1. The senate gave the republic to the consuls to be defended. CIC PHIL 8.15
2. He gave the gold to the rich man to be saved. PLAUT BACC 338
3. I see nothing to be feared, but nevertheless I fear. SEN THY 435
4. We seek things to be avoided. SEN PHAED 699
5. But the part of the fates more to be feared remains. SEN OED 793

PASSIVE PERIPHRASTIC

6. Virtue has to be/must be learned. SEN E 123.16
7. The bad thing/evil has to be/must be heard. PLAUT MERC 178
8. Antonius will have to be praised by you. SENR S6.1
9. All things will have to be done by (means of) arms. SUET DJ 31.2
10. The authority of the senate had to be defended by me. CIC ATT 1.16.1

GERUND

11. Wisdom is the art of living. CIC DE FIN 1.42
12. Nevertheless I do not see a way of doing. CIC ATT 5.4.1
13. By (means of) running he will surpass all. OV M 7.755

GERUNDIVE

14. I was the chief of defending your liberty. CIC PHIL 4.1
15. What cause did I have of giving poison to my son? QUINT DECL 319

PRACTICE SENTENCES

1.	That is the right way of teaching.	gerund	CIC DE LEG 2.8
2.	He kills me by (means of) loving.	gerund	SEN BEN 2.14.5
3.	Night made an end for you of speaking.	gerund	CIC PRO TULL 6
4.	All things must be roused by speaking.	gerund	CIC DE ORAT 2.187
5.	The wise man is content with himself for living supremely happily.	gerund	SEN E 9.13
6.	**hoc est discendī tempus.**	gerund	SEN E 36.4
7.	**mē vocās ad scrībendum.**	gerund	CIC OR BRUT 34

CHAPTER 65

1.	Nothing is easier to say.	TER PHOR 300
2.	It was easy to do.	CIC PRO TULL 21
3.	He was an aid to them.	PLAUT AMPH 92
4.	Are we going to sit?	CIC DE ORAT 3.17
5.	**it dormītum.**	PLAUT AUL 302
6.	**gaudiō erō vōbīs.**	PLAUT POEN 1217

CHAPTER 66

1.	He fears that you may sell her.	PLAUT PSEUD 284
2.	I fear that what I hear may be true/the truth.	SENR C 2.3..1
3.	**nē pereat timeō.**	OV M 7.16

TABLES OF GRAMMATICAL FORMS

NOUNS

First Declension	Second Declension				
vīta	animus	fīlius	puer	liber	fātum
vītae	animī	fīliī	puerī	librī	fātī
vītae	animō	fīliō	puerō	librō	fātō
vītam	animum	fīlium	puerum	librum	fātum
vītā	animō	fīliō	puerō	librō	fātō
vīta	anime	fīlī	puer	liber	fātum
vītae	animī	fīliī	puerī	librī	fāta
vītārum	animōrum	fīliōrum	puerōrum	librōrum	fātōrum
vītīs	animīs	fīliīs	puerīs	librīs	fātīs
vītās	animōs	fīliōs	puerōs	librōs	fāta
vītīs	animīs	fīliīs	puerīs	librīs	fātīs
vītae	animī	fīliī	puerī	librī	fāta

Third Declension				Fourth Declension		Fifth Declension
amor	corpus	nox	mare	manus	genū	diēs
amōris	corporis	noctis	maris	manūs	genūs	diēī
amōrī	corporī	noctī	marī	manuī	genū	diēī
amōrem	corpus	noctem	mare	manum	genū	diem
amōre	corpore	nocte	marī	manū	genū	diē
amor	corpus	nox	mare	manus	genū	diēs
amōrēs	corpora	noctēs	maria	manūs	genua	diēs
amōrum	corporum	noctium	marium	manuum	genuum	diērum
amōribus	corporibus	noctibus	maribus	manibus	genibus	diēbus
amōrēs	corpora	noctēs	maria	manūs	genua	diēs
amōribus	corporibus	noctibus	maribus	manibus	genibus	diēbus
amōrēs	corpora	noctēs	maria	manūs	genua	diēs

FIRST AND SECOND DECLENSION ADJECTIVES

bonus, a, um			līber, era, erum			noster, tra, trum		
bonus	bona	bonum	līber	lībera	līberum	noster	nostra	nostrum
bonī	bonae	bonī	līberī	līberae	līberī	nostrī	nostrae	nostrī
bonō	bonae	bonō	līberō	līberae	līberō	nostrō	nostrae	nostrō
bonum	bonam	bonum	līberum	līberam	līberum	nostrum	nostram	nostrum
bonō	bonā	bonō	līberō	līberā	līberō	nostrō	nostrā	nostrō
bone	bona	bonum	līber	lībera	līberum	noster	nostra	nostrum
bonī	bonae	bona	līberī	līberae	lībera	nostrī	nostrae	nostra
bonōrum	bonārum	bonōrum	līberōrum	līberārum	līberōrum	nostrōrum	nostrārum	nostrōrum
bonīs	bonīs	bonīs	līberīs	līberīs	līberīs	nostrīs	nostrīs	nostrīs
bonōs	bonās	bona	līberōs	līberās	lībera	nostrōs	nostrās	nostra
bonīs	bonīs	bonīs	līberīs	līberīs	līberīs	nostrīs	nostrīs	nostrīs
bonī	bonae	bona	līberī	līberae	lībera	nostrī	nostrae	nostra

THIRD DECLENSION ADJECTIVES

Two Terminations		One Termination		One Termination	
brevis	breve	pār	pār	libens	libens
brevis	brevis	paris	paris	libentis	libentis
brevī	brevī	parī	parī	libentī	libentī
brevem	breve	parem	pār	libentem	libens
brevī	brevī	parī	parī	libentī	libentī
brevis	breve	pār	pār	libens	libens
brevēs	brevia	parēs	paria	libentēs	libentia
brevium	brevium	parium	parium	libentium	libentium
brevibus	brevibus	paribus	paribus	libentibus	libentibus
brevēs	brevia	parēs	paria	libentēs	libentia
brevibus	brevibus	paribus	paribus	libentibus	libentibus
brevēs	brevia	parēs	paria	libentēs	libentia

COMPARATIVE/SUPERLATIVE ADJECTIVES

Comparative		Superlative		
beātior	beātius	beātissimus	beātissima	beātissimum
beātiōris	beātiōris	beātissimī	beātissimae	beātissimī
beātiōrī	beātiōrī	beātissimō	beātissimae	beātissimō
beātiōrem	beātius	beātissimum	beātissimam	beātissimum
beātiōre	beātiōre	beātissimō	beātissimā	beātissimō
beātior	beātius	beātissime	beātissima	beātissimum
beātiōrēs	beātiōra	beātissimī	beātissimae	beātissima
beātiōrum	beātiōrum	beātissimōrum	beātissimārum	beātissimōrum
beātiōribus	beātiōribus	beātissimīs	beātissimīs	beātissimīs
beātiōrēs	beātiōra	beātissimōs	beātissimās	beātissima
beātiōribus	beātiōribus	beātissimīs	beātissimīs	beātissimīs
beātiōrēs	beātiōra	beātissimī	beātissimae	beātissima

IRREGULAR ADJECTIVES

nullus et al.			ūnus			duo/trēs		
nullus	nulla	nullum	ūnus	ūna	ūnum	duo	duae	duo
nullīus	nullīus	nullīus	ūnīus	ūnīus	ūnīus	duōrum	duārum	duōrum
nullī	nullī	nullī	ūnī	ūnī	ūnī	duōbus	duābus	duōbus
nullum	nullam	nullum	ūnum	ūnam	ūnum	duōs	duās	duo
nullō	nullā	nullō	ūnō	ūnā	ūnō	duōbus	duābus	duōbus
nulle	nulla	nullum	ūne	ūna	ūnum	duo	duae	duo
nullī	nullae	nulla	ūnī	ūnae	ūna	trēs	trēs	tria
nullōrum	nullārum	nullōrum	ūnōrum	ūnārum	ūnōrum	trium	trium	trium
nullīs	nullīs	nullīs	ūnīs	ūnīs	ūnīs	tribus	tribus	tribus
nullōs	nullās	nulla	ūnōs	ūnās	ūna	trēs	trēs	tria
nullīs	nullīs	nullīs	ūnīs	ūnīs	ūnīs	tribus	tribus	tribus
nullī	nullae	nulla	ūnī	ūnae	ūna	trēs	trēs	tria

DEMONSTRATIVES

hic			ille			is		
hic	haec	hoc	ille	illa	illud	is	ea	id
huius	huius	huius	illīus	illīus	illīus	eius	eius	eius
huic	huic	huic	illī	illī	illī	eī	eī	eī
hunc	hanc	hoc	illum	illam	illud	eum	eam	id
hōc	hāc	hōc	illō	illā	illō	eō	eā	eō
hī	hae	haec	illī	illae	illa	eī/iī	eae	ea
hōrum	hārum	hōrum	illōrum	illārum	illōrum	eōrum	eārum	eōrum
hīs	hīs	hīs	illīs	illīs	illīs	eīs/iīs	eīs/iīs	eīs/iīs
hōs	hās	haec	illōs	illās	illa	eōs	eās	ea
hīs	hīs	hīs	illīs	illīs	illīs	eīs/iīs	eīs/iīs	eīs/iīs

QUI/IPSE/IDEM

Relative Pronoun			Intensifier			īdem		
quī	quae	quod	ipse	ipsa	ipsum	īdem	eadem	idem
cuius	cuius	cuius	ipsīus	ipsīus	ipsīus	eiusdem	eiusdem	eiusdem
cui	cui	cui	ipsī	ipsī	ipsī	eīdem	eīdem	eīdem
quem	quam	quod	ipsum	ipsam	ipsum	eundem	eandem	idem
quō	quā	quō	ipsō	ipsā	ipsō	eōdem	eādem	eōdem
quī	quae	quae	ipsī	ipsae	ipsa	īdem	eaedem	eadem
quōrum	quārum	quōrum	ipsōrum	ipsārum	ipsōrum	eōrundem	eārundem	eōrundem
quibus	quibus	quibus	ipsīs	ipsīs	ipsīs	īsdem	īsdem	īsdem
quōs	quās	quae	ipsōs	ipsās	ipsa	eōsdem	eāsdem	eadem
quibus	quibus	quibus	ipsīs	ipsīs	ipsīs	īsdem	īsdem	īsdem

PERSONAL PRONOUNS

First Person		Second Person		Reflexive	
ego	nōs	tu	vōs	—	—
meī	nostrum/nostrī	tuī	vestrum/vestrī	suī	suī
mihi	nōbīs	tibi	vōbīs	sibi	sibi
mē	nōs	tē	vōs	sē/sēsē	sē/sēsē
mē	nōbīs	tē	vōbīs	sē/sēsē	sē/sēsē

INTERROGATIVES/INDEFINITES

Interrogative Pronoun			Interrogative Adjective		
quis	quis	quid	quī(s)	quae	quod
cuius	cuius	cuius	cuius	cuius	cuius
cui	cui	cui	cui	cui	cui
quem	quem	quid	quem	quam	quod
quō	quō	quō	quō	quā	quō
quī	quae	quae	quī	quae	quae
quōrum	quārum	quōrum	quōrum	quārum	quōrum
quibus	quibus	quibus	quibus	quibus	quibus
quōs	quās	quae	quōs	quās	quae
quibus	quibus	quibus	quibus	quibus	quibus

Indefinite Pronoun			Indefinite Adjective		
aliquis	aliqua	aliquid	aliquī	aliqua	aliquod
alicuius	alicuius	alicuius	alicuius	alicuius	alicuius
alicui	alicui	alicui	alicui	alicui	alicui
aliquem	aliquam	aliquid	aliquem	aliquam	aliquod
aliquō	aliquā	aliquō	aliquō	aliquā	aliquō
aliquī	aliquae	aliqua	aliquī	aliquae	aliqua
aliquōrum	aliquārum	aliquōrum	aliquōrum	aliquārum	aliquōrum
aliquibus	aliquibus	aliquibus	aliquibus	aliquibus	aliquibus
aliquōs	aliquās	aliqua	aliquōs	aliquās	aliqua
aliquibus	aliquibus	aliquibus	aliquibus	aliquibus	aliquibus

INDICATIVE/ACTIVE

Present

habeō	amō	vincō	capiō	audiō
habēs	amās	vincis	capis	audīs
habet	amat	vincit	capit	audit
habēmus	amāmus	vincimus	capimus	audīmus
habētis	amātis	vincitis	capitis	audītis
habent	amant	vincunt	capiunt	audiunt

Imperfect

habēbam	amābam	vincēbam	capiēbam	audiēbam
habēbās	amābās	vincēbās	capiēbās	audiēbās
habēbat	amābat	vincēbat	capiēbat	audiēbat
habēbāmus	amābāmus	vincēbāmus	capiēbāmus	audiēbāmus
habēbātis	amābātis	vincēbātis	capiēbātis	audiēbātis
habēbant	amābant	vincēbant	capiēbant	audiēbant

Future

habēbō	amābō	vincam	capiam	audiam
habēbis	amābis	vincēs	capiēs	audiēs
habēbit	amābit	vincet	capiet	audiet

habēbimus	amābimus	vincēmus	capiēmus	audiēmus
habēbitis	amābitis	vincētis	capiētis	audiētis
habēbunt	amābunt	vincent	capient	audient

Perfect

habuī	amāvī	vīcī	cēpī	audī(v)ī
habuistī	amāvistī	vīcistī	cēpistī	audī(v)istī
habuit	amāvit	vīcit	cēpit	audī(v)it

habuimus	amāvimus	vīcimus	cēpimus	audī(v)imus
habuistis	amāvistis	vīcistis	cēpistis	audī(v)istis
habuērunt	amāvērunt	vīcērunt	cēpērunt	audī(v)ērunt

Pluperfect

habueram	amāveram	vīceram	cēperam	audī(v)eram
habuerās	amāverās	vīcerās	cēperās	audī(v)erās
habuerat	amāverat	vīcerat	cēperat	audī(v)erat

habuerāmus	amāverāmus	vīcerāmus	cēperāmus	audī(v)erāmus
habuerātis	amāverātis	vīcerātis	cēperātis	audī(v)erātis
habuerant	amāverant	vīcerant	cēperant	audī(v)erant

Future Perfect

habuerō	amāverō	vīcerō	cēperō	audī(v)erō
habueris	amāveris	vīceris	cēperis	audī(v)eris
habuerit	amāverit	vīcerit	cēperit	audī(v)erit

habuerimus	amāverimus	vīcerimus	cēperimus	audī(v)erimus
habueritis	amāveritis	vīceritis	cēperitis	audī(v)eritis
habuerint	amāverint	vīcerint	cēperint	audī(v)erint

INDICATIVE/PASSIVE

Present

habeor	amor	vincor	capior	audior
habēris	amāris	vinceris	caperis	audīris
habētur	amātur	vincitur	capitur	audītur
habēmur	amāmur	vincimur	capimur	audīmur
habēminī	amāminī	vinciminī	capiminī	audīminī
habentur	amantur	vincuntur	capiuntur	audiuntur

Imperfect

habēbar	amābar	vincēbar	capiēbar	audiēbar
habēbāris	amābāris	vincēbāris	capiēbāris	audiēbāris
habēbātur	amābātur	vincēbātur	capiēbātur	audiēbātur
habēbāmur	amābāmur	vincēbāmur	capiēbāmur	audiēbāmur
habēbāminī	amābāminī	vincēbāminī	capiēbāminī	audiēbāminī
habēbantur	amābantur	vincēbantur	capiēbantur	audiēbantur

Future

habēbor	amābor	vincar	capiar	audiar
habēberis	amāberis	vincēris	capiēris	audiēris
habēbitur	amābitur	vincētur	capiētur	audiētur
habēbimur	amābimur	vincēmur	capiēmur	audiēmur
habēbiminī	amābiminī	vincēminī	capiēminī	audiēminī
habēbuntur	amābuntur	vincentur	capientur	audientur

Perfect

habitus/a/um sum	amātus/a/um sum	victus/a/um sum	captus/a/um sum	audītus/a/um sum
habitus/a/um es	amātus/a/um es	victus/a/um es	captus/a/um es	audītus/a/um es
habitus/a/um est	amātus/a/um est	victus/a/um est	captus/a/um est	audītus/a/um est
habitī/ae/a sumus	amātī/ae/a sumus	victī/ae/a sumus	captī/ae/a sumus	audītī/ae/a sumus
habitī/ae/a estis	amātī/ae/a estis	victī/ae/a estis	captī/ae/a estis	audītī/ae/a estis
habitī/ae/a sunt	amātī/ae/a sunt	victī/ae/a sunt	captī/ae/a sunt	audītī/ae/a sunt

Pluperfect

habitus/a/um eram	amātus/a/um eram	victus/a/um eram	captus/a/um eram	audītus/a/um eram
habitus/a/um erās	amātus/a/um erās	victus/a/um erās	captus/a/um erās	audītus/a/um erās
habitus/a/um erat	amātus/a/um erat	victus/a/um erat	captus/a/um erat	audītus/a/um erat
habitī/ae/a erāmus	amātī/ae/a erāmus	victī/ae/a erāmus	captī/ae/a erāmus	audītī/ae/a erāmus
habitī/ae/a erātis	amātī/ae/a erātis	victī/ae/a erātis	captī/ae/a erātis	audītī/ae/a erātis
habitī/ae/a erant	amātī/ae/a erant	victī/ae/a erant	captī/ae/a erant	audītī/ae/a erant

Future Perfect

habitus/a/um erō	amātus/a/um erō	victus/a/um erō	captus/a/um erō	audītus/a/um erō
habitus/a/um eris	amātus/a/um eris	victus/a/um eris	captus/a/um eris	audītus/a/um eris
habitus/a/um erit	amātus/a/um erit	victus/a/um erit	captus/a/um erit	audītus/a/um erit
habitī/ae/a erimus	amātī/ae/a erimus	victī/ae/a erimus	captī/ae/a erimus	audītī/ae/a erimus
habitī/ae/a eritis	amātī/ae/a eritis	victī/ae/a eritis	captī/ae/a eritis	audītī/ae/a eritis
habitī/ae/a erunt	amātī/ae/a erunt	victī/ae/a erunt	captī/ae/a erunt	audītī/ae/a erunt

SUBJUNCTIVE/ACTIVE

Present

habeam	amem	vincam	capiam	audiam
habeās	amēs	vincās	capiās	audiās
habeat	amet	vincat	capiat	audiat
habeāmus	amēmus	vincāmus	capiāmus	audiāmus
habeātis	amētis	vincātis	capiātis	audiātis
habeant	ament	vincant	capiant	audiant

Imperfect

habērem	amārem	vincerem	caperem	audīrem
habērēs	amārēs	vincerēs	caperēs	audīrēs
habēret	amāret	vinceret	caperet	audīret
habērēmus	amārēmus	vincerēmus	caperēmus	audīrēmus
habērētis	amārētis	vincerētis	caperētis	audīrētis
habērent	amārent	vincerent	caperent	audīrent

Perfect

habuerim	amāverim	vīcerim	cēperim	audī(v)erim
habuerīs	amāverīs	vīcerīs	cēperīs	audī(v)erīs
habuerit	amāverit	vīcerit	cēperit	audī(v)erit
habuerīmus	amāverīmus	vīcerīmus	cēperīmus	audī(v)erīmus
habuerītis	amāverītis	vīcerītis	cēperītis	audī(v)erītis
habuerint	amāverint	vīcerint	cēperint	audī(v)erint

Pluperfect

habuissem	amāvissem	vīcissem	cēpissem	audī(v)issem
habuissēs	amāvissēs	vīcissēs	cēpissēs	audī(v)issēs
habuisset	amāvisset	vīcisset	cēpisset	audī(v)isset
habuissēmus	amāvissēmus	vīcissēmus	cēpissēmus	audī(v)issēmus
habuissētis	amāvissētis	vīcissētis	cēpissētis	audī(v)issētis
habuissent	amāvissent	vīcissent	cēpissent	audī(v)issent

SUBJUNCTIVE/PASSIVE

Present

habear	amer	vincar	capiar	audiar
habeāris	amēris	vincāris	capiāris	audiāris
habeātur	amētur	vincātur	capiātur	audiātur
habeāmur	amēmur	vincāmur	capiāmur	audiāmur
habeāminī	amēminī	vincāminī	capiāminī	audiāminī
habeantur	amentur	vincantur	capiantur	audiantur

Imperfect

habērer	amārer	vincerer	caperer	audīrer
habērēris	amārēris	vincerēris	caperēris	audīrēris
habērētur	amārētur	vincerētur	caperētur	audīrētur
habērēmur	amārēmur	vincerēmur	caperēmur	audīrēmur
habērēminī	amārēminī	vincerēminī	caperēminī	audīrēminī
habērentur	amārentur	vincerentur	caperentur	audīrentur

Perfect

habitus/a/um sim	amātus/a/um sim	victus/a/um sim	captus/a/um sim	audītus/a/um sim
habitus/a/um sīs	amātus/a/um sīs	victus/a/um sīs	captus/a/um sīs	audītus/a/um sīs
habitus/a/um sit	amātus/a/um sit	victus/a/um sit	captus/a/um sit	audītus/a/um sit
habitī/ae/a sīmus	amātī/ae/a sīmus	victī/ae/a sīmus	captī/ae/a sīmus	audītī/ae/a sīmus
habitī/ae/a sītis	amātī/ae/a sītis	victī/ae/a sītis	captī/ae/a sītis	audītī/ae/a sītis
habitī/ae/a sint	amātī/ae/a sint	victī/ae/a sint	captī/ae/a sint	audītī/ae/a sint

Pluperfect

habitus/a/um essem	amātus/a/um essem	victus/a/um essem	captus/a/um essem	audītus/a/um essem
habitus/a/um essēs	amātus/a/um essēs	victus/a/um essēs	captus/a/um essēs	audītus/a/um essēs
habitus/a/um esset	amātus/a/um esset	victus/a/um esset	captus/a/um esset	audītus/a/um esset
habitī/ae/a essēmus	amātī/ae/a essēmus	victī/ae/a essēmus	captī/ae/a essēmus	audītī/ae/a essēmus
habitī/ae/a essētis	amātī/ae/a essētis	victī/ae/a essētis	captī/ae/a essētis	audītī/ae/a essētis
habitī/ae/a essent	amātī/ae/a essent	victī/ae/a essent	captī/ae/a essent	audītī/ae/a essent

PARTICIPLES

habens, ntis	amans, ntis	vincens, ntis	capiens, ntis	audiens, ntis
habitus, a, um	amātus, a, um	victus, a, um	captus, a, um	audītus, a,um
habitūrus, a, um	amātūrus, a, um	victūrus, a, um	captūrus, a, um	audītūrus, a, um
habendus, a, um	amandus, a, um	vincendus, a, um	capiendus, a, um	audiendus, a, um

INFINITIVES

habēre	amāre	vincere	capere	audīre
habērī	amārī	vincī	capī	audīrī
habuisse	amāvisse	vicisse	cepisse	audī(v)isse
habitus/a/um esse	amātus/a/um esse	victus/a/um esse	captus/a/um esse	audītus/a/um esse
habitūrus/a/um esse	amātūrus/a/um esse	victūrus/a/um esse	captūrus/a/um esse	audītūrus/a/um esse
habitum īrī	amātum īrī	victum īrī	captum īrī	audītum īrī

IMPERATIVES

habē / habēte	amā / amāte	vince / vincite	cape / capite	audī / audīte

DEPONENT VERBS/INDICATIVE

Present

fateor	hortor	sequor	patior	orior
fatēris	hortāris	sequeris	pateris	orīris
fatētur	hortātur	sequitur	patitur	orītur
fatēmur	hortāmur	sequimur	patimur	orīmur
fatēminī	hortāminī	sequiminī	patiminī	orīminī
fatentur	hortantur	sequuntur	patiuntur	oriuntur

Imperfect

fatēbar	hortābar	sequēbar	patiēbar	oriēbar
fatēbāris	hortābāris	sequēbāris	patiēbāris	oriēbāris
fatēbātur	hortābātur	sequēbātur	patiēbātur	oriēbātur
fatēbāmur	hortābāmur	sequēbāmur	patiēbāmur	oriēbāmur
fatēbāminī	hortābāminī	sequēbāminī	patiēbāminī	oriēbāminī
fatēbantur	hortābantur	sequēbantur	patiēbantur	oriēbantur

Future

fatēbor	hortābor	sequar	patiar	oriar
fatēberis	hortāberis	sequēris	patiēris	oriēris
fatēbitur	hortābitur	sequētur	patiētur	oriētur
fatēbimur	hortābimur	sequēmur	patiēmur	oriēmur
fatēbiminī	hortābiminī	sequēminī	patiēminī	oriēminī
fatēbuntur	hortābuntur	sequentur	patientur	orientur

Perfect

fassus/a/um sum	hortātus/a/um sum	secūtus/a/um sum	passus/a/um sum	orsus/a/um sum
fassus/a/um es	hortātus/a/um es	secūtus/a/um es	passus/a/um es	orsus/a/um es
fassus/a/um est	hortātus/a/um est	secūtus/a/um est	passus/a/um est	orsus/a/um est
fassī/ae/a sumus	hortātī/ae/a sumus	secūtī/ae/a sumus	passī/ae/a sumus	orsī/ae/a sumus
fassī/ae/a estis	hortātī/ae/a estis	secūtī/ae/a estis	passī/ae/a estis	orsī/ae/a estis
fassī/ae/a sunt	hortātī/ae/a sunt	secūtī/ae/a sunt	passī/ae/a sunt	orsī/ae/a sunt

Pluperfect

fassus/a/um eram	hortātus/a/um eram	secūtus/a/um eram	passus/a/um eram	orsus/a/um eram
fassus/a/um erās	hortātus/a/um erās	secūtus/a/um erās	passus/a/um erās	orsus/a/um erās
fassus/a/um erat	hortātus/a/um erat	secūtus/a/um erat	passus/a/um erat	orsus/a/um erat
fassī/ae/a erāmus	hortātī/ae/a erāmus	secūtī/ae/a erāmus	passī/ae/a erāmus	orsī/ae/a erāmus
fassī/ae/a erātis	hortātī/ae/a erātis	secūtī/ae/a erātis	passī/ae/a erātis	orsī/ae/a erātis
fassī/ae/a erant	hortātī/ae/a erant	secūtī/ae/a erant	passī/ae/a erant	orsī/ae/a erant

Future Perfect

fassus/a/um erō	hortātus/a/um erō	secūtus/a/um erō	passus/a/um erō	orsus/a/um erō
fassus/a/um eris	hortātus/a/um eris	secūtus/a/um eris	passus/a/um eris	orsus/a/um eris
fassus/a/um erit	hortātus/a/um erit	secūtus/a/um erit	passus/a/um erit	orsus/a/um erit
fassī/ae/a erimus	hortātī/ae/a erimus	secūtī/ae/a erimus	passī/ae/a erimus	orsī/ae/a erimus
fassī/ae/a eritis	hortātī/ae/a eritis	secūtī/ae/a eritis	passī/ae/a eritis	orsī/ae/a eritis
fassī/ae/a erunt	hortātī/ae/a erunt	secūtī/ae/a erunt	passī/ae/a erunt	orsī/ae/a erunt

DEPONENT VERBS/SUBJUNCTIVE

Present

fatear	horter	sequar	patiar	oriar
fateāris	hortēris	sequāris	patiāris	oriāris
fateātur	hortētur	sequātur	patiātur	oriātur
fateāmur	hortēmur	sequāmur	patiāmur	oriāmur
fateāminī	hortēminī	sequāminī	patiāminī	oriāminī
fateantur	hortentur	sequantur	patiantur	oriantur

Imperfect

fatērer	hortārer	sequerer	paterer	orīrer
fatērēris	hortārēris	sequerēris	paterēris	orīrēris
fatērētur	hortārētur	sequerētur	paterētur	orīrētur
fatērēmur	hortārēmur	sequerēmur	paterēmur	orīrēmur
fatērēminī	hortārēminī	sequerēminī	paterēminī	orīrēminī
fatērentur	hortārentur	sequerentur	paterentur	orīrentur

Perfect

fassus/a/um sim	hortātus/a/um sim	secūtus/a/um sim	passus/a/um sim	orsus/a/um sim
fassus/a/um sīs	hortātus/a/um sīs	secūtus/a/um sīs	passus/a/um sīs	orsus/a/um sīs
fassus/a/um sit	hortātus/a/um sit	secūtus/a/um sit	passus/a/um sit	orsus/a/um sit
fassī/ae/a sīmus	hortātī/ae/a sīmus	secūtī/ae/a sīmus	passī/ae/a sīmus	orsī/ae/a sīmus
fassī/ae/a sītis	hortātī/ae/a sītis	secūtī/ae/a sītis	passī/ae/a sītis	orsī/ae/a sītis
fassī/ae/a sint	hortātī/ae/a sint	secūtī/ae/a sint	passī/ae/a sint	orsī/ae/a sint

Pluperfect

fassus/a/um essem	hortātus/a/um essem	secūtus/a/um essem	passus/a/um essem	orsus/a/um essem
fassus/a/um essēs	hortātus/a/um essēs	secūtus/a/um essēs	passus/a/um essēs	orsus/a/um essēs
fassus/a/um esset	hortātus/a/um esset	secūtus/a/um esset	passus/a/um esset	orsus/a/um esset
fassī/ae/a essēmus	hortātī/ae/a essēmus	secūtī/ae/a essēmus	passī/ae/a essēmus	orsī/ae/a essēmus
fassī/ae/a essētis	hortātī/ae/a essētis	secūtī/ae/a essētis	passī/ae/a essētis	orsī/ae/a essētis
fassī/ae/a essent	hortātī/ae/a essent	secūtī/ae/a essent	passī/ae/a essent	orsī/ae/a essent

PARTICIPLES

fatens, ntis	hortans, ntis	sequens, ntis	patiens, ntis	oriens, ntis
fassus, a, um	hortātus, a, um	secūtus, a, um	passus, a, um	orsus, a,um
fassūrus, a, um	hortātūrus, a, um	secūtūrus, a, um	passūrus, a, um	orsūrus, a, um
fatendus, a, um	hortandus, a, um	sequendus, a, um	patiendus, a, um	oriendus, a, um

INFINITIVES

fatērī	hortārī	sequī	patī	orīrī
fassus esse	hortātus esse	secūtus esse	passus esse	orsus esse
fassūrus esse	hortātūrus esse	secūtūrus esse	passūrus esse	orsūrus esse

IMPERATIVES

fatēre / fatēminī	hortāre/ hortāminī	sequere/ sequiminī	patere / patiminī	orīre/orīminī

IRREGULAR VERBS/INDICATIVE

Note that these verbs have no passive forms.

Present

sum	possum	volō	nōlō	mālō	eō
es	potes	vīs	nōn vīs	māvīs	īs
est	potest	vult	nōn vult	māvult	it
sumus	possumus	volumus	nōlumus	mālumus	īmus
estis	potestis	vultis	nōn vultis	māvultis	ītis
sunt	possunt	volunt	nōlunt	mālunt	eunt

Imperfect

eram	poteram	volēbam	nōlēbam	mālēbam	ībam
erās	poterās	volēbās	nōlēbās	mālēbās	ībās
erat	poterat	volēbat	nōlēbat	mālēbat	ībat
erāmus	poterāmus	volēbāmus	nōlēbāmus	mālēbāmus	ībāmus
erātis	poterātis	volēbātis	nōlēbātis	mālēbātis	ībātis
erant	poterant	volēbant	nōlēbant	mālēbant	ībant

Imperfect

eram	poteram	volēbam	nōlēbam	mālēbam	ībam
erās	poterās	volēbās	nōlēbās	mālēbās	ībās
erat	poterat	volēbat	nōlēbat	mālēbat	ībat
erāmus	poterāmus	volēbāmus	nōlēbāmus	mālēbāmus	ībāmus
erātis	poterātis	volēbātis	nōlēbātis	mālēbātis	ībātis
erant	poterant	volēbant	nōlēbant	mālēbant	ībant

Future

erō	poterō	volam	nōlam	mālam	ībō
eris	poteris	volēs	nōlēs	mālēs	ībis
erit	poterit	volet	nōlet	mālet	ībit
erimus	poterimus	volēmus	nōlēmus	mālēmus	ībimus
eritis	poteritis	volētis	nōlētis	mālētis	ībitis
erunt	poterunt	volent	nōlent	mālent	ībunt

Perfect

fuī	potuī	voluī	nōluī	māluī	ī(v)ī
fuistī	potuistī	voluistī	nōluistī	māluistī	ī(v)istī
fuit	potuit	voluit	nōluit	māluit	ī(v)it
fuimus	potuimus	voluimus	nōluimus	māluimus	ī(v)imus
fuistis	potuistis	voluistis	nōluistis	māluistis	ī(v)istis
fuērunt	potuērunt	voluērunt	nōluērunt	māluērunt	ī(v)ērunt

Pluperfect

fueram	potueram	volueram	nōlueram	mālueram	ī(v)eram
fuerās	potuerās	voluerās	nōluerās	māluerās	ī(v)erās
fuerat	potuerat	voluerat	nōluerat	māluerat	ī(v)erat
fuerāmus	potuerāmus	voluerāmus	nōluerāmus	māluerāmus	ī(v)erāmus
fuerātis	potuerātis	voluerātis	nōluerātis	māluerātis	ī(v)erātis
fuerant	potuerant	voluerant	nōluerant	māluerant	ī(v)erant

Future Perfect

fuerō	potuerō	voluerō	nōluerō	māluerō	ī(v)erō
fueris	potueris	volueris	nōlueris	mālueris	ī(v)eris
fuerit	potuerit	voluerit	nōluerit	māluerit	ī(v)erit
fuerimus	potuerimus	voluerimus	nōluerimus	māluerimus	ī(v)erimus
fueritis	potueritis	volueritis	nōlueritis	mālueritis	ī(v)eritis
fuerint	potuerint	voluerint	nōluerint	māluerint	ī(v)erint

IRREGULAR VERBS/SUBJUNCTIVE

Present

sim	possim	velim	nōlim	mālim	eam
sīs	possīs	velīs	nōlīs	mālīs	eās
sit	possit	velit	nōlit	mālit	eat
sīmus	possīmus	velīmus	nōlīmus	mālīmus	eāmus
sītis	possītis	velītis	nōlītis	mālītis	eātis
sint	possint	velint	nōlint	mālint	eant

Imperfect

essem	possem	vellem	nollem	mallem	īrem
essēs	possēs	vellēs	nollēs	mallēs	īrēs
esset	posset	vellet	nollet	mallet	īret
essēmus	possēmus	vellēmus	nollēmus	mallēmus	īrēmus
essētis	possētis	vellētis	nollētis	mallētis	īrētis
essent	possent	vellent	nollent	mallent	īrent

Perfect

fuerim	potuerim	voluerim	nōluerim	māluerim	ī(v)erim
fuerīs	potuerīs	voluerīs	nōluerīs	māluerīs	ī(v)erīs
fuerit	potuerit	voluerit	nōluerit	māluerit	ī(v)erit
fuerīmus	potuerīmus	voluerīmus	nōluerīmus	māluerīmus	ī(v)erīmus
fuerītis	potuerītis	voluerītis	nōluerītis	māluerītis	ī(v)erītis
fuerint	potuerint	voluerint	nōluerint	māluerint	ī(v)erint

Pluperfect

fuissem	potuissem	voluissem	nōluissem	māluissem	ī(v)issem
fuissēs	potuissēs	voluissēs	nōluissēs	māluissēs	ī(v)issēs
fuisset	potuisset	voluisset	nōluisset	māluisset	ī(v)isset
fuissēmus	potuissēmus	voluissēmus	nōluissēmus	māluissēmus	ī(v)issēmus
fuissētis	potuissētis	voluissētis	nōluissētis	māluissētis	ī(v)issētis
fuissent	potuissent	voluissent	nōluissent	māluissent	ī(v)issent

PARTICIPLES

futūrus, a, um	—	volens, ntis	nōlens, ntis	malens, ntis	iens, ntis
—	—	—	—	—	itūrus, a, um

INFINITIVES

esse	posse	velle	nolle	malle	īre
fuisse	potuisse	voluisse	nōluisse	māluisse	isse
futūrus esse	—	—	—	—	ītūrus esse

IMPERATIVES

es / este	—	—	nōlī / nōlīte	—	ī / īte

IRREGULAR VERB: FERO

INDICATIVE ACTIVE

Present	Imperfect	Future	Perfect	Pluperfect	Future Perfect
ferō	ferēbam	feram	tulī	tuleram	tulerō
fers	ferēbās	ferēs	tulistī	tulerās	tuleris
fert	ferēbat	feret	tulit	tulerat	tulerit
ferimus	ferēbāmus	ferēmus	tulimus	tulerāmus	tulerimus
fertis	ferēbātis	ferētis	tulistis	tulerātis	tuleritis
ferunt	ferēbant	ferent	tulērunt	tulerant	tulerint

INDICATIVE PASSIVE

Present	Imperfect	Future	Perfect	Pluperfect	Future Perfect
feror	ferēbar	ferar	lātus sum	lātus eram	lātus erō
ferris	ferēbāris	ferēris	lātus es	lātus erās	lātus eris
fertur	ferēbātur	ferētur	lātus est	lātus erat	lātus erit
ferimur	ferēbāmur	ferēmur	lātī sumus	lātī erāmus	lātī erimus
feriminī	ferēbāminī	ferēminī	lātī estis	lātī erātis	lātī eritis
feruntur	ferēbantur	ferentur	lātī sunt	lātī erant	lātī erunt

SUBJUNCTIVE ACTIVE

Present	Imperfect	Future	Perfect	Pluperfect	Future Perfect
feram	ferrem	—	tulerim	tulissem	—
ferās	ferrēs	—	tulerīs	tulissēs	—
ferat	ferret	—	tulerit	tulisset	—
ferāmus	ferrēmus	—	tulerīmus	tulissēmus	—
ferātis	ferrētis	—	tulerītis	tulissētis	—
ferant	ferrent	—	tulerint	tulissent	—

SUBJUNCTIVE PASSIVE

Present	Imperfect	Future	Perfect	Pluperfect	Future Perfect
ferar	ferrer	—	lātus sim	lātus essem	—
ferāris	ferrēris	—	lātus sīs	lātus essēs	—
ferātur	ferrētur	—	lātus sit	lātus esset	—
ferāmur	ferrēmur	—	lātī sīmus	lātī essēmus	—
ferāminī	ferrēminī	—	lātī sītis	lātī essētis	—
ferantur	ferrentur	—	lātī sint	lātī essent	—

PARTICIPLES

ferens, ntis
lātus, a, um
lātūrus, a, um
ferendus, a, um

INFINITIVES

ferre
ferrī
tulisse
lātus esse
lātūrus esse
lātum īrī

IMPERATIVES

fer
ferte

IRREGULAR VERB: FIO

INDICATIVE

Present	Imperfect	Future	Perfect	Pluperfect	Future Perfect
fīō	fīēbam	fīam	factus sum	factus eram	factus erō
fīs	fīēbās	fīēs	factus es	factus erās	factus eris
fit	fīēbat	fīet	factus est	factus erat	factus erit
fīmus	fīēbāmus	fīēmus	factī sumus	factī erāmus	factī erimus
fītis	fīēbātis	fīētis	factī estis	factī erātis	factī eritis
fīunt	fīēbant	fīent	factī sunt	factī erant	factī erunt

SUBJUNCTIVE

Present	Imperfect	Future	Perfect	Pluperfect	Future Perfect
fīam	fierem	—	factus sim	factus essem	—
fīās	fierēs	—	factus sīs	factus essēs	—
fīat	fieret	—	factus sit	factus esset	—
fīāmus	fierēmus	—	factī sīmus	factī essēmus	—
fīātis	fierētis	—	factī sītis	factī essētis	—
fīant	fierent	—	factī sint	factī essent	—

PARTICIPLES

—

factus, a, um

faciendus, a, um

INFINITIVES

fierī

factus esse

factum īrī

IMPERATIVES

fī

fīte

ENGLISH TO LATIN VOCABULARY

Instead of the full infinitive form, the number of the conjugation appears; regular first conjugation verbs are signaled by (1).

about **dē** *(prep. + abl.)* 8

accept **accipiō, 3, accēpī, acceptus** 20

according to **ex/ē** *(prep. + abl.)* 10

accuse **accūsō (1)** 7

act **faciō, 3, fēcī, factus** 20

advice **consilium, iī, n.** 5

affair **negōtium, iī, n.** 6; **rēs, reī, f.** 32

after **post** *(prep. + acc.)* 24

against **in** *(prep. + acc.)* 9; **contrā** *(prep. + acc.)* 14

age **aetas, aetātis, f.** 41

aid **auxilium, iī, n.** 20

aid **adiuvō, 1, adiūvī, adiūtus** 9

all **omnis, e** 25

allow **patior, 3, passus sum** 56

alone **sōlus, a, um** 17; **ūnus, a, um** 38, 47

also **et** 23; **etiam** 35; **quoque** 39

although **cum** *(+ subjunctive)* 51

always **semper** 9

ancient **antīquus, a, um** 35

and **et** 5; **-que** 13

and also **atque/ac** 8

and ... not **nec/neque** 15

and so **itaque** 3

anger **īra, ae, f.** 14

angry **īrātus, a, um** 37

annoying **molestus, a, um** 18

another **alius, a, ud** 10

another (of two) **alter, altera, alterum** 47

answer **respondeo, -pondēre, -pondī, -ponsus** 13

approve (of) **probō (1)** 10

any **ullus, a, um** 47

arms **arma, ōrum, n. pl.** 13

army **exercitus, ūs, m.** 30

arouse **excitō (1)** 13

art *** ars, artis, f.** 14

as **ut** 20

as though **tamquam** 40

as well **et** *(adverb)* 23

ask (for) **rogō (1)** 2

at **apud** *(prep. + acc.)* 25

at any rate **quidem** *(emphasizes previous word)* 6

at home **domī** 62

at last **tandem** 46

Athens **Athēnae, Athēnarum, f. pl.** 33

authority **auctōritās, auctōritātis, f.** 14

avoid **vītō (1)** 32

await **maneō, 2, mansī, mansūrus** 1; **exspectō (1)** 2

bad **malus, a, um** 7

be **sum, esse, fuī, futūrus** 7

be a slave **serviō, 4, servīvī, servītus** 44

be able **possum, posse, potuī, —** 7

be afraid **timeō, 2, timuī, —** 1

be born **nascor, 3, nātus sum** 56

be done **fiō, fierī, factus sum** 60

be grateful **gratiam habeō** 4

be in love **amō (1)** 2

be lacking to **dēsum, dēesse, dēfuī, dēfutūrus** *(+ dat.)* 58

be made **fiō, fierī, factus sum** 60

be pained **doleō, 2, doluī, dolitūrus** 12

be pleasing to **placeō, 2, placuī, placitus** (+ *dat.*) 57

be quiet **taceō, 2, tacuī, —** 1

be strong **valeō, 2, valuī, valitūrus** 1

be well **valeō, 2, valuī, valitūrus** 1

be wrong **errō (1)** 4

bear **ferō, ferre, tulī, lātus** 52

beautiful **pulcher, chra, chrum** 15

beauty **forma, ae, f.** 20

because **quia** 15

become **fiō, fierī, factus sum** 60

bedroom **cubiculum, ī, n.** 52

before **ante** (*prep.* + *acc.*) 14; **prior, prius** 44

beg (for) **rogō (1)** 2; **orō (1)** 59; **petō, 3, petī(v)ī, petītus** 31

begin **incipiō, 3, incēpī, inceptus** 20

behind **post** (*prep.* + *acc.*) 24

believe **crēdō, 3, crēdidī, crēditus** 35; (+ *dat. of person*) 57

belonging to another **aliēnus, a, um** 6

benefit **prōsum, prōdesse, prōfuī, prōfutūrus** (+ *dat.*) 58

best **optimus, a, um** 43

better **melior, melius** 43

beyond **praeter** (*prep.* + *acc.*) 52

bid **iubeō, 2, iussī, iussus** 8

big **magnus, a, um** 6

bigger **maior, maius** 43

biggest **maximus, a, um** 43

bitter **acerbus, a, um** 15

blame **accūsō (1)** 7

blind **caecus, a, um** 7

body **corpus, corporis, n.** 11

bold **audax, audācis** 26

book **liber, librī, m.** 27

both ... and **et ... et** 11

boy **puer, puerī, m.** 16

brave **fortis, e** 25

bribe **corrumpō, 3, corrūpī, corruptus** 27

brief **brevis, e** 25

bring **dūcō, 3, duxī, ductus** 34; **ferō, ferre, tulī, lātus** 52

bring about **efficiō, 3, effēcī, effectus** 48

bring to **adferō, adferre, attulī, allātus** (+ *dat./acc.*) 58

brother **frāter, tris, m.** 49

business **negōtium, iī, n.** 6

but **sed** 2; **at** 5

buy **emō, 3, ēmī, emptus** 22

by (with passive forms) **ā/ab** (*prep.* + *abl.*) 29

call **vocō (1)** 3

camp **castra, ōrum, n. pl.** 24

capture **capiō, 3, cēpī, captus** 20

care for **cūrō (1)** 6

carry **ferō, ferre, tulī, lātus** 52

case **causa, ae, f.** 8

cause **causa, ae, f.** 8

centurion **centurio, centuriōnis, m.** 62

certain **certus, a, um** 31

certainly **certē** 7

change **mūtō (1)** 3

charge **crīmen, crīminis, n.** 14

chest **pectus, pectoris, n.** 11

children **līberi, ōrum, m. pl.** 9

citizen ***cīvis, cīvis, m. or f.** 12

city ***urbs, urbis, f.** 22

clear **clārus, a, um** 16

come **veniō, 4, vēnī, ventus** 19

command **imperium, iī, n.** 23

command **imperō (1)** 64

common **commūnis, e** 54

condemn **damnō (1)** 35

conduct **gerō, 3, gessī, gestus** 18

confess **fateor, 2, fassus sum** 56

conquer **vincō, 3, vīcī, victus** 20

consider **habeō, 2, habuī, habitus** 29

consul **consul, consulis, m.** 30

consulship **consulātus, ūs, m.** 47

contain **capiō, 3, cēpī, captus** 20

content (with) **contentus, a, um** *(+ abl.)* 15

control **regō, regere, rexī, rectus** 15

copy **exemplum, ī, n.** 28

corrupt **corrumpō, 3, corrūpī, corruptus** 27

counsel **consilium, iī, n.** 5

crime **scelus, sceleris, n.** 11; **crīmen, crīminis, n.** 14

cure **remedium, iī, n.** 24

danger **perīculum, ī, n.** 7

dare **audeō, audēre, ausus sum** 18

daughter **fīlia, ae, f.** 18

day **diēs, diēī, m. or f.** 32

dear **cārus, a, um** 42

death ***mors, mortis, f.** 12

deceive **decipiō, 3, decēpī, deceptus** 34

deed **factum, ī, n.** 13

defend **dēfendō, 3, dēfendī, dēfensus** 15

definitely **valdē** 9

delay **mora, ae, f.** 38

delight **dēlectō (1)** 27

deliver **reddō, reddere, reddidī, redditus** 28

demand **postulō (1)** 47

deny **negō (1)** 2

deserve **mereō, 2, meruī, meritus** 54

desire **cupiō, 3, cupī(v)ī, cupītus** 20

die **morior, 3, mortuus sum** 56

different ... different **alius ... alius** 47

difficult **difficilis, e** 32

diligent **dīligens, dīligentis** 35

dine **cēnō (1)** 36

dinner **cēna, ae, f.** 49

discover **reperiō, reperīre, repperī, repertus** 35

do **agō, 3, ēgī, actus** 15; **faciō, 3, fēcī, factus** 20

doubtful **dubius, a, um** 31

drag **trahō, 3, traxī, tractus** 31

draw (out) **trahō, 3, traxī, tractus** 31

drive **agō, 3, ēgī, actus** 15

duty **officium, iī, n.** 5

each (of two) **uterque, utraque, utrumque** 47

ear ***auris, auris, f.** 20

easily **facile** 26

easy **facilis, e** 25

eat **edō, esse, ēdī, ēsus** 46

effort **opera, ae, f.** 31

either ... or **aut ... aut** 12; **vel ... vel** 31

else **alius, a, ud** 10

emperor **imperator, imperatoris, m.** 24; **princeps, principis, m.** 49

empire **imperium, iī, n.** 23

end ***fīnis, fīnis, m.** 12

enemy (national) ***hostis, hostis, m.** 37

enemy (personal) **inimīcus, ī, m.** 4

enlarge **augeō, 2, auxī, auctus** 37

enough **satis/sat** 6

equal **pār, paris** 25

esteem **dīligō, 3, dīlexī, dīlectus** 15

eternal **aeternus, a, um** 9

even **etiam** 35

ever **umquam** 24

every **omnis, e** 25

evil **malus, a, um** 7

excellence **virtūs, virtūtis, f.** 10

except **nisi** 8

except for **praeter** *(prep. + acc.)* 52

exhort **hortor, hortārī, hortātus sum** 56

express an opinion **sentiō, 4, sensī, sensus** 19

eye **oculus, ī, m.** 6

fall **cadō, 3, cecidī, cāsūrus** 36

famous **clārus, a, um** 16

fate **fātum, ī, n.** 5

father **pater, patris, m.** 14

fault (of character) **vitium, iī, n.** 5

favor **beneficium, iī, n.** 5

fear **timeō, 2, timuī, — 1; metuō, 3, metuī, — 22; vereor, verērī, veritus sum** 66

fear **timor, timōris, m.** 14; **metus, ūs, m.** 30

feel **sentiō, 4, sensī, sensus** 19

fellow **homō, hominis, m.** 10

few **paucī, ae, a** 19

fight **pugnō (1)** 5

final **ultimus, a, um** 38

finally **tandem** 46

find **inveniō, 4, invēnī, inventus** 19

first **prīmum** (adverb) 20

first **prīmus, a, um** 15

flat **plānus, a, um** 16

flee **fugiō, 3, fūgī, fugitūrus** 20

follow **sequor, sequī, secūtus sum** 56

foolish **stultus, a, um** 8

for **enim** (conjunction) 7; **nam** 17

for a long time **diū** 44

for the first time **prīmum** 20

for the sake of **causā** (with preceding genitive) 23

forbid **vetō, 1, vetuī, vetitus** 29

force **cogō, 3, coēgī, coactus** 31

force ***vīs, –, f.** 12

forgive **ignoscō, 3, ignōvī, ignōtus** (+ dat.) 57

form **forma, ae, f.** 20

fortune/Fortune **fortūna, ae, f.** 3

fortunate **fēlix, fēlīcis** 25

forum **forum, ī, n.** 35

free **līber, era, erum** 9

free **līberō (1)** 30

friend **amicus, ī, m.** 4

friendly **amīcus, a, um** 21

friendship **amīcitia, ae, f.** 39

from **dē** (prep. + abl.) 8; **ē/ex** (prep. + abl.) 13; **ā/ab** (prep. + abl.) 19

full **plēnus, a, um** 6

gather **cogō, 3, coēgī, coactus** 31

general **imperātor, tōris, m.** 24

get mad (at) **īrascor, īrascī, īrātus sum** (+ dat.) 57

get to know **cognoscō, 3, cognōvī, cognitus** 31

gift **mūnus, mūneris, n.** 27

girl **puella, ae, f.** 3

give **dō, 1, dedī, datus** 5

give back **reddō, reddere, reddidī, redditus** 28

give thanks **gratiās agō** 25

glad **libens, libentis** 26

glory **glōria, ae, f.** 6

go **eō, īre, ī(v)ī, itus** 61

go back **redeō, redīre, rediī, reditus** 61

go out **exeō, exīre, exiī, exitus** 61

god **deus, deī, m.** 4

gold **aurum, ī, n.** 5

good **bonus, a, um** 6

goodbye **valē/valēte** 1

great **magnus, a, um** 6

greater **maior, maius** 43

greatest **maximus, a, um** 43

Greece **Graecia, ae, f.** 35

greed **avāritia, ae, f.** 7

Greek **Graecus, a, um** 14

greeting **salūs, salūtis, f.** 23

hand **manus, ūs, f.** 30

handsome **pulcher, chra, chrum** 15

handwriting **manus, ūs, f.** 30

happen **accidō, 3, accidī, —** 41; **fīō, fīerī, factus sum** 60

happy **fēlix, fēlīcis** 25

harm **noceō, 2, nocuī, nocitūrus**
(+ *dat.*) 57

have **habeō, 2, habuī, habitus** 1

he/she/it is **est** 1

healthy **sānus, a, um** 12

hear **audiō, 4, audī(v)ī, audītus** 19

heart **animus, i, m.** 4; **pectus, pectoris,
n.** 11

heavy **gravis, e** 25

hello **salvē/salvēte** 4

help **adiuvō, 1, adiūvī, adiūtus** 9

help **opera, ae, f.** 31

highest **summus, a, um** 8

hinder **impediō, 4, impedī(v)i,
impedītus** 19

hire **dūcō, 3, duxī, ductus** 34

his/her/its (own) **suus, a, um** 22

hither **hūc** 46

hold **habeō, 2, habuī, habitus** 1; **teneō, 2,
tenuī, tentus** 5

home(ward) **domum** 62

homeland **patria, ae, f.** 3

honorable **honestus, a, um** 16

hope **spēs, speī, f.** 32

hope (for) **spērō (1)** 34

hour **hōra, ae, f.** 32

house **domus, ūs, f.** 30

how **quam** 7; **quōmodo** 45

how great **quantus, a, um** 23

how much **quantus, a, um** 23

however **autem** 13; **tamen** 18; **vērō** 42

human **hūmānus, a, um** 37

human being **homō, hominis, m.** 10

hurry **properō (1)** 2

hurt **doleō, 2, doluī, dolitūrus** 12

husband **vir, virī, m.** 9

I **ego** 1, 18

if **sī** 2

if not **nisi** 8

ignore **neglegō, 3, neglexī, neglectus** 15

immediately **statim** 34

immortal **immortālis, e** 25

in **in** (*prep. + abl.*) 3

in fact **equidem** 30; **vērō** 42

in order that **ut** 46

in order that ... not **nē** (*in purpose
clause*) 46

in return for **prō** (*prep. + abl.*) 23

increase **augeō, 2, auxī, auctus** 37

incredible **incrēdibilis, e** 40

injury **iniūria, ae, f.** 30

innocent **innocens, innocentis** 41

inquire **quaerō, 3, quaesivī, quaesitus** 15

insane **insānus, a, um** 24

into **in** (*prep. + acc.*) 9

invite **vocō (1)** 3

iron **ferrum, ī, n.** 18

I say, you say, he/she says **inquam,
inquis, inquit** 9

Italy **Ītalia, ae, f.** 4

journey **iter, itineris, n.** 11

joy **gaudium, iī, n.** 6

judgment **iūdicium, iī, n.** 13

Jupiter **Iuppiter, Iovis, m.** 14

juror **iūdex, iūdicis, m.** 32

just **iustus, a, um** 37

kill **occīdō, 3, occīdī, occīsus** 48

kindness **beneficium, iī, n.** 5

king **rex, rēgis, m.** 24

know **sciō, scīre, scī(v)ī, scītus** 19

know how **sciō, scīre, scī(v)ī, scītus**
(+ *inf.*) 19

lack **careō, 2, caruī, caritūrus** (+*abl.*) 11

last **ultimus, a, um** 38

Latin **Latīnus, a, um** 25

laugh (at) **rīdeō, 2, rīsī, rīsus** 36

law **lex, lēgis, f.; iūs, iūris, n.** 22

lead **dūcō, 3, duxī, ductus** 34

leader **dux, ducis, m.** 18

learn **discō, 3, didicī, —** 15

least **minimus, a, um** 43

leave (behind) **relinquō, 3, reliquī, relictus** 15

legion **legiō, legiōnis, f.** 62

less **minor, minus** 43

let fall **mittō, 3, mīsī, missus** 28

letter (an epistle) **litterae, ārum, f. pl.** 3; **epistula, ae, f.** 28

letters **litterae, ārum, f. pl.** 3

liberty **lībertās, lībertātis, f.** 23

lie (down) **iaceō, 2, iacuī, —** 37

lie hidden **lateō, 2, latuī, —** 37

lie in ruins **iaceō, 2, iacuī, —** 37

life **vīta, ae, f.** 3

light **levis, e** 42

light **lux, lūcis, f.** 42

listen to **audiō, 4, audī(v)ī, audītus** 19

little **parvus, a, um** 12

live **vīvō, 3, vixī, victus** 15

long **diū** 44

long **longus, a, um** 3; 6

look at **spectō (1)** 3

lose **āmittō, 3, āmīsī, āmissus** 31; **perdō, 3, perdidī, perditus** 32

loud **clārus, a, um** 16

love **amō (1)** 2

love **amor, amōris, m.** 10

lover **amātor, amātōris, m.** 36

madness **furor, furōris, m.** 27

make **faciō, 3, fēcī, factus** 20

man **vir, virī, m.** 9

manage **gerō, 3, gessī, gestus** 18

many **multī, ae, a** 6

marry **dūcō, 3, duxī, ductus** 34

master **dominus, ī, m.** 5

me **mē** 1

memory **memoria, ae, f.** 29

mental character **ingenium, iī, n.** 8

middle (of) **medius, a, um** 12

mind **animus, i, m.** 4; ***mens, mentis, f.** 12

mine **meus, a, um** 5, 6

misery **miseria, ae, f.** 23

miss **dēsīderō (1)** 13

model **exemplum, ī, n.** 28

money **argentum, ī, n.** 5; **pecūnia, ae, f.** 25

moral character **mōrēs, mōrum, m. pl.** 10

more **magis** 36; **plūs, plūris** 43

mortal **mortālis, e** 25

most **plūrimus, a, um** 43

mother **māter, matris, f.** 24

move **moveō, 2, mōvī, mōtus** 8

much **multus, a, um** 6

my **meus, a, um** 5, 6

name **nōmen, nōminis, n.** 19

nature **nātūra, ae, f.** 4

need **dēsīderō (1)** 13

neglect **neglegō, 3, neglexī, neglectus** 15

neither (of two) **neuter, tra, trum** 18

neither ... nor **nec/neque ... nec/neque** 4

net worth **rēs, reī, f.** 32

never **numquam** 22

nevertheless **tamen** 18

night ***nox, noctis, f.** 12

no **nullus, a, um** 6, 47

no one **nēmō, nēminis, m.** 10

none **nullus, a, um** 6, 47

not **nōn** 1

not **nē** *(with negative jussive)* 45

not even **nē ... quidem** 15

not know (how) **nesciō, 4, nescī(v)ī, nescītus** 19

not want **nōlō, nolle, nōluī, —** 53

nothing **nihil/nīl** 1

now **nunc** 2

(by) now **iam** 9

obey **pāreō, 2, pārui, – (+ dat.)** 57

observe **cernō, 3, crēvī, crētus** 27

often **saepe** 8

oh! **ō** 9

old age **senectūs, senectūtis, f.** 19

old man **senex, senis, m.** 61

on behalf of **prō** (prep. + abl.) 23

one **ūnus, a, um** 38, 47

one ... another **alius ... alius** 47

only **sōlus, a, um** 17, 47

(settled) opinion **sententia, ae, f.** 3

opinion **opiniō, opiniōnis, f.** 39

or **aut** 7

order **iubeō, 2, iussī, iussus** 8; **impero (1)** (+ dat.) 64

other **alius, a, ud** 10, 47

ought **dēbeō, 2, dēbuī, dēbitus** 17

our(s) **noster, tra, trum** 9

out of **ex/ē** (prep. + abl.) 13

owe **dēbeō, 2, dēbuī, dēbitus** 28

own **possideō, 2, possēdī, possessus** 43

owner **dominus, ī, m.** 5

pain **dolor, dolōris, m.** 10

parent **parens, parentis, m. or f.** 15

part ***pars, partis, f.** 24

peace **pax, pācis, f.** 13

people **populus, ī, m.** 10

perceive **cernō, 3, crēvī, crētus** 27

perhaps **fortasse** 62

perish **pereō, perīre, periī, peritus** 61

perpetual **perpetuus, a, um** 38

person **homō, hominis, m.** 10

philosophy **philosophia, ae, f.** 7

place **locus, ī, m.** 8

plain **plānus, a, um** 16

plan **consilium, iī, n.** 5

play **fabula, ae, f.** 37

play **lūdō, 3, lūsī, lūsus** 65

pleasant **iūcundus, a, um** 17

please **placeō, 2, placuī, placitus** (+ dat.) 57

pleasure **voluptās, voluptātis, f.** 15

poem **carmen, carminis, n.** 12

poet **poēta, ae, m.** 42

possess **possideō, 2, possēdī, possessus** 43

power **potestās, potestātis, f.** 10

praise **laudō (1)** 2

praise **laus, laudis, f.** 31

prefer **mālō, malle, māluī, —** 53

prepare **parō (1)** 29

preserve **servō (1)** 17

proper **iustus, a, um** 37

prostitute **meretrix, meretrīcis, f.** 39

prove **probō (1)** 10

provide **parō (1)** 29

punishment **poena, ae, f.** 30

put before **antepōnō, 3, anteposuī, antepositus** (+ dat./acc.) 58

put in/on **impōnō, 3, imposuī, impositus** (+ dat./acc.) 58

quickly **cito** 57

reach **perveniō, 4, pervēnī, perventus** 41

read **legō, 3, lēgī, lectus** 33

really **valdē** 9

realm **regnum, ī, n.** 34

reason **ratiō, ratiōnis, f.** 10

recognize **cognoscō, 3, cognōvī, cognitus** 31

refuse **negō (1)** 2

reign **regnō (1)** 36

rejoice **gaudeō, 2, gāvīsus sum** 8

relate **narrō (1)** 4

remain **maneō, 2, mansī, mansūrus** 1

remaining **reliquus, a, um** 24

remark **vox, vōcis, f.** 31

render **efficiō, 3, effēcī, effectus** 48

republic **rēs publica, reī publicae, f.** 32

require **dēsīderō (1)** 13

respond **respondeō, 2, respondī, responsus** 13

(the) rest **cēterī, ae, a** 8; **reliquus, a, um** 24

return **redeō, redīre, rediī, reditus** 61

reveal **ostendō, 3, ostendī, ostentus** 22

reward **praemium, iī, n.** 47

rich **dīves, dīvitis** 25

riches **dīvitiae, ārum, f. pl.** 5

right **iūs, iūris, n.** 22

right **rectus, a, um** 10

road **via, ae, f.** 3

Roman **Rōmānus, a, um** 12

Rome **Rōma, ae, f.** 6

rouse **moveō, 2, mōvī, mōtus** 8; **excitō (1)** 13

ruin **perdō, 3, perdidī, perditus** 32

rule **regō, regere, rexī, rectus** 15

(royal) rule **regnum, ī, n.** 34

rumor **rūmor, rūmōris, m.** 48

sad **tristis, e** 40

safe **tūtus, a, um** 11

safety **salūs, salūtis, f.** 23

same **īdem, eadem, idem** 39

sane **sānus, a, um** 12

save **servō (1)** 17

say **dīcō, 3, dixī, dictus** 15

say no **negō (1)** 2

scorn **contemnō, 3, contempsī, contemptus** 31

sea ***mare, maris, n.** 16

seal **signum, ī, n.** 27

(a) second **alter, altera, alterum** 47

secure **sēcūrus, a, um** 16

see **videō, 2, vīdī, vīsus** 1

seek **quaerō, 3, quaesī(v)ī, quaesītus** 15; **petō, 3, petī(v)ī, petītus** 31

seem **videor, vidērī, vīsus sum** 29

–self, –selves, **suī, sibi, sē/sēsē, sē/sēsē** *(reflexive)* 22

–self, –selves; "the very" **ipse, ipsa, ipsum** *(intensifier)* 33

sell **vendō, 3, vendidī, venditus** 22

senate **senātus, ūs, m.** 30

send **mittō, 3, mīsī, missus** 28

serious **gravis, e** 25

service **officium, iī, n.** 5

shade **umbra, ae, f.** 10

shadow **umbra, ae, f.** 10

shameful **turpis, e** 44

shared **commūnis, e** 54

short **brevis, e** 25

shout **clāmō (1)** 41

show **ostendō, 3, ostendī, ostentus** 22

sick **aeger, aegra, aegrum** 9

side ***pars, partis, f.** 24

sign **signum, ī, n.** 27

silver **argentum, ī, n.** 5

since **cum** *(+ subj.)* 51

sit **sedeō, 2, sēdī, sessus** 36

slave **servus, ī, m.** 5

slavery **servitūs, servitūtis, f.** 25

sleep **dormiō, 4, dormī(v)ī, dormītus** 24

sleep **somnus, ī, m.** 6

small **parvus, a, um** 12

smaller **minor, minus** 43

smallest **minimus, a, um** 43

snatch away from **ēripiō, 3, ēripuī, ēreptus** *(+ dat./acc.)* 58

so **ita** 9; **tam** 26; **sīc** 36

so far **adhūc** 23

so great **tantus, a, um** 44

so much **tantus, a, um** 44

soldier **mīles, mīlitis, m.** 24

some **aliquī, aliqua, aliquod** 49

some ... other **alius ... alius** 47

somebody else's **aliēnus, a, um** 6

someone/something **aliquis, aliquid** 49

son **fīlius, iī, m.** 4

soon **iam** 9

sooner **prior, prius** 44

speak **dīcō, 3, dīxī, dictus** 15; **loquor, loquī, locūtus sum** 56

spend (of time) **agō, 3, ēgī, actus** 15

state **cīvitās, cīvitātis, f.** 29

still **adhūc** 23

story **fābula, ae, f.** 37

strength ***vīrēs, vīrium, f. pl.** 12

strong **vehemens, vehementis** 26

study **studium, iī, n.** 10

stupid **stultus, a, um** 8

such **talis, e** 40

suffer **patior, patī, passus sum** 56

supremely happy **beātus, a, um** 8

sure **certus, a, um** 31

sweet **dulcis, e** 36

sword **ferrum, ī, n.** 18; **gladius, iī, m.** 27

take **capiō, 3, cēpī, captus** 20

take care (of) **cūrō (1)** 6

take up **suscipiō, 3, suscēpī, susceptus** 26

tale **fābula, ae, f.** 37

talent **ingenium, iī, n.** 8

talk **loquor, 3, locūtus sum** 56

teach **doceō, 2, docuī, doctus** 15

tear **lacrima, ae, f.** 3

tell **narrō (1)** 4

than **quam** 10

that/those **ille, illa, illud** 17; **iste, ista, istud** 54; **is, ea, id** 21

that **quī, quae, quod** *(relative pronoun)* 28

their (own) **suus, a, um** 22

then **tum** 14

there **ibi** *(adverb)* 7

there is **est** 1

therefore **igitur** 4; **ergō** 35

thing **rēs, reī, f.** 32

think **cōgitō (1)** 2; **putō (1)** 2; **existimō (1)** 30

this/these **hic, haec, hoc** 17; **is, ea, id** 21

thought **cōgitātio, cōgitātiōnis, f.** 10

three **trēs, tria** 62

through **per** *(prep. + acc.)* 3

thus **ita** 9; **sīc** 36

time **tempus, temporis, n.** 23; **diēs, diēī, m. or f.** 32

tiny **exiguus, a, um** 20

to **ad** *(prep. + acc.)* 3

to here **hūc** 46

to me **mihi** 4

to you **tibi** 6

today **hodiē** 28

toga **toga, ae, f.** *(worn in peace)* 45

tomorrow **crās** 28

too **nimis** 22

too much **nimis** 22

torture **tormentum, ī, n.** 43

torture **torqueō, 2, torsī, tortus** 29

touch **tangō, 3, tetigī, tactus** 31

towards **ad** *(prep. + acc.)* 3

trial **iūdicium, iī, n.** 13

triumph (victory parade) **triumphus, ī, m.** 45

trivial **levis, e** 42

true **vērus, a, um** 6

trust **crēdō, 3, crēdidī, crēditus** *(+ dat.)* 57

truth **vērum, ī, n.** 8

two **duo, duae, duo** 21, 62

uncertain **incertus, a, um** 32

under **sub** *(prep. + acc. or abl.)* 49

understand **intellegō, 3, intellexī, intellectus** 29

undertake **suscipiō, 3, suscēpī, susceptus** 26

unharmed **salvus, a, um** 6

universe **mundus, ī, m.** 4

unless **nisi** 8

unsound **insānus, a, um** 24

unwilling(ly) **invītus, a, um** 26

urge **hortor, hortārī, hortātus sum** 56

useful **ūtilis, e** 44

Venus **Venus, Veneris, f.** 15

very many **plūrimus, a, um** 43

victory **victōria, ae, f.** 48

view **spectō (1)** 3

virtue **virtūs, virtūtis, f.** 10

voice **vox, vōcis, f.** 31

vow **vōtum, i, n.** 45

wage **gerō, 3, gessī, gestus** 18

wait **maneō, 2, mansī, mansūrus** 1

wait for **exspectō (1)** 2

wander **errō (1)** 4

want **volō, velle, voluī, —** 53

war **bellum, ī, n.** 8

warn **moneō, 2, monuī, monitus** 59

waste **perdō, 3, perdidī, perditus** 32

watch **spectō (1)** 3

way **via, ae, f.** 3

we/us **nōs** 18

welcome **grātus, a, um** 21

well **bene** 15

what? **quī/quis, quae, quod** (*adjective*) 49

what? **quid** 1

when **cum** 24; **cum** (*+ subjunctive*) 51

where **ubi** 7

(to) where, whither **quō** 3

which (of two) **uter, utra, utrum** 47

which **quī, quae, quod** (*relative pronoun*) 28

while **dum** 15

who **quī, quae, quod** (*relative pronoun*) 28

who? what? **quis, quid** (*pronoun*) 1, 2, 49

whole **tōtus, a, um** 12, 47

why **cūr** 21

wife **uxor, uxōris, f.** 24

will **voluntās, voluntātis, f.** 21

willingness **voluntās, voluntātis, f.** 21

wine **vīnum, ī, n.** 37

wisdom **sapientia, ae, f.** 10; **prudentia, ae, f.** 47

wise **sapiens, sapientis** 25

wise man **sapiens, sapientis, m.** 17

wish **vōtum, ī, n.** 45

with **cum** (*prep. + abl.*) 5; **apud** (*prep. + acc.*) 25

without **sine** (*prep. + abl.*) 4

witness ***testis, testis, m.** 46

woe **miseria, ae, f.** 23

woman **mulier, mulieris, f.** 39

word **verbum, ī, n.** 5; **dictum, ī, n.** 13

worse **pēior, pēius** 43; **dēterior, dēterius** 48

worst **pessimus, a, um** 43

worthy (of) **dignus, a, um** (*+ abl.*) 12

wound **vulnus, vulneris, n.** 11

wretched **miser, era, erum** 9

write **scrībō, 3, scripsī, scriptus** 20

year **annus, ī, m.** 62

yield **cēdō, 3, cessī, cessus** 36

you **tē** (*object*) 1

you (singular) **tū** 2, 18

you (plural) **vōs** 18

you see **autem** 13

young man **iuvenis, iuvenis, m.** 34

your(s) (singular) **tuus, a, um** 3, 6

your(s) (plural) **vester, tra, trum** 9

zeal **studium, iī, n.** 10

LATIN TO ENGLISH VOCABULARY

Instead of the full infinitive form, the number of the conjugation appears; regular first conjugation verbs are signaled by (1).

ā/ab *from (prep. + abl.)* 19

ā/ab *(with passive forms) by* 29

ac *and also* 8

accidō, 3, accidī, — *happen* 41

accipiō, 3, accēpī, acceptus *receive; accept* 20

accūsō (1) *blame; accuse* 7

acerbus, a, um *bitter* 15

ad *to, towards (prep. + acc.)* 3

adferō, adferre, attulī, allātus *bring to (+ dat./acc.)* 58

adhūc *so far, still* 23

adiuvō, 1, adiūvī, adiūtus *aid, help* 9

aeger, aegra, aegrum *sick* 9

aetās, aetātis, f. *age* 41

aeternus, a, um *eternal* 9

agō, 3, ēgī, actus *drive; do; spend* 15

aliēnus, a, um *belonging to another, somebody else's* 6

aliquī, aliqua, aliquod *(adjective) some* 49

aliquis, aliquid *(pronoun) someone, something* 49

alius, a, ud *other, another; else* 10, 47

alius ... alius *one ... another; some ... other; different ... different* 47

alter, altera, alterum *another (of two), (a) second* 47

amātor, amātōris, m. *lover* 36

amīcitia, ae, f. *friendship* 39

amīcus, ī, m. *friend* 4

amīcus, a, um *friendly* 21

āmittō, 3, āmīsī, āmissus *lose* 31

amō (1) *love, be in love* 2

amor, amōris, m. *love* 10

animus, ī, m. *mind, heart* 4

annus, ī, m. *year* 62

ante *(prep. + acc.) before* 14

antepōnō, 3, anteposuī, antepositus *put before (+ dat./acc.)* 58

antīquus, a, um *ancient* 35

apud *with, at (prep. + acc.)* 25

argentum, ī, n. *silver, money* 5

arma, ōrum, n. pl. *arms* 13

*ars, artis, f. *art* 14

at *but* 5

Athēnae, Athēnārum, f. pl. *Athens* 33

atque *and also* 8

auctōritās, auctōritātis, f. *authority* 14

audax, audācis *bold* 26

audeō, audēre, ausus sum *dare* 18

audiō, 4, audī(v)ī, audītus *hear, listen to* 19

augeō, 2, auxī, auctus *increase, enlarge* 37

*auris, auris, f. *ear* 20

aurum, ī, n. *gold* 5

aut *or* 7

aut ... aut *either ... or* 12

autem *you see; however* 13

auxilium, iī, n. *aid* 20

avāritia, ae, f. *greed* 7

beātus, a, um *supremely happy* 8

bellum, i, n. *war* 8

bene *well* 15

beneficium, iī, n. *kindness, favor* 5

bonus, a, um *good* 6

brevis, e *short, brief* 25

cadō, 3, cecidī, cāsūrus *fall* 36

caecus, a, um *blind* 7

Caesar, Caesaris, m. *Caesar* 22

capiō, 3, cēpī, captus *take; capture; contain* 20

careō, carēre, caruī, caritūrus *lack (+abl.)* 11

carmen, carminis, n. *poem* 12

cārus, a, um *dear* 42

castra, ōrum, n. pl. *camp* 24

causa, ae, f. *cause; case* 8

causā *for the sake of (with preceding gen.)* 23

cēdō, 3, cessī, cessus *yield* 36

cēna, ae, f. *dinner* 49

cēnō (1) *dine* 36

centuriō, centuriōnis, m. *centurion* 62

cernō, 3, crēvī, crētus *observe, perceive* 27

certē *certainly* 7

certus, a, um *certain, sure* 31

cēterī, ae, a *(the) rest* 8

cito *quickly* 57

*cīvis, cīvis, m. or f. *citizen* 12

cīvitās, cīvitātis, f. *state* 29

clāmō (1) *shout* 41

clārus, a, um *loud; clear; famous* 16

cōgitātiō, cōgitātiōnis, f. *thought* 10

cōgitō (1) *think* 2

cognoscō, 3, cognōvī, cognitus *get to know, recognize* 31

cōgō, 3, coēgī, coactus *force; gather* 31

commūnis, e *common, shared* 54

consilium, iī, n. *advice, counsel, plan* 5

consul, consulis, m. *consul* 30

consulātus, ūs, m. *consulship* 47

contemnō, 3, -tempsī, -temptus *scorn* 31

contentus, a, um *content, content with (+ abl.)* 15

contrā *against (prep. + acc.)* 14

corpus, corporis, n. *body* 11

corrumpō, 3, -rūpī, -ruptus *corrupt, bribe* 27

crās *tomorrow* 28

crēdō, 3, crēdidī, crēditus *believe* 35; *believe, trust (+ dat.)* 57

crīmen, crīminis, n. *charge, crime* 14

cubiculum, ī, n. *bedroom* 52

cum *with (prep. + abl.)* 5; *when* 24; *when, since, although (+ subjunctive)* 51

cupiō, 3, cupīvī, cupītus *desire* 20

cūr *why* 21

cūrō (1) *take care (of), care for* 6

damnō (1) *condemn* 35

dē *about; from (prep. + abl.)* 8

dēbeō, 2, dēbuī, dēbitus *ought* 17; *owe* 28

dēcipiō, 3, dēcēpī, dēceptus *deceive* 34

dēfendō, 3, dēfendī, dēfensus *defend* 15

dēlectō (1) *delight* 27

dēsīderō (1) *need, require, miss* 13

dēsum, dēesse, dēfuī, dēfuturus *be lacking to (+ dat.)* 58

dēterior, ius *worse* 48

deus, deī, m. *god* 4

dīcō, 3, dīxī, dictus *say; speak* 15

dictum, ī, n. *word* 13

diēs, diēī, m. or f. *day; time* 32

difficilis, e *difficult* 32

dignus, a, um *worthy, worthy of (+ abl.)* 12

diligēns, diligentis *diligent* 35

dīligō, 3, dīlexī, dīlectus *esteem* 15

discō, 3, didicī, — *learn* 15

diū *for a long time, long* 44

dīves, dīvitis *rich* 25

dīvitiae, ārum, f. pl. *riches* 5

dō, 1, dedī, datus *give* 5

doceō, 2, docuī, doctus *teach* 15

doleō, 2, doluī, dolitūrus *hurt; be pained* 12

dolor, dolōris, m. *pain* 10

domī *at home* 62

dominus, ī, m. *owner, master* 5

domum *home(ward)* 62

domus, ūs, f. *house* 30

dormiō, 4, dormī(v)ī, dormītus *sleep* 24

dubius, a, um *doubtful* 31

dūcō, 3, duxī, ductus *bring, lead; marry; hire* 34

dulcis, e *sweet* 36

dum *while* 15

duo, duae, duo *two* 21, 62

dux, ducis, m. *leader* 18

e/ēx *according to (prep. + abl.)* 10; *out of, from (prep. + abl.)* 13

edō, esse, ēdī, ēsus *eat* 46

efficiō, 3, effēcī, effectus *render, bring about* 48

ego *I* 1, 18

emō, 3, ēmī, emptus *buy* 22

enim *for (conjunction)* 7

eō, īre, ī(v)ī, itus *go* 61

epistula, ae, f. *letter* 28

equidem *in fact* 30

ergō *therefore* 35

ēripiō, 3, ēripuī, ēreptus *snatch away from (+ dat./acc.)* 58

errō (1) *wander; be wrong* 4

est *he/she/it is, there is* 1

et *and* 5; *(adverb) also, as well* 23

et ... et *both ... and* 11

etiam *also; even* 35

ex/ē *according to (prep. + abl.)* 10; *out of, from (prep. + abl.)* 13

excitō (1) *(a)rouse* 13

exemplum, ī, n. *copy; model* 28

exeō, exīre, exiī, exitus *go out* 61

exercitus, ūs, m. *army* 30

exiguus, a, um *tiny* 20

existimō (1) *think* 30

exspectō (1) *await, wait for* 2

fābula, ae, f. *story, tale; play* 37

facile *easily* 26

facilis, e *easy* 25

faciō, 3, fēcī, factus *make, do; act* 20

factum, ī, n. *deed* 13

fateor, 2, fassus sum *confess* 56

fātum, ī, n. *fate* 5

fēlix, fēlīcis *fortunate, happy* 25

ferō, ferre, tulī, lātus *carry, bring, bear* 52

ferrum, ī, n. *iron, sword* 18

fīlia, ae, f. *daughter* 18

fīlius, iī, m. *son* 4

*fīnis, fīnis, m. *end* 12

fīō, fierī, factus sum *be made, be done; become; happen* 60

forma, ae, f. *beauty; form* 20

fortasse *perhaps* 62

fortis, e *brave* 25

fortūna, ae, f. *fortune, Fortune* 3

forum, ī, n. *forum* 35

frāter, tris, m. *brother* 49

fugiō, 3, fūgī, fugitūrus *flee* 20

furor, furōris, m. *madness* 27

gaudeō, 2, gāvīsus sum *rejoice* 8

gaudium, iī, n. *joy* 6

gerō, 3, gessī, gestus *wage, manage, conduct* 18

gladius, iī, m. *sword* 27

glōria, ae, f. *glory* 6

Graecia, ae, f. *Greece* 35

Graecus, a, um *Greek* 14

grātiam habeō *be grateful* 4

grātiās agō *give thanks* 25

grātus, a, um *welcome* 21

gravis, e *heavy, serious* 25

habeō, 2, habuī, habitus *have, hold* 1; *consider* 29

hic, haec, hoc *this, these* 17

hodiē *today* 28

homō, hominis, m. *human being, person, fellow* 10

honestus, a, um *honorable* 16

hōra, ae, f. *hour* 32

hortor, 1, hortātus sum *urge, exhort* 56

***hostis, hostis, m.** *enemy (national)* 37

hūc *hither, to here* 46

hūmānus, a, um *human* 37

iaceō, 2, iacuī, — *lie, lie down, lie in ruins* 37

iam *(by) now; soon* 9

ibi *there (adverb)* 7

īdem, eadem, idem *same* 39

igitur *therefore* 4

ignoscō, 3, ignōvī, ignōtus *forgive (+ dat.)* 57

ille, illa, illud *that, those* 17

immortālis, e *immortal* 25

impediō, 4, impedī(v)ī, impedītus *hinder* 19

imperātor, tōris, m. *general; emperor* 24

imperium, iī, n. *command; empire* 23

imperō (1) *order, command* 64

impōnō, 3, -posuī, -positus *put in/on (+ dat./acc.)* 58

in *in (prep. + abl.)* 3

in *into; against (prep. + acc.)* 9

incertus, a, um *uncertain* 32

incipiō, 3, -cēpī, -ceptus *begin* 20

incrēdibilis, e *incredible* 40

ingenium, iī, n. *mental character; talent* 8

inimīcus, ī, m. *enemy (personal)* 4

iniūria, ae, f. *injury* 30

innocens, innocentis *innocent* 41

inquam, inquis, inquit *I say, you say, he/she says* 9

insānus, a, um *insane, unsound* 24

intellegō, 3, -tellexī, -tellectus *understand* 29

inveniō, 4, invēnī, inventus *find* 19

invītus, a, um *unwilling(ly)* 26

ipse, ipsa, ipsum *-self, -selves; "the very"* 33

īra, ae, f. *anger* 14

īrāscor, 3, īrātus sum *get mad (at)* 57

īrātus, a, um *angry* 37

is, ea, id *this, that; he, she, it* 21

iste, ista, istud *that* 54

ita *so, thus* 9

Ītalia, ae, f. *Italy* 4

itaque *and so* 3

iter, itineris, n. *journey* 11

iubeō, 2, iussī, iussus *bid, order* 8

iūcundus, a, um *pleasant* 17

iūdex, iūdicis, m. *juror* 32

iūdicium, iī, n. *trial; judgment* 13

Iuppiter, Iovis, m. *Jupiter* 14

iūs, iūris, n. *law, right* 22

iustus, a, um *just; proper* 37

iuvenis, iuvenis, m. *young man* 34

lacrima, ae, f. *tear* 3

lateō, 2, latuī, — *lie hidden* 37

Latīnus, a, um *Latin* 25

laudō (1) *praise* 2

laus, laudis, f. *praise* 31

legiō, legiōnis, f. *legion* 62

legō, 3, lēgī, lectus *read* 33

levis, e *light, trivial* 42

lex, lēgis, f. *law* 10

libens, libentis *glad* 26

liber, librī, m. *book* 27

līber, era, erum *free* 9

līberī, ōrum, m. pl. *children* 9

līberō (1) *free* 30

lībertās, lībertātis, f. *liberty* 23

litterae, ārum, f. pl. *a letter (epistle), letters* 3

locus, ī, m. *place* 8

longus, a, um *long* 3, 6

loquor, 3, locūtus sum *talk, speak* 56

lūdō, 3, lūsī, lūsus *play* 65

lux, lūcis, f. *light* 42

magis *more* 36

magnus, a, um *big, great* 6

maior, maius *bigger, greater* 43

mālō, malle, māluī, — *prefer* 53

malus, a, um *bad; evil* 7

maneō, 2, mansī, mansūrus *(a)wait, remain* 1

manus, ūs, f. *hand; handwriting* 30

*mare, maris, n. *sea* 16

māter, matris, f. *mother* 24

maximus, a, um *biggest, greatest* 43

mē *me* 1

medius, a, um *middle (of)* 12

melior, melius *better* 43

memoria, ae, f. *memory* 29

*mens, mentis, f. *mind* 12

mereō, 2, meruī, meritus *deserve* 54

meretrix, meretrīcis, f. *prostitute* 39

metuō, 3, metuī, — *fear* 22

metus, ūs, m. *fear* 30

meus, a, um *my, mine* 5, 6

mihi *to/for me* 4

mīles, mīlitis, m. *soldier* 24

minimus, a, um *smallest, least* 43

minor, minus *smaller, less* 43

miser, era, erum *wretched* 9

miseria, ae, f. *misery, woe* 23

mittō, 3, mīsī, missus *send; let fall* 28

molestus, a, um *annoying* 18

moneō, 2, monuī, monitus *warn* 59

mora, ae, f. *delay* 38

mōres, mōrum m. pl. *moral character* 10

morior, 3, mortuus sum *die* 56

*mors, mortis, f. *death* 12

mortālis, e *mortal* 25

moveō, 2, mōvī, mōtus *move, rouse* 8

mulier, mulieris, f. *woman* 39

multus, a, um *much, many* 6

mundus, ī, m. *universe* 4

mūnus, mūneris, n. *gift* 27

mūtō (1) *change* 3

nam *for (explanatory)* 17

narrō (1) *tell, relate* 4

nascor, 3, nātus sum *be born* 56

nātūra, ae, f. *nature* 4

nē *not (with negative jussive)* 45

nē *in order that ... not* 46

-ne *(indicates a question)* 4

nē ... quidem *not even* 15

nec/neque *and ... not* 15

nec/neque ... nec/neque *neither ... nor* 4

neglegō, 3, neglexī, neglectus *ignore; neglect* 15

negō (1) *deny, say no, refuse* 2

negōtium, iī, n. *business, affair* 6

nēmō, nēminis, m. *no one* 10

neque/nec *and... not* 15

neque/nec ... neque/nec *neither... nor* 4

nesciō, 4, nescī(v)ī, nescītus *not know (how)* 19

neuter, tra, trum *neither (of two)* 18, 47

nihil/nīl *nothing* 1

nimis *too much* 22

nisi *unless, if not; except* 8

noceō, 2, nocuī, nocitūrus *harm (+ dat.)* 57

nōlō, nolle, nōluī, — *not want* 53

nōmen, nōminis, n. *name* 19

nōn *not* 1

nōs *we* 18

noster, tra, trum *our(s)* 9

***nox, noctis, f.** *night* 12

nullus, a, um *no, none* 6, 47

numquam *never* 22

nunc *now* 2

ō *oh!* 9

occīdō, 3, occīdī, occīsus *kill* 48

oculus, ī, m. *eye* 6

officium, ii, n. *duty, service* 5

omnis, e *all, every* 25

opera, ae, f. *effort, help* 31

opīniō, opīniōnis, f. *opinion* 39

optimus, a, um *best* 43

ōrō (1) *beg (for)* 59

ostendō, 3, ostendī, ostentus *show, reveal* 22

pār, paris *equal, equal to (+ dat.)* 25

parens, parentis, m. or f. *parent* 15

pāreō, 2, pāruī, — *obey (+ dat.)* 57

parō (1) *prepare, provide* 29

***pars, partis, f.** *part; side* 24

parvus, a, um *small, little* 12

pater, patris, m. *father* 14

patior, 3, passus sum *suffer; allow* 56

patria, ae, f. *homeland* 3

paucī, ae, a *(a) few* 19

pax, pācis, f. *peace* 13

pectus, pectoris, n. *chest; heart* 11

pecūnia, ae, f. *money* 25

pēior, pēius *worse* 43

per *through (prep. + acc.)* 3

perdō, 3, perdidī, perditus *ruin, waste; lose* 32

pereō, perīre, periī, peritus *perish* 61

perīculum, ī, n. *danger* 7

perpetuus, a, um *perpetual* 38

perveniō, 4, -vēnī, -ventus *reach* 41

pessimus, a, um *worst* 43

petō, 3, petī(v)ī, petītus *seek; beg* 31

philosophia, ae, f. *philosophy* 7

placeō, 2, placuī, placitus *please, be pleasing to (+ dat.)* 57

plānus, a, um *plain, flat* 16

plēnus, a, um *full* 6

plūrēs, plūra *more* 43

plūrimus, a, um *very many, most* 43

plūs *more* 43

poena, ae, f. *punishment* 30

poēta, ae, m. *poet* 42

populus, ī, m. *people* 10

possideō, 2, possēdī, possessus *possess, own* 43

possum, posse, potuī, — *be able* 7

post *after, behind (prep. + acc.)* 24

postulō (1) *demand* 47

potestās, potestātis, f. *power* 10

praemium, ii, n. *reward* 47

praeter *except for, beyond (prep. + acc.)* 52

prīmum *first for the (adverb) first, time* 20

prīmus, a, um *first* 15

princeps, principis, m. *emperor* 49

prior, prius *sooner; before* 44

prō *in return for; on behalf of (prep. + abl.)* 23

probō (1) *approve (of); prove* 10

properō (1) *hurry* 2

prōsum, prōdesse, prōfuī, prōfutūrus *benefit (+ dat.)* 58

prūdentia, ae, f. *wisdom* 47

puella, ae, f. *girl* 3

puer, puerī, m. *boy* 16

pugnō (1) *fight* 5

pulcher, chra, chrum *beautiful, handsome* 15

putō (1) *think* 2

quaerō, 3, quaesīvī, quaesītus *seek, inquire* 15

quam *how* 7; *than* 10

quantus, a, um *how great, how much* 23

-que *and* 13

quī, quae, quod *who, which, that* 28

qui(s), quae, quod *what? (adjective)* 49

quia *because* 15

quid *what* 1

quidem *at any rate (emphasizes previous word)* 6

quis, quis, quid *who? what? (pronoun)* 2, 49

quō *(to) where, whither* 3

quōmodo *how* 45

quoque *also* 39

ratiō, ratiōnis, f. *reason* 10

rectus, a, um *right* 10

reddō, 3, reddidī, redditus *give back; deliver* 28

redeō, redīre, rediī, reditus *go back, return* 61

regnō (1) *reign* 36

regnum, ī, n. *(royal) rule; realm* 34

regō, 3, rexī, rectus *rule, control* 15

relinquō, 3, relīquī, relictus *leave (behind)* 15

reliquus, a, um *remaining, rest (of)* 24

remedium, iī, n. *cure* 24

reperiō, 4, repperī, repertus *discover* 35

rēs, reī, f. *thing; affair; net worth* 32

rēs publica, reī publicae, f. *republic* 32

respondeō, 2, -pondī, -ponsus *answer, respond* 13

rex, rēgis, m. *king* 24

rīdeō, 2, rīsī, rīsus *laugh (at)* 36

rogō (1) *ask (for), beg (for)* 2

Rōma, ae, f. *Rome* 6

Rōmānus, a, um *Roman* 12

rūmor, ōris, m. *rumor* 48

saepe *often* 8

salūs, salūtis, f. *safety; greeting* 23

salvē/salvēte *hello* 4

salvus, a, um *unharmed* 6

sānus, a, um *healthy; sane* 12

sapiens, sapientis, m. *wise man* 17

sapiens, sapientis *wise* 25

sapientia, ae, f. *wisdom* 10

satis/sat *enough* 6

scelus, sceleris, n. *crime* 11

sciō, 4, scī(v)ī, scītus *know; know how (+ inf.)* 19

scrībō, 3, scripsī, scriptus *write* 20

sēcūrus, a, um *secure* 16

sed *but* 2

sedeō, 2, sēdī, sessus *sit* 36

semper *always (adverb)* 9

senātus, ūs, m. *senate* 30

senectūs, senectūtis, f. *old age* 19

senex, senis, m. *old man* 61

sententia, ae, f. *(settled) opinion* 3

sentiō, 4, sensī, sensus *feel; express an opinion* 19

sequor, sequī, secūtus sum *follow* 56

serviō, 4, servīvī, servītus *be a slave* 44

servitūs, servitūtis, f. *slavery* 25

servō (1) *save, preserve* 17

servus, ī, m. *slave* 5

sī *if* 2

sīc *thus, so* 36

signum, ī, n. *sign; seal* 27

sine *without (prep. + abl.)* 4

sōlus, a, um *alone; only* 17, 47

somnus, ī, m. *sleep* 6

spectō (1) *watch, look at, view* 3

spērō (1) *hope (for)* 34

spēs, speī, f. *hope* 32

statim *immediately* 34

studium, iī, n. *zeal; study* 10

stultus, a, um *stupid, foolish* 8

sub *under (prep. + acc. or abl.)* 49

–, suī, sibi, sē/sēsē, sē/sēsē *–self, –selves* 22

sum, esse, fuī, futūrus *be* 7

summus, a, um *highest* 8

suscipiō, 3, -cēpī, -ceptus *take up, undertake* 26

suus, a, um *his/her/its (own); their (own)* 22

taceō, 2, tacuī, — *be quiet* 1

tālis, e *such* 40

tam *so* 26

tamen *nevertheless, however* 18

tamquam *as though* 40

tandem *finally, at last* 46

tangō, 3, tetigī, tactus *touch* 31

tantus, a, um *so great, so much* 44

tē *you (object)* 1

tempus, temporis, n. *time* 23

teneō, 2, tenuī, tentus *hold* 5

*testis, testis, m. *witness* 46

tibi *to/for you* 6

timeō, 2, timuī, — *fear, be afraid* 1

timor, timōris, m. *fear* 14

toga, ae, f. *toga (worn in peace)* 45

tormentum, ī, n. *torture* 43

torqueō, 2, torsī, tortus *torture* 29

tōtus, a, um *whole* 12, 47

trahō, 3, traxī, tractus *drag, draw (out)* 31

trēs, tria *three* 62

tristis, e *sad* 40

triumphus, ī, m. *triumph (victory parade)* 45

tū *you (subject)* 2, 18

tum *then (adverb)* 14

turpis, e *shameful* 44

tūtus, a, um *safe* 11

tuus, a, um *your, yours* 3, 6

ubi *where* 7

ullus, a, um *any* 47

ultimus, a, um *last, final* 38

umbra, ae, f. *shadow, shade* 10

umquam *ever* 24

ūnus, a, um *one* 38, 47

*urbs, urbis, f. *city* 22

ut *as* 20

ut *in order that* 46

uter, utra, utrum *which (of two)* 47

uterque, utraque, utrumque *each (of two)* 47

ūtilis, e *useful* 44

utrum ... an *— ... or (signals two-pronged question)* 50

uxor, uxōris, f. *wife* 24

valdē *really, definitely (adverb)* 9

valeō, 2, valuī, valitūrus *be well, be strong* 1

valē /valēte *goodbye* 1

vehemens, vehementis *strong* 26

vel ... vel *either ... or* 31

vendō, 3, vendidī, venditus *sell* 22

veniō, 4, vēnī, ventus *come* 19

Venus, Veneris, f. *Venus* 15

verbum, ī, n. *word* 5

vereor, 2, veritus sum *fear* 66

vērō *in fact; however* 42

vērum, ī, n. *truth* 8

vērus, a, um *true* 6

vester, tra, trum *your(s)* 9

vetō, 1, vetuī, vetitus *forbid* 29

via, ae, f. *road, way* 3

victōria, ae, f. *victory* 48

videō, 2, vīdī, vīsus *see* 1

videor, 2, vīsus sum *seem* 29

vincō, 3, vīcī, victus *conquer* 20

vīnum, ī, n. *wine* 37

vir, virī, m. *man; husband* 9

*vīrēs, vīrium, f. pl. *strength* 12

virtūs, virtūtis, f. *virtue, excellence* 10

*vīs, –, f. *force* 12

vīta, ae, f. *life* 3

vitium, iī, n. *fault (of character)* 5

vītō (1) *avoid* 32

vīvō, 3, vixī, victus *live* 15

vocō (1) *call; invite* 3

volō, velle, voluī, — *want* 53

voluntās, voluntātis, f. *willingness, will* 21

voluptās, voluptātis, f. *pleasure* 15

vōs *you (plural)* 18

vōtum, ī, n. *vow, wish* 45

vox, vōcis, f. *voice; remark* 31

vulnus, vulneris, n. *wound* 11

AUTHORS/WORKS/ABBREVIATIONS

Aulus Gellius	**Noctes Atticae**	AG
[author unknown]	**Ad Herennium**	AUCHER
Augustine	**De Civitate Dei**	AUG CD
	Confessiones	AUG CONF
Caesar	**De Bello Civili**	CAES BC
	De Bello Gallico	CAES BG
	De Bello Alexandrino	CAES BELL ALEX
[author unknown]	**De Bello Africano**	[CAES]BELAFR
Dionysius Cato	**Disticha Catonis**	CATO DISTICHS
Catullus	**Carmina**	CATULLUS
Celsus	**De Medicina**	CELS
Cicero	**Academica Posteriora**	CIC ACADPOS
	Epistulae Ad Brutum	CIC AD BRUT
	Epistulae Ad Atticum	CIC ATT
	Brutus	CIC BRUTUS
	In Caecilium Divinatio	CIC CAEC DIV
	Pro Cluentio	CIC CLUENT
	De Amicitia	CIC DE AMIC
	De Divinatione	CIC DE DIVIN
	De Fato	CIC DE FATO
	De Finibus	CIC DE FIN
	De Legibus	CIC DE LEG
	De Officiis	CIC DE OFF
	De Oratore	CIC DE ORAT
	De Senectute	CIC DE SENEC
	De Domo Sua	CIC DOMO SUA
	Epistulae ad Familiares	CIC FAM
	De Haruspicum Responsis	CIC HAR RESP
	De Imperio Pompei	CIC IMP POMP
	In Catilinam	CIC IN CAT
	In Pisonem	CIC IN PIS
	In Vatinium	CIC IN VAT
	De Inventione	CIC INVENT

	De Lege Agraria	CIC LEG AGR
	De Natura Deorum	CIC ND
	Orator Ad M. Brutum	CIC OR BRUT
	Paradoxa Stoicorum	CIC PARADOX
	Philippics	CIC PHIL
	Pro Archia	CIC PRO ARCH
	Pro Caecina	CIC PRO CAEC
	Pro Caelio	CIC PRO CAEL
	Pro Deiotaro	CIC PRO DEIOT
	Pro Flacco	CIC PRO FLACC
	Pro Fonteio	CIC PRO FONT
	Pro Ligario	CIC PRO LIG
	Pro Marcello	CIC PRO MARC
	Pro Milone	CIC PRO MIL
	Pro Murena	CIC PRO MUR
	Pro Plancio	CIC PRO PLANC
	Pro Quinctio	CIC PRO QUINCT
	Pro Rabirio Perduellionis Reo	CIC PRO RAB
	Pro Sestio	CIC PRO SEST
	Pro Sulla	CIC PRO SULLA
	Pro Tullio	CIC PRO TULL
	De Provinciis Consularibus	CIC PROV CONS
	Epistulae ad Q. Fratrem	CIC Q FR
	Pro Rabirio Postumo	CIC RAB POST
	Post Reditum Ad Quirites	CIC RED POP
	Post Reditum In Senatu	CIC RED SEN
	De Re Publica	CIC REPUB
	Pro Roscio Amerino	CIC ROSCAM
	Pro Roscio Comoedo	CIC ROSCC
	Tusculanae Disputationes	CIC TD
	In Verrem	CIC VER
Quintus Cicero	Commentariolum Petitionis	QCIC COMM PET
[many authors]	Corpus Inscriptionum Latinarum	CIL
Columella	De Re Rustica	COL
Gaius	Institutionum Commentarii	GAIUS
Horace	Ars Poetica	HOR AP

	Epistulae	HOR E
	Epodes	HOR EPO
	Odes	HOR O
	Sermones	HOR S
Juvenal	Saturae	JUV
Livy	Ab Urbe Condita	LIVY
Lucan	De Bello Civili	LUCAN
Lucretius	De Rerum Natura	LUCR
Martialis	Epigrammata	MART
Nepos	De Excellentibus Ducibus	NEPOS
Ovid	Amores	OV A
	Ars Amatoria	OV AA
	Fasti	OV F
	Heroides	OV HER
	Ibis	OV IBIS
	Metamorphoses	OV M
	Ex Ponto	OV PONT
	Remedia Amoris	OV RA
	Tristia	OV TRIST
Persius	Saturae	PERS
Petronius	Satyricon	PETR
Phaedrus	Fabulae	PHAEDR
Plautus	Amphitruo	PLAUT AMPH
	Asinaria	PLAUT ASIN
	Aulularia	PLAUT AUL
	Bacchides	PLAUT BACC
	Captivi	PLAUT CAPT
	Casina	PLAUT CAS
	Cistellaria	PLAUT CIST
	Curculio	PLAUT CURC
	Epidicus	PLAUT EPID
	Menaechmi	PLAUT MEN
	Mercator	PLAUT MERC
	Miles Gloriosus	PLAUT MG
	Mostellaria	PLAUT MOST
	Persa	PLAUT PERS

	Poenulus	PLAUT POEN
	Pseudolus	PLAUT PSEUD
	Rudens	PLAUT RUD
	Stichus	PLAUT STICH
	Trinummus	PLAUT TRIN
	Truculentus	PLAUT TRUC
Pliny Minor	**Epistulae**	PLINY E
	Panegyricus	PLINY PANEG
Pliny Maior	**Naturalis Historia**	PLINY NH
Propertius	**Elegiae**	PROP
Publilius Syrus	**Sententiae**	PUBLSYR
Quintilian	**Institutiones**	QUINT
	Declamationes Minores	QUINT DECL
pseudo-Quintilian	**Declamationes Maiores**	[QUINT] DECL
Sallust	**Bellum Jugurthinum**	SALL BJ
	Bellum Catilinae	SALL C
	Historiae	SALL HIST
pseudo-Sallust	**Epistulae ad Caesarem**	[SALL] CAES
Seneca Minor	**Consolatio ad Helviam**	SEN AD HELV
	Consolatio ad Marciam	SEN AD MARC
	Consolatio ad Polybium	SEN AD POLY
	Agamemnon	SEN AGAM
	Apocolocyntosis	SEN APOCO
	De Beneficiis	SEN BEN
	De Brevitate Vitae	SEN BREV VIT
	De Clementia	SEN CLEM
	De Constantia Sapientis	SEN CONS SAP
	De Otio	SEN DE OTIO
	Epistulae	SEN E
	Hercules	SEN HERC
	De Ira	SEN IRA
	Medea	SEN MED
	Oedipus	SEN OED
	Phaedra	SEN PHAED
	Phoenissae	SEN PHOEN
	De Providentia	SEN PROV

	Quaestiones Naturales	SEN QN
	Thyestes	SEN THY
	De Tranquillitate Animi	SEN TRANQ AN
	Troades	SEN TROAD
	De Vita Beata	SEN VIT BEAT
pseudo-Seneca Minor	**Octavia**	[SEN] OCT
Seneca Maior	**Controversiae**	SENR C
	Suasoriae	SENR S
Suetonius	**De Vita Caesarum**	SUET
Tacitus	**Agricola**	TAC AGRIC
	Annales	TAC ANN
	Historiae	TAC HIST
Terence	**Adelphoe**	TER ADEL
	Andria	TER AND
	Eunuchus	TER EUN
	Heauton Timoroumenos	TER HT
	Hecyra	TER HEC
	Phormio	TER PHOR
Tibullus	**Carmina**	TIB
Valerius Maximus	**Facta Et Dicta Memorabilia**	VALMAX
Varro	**De Lingua Latina**	VARRO LL
Vegetius	**Epitoma Rei Militaris**	VEG
Velleius Paterculus	**Historiae**	VP
Vergil	**Aeneid**	VERG A
	Eclogues	VERG E
	Georgics	VERG G

CITATIONS

Number indicates chapter; **L-E** = Latin to English; **E-L** = English to Latin; **Gl** = Glossed; **Pr** = practice; **Pas** = passage; **Ex** = illustrative example in body of chapter; **Rev** = review sentences

AFRANIUS FR 221	*20*	*L-E*	CAES BG 5.31.3	*4*	*Gl*
AG 1.17	*52*	*Gl*	CAES BG 6.38.4	*37*	*L-E*
AUCHER 1.11	*50*	*E-L*	CAES BG 7.4.4	*59*	*L-E*
AUCHER 2.35	*56*	*L-E*	CAES BG 7.77.9	*23*	*L-E*
AUCHER 2.37	*65*	*E-L*	CAES BELL ALEX 67.1	*65*	*L-E*
AUCHER 2.37	*25*	*Ex*	[CAES] BELL AFR 97.1	*52*	*E-L*
AUCHER 4.19	*14*	*Pas*	CATHOLIC MASS	*18*	*Ex*
AUCHER 4.24	*22*	*L-E*	CATO DISTICHS 1.11	*48*	*L-E*
AUCHER 4.53	*65*	*L-E*	CATULLUS 5.1	*45*	*L-E*
AUCHER 4.54	*21*	*Pr*	CATULLUS 5.6	*38*	*L-E*
AUCHER 4.57	*32*	*L-E*	CATULLUS 8.12	*3*	*L-E*
AUCHER 4.57	*61*	*L-E*	CATULLUS 8.15	*49*	*Pr*
AUCHER 4.63	*61*	*Ex*	CATULLUS 13.1-5	*58*	*Pas*
AUCHER 4.67	*53*	*Pr*	CATULLUS 23.8	*1*	*E-L*
AUCHER 4.68	*1*	*L-E*	CATULLUS 29.1	*17*	*Pr*
AUG CD 3.17	*41*	*Ex*	CATULLUS 49	*43*	*Pas*
AUG CD 5.25	*23*	*Ex*	CATULLUS 55.15	*50*	*L-E*
AUG CD 8.5	*11*	*E-L*	CATULLUS 61.191-2	*15*	*L-E*
AUG CD 8.8	*38*	*Ex*	CATULLUS 68.9	*21*	*Ex*
AUG CD 8.9	*58*	*Pr*	CATULLUS 106.2	*45*	*Ex*
AUG CD 8.13	*7*	*E-L*	CELS 1.PR.P.12.35-6	*36*	*Pas*
AUG CD 9.23	*53*	*Pr*	CELS 2.8.P.50.12	*12*	*Pr*
AUG CD 22.6	*23*	*Gl*	CELS 6.11.P.249.16	*39*	*E-L*
AUG CONF 2.1.2	*29*	*L-E*	CELS 8.9.P.344.4	*38*	*E-L*
CAES BC 1.2.8	*31*	*Pr*	CIC ACADPOS 5	*39*	*Pr*
CAES BC 1.5.5	*62*	*Pr*	CIC ACADPOS 18	*9*	*L-E*
CAES BC 2.32.5	*34*	*Pas*	CIC ACADPOS 21	*31*	*L-E*
CAES BC 3.82.1	*22*	*Ex*	CIC AD BRUT 1.2.2	*26*	*Ex*
CAES BC 3.99.2	*44*	*Gl*	CIC AD BRUT 1.3A	*37*	*Pr*
CAES BG 3.18.6	*53*	*L-E*	CIC AD BRUT 1.4A.4	*4*	*E-L*
CAES BG 4.29.1	*48*	*Ex*	CIC AD BRUT 1.9.3	*30*	*Pr*

CIC AD BRUT 1.15.11	*10*	*L-E*	CIC ATT 3.6	*8*	*Gl*
CIC AD BRUT 1.15.12	*4*	*Gl*	CIC ATT 3.7.1	*62*	*Pr*
CIC ATT 1.3.2	*23*	*Pr*	CIC ATT 3.7.1	*1*	*E-L*
CIC ATT 1.3.2	*64*	*L-E*	CIC ATT 3.7.2	*3*	*L-E*
CIC ATT 1.5.3	*29*	*Pr*	CIC ATT 3.8.2	*25*	*Ex*
CIC ATT 1.5.3	*62*	*Ex*	CIC ATT 3.8.3	*41*	*Ex*
CIC ATT 1.5.8	*59*	*Ex*	CIC ATT 3.8.4	*43*	*Pr*
CIC ATT 1.6.1	*53*	*Pr*	CIC ATT 3.10.3	*44*	*Pr*
CIC ATT 1.10.3	*36*	*Pr*	CIC ATT 3.17.3	*44*	*Ex*
CIC ATT 1.13.5	*31*	*Pr*	CIC ATT 3.22.1	*50*	*L-E*
CIC ATT 1.14.5	*30*	*Pr*	CIC ATT 4.2.7	*29*	*Ex*
CIC ATT 1.15.1	*48*	*Ex*	CIC ATT 4.2.7	*2*	*E-L*
CIC ATT 1.16.1	*64*	*Rev*	CIC ATT 4.4	*41*	*L-E*
CIC ATT 1.16.1	*38*	*L-E*	CIC ATT 4.4	*36*	*Ex*
CIC ATT 1.16.9	*4*	*E-L*	CIC ATT 4.5.1	*39*	*Ex*
CIC ATT 1.17.6	*45*	*Ex*	CIC ATT 4.8A.1	*44*	*Ex*
CIC ATT 1.20.7	*41*	*Pr*	CIC ATT 4.12	*55*	*E-L*
CIC ATT 2.1.5	*21*	*L-E*	CIC ATT 4.15.9	*31*	*Pr*
CIC ATT 2.1.9	*24*	*Pr*	CIC ATT 5.4.1	*64*	*Rev*
CIC ATT 2.1.12	*42*	*Ex*	CIC ATT 5.7	*42*	*Pr*
CIC ATT 2.3.1	*24*	*Pr*	CIC ATT 5.8.3	*43*	*Ex*
CIC ATT 2.3.2	*8*	*L-E*	CIC ATT 5.10.1	*18*	*Pr*
CIC ATT 2.3.4	*3*	*E-L*	CIC ATT 5.11.3	*44*	*L-E*
CIC ATT 2.6.1	*27*	*L-E*	CIC ATT 5.12.1	*62*	*Ex*
CIC ATT 2.11.2	*62*	*L-E*	CIC ATT 5.12.2	*51*	*Ex*
CIC ATT 2.12.2	*62*	*Ex*	CIC ATT 5.12.3	*16*	*L-E*
CIC ATT 2.12.3	*59*	*E-L*	CIC ATT 5.14.3	*42*	*Pr*
CIC ATT 2.12.4	*35*	*Pr*	CIC ATT 5.17.2	*2*	*L-E*
CIC ATT 2.14.2	*60*	*Pr*	CIC ATT 5.20.1	*23*	*Pr*
CIC ATT 2.15.1	*62*	*Ex*	CIC ATT 5.21.10	*9*	*Pr*
CIC ATT 2.17.1	*63*	*E-L*	CIC ATT 6.1.1	*21*	*Ex*
CIC ATT 2.18.2	*20*	*E-L*	CIC ATT 6.1.2	*18*	*Pr*
CIC ATT 2.19.1	*8*	*Gl*	CIC ATT 6.1.13	*22*	*Ex*
CIC ATT 2.19.1	*57*	*L-E*	CIC ATT 6.1.16	*5*	*L-E*
CIC ATT 2.19.3	*27*	*L-E*	CIC ATT 6.1.17	*33*	*Ex*
CIC ATT 2.24.4	*42*	*L-E*	CIC ATT 6.1.26	*33*	*L-E*
CIC ATT 3.2.1	*43*	*Ex*	CIC ATT 6.2.7	*28*	*Ex*

CIC ATT 6.4.1	*23*	*Ex*	CIC ATT 9.13A	*32*	*Pr*
CIC ATT 6.4.1	*19*	*Pr*	CIC ATT 9.13A	*45*	*E-L*
CIC ATT 6.4.2	*66*	*L-E*	CIC ATT 9.13A	*42*	*E-L*
CIC ATT 6.6.2	*57*	*Pr*	CIC ATT 9.14.2	*28*	*Ex*
CIC ATT 6.6.4	*4*	*Gl*	CIC ATT 9.18.1	*41*	*Ex*
CIC ATT 6.9.2	*65*	*Ex*	CIC ATT 9.18.2	*12*	*Pr*
CIC ATT 7.1.9	*21*	*E-L*	CIC ATT 9.18.3	*24*	*L-E*
CIC ATT 7.2.7	*52*	*Pr*	CIC ATT 9.18.4	*16*	*Pr*
CIC ATT 7.4.3	*28*	*E-L*	CIC ATT 9.19.3	*64*	*L-E*
CIC ATT 7.9.4	*32*	*L-E*	CIC ATT 10.1.2	*21*	*L-E*
CIC ATT 7.15.2	*53*	*Pr*	CIC ATT 10.2.2	*27*	*Pr*
CIC ATT 7.21.3	*56*	*E-L*	CIC ATT 10.4.1	*39*	*L-E*
CIC ATT 7.25	*32*	*L-E*	CIC ATT 10.4.4	*54*	*L-E*
CIC ATT 8.2.1	*62*	*Ex*	CIC ATT 10.5.1	*23*	*L-E*
CIC ATT 8.3.5	*49*	*E-L*	CIC ATT 10.10.2	*3*	*E-L*
CIC ATT 8.9.1	*56*	*Pr*	CIC ATT 10.10.2	*6*	*Pr*
CIC ATT 8.9A.1	*44*	*E-L*	CIC ATT 10.10.4	*4*	*E-L*
CIC ATT 8.10	*59*	*E-L*	CIC ATT 10.10.4	*29*	*L-E*
CIC ATT 8.11D.3	*39*	*L-E*	CIC ATT 10.10.6	*41*	*L-E*
CIC ATT 8.11D.6	*24*	*L-E*	CIC ATT 10.15.1	*58*	*E-L*
CIC ATT 8.11D.6	*20*	*Pr*	CIC ATT 10.17.1	*37*	*Pr*
CIC ATT 8.13.2	*28*	*Ex*	CIC ATT 11.2.3	*42*	*Pr*
CIC ATT 8.14.2	*52*	*L-E*	CIC ATT 11.5.1	*43*	*E-L*
CIC ATT 8.14.2	*56*	*E-L*	CIC ATT 11.6.1	*55*	*L-E*
CIC ATT 8.15.2	*48*	*L-E*	CIC ATT 11.7.1	*20*	*L-E*
CIC ATT 8.15.3	*55*	*E-L*	CIC ATT 11.7.2	*59*	*L-E*
CIC ATT 9.5.2	*15*	*Ex*	CIC ATT 11.11.1	*63*	*Pr*
CIC ATT 9.6.4	*61*	*Pr*	CIC ATT 11.11.1	*41*	*Pr*
CIC ATT 9.7.7	*58*	*Pr*	CIC ATT 11.13.4	*39*	*L-E*
CIC ATT 9.7A.1	*59*	*L-E*	CIC ATT 11.16.3	*3*	*L-E*
CIC ATT 9.7A.1	*13*	*Pr*	CIC ATT 11.17A.3	*21*	*L-E*
CIC ATT 9.7B.1	*28*	*L-E*	CIC ATT 11.18.1	*40*	*E-L*
CIC ATT 9.10.5	*4*	*E-L*	CIC ATT 11.23.3	*59*	*Pr*
CIC ATT 9.10.8	*41*	*L-E*	CIC ATT 12.18.1	*29*	*Pas*
CIC ATT 9.10.8	*3*	*E-L*	CIC ATT 12.26.2	*21*	*L-E*
CIC ATT 9.12.1	*58*	*Pr*	CIC ATT 12.27.3	*64*	*Ex*
CIC ATT 9.13.6	*55*	*Pr*	CIC ATT 12.41.2	*52*	*L-E*

CIC DE FIN 2.63	29	L-E	CIC DE ORAT 2.38	12	L-E
CIC DE FIN 2.65	33	E-L	CIC DE ORAT 2.187	64	Pr
CIC DE FIN 2.65	24	Pr	CIC DE ORAT 2.198	50	Pr
CIC DE FIN 2.79	54	E-L	CIC DE ORAT 3.17	65	Pr
CIC DE FIN 2.84	31	E-L	CIC DE ORAT 3.87	38	Pr
CIC DE FIN 2.85	40	Ex	CIC DE ORAT 3.168	18	Pr
CIC DE FIN 2.86	31	L-E	CIC DE SENEC 2	29	L-E
CIC DE FIN 2.87	10	Pr	CIC DE SENEC 3	23	L-E
CIC DE FIN 2.104	10	L-E	CIC DE SENEC 5	57	L-E
CIC DE FIN 3.8	55	E-L	CIC DE SENEC 10	24	L-E
CIC DE FIN 3.8	65	Ex	CIC DE SENEC 11	55	Pas
CIC DE FIN 3.62	60	Ex	CIC DE SENEC 15	62	L-E
CIC DE FIN 3.64	58	Gl	CIC DE SENEC 34	12	Gl
CIC DE FIN 4.16	23	Gl	CIC DE SENEC 42	19	E-L
CIC DE FIN 4.25	11	Gl	CIC DE SENEC 44	61	L-E
CIC DE FIN 4.54	16	L-E	CIC DE SENEC 67	19	L-E
CIC DE FIN 5.6	56	Ex	CIC DOMO SUA 8	50	Pr
CIC DE FIN 5.6	56	Ex	CIC DOMO SUA 16	34	Pr
CIC DE FIN 5.15	35	Pr	CIC DOMO SUA 16	37	L-E
CIC DE FIN 5.38	60	L-E	CIC DOMO SUA 57	14	E-L
CIC DE FIN 5.47	12	L-E	CIC FAM 1.8.7	29	Pr
CIC DE LEG 1.1	13	Pr	CIC FAM 2.11.1	12	L-E
CIC DE LEG 1.8	48	L-E	CIC FAM 2.13.2	49	Pr
CIC DE LEG 1.14	56	L-E	CIC FAM 2.15.2	45	Ex
CIC DE LEG 1.18	10	Pr	CIC FAM 2.15.3	44	Ex
CIC DE LEG 2.8	64	Pr	CIC FAM 2.15.3	12	E-L
CIC DE LEG 2.11	17	Gl	CIC FAM 2.15.4	55	Pr
CIC DE LEG 3.4	10	Pr	CIC FAM 3.6.2	34	L-E
CIC DE OFF 1.4	47	L-E	CIC FAM 3.13.1	43	Pr
CIC DE OFF 1.11	32	Ex	CIC FAM 4.2.3	47	Gl
CIC DE OFF 1.80	48	L-E	CIC FAM 4.4.4	34	E-L
CIC DE OFF 1.91	48	L-E	CIC FAM 4.4.4	43	E-L
CIC DE OFF 2.11	44	L-E	CIC FAM 4.4.5	44	Ex
CIC DE OFF 3.114	62	E-L	CIC FAM 4.10.1	20	L-E
CIC DE ORAT 1.132	44	Ex	CIC FAM 5.2.1	30	E-L
CIC DE ORAT 1.197	58	L-E	CIC FAM 5.10A.1	52	L-E
CIC DE ORAT 1.209	7	L-E	CIC FAM 5.10A.2	17	L-E

CIC FAM 5.12.8	*33*	*Ex*		CIC FAM 10.24.6	*38*	*Pr*
CIC FAM 5.19.2	*55*	*L-E*		CIC FAM 10.33.1	*55*	*L-E*
CIC FAM 6.5.1	*35*	*L-E*		CIC FAM 11.4.2	*27*	*E-L*
CIC FAM 6.6.1	*66*	*L-E*		CIC FAM 11.5.2	*32*	*L-E*
CIC FAM 6.11.2	*18*	*Ex*		CIC FAM 11.10.2	*50*	*Pr*
CIC FAM 7.3.1	*33*	*L-E*		CIC FAM 11.10.4	*30*	*E-L*
CIC FAM 7.3.2	*44*	*L-E*		CIC FAM 11.10.4	*66*	*E-L*
CIC FAM 7.9.2	*58*	*Pr*		CIC FAM 11.18.1	*30*	*Gl*
CIC FAM 7.13.1	*52*	*L-E*		CIC FAM 11.19.2	*43*	*Ex*
CIC FAM 7.29.2	*53*	*L-E*		CIC FAM 11.20.2	*42*	*E-L*
CIC FAM 7.30.1	*62*	*L-E*		CIC FAM 11.23.1	*37*	*L-E*
CIC FAM 7.30.1	*65*	*E-L*		CIC FAM 11.24.1	*2*	*L-E*
CIC FAM 7.31.1	*31*	*E-L*		CIC FAM 11.27.2	*42*	*L-E*
CIC FAM 8.11.2	*38*	*Pr*		CIC FAM 11.28.4	*25*	*L-E*
CIC FAM 8.16.4	*41*	*Pr*		CIC FAM 12.1.1	*32*	*Pr*
CIC FAM 8.16.4	*59*	*Ex*		CIC FAM 12.1.1	*34*	*L-E*
CIC FAM 8.17.2	*29*	*L-E*		CIC FAM 12.2.3	*57*	*Ex*
CIC FAM 8.17.2	*47*	*L-E*		CIC FAM 12.2.3	*58*	*L-E*
CIC FAM 9.6.2	*41*	*Ex*		CIC FAM 12.3.1	*63*	*L-E*
CIC FAM 9.16.2	*27*	*L-E*		CIC FAM 12.9.2	*32*	*E-L*
CIC FAM 9.17.1	*13*	*L-E*		CIC FAM 12.13.1	*33*	*Ex*
CIC FAM 9.18.3	*60*	*Pr*		CIC FAM 12.13.1	*15*	*Pr*
CIC FAM 9.18.3	*19*	*L-E*		CIC FAM 12.19.1	*44*	*Pr*
CIC FAM 9.18.4	*41*	*Pr*		CIC FAM 12.19.1	*66*	*Ex*
CIC FAM 9.20.3	*17*	*E-L*		CIC FAM 12.25.1	*32*	*Pr*
CIC FAM 9.20.3	*29*	*Ex*		CIC FAM 12.25A.2	*63*	*L-E*
CIC FAM 9.21.3	*24*	*Ex*		CIC FAM 12.30.6	*60*	*Pr*
CIC FAM 9.24.1	*21*	*L-E*		CIC FAM 13.4.1	*44*	*Pr*
CIC FAM 9.26.1	*55*	*Gl*		CIC FAM 13.8.3	*43*	*E-L*
CIC FAM 10.1.1	*3*	*Gl*		CIC FAM 13.19.1	*47*	*E-L*
CIC FAM 10.2.2	*13*	*L-E*		CIC FAM 13.24.2	*13*	*L-E*
CIC FAM 10.3.1	*36*	*L-E*		CIC FAM 13.77.3	*33*	*E-L*
CIC FAM 10.4.1	*42*	*Ex*		CIC FAM 13.77.3	*10*	*E-L*
CIC FAM 10.11.1	*25*	*L-E*		CIC FAM 14.1.2	*18*	*Gl*
CIC FAM 10.12.2	*38*	*Pr*		CIC FAM 14.3.4	*35*	*E-L*
CIC FAM 10.23.6	*45*	*Ex*		CIC FAM 14.4.3	*58*	*Ex*
CIC FAM 10.23.6	*45*	*Ex*		CIC FAM 14.4.4	*50*	*Ex*

CIC FAM 14.5.2	*59*	*Pr*		CIC INVENT 2.140	*55*	*Ex*
CIC FAM 14.8	*1*	*Gl*		CIC INVENT 2.140	*55*	*Pr*
CIC FAM 14.12	*11*	*L-E*		CIC LEG AGR 1.15	*64*	*Ex*
CIC FAM 14.14	*18*	*E-L*		CIC LEG AGR 1.15	*63*	*Pr*
CIC FAM 14.5.2	*24*	*L-E*		CIC LEG AGR 2.10	*16*	*Pr*
CIC FAM 14.15	*23*	*Ex*		CIC LEG AGR 2.16	*13*	*E-L*
CIC FAM 14.16	*9*	*Pr*		CIC LEG AGR 2.24	*8*	*E-L*
CIC FAM 15.1.2	*39*	*E-L*		CIC ND 1.12	*63*	*L-E*
CIC FAM 16.7.1	*63*	*E-L*		CIC ND 1.39	*41*	*Pr*
CIC FAM 16.10.1	*20*	*E-L*		CIC ND 1.85	*33*	*Pr*
CIC FAM 16.11.1	*25*	*Pr*		CIC ND 1.90	*23*	*E-L*
CIC FAM 16.12.6	*32*	*Ex*		CIC ND 1.90	*56*	*L-E*
CIC FAM 16.14.1	*23*	*L-E*		CIC ND 1.94	*23*	*E-L*
CIC HAR RESP 31	*8*	*L-E*		CIC ND 1.114	*9*	*L-E*
CIC IMP POMP 28	*43*	*L-E*		CIC ND 1.123	*8*	*Gl*
CIC IMP POMP 37	*57*	*E-L*		CIC ND 2.12	*40*	*L-E*
CIC IN CAT 1.2	*30*	*L-E*		CIC ND 2.18	*43*	*Pr*
CIC IN CAT 1.6	*42*	*E-L*		CIC ND 2.36	*60*	*Ex*
CIC IN CAT 1.9	*49*	*L-E*		CIC ND 2.154	*60*	*L-E*
CIC IN CAT 1.17	*25*	*E-L*		CIC ND 2.167	*8*	*L-E*
CIC IN CAT 1.18	*58*	*Ex*		CIC ND 2.167	*15*	*L-E*
CIC IN CAT 2.1	*37*	*L-E*		CIC ND 3.14	*40*	*Gl*
CIC IN CAT 2.3	*54*	*Gl*		CIC ND 3.23	*4*	*L-E*
CIC IN CAT 2.11	*34*	*Gl*		CIC ND 3.26	*30*	*L-E*
CIC IN CAT 2.22	*48*	*Ex*		CIC ND 3.38	*7*	*Gl*
CIC IN CAT 4.1	*18*	*L-E*		CIC ND 3.39	*10*	*Gl*
CIC IN CAT 4.3	*15*	*Gl*		CIC ND 3.49	*36*	*L-E*
CIC IN CAT 4.3	*32*	*Pr*		CIC ND 3.86	*43*	*E-L*
CIC IN CAT 4.23	*47*	*L-E*		CIC ND 3.89	*41*	*L-E*
CIC IN CAT 4.23	*18*	*Gl*		CIC OR BRUT 31	*35*	*Pr*
CIC IN PIS 1	*35*	*E-L*		CIC OR BRUT 33	*23*	*L-E*
CIC IN PIS 13	*20*	*Pr*		CIC OR BRUT 34	*64*	*Pr*
CIC IN PIS 29	*41*	*Pr*		CIC PARADOX 6	*44*	*L-E*
CIC IN VAT 7	*59*	*Ex*		CIC PARADOX 8	*17*	*E-L*
CIC INVENT 1.95	*8*	*Pr*		CIC PARADOX 15	*16*	*L-E*
CIC INVENT 1.95	*43*	*Pr*		CIC PARADOX 17	*50*	*L-E*
CIC INVENT 2.122	*56*	*Ex*		CIC PARADOX 41	*30*	*E-L*

CIC TD 2.6	*39*	*Pr*	CIC VER 3.61	*40*	*Pr*
CIC TD 2.32	*31*	*Ex*	CIC VER 3.132	*8*	*Pr*
CIC TD 2.53	*52*	*Pr*	CIC VER 3.158	*28*	*Pr*
CIC TD 2.58	*32*	*Gl*	CIC VER 3.161	*32*	*Pr*
CIC TD 3.1	*27*	*Gl*	CIC VER 3.208	*57*	*Pr*
CIC TD 3.5	*9*	*L-E*	CIC VER 3.209	*14*	*L-E*
CIC TD 3.20	*44*	*Ex*	CIC VER 4.11	*38*	*Ex*
CIC TD 3.32	*24*	*Pr*	CIC VER 4.18	*29*	*Ex*
CIC TD 3.35	*8*	*L-E*	CIC VER 4.19	*45*	*Ex*
CIC TD 3.36	*12*	*E-L*	CIC VER 4.25	*13*	*L-E*
CIC TD 3.47	*33*	*Pr*	CIC VER 4.27	*44*	*Pr*
CIC TD 3.51	*36*	*L-E*	CIC VER 4.92	*23*	*Ex*
CIC TD 5.25	*15*	*L-E*	CIC VER 4.104	*49*	*Ex*
CIC TD 5.31	*29*	*Ex*	CIC VER 5.66	*42*	*Pr*
CIC TD 5.39	*58*	*Pr*	CIC VER 5.120	*37*	*L-E*
CIC TD 5.40	*14*	*E-L*	CIC VER 5.121	*26*	*L-E*
CIC TD 5.50	*56*	*Pr*	CIC VER 5.161	*41*	*L-E*
CIC TD 5.62	*29*	*Gl*	CIC VER 5.162	*12*	*L-E*
CIC TD 5.63	*63*	*L-E*	QCIC COMM PET 9	*22*	*E-L*
CIC TD 5.63	*8*	*Gl*	CIL 12.5193, 3	*9*	*Pas*
CIC TD 5.67	*12*	*Pr*	CATO AP COL 11.1.26	*64*	*L-E*
CIC TD 5.82	*60*	*Ex*	GAIUS 1.9-11	*56*	*Pas*
CIC TD 5.111	*28*	*Pr*	GAIUS 1.52	*10*	*L-E*
CIC TD 5.111	*64*	*Ex*	GAIUS 1.55	*10*	*E-L*
CIC TD 5.112	*32*	*Ex*	HOR AP 25-6	*60*	*Gl*
CIC TD 5.113	*62*	*Ex*	HOR AP 63	*29*	*L-E*
CIC VER 1.12	*56*	*L-E*	HOR AP 68	*61*	*L-E*
CIC VER 1.35	*50*	*Pr*	HOR AP 333	*58*	*E-L*
CIC VER 1.66	*52*	*Ex*	HOR E 1.1.97	*22*	*L-E*
CIC VER 1.66	*45*	*Pr*	HOR E 1.2.62	*15*	*Pr*
CIC VER 1.70	*52*	*L-E*	HOR E 1.4.6	*14*	*L-E*
CIC VER 2.1	*32*	*Ex*	HOR E 1.4.6-7	*23*	*L-E*
CIC VER 2.24	*20*	*L-E*	HOR E 1.4.12-3	*41*	*Pas*
CIC VER 2.68	*51*	*L-E*	HOR E 1.7.44	*8*	*Gl*
CIC VER 2.76	*54*	*Ex*	HOR E 1.8.17	*52*	*L-E*
CIC VER 2.185	*2*	*L-E*	HOR E 1.10.32	*20*	*Pr*
CIC VER 2.191	*2*	*L-E*	HOR E 1.12.10	*19*	*Gl*

HOR E 1.16.66	36	L-E	HOR S 2.5.1-2	36	Pr
HOR E 1.19.2-3	31	Pas	HOR S 2.5.33	23	L-E
HOR E 2.1.156	34	Gl	HOR S 2.5.34	15	Pr
HOR EPO 7.17	15	L-E	HOR S 2.6.49	4	L-E
HOR EPO 16.1-2	33	Pas	HOR S 2.7.22-3	10	Gl
HOR O 1.11.7-8	56	Gl	HOR S 2.7.112	32	E-L
HOR O 1.16.1	42	L-E	JUV 3.60-1	52	Gl
HOR O 1.22.23	36	Ex	JUV 3.171-2	28	Pas
HOR O 3.2.13-4	56	Pas	JUV 5.157	46	Ex
HOR O 3.16.42-3	58	L-E	JUV 5.166	64	E-L
HOR O 3.27.74-5	52	Pr	JUV 6.112	28	L-E
HOR O 4.9.34	24	E-L	JUV 6.292	56	L-E
HOR O 4.13.17	23	Gl	JUV 6.347-8	33	Gl
HOR S 1.1.16	53	Pr	JUV 7.197-8	60	Pas
HOR S 1.1.24-5	36	L-E	JUV 7.201	13	Gl
HOR S 1.1.69-70	37	L-E	JUV 8.125	8	L-E
HOR S 1.1.95	7	Gl	JUV 9.32	15	E-L
HOR S 1.2.11	29	Gl	JUV 9.128-9	34	Pas
HOR S 1.3.10	36	Ex	JUV 10.4-5	20	L-E
HOR S 1.3.20	6	L-E	JUV 10.66-9	49	Pas
HOR S 1.3.68	56	Ex	JUV 10.78-81	32	Pas
HOR S 1.3.102	27	Ex	JUV 10.295-7	11	Pas
HOR S 1.5.48	65	L-E	JUV 10.356	12	L-E
HOR S 1.5.82-3	12	L-E	JUV 11.197	20	Gl
HOR S 1.5.82-3	42	Pas	JUV 13.100	6	Gl
HOR S 1.7.33-4	6	Gl	JUV 14.321	47	Ex
HOR S 1.9.26	24	Ex	LIVY PRAEF 9	56	L-E
HOR S 1.9.52	8	Ex	LIVY 1.4.1	29	Gl
HOR S 1.9.55	63	Ex	LIVY 1.21.6	62	L-E
HOR S 1.9.57	27	L-E	LIVY 1.23.9	18	Pr
HOR S 1.9.59-60	25	Gl	LIVY 1.33.1	64	Gl
HOR S 2.2.8	55	Ex	LIVY 1.37.6	35	Pr
HOR S 2.2.19-20	33	L-E	LIVY 1.39.3	17	Ex
HOR S 2.3.19	6	L-E	LIVY 1.48.8	62	Pr
HOR S 2.3.67	24	L-E	LIVY 1.58.2	30	L-E
HOR S 2.3.302	29	Pr	LIVY 2.12.9	56	Pas
HOR S 2.4.1	24	Ex	LIVY 2.33.4	62	E-L

LIVY 2.45.6	59	E-L	LUCAN 8.386	27	E-L
LIVY 2.45.14	20	Pr	LUCAN 8.395-6	38	L-E
LIVY 2.64.6	41	Ex	LUCR 2.1044	15	Pr
LIVY 3.4.2	29	L-E	LUCR 3.831	29	Ex
LIVY 3.21.6	65	L-E	LUCR 3.1067	36	Pr
LIVY 4.38.4	20	E-L	MART 1.9	53	Pas
LIVY 5.6.6	17	Gl	MART 1.17	32	Pas
LIVY 5.22.5	62	Pr	MART 1.32	17	Pas
LIVY 5.33.1	31	L-E	MART 1.38	28	Pas
LIVY 5.37.1	4	Gl	MART 1.63	59	Pas
LIVY 6.7.6	20	L-E	MART 1.64.2	7	E-L
LIVY 6.26.2	62	Pr	MART 1.91	53	Pas
LIVY 6.26.5	30	L-E	MART 1.107.2	49	Ex
LIVY 6.26.5	57	L-E	MART 2.3	56	Pas
LIVY 7.40.5	38	Pr	MART 2.20	63	Pas
LIVY 7.41.1	59	Ex	MART 2.21	53	Pas
LIVY 8.5.6	45	Ex	MART 2.25	36	Pas
LIVY 8.5.8	19	L-E	MART 2.38	50	Pas
LIVY 9.17.11	24	Ex	MART 2.86.6	7	Gl
LIVY 22.14.14	64	Gl	MART 3.9	29	Pas
LIVY 22.39.21	45	Pr	MART 3.70	57	Pas
LIVY 22.39.22	36	E-L	MART 4.38	53	Pas
LIVY 23.13.1	65	E-L	MART 4.49.10	54	Ex
LIVY 23.42.6	62	L-E	MART 5.19.6	49	L-E
LIVY 28.42.20	51	E-L	MART 5.43	49	Pas
LIVY 33.34.10	30	L-E	MART 5.81	29	Pas
LIVY 35.16.6	31	Pr	MART 6.56.5	41	Pr
LIVY 35.21.7	62	Ex	MART 6.60.4	57	Ex
LIVY 42.30.5	53	E-L	MART 6.78.4	55	Ex
LIVY 42.34.11	62	Pr	MART 7.3	46	Pas
LUCAN 1.522	37	Ex	MART 7.59	9	Pas
LUCAN 3.21	35	Pr	MART 8.12	60	Pas
LUCAN 3.118-9	19	L-E	MART 8.20	51	Pas
LUCAN 3.139-40	29	Ex	MART 8.35	56	Pas
LUCAN 4.259	43	Ex	MART 8.76.8	26	Ex
LUCAN 7.110	38	L-E	MART 9.21	50	Pas
LUCAN 7.706	43	E-L	MART 10.8	57	Pas

MART 10.35.1–4	57	Pas		OV A 1.13.3	3	L-E
MART 10.43	47	Pas		OV A 1.13.40	16	Gl
MART 10.69	33	Pas		OV A 1.15.32	12	L-E
MART 11.2.8	54	Ex		OV A 1.15.33	45	L-E
MART 11.8.13	20	Pr		OV A 2.9.15	10	Gl
MART 11.24.15	62	E-L		OV A 2.10.7–8	57	Pas
MART 11.58.2	8	Ex		OV A 3.6.2	3	Gl
MART 11.64	50	Pas		OV A 3.11.20	23	E-L
MART 11.68.2	8	Pr		OV A 3.11.25–6	35	Pas
MART 11.79.3	3	Gl		OV A 3.11B.17	14	Pr
MART 12.10	47	Pas		OV A 3.12.33	22	Gl
MART 12.20	50	Pas		OV A 3.12.16	23	L-E
MART 12.30	9	Pas		OV AA 1.34	14	L-E
MART 12.33	46	Pas		OV AA 1.99	65	L-E
MART 12.41	31	Pas		OV AA 2.12	38	L-E
MART 12.46	39	Pas		OV AA 2.43	8	L-E
MART 12.46.2	18	E-L		OV AA 2.58	37	Ex
MART 12.63.13	42	L-E		OV AA 2.166	51	Ex
MART 12.73	55	Pas		OV AA 2.249	14	L-E
MART 12.80	46	Pas		OV AA 2.275	31	L-E
MART 12.86	62	Pas		OV AA 2.277	16	Gl
MART 12.96.9	39	Pr		OV AA 2.648	36	Ex
NEPOS 2.1.2	44	Ex		OV AA 2.717	38	E-L
NEPOS 2.1.3	43	Ex		OV AA 2.727	3	Gl
NEPOS 2.5.3	47	L-E		OV AA 2.741	23	Pr
NEPOS 4.3.3	62	Ex		OV AA 3.41	50	E-L
NEPOS 6.3.3	31	Pr		OV AA 3.79	20	L-E
NEPOS 7.4.6	23	Gl		OV AA 3.113	6	Gl
NEPOS 7.5.7	62	Ex		OV AA 3.667	52	L-E
NEPOS 10.6.2	42	L-E		OV F 1.212	51	L-E
NEPOS 11.1.4	42	Ex		OV F 1.421	37	L-E
NEPOS 13.3.2	48	E-L		OV F 2.9	52	Pr
NEPOS 18.1.1	56	Gl		OV F 2.117	6	Gl
OV A 1.2.27	34	L-E		OV F 2.661	31	Pr
OV A 1.3.15	62	Ex		OV F 2.745	3	L-E
OV A 1.4.45	9	L-E		OV F 2.795	18	L-E
OV A 1.9.1	36	Gl		OV F 5.248	14	L-E

OV F 6.5	18	E-L	OV M 5.345	16	Gl
OV HER 2.27	26	L-E	OV M 6.40	18	L-E
OV HER 2.110	40	L-E	OV M 6.193	25	Pr
OV HER 3.14-5	23	Gl	OV M 7.10-1	27	L-E
OV HER 3.46	24	L-E	OV M 7.16	66	Pr
OV HER 4.64	20	E-L	OV M 7.18	55	Ex
OV HER 6.28	5	Gl	OV M 7.20-1	56	L-E
OV HER 6.71	3	L-E	OV M 7.93	29	Pr
OV HER 7.13	38	Pr	OV M 7.719	36	Gl
OV HER 8.89	52	Pr	OV M 7.755	64	Rev
OV HER 8.97	56	Pr	OV M 7.826	32	Gl
OV HER 10.27	13	E-L	OV M 8.503	27	Pr
OV HER 11.55	14	E-L	OV M 8.689	7	Ex
OV HER 11.61	45	Pr	OV M 8.861	50	Ex
OV HER 13.84	45	Pr	OV M 9.541-2	46	L-E
OV HER 13.120	20	Gl	OV M 9.781	56	E-L
OV HER 15.109	20	Pr	OV M 10.26	23	Ex
OV HER 15.126	6	L-E	OV M 10.32	29	Pr
OV HER 16.83	26	Ex	OV M 10.204	18	Ex
OV HER 16.237	19	L-E	OV M 10.368-9	24	Gl
OV HER 16.352	24	Pr	OV M 10.637	19	L-E
OV HER 17.243	6	E-L	OV M 12.144	34	Pr
OV HER 18.196	14	Gl	OV M 12.476	15	Pr
OV HER 19.109	23	Pr	OV M 13.262-3	24	Pr
OV HER 20.33	36	Ex	OV M 13.267	11	L-E
OV HER 20.107	15	Pr	OV M 13.364	7	Pr
OV HER 20.178	14	E-L	OV M 13.380-1	17	L-E
OV HER 21.5	40	Ex	OV M 14.81	34	L-E
OV HER 21.103	36	L-E	OV M 15.165	29	Pr
OV HER 21.194	37	L-E	OV M 15.746	22	E-L
OV IBIS 137	18	Pr	OV PONT 1.1.60	33	L-E
OV M 1.481-2	23	Pas	OV PONT 1.2.27	12	L-E
OV M 2.62	44	Ex	OV PONT 1.4.29	57	Pr
OV M 3.135-6	38	L-E	OV PONT 2.3.54	58	L-E
OV M 3.425-6	33	Pas	OV PONT 2.6.33-4	40	L-E
OV M 4.467	56	E-L	OV PONT 3.1.34	55	Pr
OV M 5.310-1	31	L-E	OV PONT 3.4.75	16	Gl

OV PONT 3.4.93	*11*	*E-L*	PETR 72.5	*2*	*L-E*
OV PONT 3.4.93	*54*	*L-E*	PETR 73.1	*45*	*L-E*
OV RA 41	*34*	*Gl*	PETR 75.1	*10*	*E-L*
OV RA 71-2	*39*	*Pas*	PETR 76.8	*60*	*L-E*
OV RA 104	*60*	*L-E*	PETR 79.4	*36*	*E-L*
OV RA 277	*59*	*Ex*	PETR 79.8.4-5	*25*	*Ex*
OV RA 583	*55*	*Ex*	PETR 82.6	*22*	*Pr*
OV TRIST 1.1.127	*3*	*L-E*	PETR 83.9	*25*	*L-E*
OV TRIST 1.3.62	*38*	*Ex*	PETR 90.2	*66*	*E-L*
OV TRIST 1.4.4	*31*	*L-E*	PETR 91.3	*13*	*Gl*
OV TRIST 1.5.7	*50*	*Pr*	PETR 92.1	*14*	*Pr*
OV TRIST 1.5.66	*34*	*Pr*	PETR 98.2	*62*	*Ex*
OV TRIST 2.12	*35*	*Pr*	PETR 99.4	*56*	*L-E*
OV TRIST 2.38	*43*	*Pr*	PETR 105.4	*60*	*Ex*
OV TRIST 2.89	*13*	*L-E*	PETR 108.14.5	*34*	*L-E*
OV TRIST 3.1.41	*54*	*L-E*	PETR 108.14.7	*49*	*L-E*
OV TRIST 3.3.36	*35*	*Pr*	PETR 109.10.5	*36*	*E-L*
OV TRIST 3.5.25	*32*	*L-E*	PETR 129.4	*44*	*Ex*
OV TRIST 3.6.25	*11*	*L-E*	PETR 130.4	*34*	*L-E*
OV TRIST 3.7.3	*36*	*L-E*	PETR 132.4	*50*	*Ex*
OV TRIST 4.2.28	*24*	*Ex*	PETR 137.8	*59*	*L-E*
OV TRIST 4.10.23	*35*	*Ex*	PHAEDR 4.10.4	*9*	*L-E*
OV TRIST 5.9.22	*42*	*Ex*	PHAEDR 4.22.1	*34*	*L-E*
OV TRIST 5.12.37	*12*	*L-E*	PHAEDR 5.4.12	*65*	*Gl*
PERS 5.84-5	*42*	*Ex*	PHAEDR APP 3.3	*13*	*Pr*
PERS 6.27	*5*	*L-E*	PHAEDR APP 18.3	*16*	*E-L*
PETR 1.3	*60*	*Pas*	PHAEDR APP 29.10	*50*	*L-E*
PETR 3.1	*12*	*Pr*	PLAUT AMPH 32	*52*	*Ex*
PETR 34.7	*5*	*Gl*	PLAUT AMPH 92	*65*	*Pr*
PETR 43.7	*60*	*Gl*	PLAUT AMPH 113	*60*	*Ex*
PETR 45.2	*28*	*L-E*	PLAUT AMPH 167	*25*	*Ex*
PETR 45.13	*43*	*E-L*	PLAUT AMPH 331	*1*	*E-L*
PETR 57.4	*33*	*E-L*	PLAUT AMPH 447	*39*	*Ex*
PETR 57.9	*50*	*L-E*	PLAUT AMPH 610	*7*	*Ex*
PETR 66.1	*55*	*Ex*	PLAUT AMPH 792-3	*28*	*Pr*
PETR 67.1	*4*	*L-E*	PLAUT AMPH 870	*52*	*L-E*
PETR 71.5	*42*	*Pr*	PLAUT AMPH 931	*1*	*L-E*

PLAUT AMPH 965	*60*	*Pr*		PLAUT AUL 823	*21*	*E-L*
PLAUT AMPH 1035	*24*	*Pr*		PLAUT BACC 92	*63*	*Ex*
PLAUT AMPH 1146	*16*	*Gl*		PLAUT BACC 93	*53*	*Ex*
PLAUT ASIN 126	*61*	*E-L*		PLAUT BACC 124	*19*	*Pr*
PLAUT ASIN 189	*1*	*L-E*		PLAUT BACC 145	*51*	*Ex*
PLAUT ASIN 338	*21*	*Ex*		PLAUT BACC 146	*62*	*Pr*
PLAUT ASIN 413	*24*	*Pr*		PLAUT BACC 149	*7*	*E-L*
PLAUT ASIN 531	*21*	*Ex*		PLAUT BACC 189	*50*	*Pr*
PLAUT ASIN 578	*28*	*Pr*		PLAUT BACC 269	*5*	*E-L*
PLAUT ASIN 592	*1*	*L-E*		PLAUT BACC 324	*19*	*L-E*
PLAUT ASIN 597	*55*	*Ex*		PLAUT BACC 338	*38*	*L-E*
PLAUT ASIN 616	*28*	*Pr*		PLAUT BACC 338	*64*	*Rev*
PLAUT ASIN 631	*17*	*L-E*		PLAUT BACC 449	*17*	*Ex*
PLAUT ASIN 652	*49*	*Pr*		PLAUT BACC 494	*59*	*L-E*
PLAUT ASIN 659	*30*	*Ex*		PLAUT BACC 537	*45*	*Ex*
PLAUT ASIN 712	*5*	*L-E*		PLAUT BACC 572-3	*1*	*L-E*
PLAUT ASIN 732-3	*52*	*E-L*		PLAUT BACC 575	*61*	*Pr*
PLAUT ASIN 745	*16*	*E-L*		PLAUT BACC 691	*38*	*Ex*
PLAUT ASIN 837	*41*	*Pr*		PLAUT BACC 713	*9*	*Gl*
PLAUT ASIN 845	*54*	*Ex*		PLAUT BACC 731	*45*	*L-E*
PLAUT ASIN 940	*62*	*Pr*		PLAUT BACC 739	*35*	*Ex*
PLAUT AUL 23	*24*	*Ex*		PLAUT BACC 758	*35*	*E-L*
PLAUT AUL 42	*46*	*Gl*		PLAUT BACC 760	*9*	*Pr*
PLAUT AUL 88	*52*	*Pr*		PLAUT BACC 760	*18*	*Pr*
PLAUT AUL 114-5	*44*	*Gl*		PLAUT BACC 775	*6*	*L-E*
PLAUT AUL 137	*2*	*E-L*		PLAUT BACC 801	*2*	*E-L*
PLAUT AUL 235	*17*	*Ex*		PLAUT CAPT 104	*25*	*Ex*
PLAUT AUL 263	*61*	*E-L*		PLAUT CAPT 142-3	*28*	*Pas*
PLAUT AUL 289	*49*	*Ex*		PLAUT CAPT 249	*41*	*L-E*
PLAUT AUL 302	*65*	*Pr*		PLAUT CAPT 297	*23*	*Pr*
PLAUT AUL 330	*61*	*L-E*		PLAUT CAPT 317	*56*	*L-E*
PLAUT AUL 444	*19*	*Pr*		PLAUT CAPT 461-3	*42*	*Pas*
PLAUT AUL 579	*65*	*Ex*		PLAUT CAPT 628	*23*	*Pr*
PLAUT AUL 580	*6*	*L-E*		PLAUT CAPT 630	*26*	*L-E*
PLAUT AUL 657	*17*	*Ex*		PLAUT CAPT 632	*55*	*Ex*
PLAUT AUL 713	*45*	*Ex*		PLAUT CAPT 640	*21*	*Ex*
PLAUT AUL 781	*18*	*L-E*		PLAUT CAPT 773	*58*	*L-E*

PLAUT CAPT 863	*18*	*L-E*	PLAUT CIST 289	*28*	*Ex*
PLAUT CAPT 889	*64*	*L-E*	PLAUT CIST 499	*24*	*L-E*
PLAUT CAPT 921	*14*	*L-E*	PLAUT CIST 521	*46*	*E-L*
PLAUT CAPT 933-4	*14*	*L-E*	PLAUT CIST 543	*35*	*L-E*
PLAUT CAPT 934	*21*	*Pr*	PLAUT CIST 547	*61*	*E-L*
PLAUT CAPT 938	*59*	*Ex*	PLAUT CIST 649	*7*	*Pr*
PLAUT CAPT 974	*21*	*Pr*	PLAUT CIST 689	*16*	*L-E*
PLAUT CAPT 983	*24*	*Ex*	PLAUT CIST 742	*21*	*Ex*
PLAUT CAPT 989	*21*	*Pr*	PLAUT CIST 745	*17*	*Ex*
PLAUT CAS 35	*24*	*Ex*	PLAUT CURC 12-3	*55*	*Ex*
PLAUT CAS 225	*3*	*E-L*	PLAUT CURC 133	*35*	*Pr*
PLAUT CAS 413	*50*	*Pr*	PLAUT CURC 178	*45*	*L-E*
PLAUT CAS 422	*59*	*Ex*	PLAUT CURC 187	*64*	*L-E*
PLAUT CAS 510	*34*	*E-L*	PLAUT CURC 189	*47*	*L-E*
PLAUT CAS 549	*45*	*Pr*	PLAUT CURC 333	*23*	*L-E*
PLAUT CAS 610	*40*	*E-L*	PLAUT CURC 362	*61*	*Pr*
PLAUT CAS 629	*58*	*Ex*	PLAUT CURC 373	*28*	*L-E*
PLAUT CAS 634	*46*	*Ex*	PLAUT CURC 530	*5*	*L-E*
PLAUT CAS 680-1	*46*	*E-L*	PLAUT CURC 551	*42*	*Pr*
PLAUT CAS 724	*9*	*E-L*	PLAUT CURC 591-2	*43*	*Pas*
PLAUT CAS 725	*41*	*Ex*	PLAUT CURC 607	*56*	*Pr*
PLAUT CAS 733	*1*	*E-L*	PLAUT CURC 702	*15*	*Pr*
PLAUT CAS 736	*9*	*E-L*	PLAUT CURC 707	*24*	*Ex*
PLAUT CAS 738	*7*	*E-L*	PLAUT EPID 24	*31*	*L-E*
PLAUT CAS 766	*2*	*E-L*	PLAUT EPID 67A	*62*	*E-L*
PLAUT CAS 826	*1*	*L-E*	PLAUT EPID 150	*2*	*L-E*
PLAUT CAS 908	*66*	*Ex*	PLAUT EPID 152	*7*	*E-L*
PLAUT CAS 978	*2*	*L-E*	PLAUT EPID 196	*25*	*Ex*
PLAUT CIST 7	*18*	*Pr*	PLAUT EPID 207	*60*	*Pr*
PLAUT CIST 113	*18*	*Ex*	PLAUT EPID 241	*46*	*E-L*
PLAUT CIST 116	*55*	*Pr*	PLAUT EPID 265	*53*	*Pr*
PLAUT CIST 122	*56*	*Pr*	PLAUT EPID 507	*28*	*E-L*
PLAUT CIST 145	*21*	*L-E*	PLAUT EPID 648	*7*	*Pr*
PLAUT CIST 166	*21*	*L-E*	PLAUT EPID 649	*17*	*Ex*
PLAUT CIST 211-2	*7*	*L-E*	PLAUT EPID 668	*46*	*Ex*
PLAUT CIST 284	*58*	*Ex*	PLAUT EPID 728-9	*59*	*E-L*
PLAUT CIST 284	*61*	*Pr*	PLAUT MEN 129	*26*	*Ex*

PLAUT MEN 192	26	Ex	PLAUT MG 1236	33	Pr
PLAUT MEN 278	13	Pr	PLAUT MG 1254	46	Ex
PLAUT MEN 302	50	Ex	PLAUT MG 1259	27	Ex
PLAUT MEN 458	29	E-L	PLAUT MG 1299	61	L-E
PLAUT MEN 461	41	Ex	PLAUT MG 1312	44	Ex
PLAUT MEN 498	24	L-E	PLAUT MG 1429	55	L-E
PLAUT MEN 736	15	Pr	PLAUT MOST 22	32	Ex
PLAUT MEN 882	64	E-L	PLAUT MOST 48	9	Gl
PLAUT MEN 1062	1	L-E	PLAUT MOST 181	8	E-L
PLAUT MEN 1131	24	E-L	PLAUT MOST 209	9	L-E
PLAUT MEN 1148	51	Ex	PLAUT MOST 303	2	L-E
PLAUT MEN 1152	53	Ex	PLAUT MOST 305	2	L-E
PLAUT MERC 161	52	Ex	PLAUT MOST 431	6	L-E
PLAUT MERC 178	64	Rev	PLAUT MOST 513	45	Ex
PLAUT MERC 206	42	Ex	PLAUT MOST 928	20	Pr
PLAUT MERC 214	2	L-E	PLAUT MOST 1105-6	1	L-E
PLAUT MERC 366	28	E-L	PLAUT PERS 5	64	Ex
PLAUT MERC 443	17	L-E	PLAUT PERS 144	50	Ex
PLAUT MERC 456	44	E-L	PLAUT PERS 179	28	Ex
PLAUT MERC 456	44	L-E	PLAUT PERS 191	62	Ex
PLAUT MERC 515	36	Pr	PLAUT PERS 212	10	L-E
PLAUT MERC 577	41	Ex	PLAUT PERS 239	35	L-E
PLAUT MERC 750	40	Pr	PLAUT PERS 272	62	Ex
PLAUT MERC 923	57	Pr	PLAUT PERS 284	1	L-E
PLAUT MERC 951	17	Ex	PLAUT PERS 293	7	Ex
PLAUT MERC 961	61	L-E	PLAUT PERS 303	41	Ex
PLAUT MG 60	23	Pr	PLAUT PERS 304	22	L-E
PLAUT MG 123	27	L-E	PLAUT PERS 357	66	L-E
PLAUT MG 144	37	Ex	PLAUT PERS 385	8	Ex
PLAUT MG 347	6	L-E	PLAUT PERS 385	10	Pr
PLAUT MG 376	1	E-L	PLAUT PERS 413	5	E-L
PLAUT MG 625	2	E-L	PLAUT PERS 422	5	E-L
PLAUT MG 625	36	L-E	PLAUT PERS 548	6	Pr
PLAUT MG 630	27	Ex	PLAUT PERS 618	22	Ex
PLAUT MG 648	62	Ex	PLAUT PERS 624	66	Ex
PLAUT MG 1114	5	E-L	PLAUT PERS 741	17	Pr
PLAUT MG 1206	45	E-L	PLAUT PERS 772	30	Pr

PLAUT PERS 847	*23*	*L-E*	PLAUT PSEUD 1314	*41*	*Ex*
PLAUT POEN 55-6	*20*	*Pr*	PLAUT RUD 156	*21*	*Ex*
PLAUT POEN 126	*60*	*E-L*	PLAUT RUD 162	*1*	*E-L*
PLAUT POEN 365-7	*10*	*Pas*	PLAUT RUD 169	*7*	*Ex*
PLAUT POEN 404	*7*	*Gl*	PLAUT RUD 243	*15*	*Ex*
PLAUT POEN 660	*5*	*L-E*	PLAUT RUD 437	*22*	*L-E*
PLAUT POEN 678	*61*	*Ex*	PLAUT RUD 523	*3*	*E-L*
PLAUT POEN 706	*53*	*Ex*	PLAUT RUD 711	*58*	*L-E*
PLAUT POEN 761-2	*41*	*Pr*	PLAUT RUD 724	*18*	*Pr*
PLAUT POEN 866	*7*	*Pr*	PLAUT RUD 879	*61*	*Ex*
PLAUT POEN 1217	*65*	*Pr*	PLAUT RUD 906	*17*	*Ex*
PLAUT POEN 1231	*53*	*Pr*	PLAUT RUD 1166	*27*	*Pr*
PLAUT POEN 1237	*61*	*E-L*	PLAUT RUD 1164	*34*	*L-E*
PLAUT POEN 1248	*21*	*E-L*	PLAUT RUD 1183	*65*	*Ex*
PLAUT POEN 1260-1	*34*	*Ex*	PLAUT RUD 1343	*46*	*L-E*
PLAUT POEN 1299	*27*	*Pr*	PLAUT STICH 56	*22*	*E-L*
PLAUT POEN 1375-6	*49*	*L-E*	PLAUT STICH 96	*22*	*L-E*
PLAUT PSEUD 13	*16*	*E-L*	PLAUT STICH 284	*22*	*Ex*
PLAUT PSEUD 80	*9*	*Pr*	PLAUT STICH 326	*50*	*Ex*
PLAUT PSEUD 139	*21*	*Ex*	PLAUT STICH 539-40	*24*	*Ex*
PLAUT PSEUD 152	*32*	*Pr*	PLAUT STICH 583-4	*34*	*L-E*
PLAUT PSEUD 284	*66*	*Pr*	PLAUT STICH 591	*19*	*Pr*
PLAUT PSEUD 377	*17*	*Pr*	PLAUT STICH 599	*62*	*Pr*
PLAUT PSEUD 379	*17*	*Pr*	PLAUT STICH 731	*7*	*L-E*
PLAUT PSEUD 380	*7*	*L-E*	PLAUT TRIN 55-6	*40*	*L-E*
PLAUT PSEUD 404	*60*	*E-L*	PLAUT TRIN 89	*4*	*L-E*
PLAUT PSEUD 504	*15*	*Pr*	PLAUT TRIN 94	*42*	*L-E*
PLAUT PSEUD 610	*9*	*Gl*	PLAUT TRIN 148	*56*	*Pr*
PLAUT PSEUD 637	*24*	*Ex*	PLAUT TRIN 329	*28*	*L-E*
PLAUT PSEUD 657	*55*	*Ex*	PLAUT TRIN 449-50	*59*	*Gl*
PLAUT PSEUD 915	*59*	*L-E*	PLAUT TRIN 490	*25*	*Ex*
PLAUT PSEUD 971	*2*	*L-E*	PLAUT TRIN 563-4	*60*	*Pr*
PLAUT PSEUD 977	*24*	*Ex*	PLAUT TRIN 576	*13*	*Gl*
PLAUT PSEUD 1087	*45*	*Ex*	PLAUT TRIN 651	*5*	*Gl*
PLAUT PSEUD 1115	*32*	*Pr*	PLAUT TRIN 679	*65*	*L-E*
PLAUT PSEUD 1169	*17*	*Pr*	PLAUT TRIN 714	*28*	*Pr*
PLAUT PSEUD 1171	*62*	*L-E*	PLAUT TRIN 727	*61*	*Ex*

PLAUT TRIN 811	*32*	*Pr*	PLINY PANEG 21.3	*14*	*L-E*
PLAUT TRIN 906	*24*	*E-L*	PLINY PANEG 21.4	*15*	*GI*
PLAUT TRIN 1076	*53*	*E-L*	PLINY PANEG 44.1	*23*	*Ex*
PLAUT TRUC 134	*60*	*Ex*	PLINY PANEG 45.6	*44*	*E-L*
PLAUT TRUC 217	*1*	*GI*	PLINY NH PR 18	*3*	*GI*
PLAUT TRUC 295	*43*	*Pr*	PLINY NH 2.22	*31*	*Pas*
PLAUT TRUC 313	*61*	*L-E*	PLINY NH 3.66	*36*	*GI*
PLAUT TRUC 774	*66*	*L-E*	PLINY NH 7.5	*43*	*L-E*
PLAUT TRUC 817	*23*	*Pr*	PLINY NH 7.130	*25*	*Pr*
PLAUT TRUC 922	*29*	*Ex*	PLINY NH 11.145	*4*	*GI*
PLAUT TRUC 960	*40*	*Pr*	PLINY NH 11.146	*27*	*L-E*
PLINY E 1.3.5	*56*	*L-E*	PLINY NH 19.4	*26*	*E-L*
PLINY E 1.5.15	*43*	*Ex*	PLINY NH 23.42	*36*	*GI*
PLINY E 1.11	*63*	*Pas*	PLINY NH 33.4	*15*	*Pr*
PLINY E 1.16.1	*21*	*Ex*	PROP 1.1.1	*27*	*GI*
PLINY E 1.20.12	*47*	*Ex*	PROP 1.5.3	*53*	*L-E*
PLINY E 1.22.3	*63*	*E-L*	PROP 1.12.11	*3*	*L-E*
PLINY E 1.23.2	*49*	*Pr*	PROP 1.12.12	*23*	*L-E*
PLINY E 2.1.11	*15*	*Ex*	PROP 1.12.13-4	*31*	*L-E*
PLINY E 2.2.2	*62*	*Pr*	PROP 1.12.20	*23*	*L-E*
PLINY E 2.14.3	*65*	*Ex*	PROP 1.14.8	*19*	*GI*
PLINY E 2.20.8	*7*	*E-L*	PROP 1.17.1	*23*	*Ex*
PLINY E 3.9.13	*62*	*Ex*	PROP 2.1.4	*33*	*L-E*
PLINY E 3.21.6	*43*	*L-E*	PROP 2.7.19	*57*	*Ex*
PLINY E 4.2.6	*53*	*Pr*	PROP 2.8.1-2	*58*	*Pas*
PLINY E 4.17.8	*20*	*E-L*	PROP 2.8.8	*31*	*GI*
PLINY E 4.23.1	*23*	*Ex*	PROP 2.8.17-8	*56*	*L-E*
PLINY E 4.24.3	*30*	*Ex*	PROP 2.12.22	*6*	*L-E*
PLINY E 5.1.8	*59*	*L-E*	PROP 2.15.12	*10*	*GI*
PLINY E 5.9.6	*44*	*Ex*	PROP 2.20.27	*51*	*L-E*
PLINY E 8.23.8	*51*	*E-L*	PROP 2.21.4	*17*	*GI*
PLINY E 9.12.1	*49*	*Ex*	PROP 2.23.24	*14*	*Pr*
PLINY E 9.32	*40*	*Ex*	PROP 2.30B.40	*18*	*L-E*
PLINY E 9.33.6	*29*	*Ex*	PROP 2.32.1	*28*	*Ex*
PLINY E 9.36.4	*36*	*L-E*	PROP 3.5.1	*13*	*Pr*
PLINY E 9.39.2	*32*	*Pr*	PROP 3.8.10	*25*	*GI*
PLINY PANEG 5.6	*38*	*Pr*	PROP 3.13.50	*56*	*Pr*

QUINT DECL 315	*53*	*Ex*	[QUINT] DECL 1.9	*24*	*L-E*
QUINT DECL 315	*57*	*L-E*	[QUINT] DECL 1.11	*23*	*Pr*
QUINT DECL 318	*18*	*L-E*	[QUINT] DECL 2.23	*27*	*Pr*
QUINT DECL 319	*64*	*Rev*	[QUINT] DECL 3.9	*38*	*Ex*
QUINT DECL 321	*49*	*L-E*	[QUINT] DECL 3.13	*34*	*Ex*
QUINT DECL 322	*17*	*Ex*	[QUINT] DECL 3.15	*24*	*L-E*
QUINT DECL 326	*33*	*Pr*	[QUINT] DECL 3.19	*36*	*Ex*
QUINT DECL 328	*24*	*L-E*	[QUINT] DECL 4.18	*7*	*Ex*
QUINT DECL 328	*50*	*E-L*	[QUINT] DECL 4.19	*31*	*Ex*
QUINT DECL 330	*34*	*E-L*	[QUINT] DECL 6.1	*27*	*E-L*
QUINT DECL 332	*39*	*Ex*	[QUINT] DECL 6.7	*49*	*Ex*
QUINT DECL 332	*47*	*L-E*	[QUINT] DECL 6.13	*16*	*E-L*
QUINT DECL 335	*22*	*Gl*	[QUINT] DECL 6.16	*27*	*Ex*
QUINT DECL 335	*4*	*E-L*	[QUINT] DECL 6.17	*49*	*L-E*
QUINT DECL 335	*27*	*L-E*	[QUINT] DECL 6.21	*56*	*Ex*
QUINT DECL 335	*54*	*L-E*	[QUINT] DECL 6.23	*56*	*Ex*
QUINT DECL 337	*64*	*Ex*	[QUINT] DECL 7.3	*57*	*Ex*
QUINT DECL 337	*39*	*L-E*	[QUINT] DECL 7.4	*29*	*E-L*
QUINT DECL 337	*25*	*Pr*	[QUINT] DECL 9.15	*51*	*L-E*
QUINT DECL 339	*49*	*E-L*	[QUINT] DECL 9.22	*40*	*E-L*
QUINT DECL 340	*56*	*Ex*	[QUINT] DECL 11.7	*48*	*L-E*
QUINT DECL 344	*49*	*Ex*	[QUINT] DECL 14.8	*52*	*Pr*
QUINT DECL 344	*39*	*L-E*	[QUINT] DECL 14.10	*10*	*Pr*
QUINT DECL 345	*46*	*Ex*	[QUINT] DECL 15.7	*35*	*Ex*
QUINT DECL 348	*55*	*L-E*	[QUINT] DECL 17.19	*14*	*Pr*
QUINT DECL 348	*45*	*L-E*	[QUINT] DECL 19.1	*46*	*Ex*
QUINT DECL 348	*60*	*Ex*	[QUINT] DECL 19.5	*2*	*E-L*
QUINT DECL 348	*57*	*Pr*	SALL BJ 1.3	*25*	*L-E*
QUINT DECL 349	*55*	*Ex*	SALL BJ 5.1	*40*	*L-E*
QUINT DECL 352	*55*	*L-E*	SALL BJ 8.1	*62*	*Gl*
QUINT DECL 369	*29*	*Pr*	SALL BJ 20.2	*38*	*Ex*
QUINT DECL 369	*9*	*E-L*	SALL BJ 25.7	*30*	*Pr*
QUINT DECL 369	*41*	*E-L*	SALL C 1.4	*29*	*L-E*
QUINT DECL 377	*39*	*Ex*	SALL C 2.9	*47*	*L-E*
QUINT DECL 377	*61*	*Pr*	SALL C 9.2	*13*	*Gl*
[QUINT] DECL 1.3	*24*	*Pr*	SALL C 17.6	*53*	*L-E*
[QUINT] DECL 1.6	*9*	*L-E*	SALL C 51.32	*21*	*L-E*

SALL C 53.1	*29*	*Ex*		SEN BEN 3.18.4	*7*	*L-E*
SALL C 54.6	*53*	*Ex*		SEN BEN 3.22.3	*20*	*Pr*
SALL HIST IV.69.5	*64*	*Pas*		SEN BEN 3.29.1	*38*	*Ex*
SALL HIST IV.69.18	*53*	*L-E*		SEN BEN 3.31.2	*36*	*Ex*
[SALL] CAES 1.2.2	*24*	*L-E*		SEN BEN 3.31.4	*15*	*L-E*
SEN AD HELV 5.2	*25*	*Pr*		SEN BEN 3.38.2	*57*	*Pr*
SEN AD HELV 5.4	*57*	*Pr*		SEN BEN 4.6.1	*41*	*Pr*
SEN AD HELV 10.3	*46*	*Gl*		SEN BEN 4.6.3	*47*	*Ex*
SEN AD HELV 13.6	*35*	*Gl*		SEN BEN 4.8.2	*4*	*L-E*
SEN AD HELV 14.3	*56*	*Ex*		SEN BEN 4.8.3	*39*	*L-E*
SEN AD HELV 19.4	*42*	*Pr*		SEN BEN 4.10.2	*38*	*E-L*
SEN AD MARC 9.2	*12*	*Pr*		SEN BEN 4.11.1	*35*	*E-L*
SEN AD MARC 16.1	*50*	*Ex*		SEN BEN 4.13.3	*18*	*Ex*
SEN AD MARC 19.5	*12*	*Pr*		SEN BEN 4.19.1	*10*	*Gl*
SEN AD MARC 21.6	*44*	*Pr*		SEN BEN 4.21.6	*58*	*Pr*
SEN AD MARC 23.1	*40*	*Pr*		SEN BEN 4.26.3	*13*	*E-L*
SEN AD POLY 1.1	*30*	*L-E*		SEN BEN 4.32.2	*53*	*Ex*
SEN AD POLY 4.1	*7*	*L-E*		SEN BEN 4.40.3	*9*	*Gl*
SEN AD POLY 11.2	*12*	*L-E*		SEN BEN 5.4.1	*8*	*Pr*
SEN AGAM 26	*45*	*Ex*		SEN BEN 5.7.2	*18*	*Pr*
SEN AGAM 115	*11*	*L-E*		SEN BEN 5.8.6	*64*	*Ex*
SEN AGAM 611	*36*	*Gl*		SEN BEN 5.9.1	*22*	*Ex*
SEN AGAM 758	*9*	*Pr*		SEN BEN 5.9.4	*47*	*Ex*
SEN APOCO 6.2	*50*	*L-E*		SEN BEN 5.12.4	*10*	*E-L*
SEN APOCO 8.3	*60*	*Ex*		SEN BEN 5.18	*24*	*E-L*
SEN APOCO 13.1	*29*	*Ex*		SEN BEN 6.18.2	*29*	*Pr*
SEN BEN 1.1.1	*20*	*L-E*		SEN BEN 6.26.1	*12*	*Gl*
SEN BEN 1.5.2	*31*	*E-L*		SEN BEN 6.36.2	*27*	*Ex*
SEN BEN 2.7.3	*56*	*Ex*		SEN BEN 7.6.1	*47*	*Pas*
SEN BEN 2.14.4	*13*	*E-L*		SEN BEN 7.14.4	*46*	*Ex*
SEN BEN 2.14.5	*64*	*Pr*		SEN BEN 7.17.2	*22*	*Ex*
SEN BEN 2.15.2	*13*	*Pr*		SEN BEN 7.18.1	*63*	*Ex*
SEN BEN 2.18.3	*49*	*Ex*		SEN BEN 7.18.2	*47*	*Ex*
SEN BEN 2.19.1	*23*	*Gl*		SEN BEN 7.20.2	*21*	*Pr*
SEN BEN 3.5.2	*36*	*Ex*		SEN BEN 7.29.2	*39*	*Pr*
SEN BEN 3.13.2	*26*	*E-L*		SEN BREV VIT 2.4	*25*	*L-E*
SEN BEN 3.18.3	*5*	*L-E*		SEN BREV VIT 3.2	*41*	*L-E*

SEN BREV VIT 3.4	*40*	*E-L*	SEN E 12.8	*52*	*E-L*
SEN BREV VIT 9.1	*40*	*L-E*	SEN E 12.10	*53*	*Ex*
SEN BREV VIT 10.2	*40*	*Pas*	SEN E 12.10	*45*	*Pr*
SEN CLEM 1.5.5	*6*	*Gl*	SEN E 12.10	*29*	*Pr*
SEN CLEM 1.19.9	*22*	*L-E*	SEN E 13.9	*17*	*L-E*
SEN CLEM 1.24.1	*57*	*Ex*	SEN E 13.10	*34*	*L-E*
SEN CLEM 1.26.2	*33*	*Pr*	SEN E 13.11	*14*	*Gl*
SEN CLEM 2.4.4	*5*	*E-L*	SEN E 13.13	*53*	*Pr*
SEN CONS SAP 3.4	*57*	*Pr*	SEN E 14.7	*63*	*L-E*
SEN CONS SAP 5.7	*22*	*Ex*	SEN E 14.13	*43*	*Pr*
SEN CONS SAP 6.6	*23*	*Pr*	SEN E 14.15	*41*	*L-E*
SEN CONS SAP 8.3	*41*	*Pr*	SEN E 15.1	*12*	*Pr*
SEN CONS SAP 10.3	*31*	*L-E*	SEN E 16.2	*50*	*Ex*
SEN DE OTIO 1.2	*34*	*Pr*	SEN E 16.8	*8*	*Gl*
SEN E 2.5	*33*	*Ex*	SEN E 17.9	*43*	*Ex*
SEN E 3.4	*57*	*L-E*	SEN E 17.9	*22*	*Gl*
SEN E 4.1	*7*	*Gl*	SEN E 17.12	*33*	*Ex*
SEN E 5.6	*39*	*Pr*	SEN E 20.2	*20*	*L-E*
SEN E 5.9	*57*	*L-E*	SEN E 20.5	*53*	*L-E*
SEN E 6.3	*63*	*L-E*	SEN E 20.13	*56*	*E-L*
SEN E 6.4	*49*	*L-E*	SEN E 21.1	*18*	*L-E*
SEN E 6.5	*33*	*E-L*	SEN E 21.1	*53*	*E-L*
SEN E 7.8	*15*	*L-E*	SEN E 21.2	*4*	*L-E*
SEN E 7.9	*63*	*E-L*	SEN E 22.9	*45*	*L-E*
SEN E 7.12	*8*	*E-L*	SEN E 22.15	*9*	*Pr*
SEN E 8.1	*18*	*Gl*	SEN E 22.17	*50*	*L-E*
SEN E 8.3	*11*	*Gl*	SEN E 23.4	*32*	*Gl*
SEN E 9.3	*53*	*Ex*	SEN E 23.4	*6*	*E-L*
SEN E 9.5	*22*	*L-E*	SEN E 23.6	*8*	*E-L*
SEN E 9.13	*64*	*Pr*	SEN E 23.9	*28*	*L-E*
SEN E 10.1	*3*	*E-L*	SEN E 24.7	*23*	*L-E*
SEN E 10.2	*32*	*E-L*	SEN E 24.19	*56*	*L-E*
SEN E 11.1	*56*	*Pr*	SEN E 24.24	*45*	*Ex*
SEN E 11.6	*29*	*E-L*	SEN E 24.25	*61*	*L-E*
SEN E 11.8	*46*	*Pas*	SEN E 25.4	*35*	*Ex*
SEN E 12.3	*54*	*E-L*	SEN E 26.2	*51*	*L-E*
SEN E 12.7	*62*	*L-E*	SEN E 27.9	*31*	*L-E*

SEN E 28.1	5	Gl		SEN E 54.6	14	L-E
SEN E 28.4	17	L-E		SEN E 54.7	20	Gl
SEN E 29.1	19	E-L		SEN E 55.5	42	Ex
SEN E 29.4	17	L-E		SEN E 57.6	19	Pr
SEN E 30.10	53	Ex		SEN E 57.7	29	Pr
SEN E 30.10	31	L-E		SEN E 58.22	39	E-L
SEN E 30.17	12	L-E		SEN E 58.27	45	L-E
SEN E 31.10	25	L-E		SEN E 58.37	58	E-L
SEN E 31.10	20	L-E		SEN E 59.1	41	E-L
SEN E 32.2	66	L-E		SEN E 59.4	50	L-E
SEN E 35.1	7	L-E		SEN E 59.9	35	L-E
SEN E 35.3	28	Gl		SEN E 59.11	43	Pr
SEN E 35.3	41	Ex		SEN E 59.11	57	L-E
SEN E 35.4	18	Pr		SEN E 59.13	45	Pr
SEN E 36.4	64	Pr		SEN E 59.17	8	L-E
SEN E 37.1	53	E-L		SEN E 61.1	53	Gl
SEN E 37.3	17	E-L		SEN E 61.2	46	L-E
SEN E 37.4	55	E-L		SEN E 62.3	42	Gl
SEN E 38.1	7	L-E		SEN E 64.8	35	L-E
SEN E 38.1	16	L-E		SEN E 65.16	17	Gl
SEN E 42.9	61	Pr		SEN E 66.8	42	L-E
SEN E 42.9	43	Pr		SEN E 66.32	10	L-E
SEN E 43.1	48	E-L		SEN E 66.39	10	L-E
SEN E 45.6	9	Gl		SEN E 66.44	39	Ex
SEN E 46.3	19	Pr		SEN E 66.45	11	L-E
SEN E 47.4	56	Gl		SEN E 67.4	48	Ex
SEN E 47.12	6	Pr		SEN E 68.8	37	L-E
SEN E 47.18	29	Gl		SEN E 70.6	38	L-E
SEN E 49.3	32	Pr		SEN E 70.15	27	L-E
SEN E 50.2	41	E-L		SEN E 71.7	56	Pr
SEN E 50.3	18	L-E		SEN E 71.16	57	E-L
SEN E 50.7	15	Gl		SEN E 71.18	8	L-E
SEN E 51.5	35	L-E		SEN E 71.30	27	L-E
SEN E 51.8	18	E-L		SEN E 71.33	47	Ex
SEN E 53.7	41	Pr		SEN E 73.16	12	L-E
SEN E 53.8	18	E-L		SEN E 74.11	18	Gl
SEN E 54.4	28	L-E		SEN E 75.9	41	Ex

SEN E 76.6	2	E-L	SEN E 93.2	6	L-E
SEN E 76.27	46	E-L	SEN E 94.15	25	E-L
SEN E 76.27	56	Pr	SEN E 94.28	36	Ex
SEN E 77.18	54	E-L	SEN E 94.39	10	Pr
SEN E 78.3	65	L-E	SEN E 95.2	15	L-E
SEN E 78.7	16	Gl	SEN E 95.52	11	Gl
SEN E 78.14	52	L-E	SEN E 97.14	11	Gl
SEN E 78.15	55	Pr	SEN E 97.16	30	L-E
SEN E 78.17	25	Pr	SEN E 99.2	55	Ex
SEN E 78.21	33	L-E	SEN E 99.4	28	L-E
SEN E 79.11	56	Ex	SEN E 99.12	8	L-E
SEN E 79.13	10	E-L	SEN E 101.1	50	L-E
SEN E 80.1	19	L-E	SEN E 104.12	32	L-E
SEN E 80.2	50	Gl	SEN E 104.26	53	Pr
SEN E 81.5	53	Pr	SEN E 105.4	29	Pr
SEN E 81.12	19	E-L	SEN E 106.12	15	Gl
SEN E 81.14	29	E-L	SEN E 107.5	23	Ex
SEN E 81.21	47	L-E	SEN E 107.11	53	L-E
SEN E 82.3	12	Gl	SEN E 108.6	46	L-E
SEN E 82.13	41	Ex	SEN E 108.13	41	Pr
SEN E 82.15	22	Ex	SEN E 108.24	31	Pr
SEN E 82.19	47	Ex	SEN E 109.4	57	L-E
SEN E 84.11	15	L-E	SEN E 110.7	1	E-L
SEN E 84.13	19	L-E	SEN E 110.18	15	L-E
SEN E 85.11	14	E-L	SEN E 113.5	18	Ex
SEN E 87.18	6	E-L	SEN E 115.16	43	L-E
SEN E 87.22	60	L-E	SEN E 116.8	15	L-E
SEN E 87.24	56	Pr	SEN E 117.2	41	Ex
SEN E 88.17	60	Pr	SEN E 118.8	50	Pr
SEN E 88.37	62	Ex	SEN E 118.8	8	L-E
SEN E 89.4	12	Gl	SEN E 119.2	29	Ex
SEN E 89.4	10	L-E	SEN E 119.6	53	L-E
SEN E 89.8	10	L-E	SEN E 119.9	25	Pr
SEN E 89.8	10	L-E	SEN E 121.16	39	Gl
SEN E 91.5	60	Pr	SEN E 122.5	25	E-L
SEN E 91.16	64	L-E	SEN E 122.14	8	Gl
SEN E 91.21	51	L-E	SEN E 123.16	64	Rev

SEN HERC 1-2	35	E-L		SEN PHOEN 557	49	Pr
SEN HERC 112	45	E-L		SEN PHOEN 642-3	30	Pr
SEN HERC 341	8	Pr		SEN PROV 1.5	9	Gl
SEN HERC 365	15	L-E		SEN PROV 4.2	9	E-L
SEN HERC 503-4	58	E-L		SEN PROV 5.2	8	E-L
SEN IRA 1.13.5	64	E-L		SEN PROV 5.4	31	Pr
SEN IRA 1.14.2	57	Pr		SEN PROV 5.4	56	Pr
SEN IRA 2.10.6	57	L-E		SEN PROV 5.7	61	L-E
SEN IRA 2.13.2	25	L-E		SEN PROV 5.9	24	L-E
SEN IRA 2.28.8	6	L-E		SEN PROV 6.5	40	Ex
SEN IRA 2.29.1	43	Ex		SEN PROV 6.6	52	Ex
SEN IRA 2.32.1	49	Pr		SEN QN 1.PR.5	34	Ex
SEN IRA 2.34.5	35	Pr		SEN QN 1.PR.6	54	Pas
SEN IRA 3.8.1	46	L-E		SEN QN 1.PR.13	28	Pas
SEN IRA 3.8.1	22	Gl		SEN QN 1.3.7	42	Ex
SEN IRA 3.8.5	14	E-L		SEN QN 1.11.2	58	Pr
SEN IRA 3.12.1	44	L-E		SEN QN 2.34.2	42	Pr
SEN IRA 3.24.2	57	E-L		SEN QN 2.37.3	60	Pas
SEN IRA 3.25.4	57	L-E		SEN QN 2.38.2	38	Ex
SEN IRA 3.26.4	25	Ex		SEN QN 2.38.3	5	L-E
SEN IRA 3.30.3	43	L-E		SEN QN 3.30.8	31	Gl
SEN MED 159	25	Pr		SEN QN 4A.PR.2	33	L-E
SEN MED 168	24	E-L		SEN QN 4A.PR.4	40	L-E
SEN MED 295	64	Ex		SEN QN 5.18.15	49	Pr
SEN MED 416	10	L-E		SEN QN 6.2.1	24	L-E
SEN MED 494	25	E-L		SEN QN 6.2.3	53	L-E
SEN OED 296	3	L-E		SEN QN 6.3.2	27	Gl
SEN OED 629-30	62	Gl		SEN QN 6.28.2	43	L-E
SEN OED 793	64	Rev		SEN QN 6.32.12	12	E-L
SEN OED 980	31	Pr		SEN QN 7.30.4	43	L-E
SEN OED 1009	45	Pr		SEN THY 313	66	Ex
SEN OED 1031-2	45	Pr		SEN THY 435	38	E-L
SEN PHAED 699	64	Rev		SEN THY 435	64	Rev
SEN PHAED 699	38	Ex		SEN THY 551	28	Pr
SEN PHAED 880	9	L-E		SEN THY 572	43	L-E
SEN PHAED 1267	18	Ex		SEN TRANQ AN 5.5	38	Pr
SEN PHOEN 5-6	44	L-E		SEN TRANQ AN 8.2.	43	L-E

SENR C 9.5.11	54	L-E	TAC HIST 1.38	18	L-E
SENR C 9.5.12	24	E-L	TAC HIST 1.48	24	Gl
SENR C 9.5.17	28	Gl	TAC HIST 1.81	51	Ex
SENR C 9.6.6	48	Gl	TAC HIST 4.42	43	L-E
SENR S 1.15	52	Ex	TER ADEL 69	22	Ex
SENR S 2.2	12	E-L	TER ADEL 97	31	Ex
SENR S 2.4	45	Ex	TER ADEL 125	28	L-E
SENR S 2.9	5	L-E	TER ADEL 149	49	L-E
SENR S 2.17	35	L-E	TER ADEL 155	52	L-E
SENR S 5.4	55	Pr	TER ADEL 266	1	E-L
SENR S 5.5	13	Pr	TER ADEL 266	33	Ex
SENR S 6.1	64	Rev	TER ADEL 288	60	Pr
SENR S 6.1	38	Ex	TER ADEL 322	2	L-E
SENR S 6.4	40	Pr	TER ADEL 385-8	40	Pas
SENR S 6.22	62	L-E	TER ADEL 552	42	Ex
SENR S 6.27	54	E-L	TER ADEL 555	49	Ex
SUET DJ 30.4	55	Pas	TER ADEL 571-2	19	E-L
SUET DJ 31.2	38	L-E	TER ADEL 739	10	Pr
SUET DJ 31.2	64	Rev	TER ADEL 748	41	Ex
SUET DJ 33	35	Gl	TER AND 155	53	Gl
SUET DJ 37.2	23	Ex	TER AND 240	49	Ex
SUET DJ 49.4	28	Pas	TER AND 260	19	Gl
SUET DJ 80.3	60	E-L	TER AND 309	26	Gl
SUET T 21.4	42	L-E	TER AND 312	17	Ex
SUET T 61.2	35	L-E	TER AND 338	45	Pr
SUET CAL 6.1	6	L-E	TER AND 385	60	Pr
SUET CAL 30.1	56	Gl	TER AND 407	41	Ex
SUET CLAU 4.3	9	E-L	TER AND 453	49	E-L
SUET N 47.3	4	L-E	TER AND 464-5	19	Pr
SUET N 49.1	61	Gl	TER AND 533	33	L-E
SUET VES 23.4	60	Gl	TER AND 579	21	E-L
SUET TIT. 8.1	32	E-L	TER AND 612	45	E-L
SUET VIT HORAT	64	Ex	TER AND 621	41	Pr
TAC AGRIC 30.4	20	Gl	TER AND 751	40	Ex
TAC ANN 1.42	42	E-L	TER AND 763	15	Ex
TAC ANN 2.37	34	E-L	TER AND 780-1	34	Ex
TAC ANN 2.51	51	Ex	TER AND 791	50	E-L

TER AND 896	56	Pr	TER PHOR 1053	3	Gl
TER AND 915	17	Pr	TIB 1.2.16	33	E-L
TER AND 933	7	E-L	TIB 1.3.35	37	Ex
TER AND 973	63	Ex	TIB 1.5.43	27	Pr
TER AND 973	17	L-E	TIB 1.5.57	5	Gl
TER EUN 560	4	E-L	TIB 1.9.11	35	L-E
TER EUN 561	63	L-E	TIB 1.10.13	31	E-L
TER EUN 834	7	Ex	TIB 2.2.1	45	Ex
TER EUN 835	33	Ex	TIB 2.6.44	33	Pr
TER EUN 1009	42	Pr	VALMAX 1.PRAEF	23	Gl
TER HT 105	57	Ex	VALMAX 5.4.7	15	L-E
TER HT 190	21	E-L	VARRO LL 9.15	46	Gl
TER HT 263	42	Ex	VEG 1.15	30	Gl
TER HT 971	50	Pr	VEG 2.5	41	Pas
TER HEC 133	52	Ex	VEG 2.8	62	L-E
TER HEC 224	65	Ex	VP 1.12.3	38	L-E
TER HEC 422	13	L-E	VP 2.4.2	24	Gl
TER HEC 461	23	Pr	VERG A 1.47-8	32	Ex
TER HEC 653	4	L-E	VERG A 1.279	23	E-L
TER PHOR 103-4	61	Pr	VERG A 1.462	32	L-E
TER PHOR 188	21	Ex	VERG A 1.630	57	Gl
TER PHOR 203	25	Ex	VERG A 4.290	45	Pr
TER PHOR 215	28	Ex	VERG A 5.231	29	Ex
TER PHOR 300	65	Pr	VERG A 6.268	61	Pas
TER PHOR 460	38	Ex	VERG A 6.466	49	Ex
TER PHOR 488	63	L-E	VERG A 10.113	19	E-L
TER PHOR 492	57	Ex	VERG A 11.180	15	E-L
TER PHOR 506	27	Gl	VERG A 11.160	64	Ex
TER PHOR 539	17	L-E	VERG A 12.435-6	15	Pas
TER PHOR 549	56	Pr	VERG E 1.3-4	20	Pr
TER PHOR 575	33	Gl	VERG E 4.36	31	Gl
TER PHOR 575-6	41	Ex	VERG E 8.43	50	E-L
TER PHOR 682	50	Ex	VERG E 10.69	45	L-E
TER PHOR 724	23	Ex	VERG E 10.69	25	Pr
TER PHOR 899	61	Pr	VERG G 2.490	32	L-E
TER PHOR 1022	45	Pr	VERG G 4.218	15	Gl
TER PHOR 1047	7	Pr	VERG G 4.465-6	37	Pas

INDEX